Africa Reset

A NEW WAY FORWARD

Africa Reset

A NEW WAY FORWARD

Editors
THEODORE AHLERS
HARINDER S. KOHLI

CENTENNIAL GROUP
policy and strategic advisors

JICA

OXFORD
UNIVERSITY PRESS

OXFORD
UNIVERSITY PRESS

Oxford University Press is a department of the University of Oxford.
It furthers the University's objective of excellence in research, scholarship,
and education by publishing worldwide. Oxford is a registered trademark of
Oxford University Press in the UK and in certain other countries.

Published in India by
Oxford University Press
2/11 Ground Floor, Ansari Road, Daryaganj, New Delhi 110 002, India

Centennial Group International
2600 Virginia Avenue NW,
Suite 201, Washington, DC 20037

Japan International Cooperation Agency Research Institute
10-5 Ichigaya Honmura-cho Shinjuku-ku
Tokyo 162-8433, Japan

First Edition published in 2017

ISBN-13: 978-0-19-948502-4
ISBN-10: 0-19-948502-X

Printed in India by Replika Press Pvt. Ltd
Title page photo credit: michaeljung/Shutterstock.com

Table of Contents

List of Figures, Tables, and Boxes

List of Figures

Chapter 1

Chapter 2

Chapter 3

Chapter 4

Chapter 5

Chapter 6

Chapter 7

Chapter 8

Chapter 9

List of Tables

Chapter 6

Chapter 7

Chapter 8

Chapter 9

Chapter 10

List of Boxes

Chapter 3

Chapter 6

Chapter 7

Chapter 8

Chapter 9

Chapter 10

List of acronyms

ACP	African, Caribbean and Pacific Group of States
AfDB	African Development Bank
AGOA	African Growth and Opportunity Act
AMU	Arab Maghreb Union
ASYCUDA	Automated System for Customs Data
AU	African Union
BDS	Business Development Services
CAPP	Central Africa Power Pool
CCU	Continental Customs Union
CEMAC	Central African Economic and Monetary Community
CEN-SAD	Community of Sahel-Saharan States
CFTA	Continental Free Trade Agreement
CIS	Commonwealth of Independent States
COMELEC	Comité Maghrébin de l'Électricité
COMESA	Common Market for Eastern and Southern Africa
CONFEMEN	Conférence des Ministres de l'Éducation de pays ayant le français en partage
DAC	Development Assistance Committee
EAC	East African Community
EAPP	Eastern Africa Power Pool
ECCAS	Economic Community of Central African States
ECOWAS	Economic Community of West African States
EPZ	export processing zone
FAO	Food and Agricultural Organization
FDI	foreign direct investment
FTA	free trade areas
GVC	global value chain
HE	household enterprise
IBRD	International Bank for Reconstruction and Development
ICA	Infrastructure Consortium of Africa
ICT	information and communication technology
IDA	International Development Association
IFAD	International Fund for Agricultural Development
IGAD	Intergovernmental Authority on Development
IFI	international financial institution
IFPRI	International Food Policy Research Institute
ILO	International Labour Organization
INDCs	Intended National Determined Contributions
IOC	Indian Ocean Commission
IPCC	Intergovernmental Panel on Climate Change

IPPs	Independent Power Producers
LDCs	Least Developed Countries
LPA	Lagos Plan of Action
MDB	multilateral development bank
MDGs	Millennium Development Goals
MIP	Minimum Integration Program
NAFTA	North American Free Trade Agreement
NEPAD	New Partnership for African Development
NICs	Newly Industrialized Countries
NRW	nonrevenue water
ODA	official development assistance
OECD	Organisation for Economic Co-operation and Development
OHADA	Organisation for the Harmonization of Business Law in Africa
OPEC	Organization of the Petroleum Countries
OSBP	One-Stop Border Posts
PASEC	Programme d'analyse des systèmes éducatifs de la CONFEMEN
PIDA	Programme for Infrastructure Development in Africa
PISA	Program for International Student Assessment
PPI	private participation in infrastructure
PPP	public-private partnership
REC	Regional Economic Community
REIPPP	Renewable Energy Independent Power Producer Procurement
SADC	Southern African Development Community
SACMEQ	Southern and Eastern Africa Consortium for Monitoring Educational Quality
SAPP	Southern African Power Pool
SDE	Sénégalise des Eaux
SDI	Service Delivery Indicators
SEZ	special economic zone
SGR	standard gauge
SOEs	state-owned enterprises
SSA	Sub-Saharan Africa
STEM	short-term energy market
TEU	twenty-foot equivalent unit
TFP	total factor productivity
TIMSS	Trends in International Mathematics and Science Study
TVET	technical and vocational education and training
UNCTAD	United Nations Conference on Trade and Development
UNECA	United Nations Economic Commission for Africa
UNESCO	United Nations Educational, Scientific and Cultural Organization
WAEMU	West African Economic and Monetary Union
WAGP	West African Gas Pipeline
WAPP	Western African Power Pool
WSS	water supply and sanitation

Foreword

It is with great pleasure that we bring this volume to publication. It discusses the long-term development prospects and challenges of Africa, while providing medium-term recommendations for how African leaders and stakeholders could address these challenges. The volume is a culmination of a cooperation project between the Japan International Cooperation Agency (JICA) and Centennial Group International, who started to work together on Africa five years ago.

In the international community's efforts to eradicate poverty, promote global peace and security, and achieve the United Nation's Sustainable Development Goals, the economic and social development of Africa is of utmost priority. As such, I see it as an important responsibility of JICA to support the creation and dissemination of analytical work such as this volume, which so keenly identifies the challenges Africa faces in its development as well as many opportunities before it.

The initial outcome of the cooperation effort between JICA and Centennial Group International was presented at the fifth Tokyo International Conference on African Development (TICAD V) in 2013, as a volume titled *Africa 2050: Realizing the Continent's Full Potential*. In it, the authors argued that it was possible for Africa to catch up—or converge—with the rest of the world in terms of income and productivity by 2050. Three years later, an updated version was presented first at TICAD VI in Nairobi, Kenya in August 2016, and then a further revised and expanded set of reports, including updated analyses as well as some new chapters, was presented at the Fifth Africa Emerging Markets Forum in Abidjan, Côte d'Ivoire in March 2017.

This current volume represents the culmination of that process, following commentary and discussion in both Nairobi and Abidjan. It presents two alternative scenarios on how the continent may look like two generations from now, depending on how its leaders tackle the main challenges outlined in the volume.

Behind these continuous revisions and updating of the various chapters are the changes in global economic environment in which Africa has been placed, as well as internal developments in different countries since 2013. True, Africa is still growing in nominal terms, but it is no longer converging with the rest of the world. For it to resume its path toward the convergence scenario, it is necessary that African countries strengthen policy responses to the changing circumstances in various domains, in demographics, domestic resource mobilization, human development (particularly education quality), inclusive growth and job creation, agriculture, infrastructure, as well as global economic environment.

I hope you will find this volume useful and interesting, as I myself and all my colleagues at JICA have found it.

Shinichi Kitaoka
President
Japan International Cooperation Agency (JICA)

Preface

Three years ago, *Africa 2050: Realizing the Continent's Full Potential*, was released. That book offered a vision of what could be—an Africa that meets the aspiration of its people and is catching up with the rest of the world in living standards and competitiveness.

The global economic environment has changed dramatically since the book was published. Even as it was being finalized, the commodity super cycle, which peaked in 2012, was starting to turn down. However, the bust was even more dramatic than anticipated, resulting in a historic collapse in global commodity prices. By early 2016, the price of oil fell to less than $30 per barrel, the lowest in over a decade. The collapse went far beyond oil though, as nearly every major commodity, and even food prices, underwent major downturns. As would be expected, the end of the commodity super cycle had a profound effect on the continent, but was particularly devastating for many of the resource-rich African economies, which had been experiencing a boom for over a decade.

Financial markets have also tightened in the past four years. Many countries which had, in the past, benefited from cheap finance and the global search for higher yields are longer able to do so. As global interest rates appear to be bottoming out, and risk aversion has become greater, international investors are less willing to channel their funds to the developing world.

We have also witnessed an ebb in globalization. This has resulted in further global economic challenges that impact Africa. Global trade has slowed as developed countries face populist pushback against free trade. The Doha round of WTO negotiations is functionally moribund. Major global free trade agreements like TPP and TTIP have faced significant backlash, and negotiations have stalled to the point of irrelevance and lost the support of major economic actors like the US and the UK. The inability of the G20 leaders in June 2017 to agree even on their usual routine support for an open global trading system is the latest illustration of the loss of political support from the major powers.

The growing anti-globalization sentiment has also led to a backlash against immigration and refugees that again impacts Africa. Opportunities for economic migrants to the developed world grow increasingly slim, and migrants face ever more hostile political environments when they arrive. As such, many European countries are reorienting official development assistance towards domestic refugee resettlement, rather than overseas development flows. This, combined with growing fiscal deficits throughout the developed world, means a much lower appetite for aid toward Africa in traditional donors.

These global headwinds, combined with new domestic developments in many African countries, has led us to reassess our previous analysis. Building off the basic analytical work undertaken for Africa 2050, this book charts a renewed course for the continent.

The authors are persuaded that while the challenges the continent faces are even more daunting today, vast opportunities remain for Africa. It must not let these opportunities slip away. Africa's advantages include: a still huge scope to catch up with global best practice; a growing, young labor force; a fast-expanding urban middle class; exploding technological innovations worldwide; greater market opportunities in Asia and other emerging markets; and a strong natural resource base. But it cannot afford to miss the chance to exploit these opportunities. This book has tried to strike a balance between recognizing the challenges the continent faces and putting forth a strategic agenda for exploiting these opportunities. By presenting two scenarios—an aspirational one and a business as usual one—the book also attempts to present the cost of missing the opportunities.

The tougher global environment does require that Africa take charge of its own future and pursue a path of greater self-reliance and economic diversity. African countries must decrease their reliance on traditional aid flows and focus on increasing domestic savings and resource mobilization, so they can better weather these global headwinds.

Our chosen title for this book, *Africa Reset: A New Way Forward*, emphasizes the need for an urgent break with the past and rethinking of old paradigms and approaches. Rather than just aiming towards prosperity in the distant future, the chapters in this book also deal with the medium-term, assessing the challenges and providing concrete policy recommendations that Africa's leaders and citizens can now take in the key areas to reset their economic trajectory, achieve their desired convergence, and meet the aspirations of their people. It also emphasizes what we see to be the two most important priorities for Africa: creating quality jobs to meet the needs of the continent's growing working-age population and eradicating extreme poverty through inclusive economic growth that targets the continent's poorest.

As with *Africa 2050*, this book is overall optimistic in its long-term prospects for the continent. However, given the changes in the global economic environment, it focuses much more on the immediate challenges resulting from these changes and examines how Africa can best overcome them in the medium-term to achieve the aspirational long-term scenario. We believe that with the right set of policies and, even more importantly, the political will to implement them, jobs can be created, the continent can be empowered, and Africa's development trajectory can be reset.

In the process, the world would conquer its final development frontier.

Harinder S. Kohli

President and Chief Executive Officer,
Centennial Group International
Founding Director and Chief Executive,
Emerging Markets Forum

Acknowledgments

This book originates from a series of policy papers commissioned by the Japan International Cooperation Agency (JICA) for the 6th TICAD meeting in Nairobi in August 2016. Some of these papers were revised and additional draft chapters of the book were subsequently presented and discussed at the 5th Africa Emerging Markets Forum in Abidjan in March 2017. The editors would like to thank all the participants in Nairobi and Abidjan for their comments and suggestions.

The book was made possible by generous financial and intellectual support from JICA and particularly the support of Tomoki Kobayashi and Hideki Watanabe. The editors would like to particularly thank Hiroshi Kato, Vice-President at JICA, for inspiring this book and serving as a co-author for the Epilogue chapter.

The editors are much obliged to Kaisa Alavuotunki, James Bond, Kevin Cleaver, Louise Fox, Gregory K. Ingram, Claudio Loser, Serge Michailof, Ritva Reinikka, and Hasan Tuluy, who generously accepted the invitation to contribute chapters and undertook numerous revisions following commentary in Nairobi and Abidjan, as well as numerous suggestions by the editors to make the book more cohesive and internally consistent.

Several colleagues at Centennial Group International also contributed to the realization of this volume. Harpaul Kohli undertook extensive modelling work underlying the scenarios presented in the book. Alden LeClair and Ieva Vilkelyte, who both co-authored chapters, as well as Michael Whelan and Ben Goodwin, provided invaluable research and production support. Additionally, Anil Sood provided support and commentary throughout the process.

The editors are deeply indebted to Michel Camdessus for his valuable insights, guidance, and suggestions throughout preparation of the papers and the final book.

The editors and the Emerging Markets Forum would like to express their immense gratitude to President Alassane Ouatarra for his strong support for the book, for hosting the Emerging Markets Forum in Abidjan, and for his continuing advocacy of the book's findings to his fellow Heads of State and other leading policymakers in Africa. In addition, they would like to thank Vice President Daniel Kablan Duncan for his active participation in the Forum and insightful comments in the panels, as well as Nialé Kaba, Minister of Planning and Development of Côte d'Ivoire, for serving as the official co-host of the Forum.

The editors thank Sylvie Naville and Hanzhi Jiang for their commitment to the planning and realization of the 5th Africa Emerging Markets Forum. They also thank Jean-Paul Dailly and the entire team at JPD Systems for their fast and high-quality French translations of several chapters for presentation at the Forum in Abidjan.

Finally, the editors and contributors acknowledge Oxford University Press India for their support and willingness to publish the book in record time.

Editors

Theodore Ahlers   Harinder S. Kohli

Introduction

Chapter 1

Harinder S. Kohli and Alden LeClair

A massive, highly diverse, and heterogeneous region

Continental Africa is one of the largest and, arguably, the most heterogeneous region of the world. With its 54 countries and a land mass roughly three times that of Europe, it has more countries than any other continent and, with 1.2 billion people, the second largest population after Asia with 4.2 billion. Given its size and number of countries, Africa is also exceptionally diverse. Its history ranges from ancient kingdoms to colonially-determined states that, with a few exceptions, became independent only in the middle of the 20th century. Its geography runs the gamut from deserts to tropical forests. Its natural resource endowments vary by country from extensive oil and mineral wealth to little more than poor soils. Its countries vary greatly in size: six have populations under one million, while four (Democratic Republic of the Congo, Egypt, Ethiopia, and Nigeria) have populations over 80 million in 2017.

At the national level, this diversity is further complicated in much of the continent by borders drawn by colonial authorities that frequently divided ethnic, geographic, or historical identities. There is, thus, no "one Africa" but rather several that share a single land mass, common borders, and a history of exchanges between local kingdoms centuries ago and foreign control through much of the 19th and early 20th centuries.

The economic diversity is as striking as the geographic, historic, or cultural (see Figure 1). The continent has 26 middle-income countries,[1] including upper-middle-income countries, such as Algeria, Botswana, South Africa, and Mauritius, that have been solidly middle-income for decades. Of the 18 African countries that were middle-income countries 25 years ago, however, only one, Seychelles, is high-income today. Africa also has 27 low-income countries[2] with a total population of 557 million (46 percent of Africans), including two where the average per capita income is below $1.90 a day (2015 PPP terms).

Overall, the region has the lowest per capita income in the world and the highest proportion of absolute poor. According to the World Bank, in 2015, 40 percent of people in Sub-Saharan Africa lived below the absolute poverty line.

Many of the low-income countries are landlocked, small, fragile, or conflict-affected. Sixteen countries are landlocked. Thirty-six countries have annual economic output of less than US$25 billion making it very difficult for their firms to generate economies of scale. And, one in three countries were classified as fragile according to the World Bank/African Development Bank (AfDB) Harmonized List in FY2017. These realities make economic and social development of the region very challenging.

The ongoing global geopolitical, economic, and environmental changes also expose Africa to additional challenges, but some of these developments could also present potential opportunities. Slower global economic growth, lower commodity prices, pushback against globalization in many countries, climate change, and tighter global financial markets make Africa's development and faster convergence with global best practice tougher to achieve but by no means impossible.

While the continent confronts these many daunting challenges, it must not let slip away the vast opportunities before it. Africa can harvest a huge potential demographic dividend in the coming decades. Indeed, by 2050, it will be the only region with a growing working-age population as the rest of the world faces aging and even declining populations; 72 percent of the world's growth in the working-age population between now and 2050 will be in Africa. Its natural resources will be sought by the resource-deficient economies in Asia, Europe, and elsewhere. Its local entrepreneurs could provide a spark to unleash domestic

1. Algeria, Angola, Botswana, Cameroon, Cape Verde, Republic of the Congo, Côte d'Ivoire, Djibouti, Egypt, Equatorial Guinea, Gabon, Ghana, Kenya, Lesotho, Libya, Mauritania, Mauritius, Morocco, Namibia, Nigeria, Sao Tome and Principe, South Africa, Sudan, Swaziland, Tunisia, and Zambia.

2. . Benin, Burkina Faso, Burundi, Central African Republic, Chad, Comoros, Democratic Republic of the Congo, Eritrea, Ethiopia, The Gambia, Guinea, Guinea-Bissau, Liberia, Madagascar, Malawi, Mali, Mozambique, Niger, Rwanda, Senegal, Sierra Leone, Somalia, South Sudan, Tanzania, Togo, Uganda, and Zimbabwe.

Africa has a very large scope to catch up with the global productivity frontier and attract international investors, as Asia did in the past 50 years.

Figure 1: Africa is largely made up of low- and lower-middle income countries

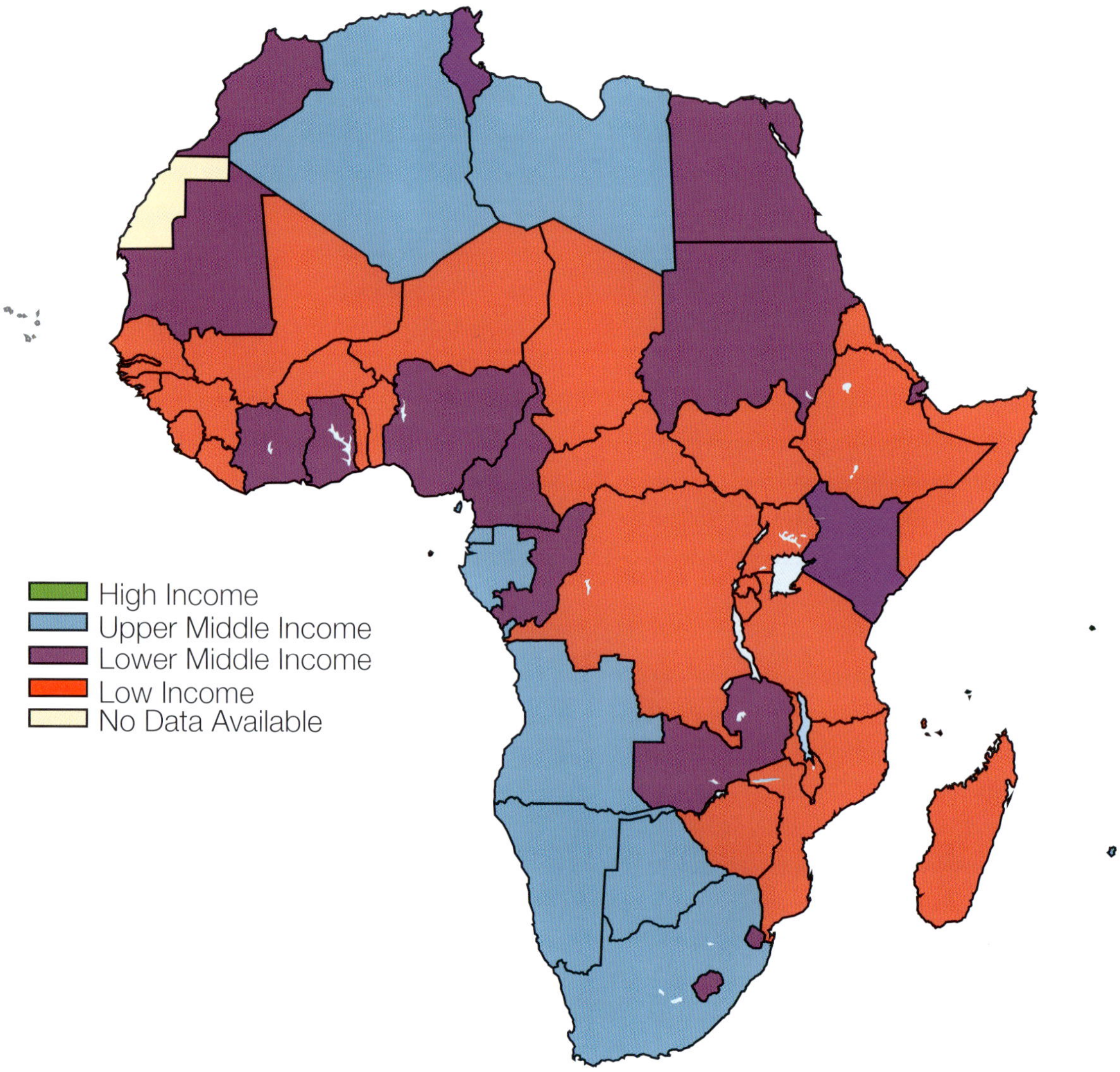

Source: World Bank (2016d)

private enterprise and harness unfolding technological changes. And, finally, Africa has a very large scope to catch up with the global productivity frontier and attract international investors, as Asia did in the past 50 years.[3]

3. This section and some other parts of the book build on the work done by the authors for the African Development Bank's Special Panel on Accelerating Development Impact of the High 5s (see its report of May 2017).

Some African countries are already on track to achieve such convergence. One out of six countries has averaged a per capita income growth above 3½ percent since 2010, the rate achieved by the successful Asian economies in the 1970s and 1980s. But, in the aggregate, growth in Africa has been slowing in recent years, partly because of the weak performance of two of its largest economies (Nigeria

It is possible to reverse the recent trends, significantly raise Africa's economic growth, and create more quality jobs, provided that decisive actions are taken soon to exploit the available opportunities.

and South Africa). For the first time in 20 years, per capita income in Africa declined in 2016. Overall, during the past decade, the continent's growth was slower than the rest of world and its share of global output fell back to 3 percent, where it was twenty years ago. Equally worrisome, African economies are not creating good jobs on nearly the scale needed for the 200 million young people who are projected to enter the labor market during the next decade.[4] It is urgent to address this widening gap.

The authors of this volume are persuaded that it is possible to reverse the recent trends, significantly raise Africa's economic growth, and create more quality jobs, provided that decisive actions are taken soon to exploit the available opportunities. This would put Africa on a fast track to converge with the rest of the world and achieve robust growth in per capita income. Promoting such convergence is the underlying motivation of the book.

Region-wide approaches and studies such as this book have both value and limitations. They are useful vehicles for developing and debating a broad vision for the region as a whole, identifying common opportunities and challenges, and agreeing on a general framework for realizing the vision. But beyond this, the specific strategies as well as the action agenda and its timetable must be developed at the level of each economy depending on its unique circumstances, including its economic and political history, aspirations of its people, stage of development, resource endowment, and sophistication of institutions and governance.

What is unique about this book?

The point of departure of this book is a vision of where Africa can be 40 years—or two generations— from now. The vision is deliberately based on stretch goals in key social and economic areas. While clearly ambitious, the vision is certainly plausible. To illustrate the economic and social costs of inaction, Chapter 2 presents two scenarios: the convergence scenario and the central scenario (under which productivity growth is much slower). The differences in the outcomes in 2060 (GDP per capita, poverty levels, size of the middle class, Africa's share of global GDP) are staggering.

The chapter identifies the key multi-generational and crosscutting issues, challenges, and risks that must be tackled starting now in order to realize the vision. The intent is to inspire and lift the ambitions of all Africans and their leaders. Subsequent chapters highlight sectoral issues that require action on an urgent basis and suggest possible strategies to tackle them so that the longer-term aspirational vision can indeed be realized.

There are four other distinguishing features of the book:

- It focuses on multi-generational issues that require long lead times and are critical for Africa to meet the rising aspirations of its people.
- It results from the efforts of a highly experienced international team that has no institutional or ideological agenda.
- It combines analytical work on the lessons from other regions, particularly from Asia and Latin America, with the best existing work on Africa.
- It puts forth a framework that transcends the traditional ideological debates and gives equal priority to three overarching prerequisites for realizing the vision: putting greater focus on people, inclusion, and social cohesion; enhancing the competitiveness of African economies; and achieving greater cooperation, trade, and capital flows within the continent and with the rest of the world.

Assumptions and organization

The work underlying this book is based on several assumptions about the global economy. First, it is assumed that overall the world will remain peaceful and that there will be neither a widespread military conflict nor a natural or man-made calamity (e.g., nuclear war) affecting

4. This number is based on the increase in the working-age population as projected in United Nations. (2015). *World Population Prospects: The 2015 Revision*. New York: Department of Economic and Social Affairs, Population Division, CD-ROM edition.

Today, some 18 million youth enter the job market each year. Creating jobs for them is most urgent, and the jobs need to be created where the young live (i.e., mostly in the rural areas).

a wide swath of humanity. Second, that the ongoing historic shift in the balance of the global economy from North America and Europe to emerging markets will continue peacefully, as over the past 70 years. Third, that the global financial and trading systems will remain stable and continue to drive further globalization, though with the usual ups and downs associated with business cycles. Fourth, that changes in the Earth's climate will remain within the range currently anticipated by the scientific community. And, finally, that the pace of technological progress and improvements in the productivity frontier will be similar to that over the past century. If one or more of these assumptions fail to hold, then the outcomes for the world economy as a whole, including Africa, could well be outside the scenarios portrayed in the book.

The book is intentionally not comprehensive. Instead, it covers a limited number of topics that, in the view of the book's authors, will have a decisive impact on African economies over the next 40 years. Other criteria for selecting the topics included: intergenerational nature of the issues, horizontal interplay between the issues, and availability of data for all or the vast majority of countries. In addition, the book does not cover certain important topics covered in recent work elsewhere or in our earlier book, *Africa 2050*, published in 2014 (e.g., demographics, climate change, governance).[5] These subjects are recognized in the book, but detailed analysis and the related action agendas are not developed here.

This volume comprises twelve chapters. After this introduction, Chapter 2 by Theodore Ahlers, "Imagining Africa 40 Years from Now," paints two dramatically different scenarios for the continent depending on what actions its leaders take in seven key policy areas beginning today. In developing the scenarios, Ahlers looks at the actual performance during the past decade, compares key indicators for Africa and Asia to draw lessons for the future, and suggests that for Africa to converge rapidly with the rest of the world it needs to aim at annual per capita income growth of 3½ percent. Chapter 3 by Louise Fox, "Africa's Inclusive Growth Challenge: Reducing Deprivation and Creating Jobs," points out that despite a decade and half of growth, poverty and inequality in Africa remain high and almost half of the population still lives in a state of extreme deprivation. Today, some 18 million youth enter the job market each year.[6] Creating jobs for them is most urgent, and the jobs need to be created where the young live (i.e., mostly in the rural areas). Improving productivity in agriculture is crucial as is creating and growing labor-intensive, non-SMEs. Chapter 4 by Kaisa Alavuotunki and Ritva Reinikka, "Building Human Capital: Improving Education Quality," develops a vision for education in Africa consistent with the convergence scenario articulated by Ahlers and tries to formulate a road map for how to get there. In assessing the situation today, they present the good news that the continent has made good progress on public spending targets and raising primary school enrollment rates in most countries. But they raise serious concerns about the quality of education and the reality that students are not learning basics skills. Without urgent actions on this front, the continent will not be able to realize the so-called demographic dividend or see its firms become competitive in a globalized economy.

Chapter 5, "Transforming Rural Africa: Growing a Productive Agriculture Sector" by Kevin Cleaver, is a bridge between Chapters 3 and 6 on people and social issues and the next six chapters on individual sectors. Given that some 60 percent of all Africans live in rural areas, most of the poor are rural and the immediate scope for creating large number of jobs possibly lies in agriculture-related activities, particularly in low- and lower-middle-income countries. Cleaver demonstrates the tremendous scope for improving agricultural productivity through greater private investment and management, improved rural institutions and infrastructure, better donor coordination, and more aggressive climate change adaptation and mitigation.

5. Ahlers, T. Kato, H., Kohli, H., Madavo, C., & Sood. A. (eds.). *Africa 2050: Realizing the Continent's Full Potential*. New Delhi: Oxford University Press.

6. United Nations (2015)

Openness to the global markets (including joining global value chains), promotion of industrial clusters, better infrastructure, faster progress on creating regional markets, and improvement of the local skills base are all high priority for economic diversification to succeed.

Chapter 6, "The Impact of Commodity Terms of Trade in Africa: Curse, Blessing or Manageable Reality?" by Claudio and Ieva Vilkelyte, discusses the important issue of the strong interplay between commodity cycles in international markets and the fortunes of many African economies. The authors quantify the impact of commodity prices and countries' terms of trade in commodity-exporting economies. They show that Africa remains more dependent on commodity exports than Latin America and suggest policy measures to reduce the continent's vulnerabilities to future shocks. Next, in Chapter 7, "Economic Diversification of African Economies," James Bond discusses the longer-term objective of reducing Africa's heavy dependence on commodity exports while creating well-paying jobs in manufacturing and services. He suggests that policy makers need to focus on creating the right economic (business) environment and work closely with the private sector to proactively promote new sources of economic growth. Openness to the global markets (including joining global value chains), promotion of industrial clusters, better infrastructure, faster progress on creating regional markets, and improvement of the local skills base are all high priority for economic diversification to succeed. The next three chapters address some of these issues. Chapter 8, "Africa's Infrastructure Deficit: Closing the Gap," also by James Bond, highlights the infrastructure constraint to Africa's economic and social development. This chapter demonstrates that Africa is the least-endowed region in the world in terms of infrastructure. It also does not perform well on the quality of services delivered to users; they are costly and undependable. The chapter outlines the need for developing new models of infrastructure delivery that move away from state-owned enterprises, improving management of assets with more cost-reflective tariffs and government payment, and increasing private financing of infrastructure. Chapter 9, "Urbanization and Demographics: Planning Cities That Work" by Gregory K. Ingram, is closely related to the previous two chapters. Cities that work are critical for the long-term future of Africa both because that is where the majority of Africans will live and because they provide the location for most modern economic activities (industry and high-value services). Ingram points out that a large proportion of Africa's infrastructure will be built in and around cities. Given the rapid pace of urbanization expected between now and 2060, it is urgent that countries pay much more attention to better urban planning, improved urban governance, strengthened urban institutions, and financing sources. Ingram also highlights the link between climate change and urban development on the one hand and between urbanization and loss of agriculture land on the other.

Chapter 10, "Regional Economic Integration in Africa" by Hasan Tuluy, highlights an issue important to the region because of its many small economies and land-locked countries. The chapter points out that despite the importance of deeper economic integration to the region as a whole and its adoption as a political objective at the highest levels—including at the African Union Summits—the actual progress has been meager. Tuluy calls for a new, more pragmatic, bottom-up approach that will serve business needs along the lines of the integration achieved by East Asia. This chapter is followed by the last substantive chapter, which discusses the very worrisome conflict phenomena that currently threaten the safety and well-being of people in countries with almost one fourth of all Africans. Chapter 11, "New Threats to Africa's Stability and Growth" by Serge Michailof, discusses the key factors that have led to fragility in many parts of Africa, particularly in the Sahel. He then suggests a possible program of action to be supported by the international community that will rebuild the state apparatus in the countries concerned, help reduce rural poverty, reform the education systems, create new jobs, and bring down the rate of population growth. The book concludes with a brief epilogue by Harinder Kohli and Hiroshi Kato highlighting the book's messages on how to realize the aspirational vision (convergence scenarios) advocated by the authors.

Imagining Africa 40 Years from Now

Chapter 2

Theodore Ahlers

The next 40 years—which Africa will emerge?

Africa faces both big opportunities and worrisome threats, and which Africa emerges over the next 40 years—a dynamic continent with a growing influence in the world or an economic backwater that exports its people and capital—depends on what countries do now. This chapter presents two indicative scenarios to 2060, looks at actual performance in the current decade, highlights the differences in performance among countries, and identifies the biggest policy issues to be addressed if Africa is to converge with the rest of the world and avoid the potential social and political turmoil associated with its projected demographics.

The pace of population, productivity, and investment growth has staggering implications for people's lives over the next 40 years. These implications are illustrated by the differences in per capita incomes, poverty, and size of the middle class under two indicative scenarios: the central scenario of the latest Centennial Group global economic model[1] and an Africa convergence scenario.[2] As discussed in greater detail below, the difference between the two scenarios is driven by differences in the level of investment in Africa and in the pace at which structural reforms are undertaken to increase productivity. While it is possible to argue for more pessimistic or more optimistic scenarios, a comparison of these two scenarios illustrates what is at stake.

Need annual per capita income growth of 3½ percent

In the central scenario, Africa would grow over the next 40 years but make no further progress in catching up with the rest of the world in terms of per capita income. Africa's share of global GDP would almost double to around 9 percent (in line with its population growth) after averaging only around 4 percent (2014 PPP$) for the last 40 years (Figure 1). Under such a scenario, Africa would be economically more important and its people somewhat better off. It would not, however, be converging with the rest of the world. Africa's share of world GDP under the central scenario is considerably less than envisaged in the Africa convergence scenario, under which Africa's share would more than triple to 15 percent of global GDP by 2060.

Faster economic growth since the mid-1990s slowed the long slide in Africa's per capita GDP as a share of the global average. But it has remained around one third of the global average for the last 15 years (Figure 2) while that for Asia has continued to grow rapidly. The African averages, of course, mask a high level of variation among countries. The issue is not that all African countries are slipping but that divergence in performance across Africa is growing. For Africa to converge with the rest of the world, a much larger number of countries will need to pursue African best practice policies.

In the central scenario, Africa's per capita incomes would rise (Figure 3) but, even 40 years from now, per capita incomes would still be stuck at less than a third of the global average (Figure 4). The rest of the world would be growing faster and Africans would not be on track to catch up. Such an increase in per capita incomes is much less than that envisaged under the Africa convergence scenario where by 2060 per capita incomes would increase five-fold relative to today's level and increase from one-third of the global average to over one-half. This is what Africa needs to meet people's fast rising expectations.

If Africa is to catch up with the rest of the world, it needs annual per capita GDP growth of 3½ percent or more between now and 2060. In the central scenario, global per capita income growth over the next 40 years would be around 2½ percent per year. If Africa is to converge, it must aim for per capita growth at least a percentage point higher. In the central scenario, Africa's annual per capita income growth would be only around 2.2 percent through

1. See Kohli, H. (ed.). (2016). *The World in 2050: Striving for a more just, prosperous, and harmonious global community*. New Delhi: Oxford University Press, for a discussion of the global central scenario.

2. The Africa convergence scenario in this paper is an update of the convergence scenario that originally appeared in Ahlers et al. (2014). It applies the original Africa convergence parameters (increasing investment and accelerated productivity growth in Africa) to the updated Centennial global model and extends the scenario to 2060.

In the central scenario, Africa would grow over the next 40 years but make no further progress in catching up with the rest of the world.

Figure 1: Africa's share of world GDP (PPP), 2015–60

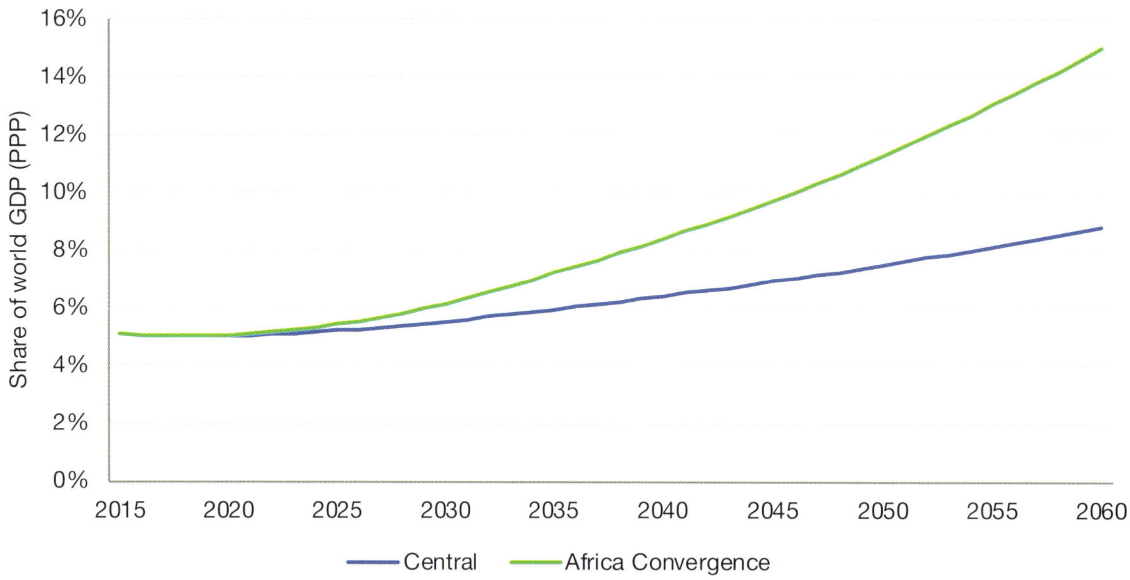

Source: Centennial Group International (2017)

Figure 2: GDP per capita as a share of the world average, Africa and Asia, 1960–2016

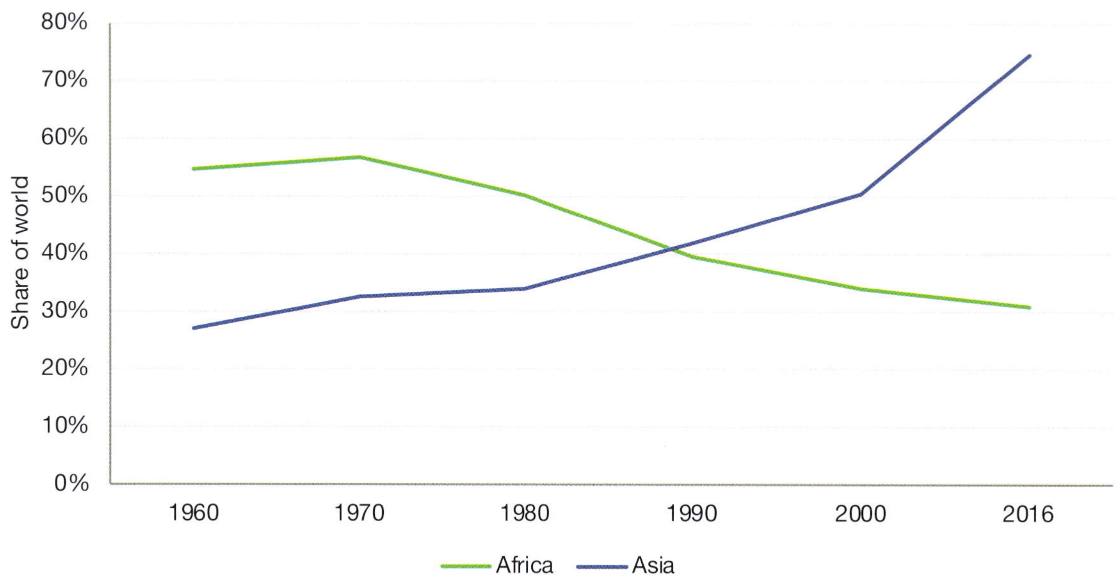

Source: IMF (2017)

In the central scenario, Africa's per capita incomes would rise but, even 40 years from now, per capita incomes would still be stuck at only a third of the global average.

Figure 3: GDP per capita (PPP), 2015–60

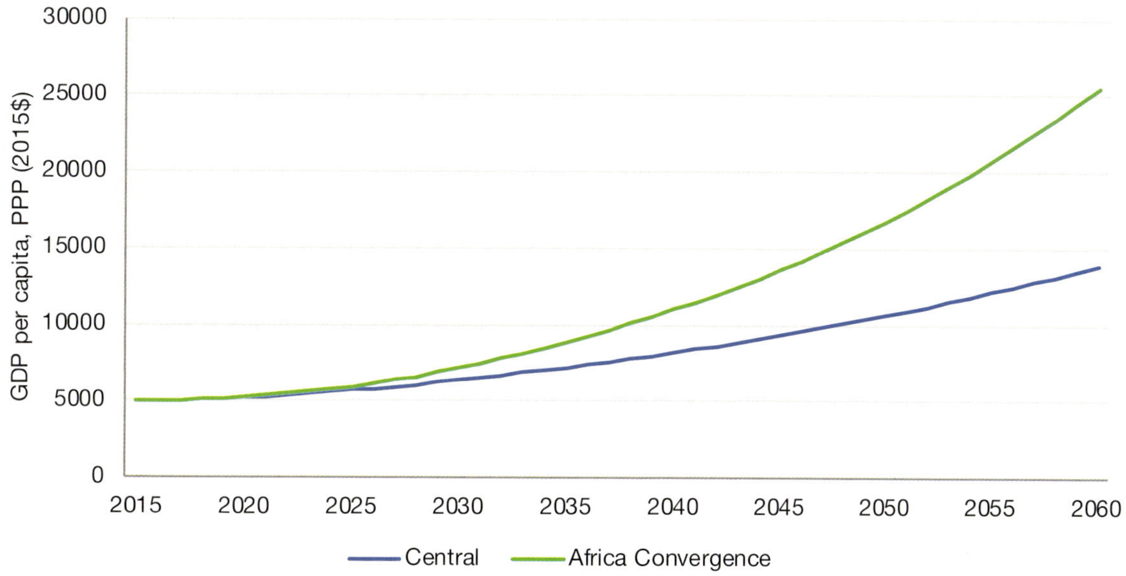

Source: Centennial Group International (2017)

Figure 4: Africa's GDP per capita as share of global average (PPP), 2015–60

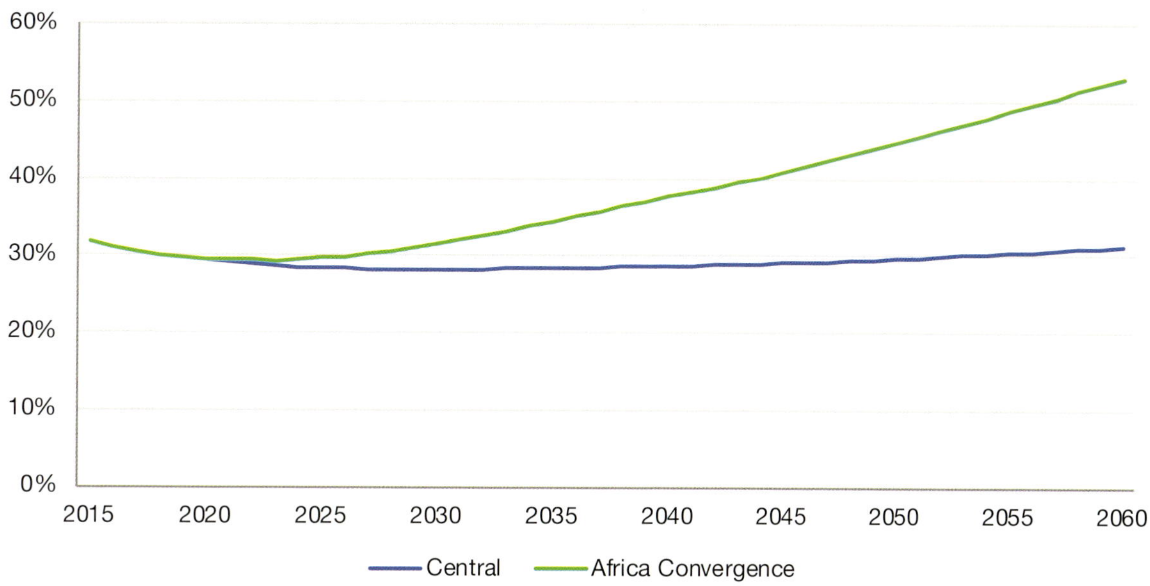

Source: Centennial Group International (2017)

The evolution of GDP and per capita incomes in the central scenario means 200 million more people in poverty than in the convergence scenario.

2040 and 2.7 percent from there to 2060. Under the convergence scenario, it would be 3.6 percent and then rise to 4.3 percent.

Convergence means millions fewer poor and half a billion more middle class Africans

The evolution of GDP and per capita incomes in the central scenario means 200 million more people in poverty than in the convergence scenario. Under the central scenario, the poverty headcount ratio in Africa would decline from 34 percent in 2015 to around 14 percent in 2060 (Figure 5). The number of poor would be more than 200 million higher than under the convergence scenario where poverty falls to less than 3 percent.

The central scenario also implies more than half a billion fewer Africans in the middle class by 2060 than in the convergence scenario. Under the central scenario, the proportion of Africans in the middle class rises from some 20 percent today to about 50 percent in 2060 (Figure 6).[3] This is far below the more than 70 percent middle class envisioned in the Africa convergence scenario. Again, the difference in human terms is large—more than half a billion fewer Africans in the middle class.

Africa diverging

The big question for African leaders in all fields is how to restart and sustain the convergence that has stalled in recent years. Africa's share of world population has been rising since the early 1900s but its share of world GDP continued to decline for almost a century (Figure 7). In practical terms, this means that people's incomes fell dramatically relative to the rest of the world. This long-term secular trend was reversed in the mid-1990s, when Africa's share

3. Middle class is defined as per capita income between $10 and $100 per day in 2005 PPP$ as set out in Kharas, H. (2010). The Emerging Middle Class in Developing Countries. *OECD Development Centre Working Paper* (285).. In 2014 PPP$ this corresponds to per capita income between $12 and $108 per day.

Figure 5: Poverty level in Africa, 2015–60 (% of population)

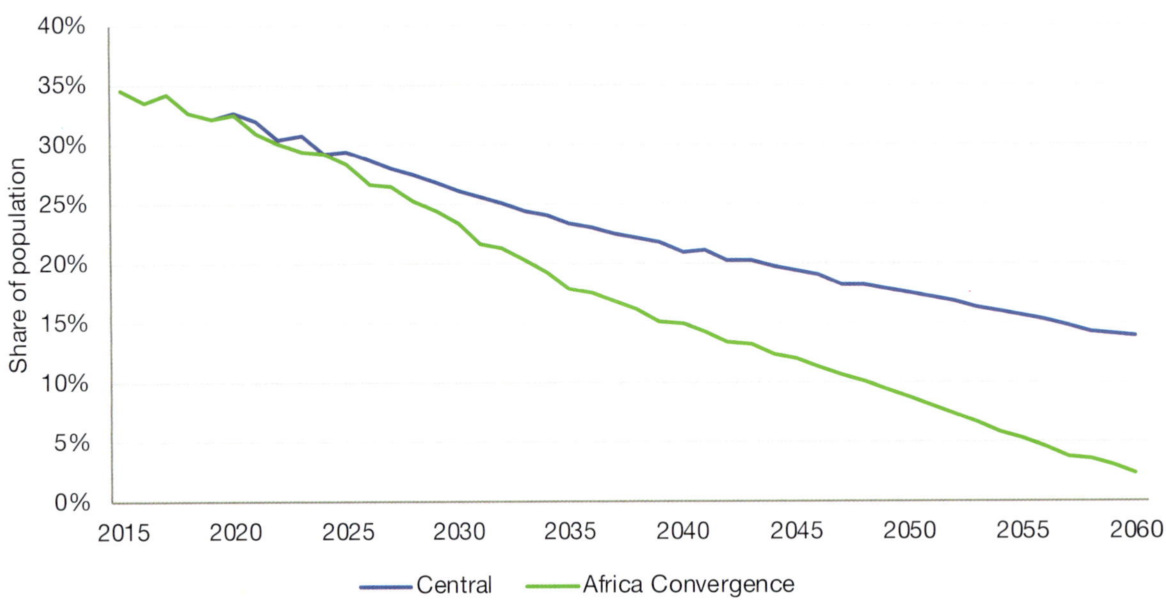

Source: Centennial Group International (2017)

The big question for African leaders in all fields is how to restart and sustain the convergence that has stalled in recent years.

Figure 6: Share of middle class in Africa, 2015–60 (% of population)

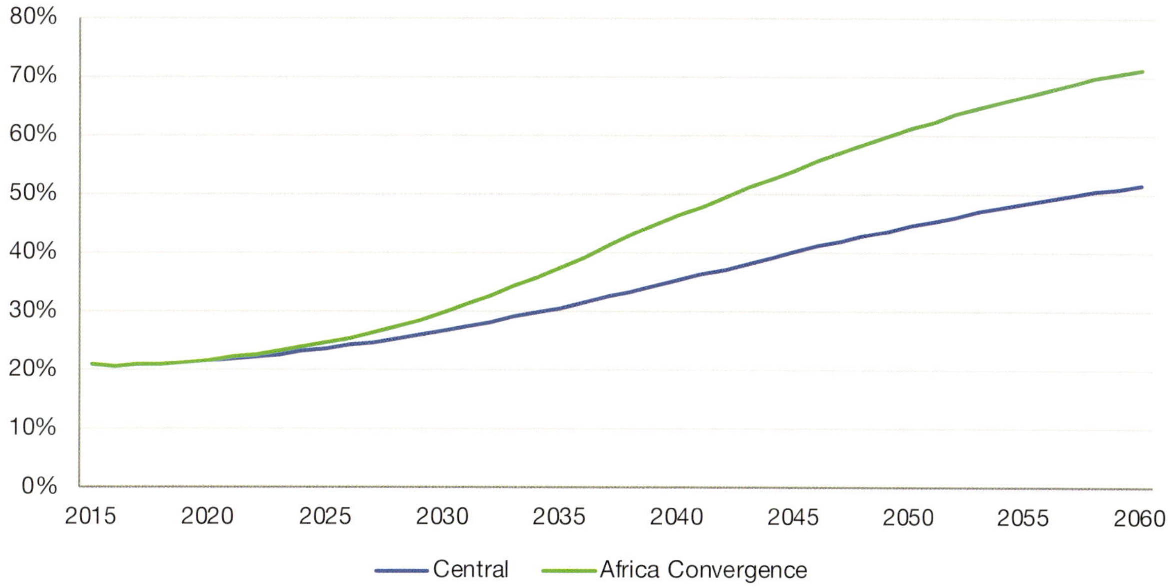

Source: Centennial Group International (2017)

Figure 7: Africa's share of world population and world GDP, 1700–2016

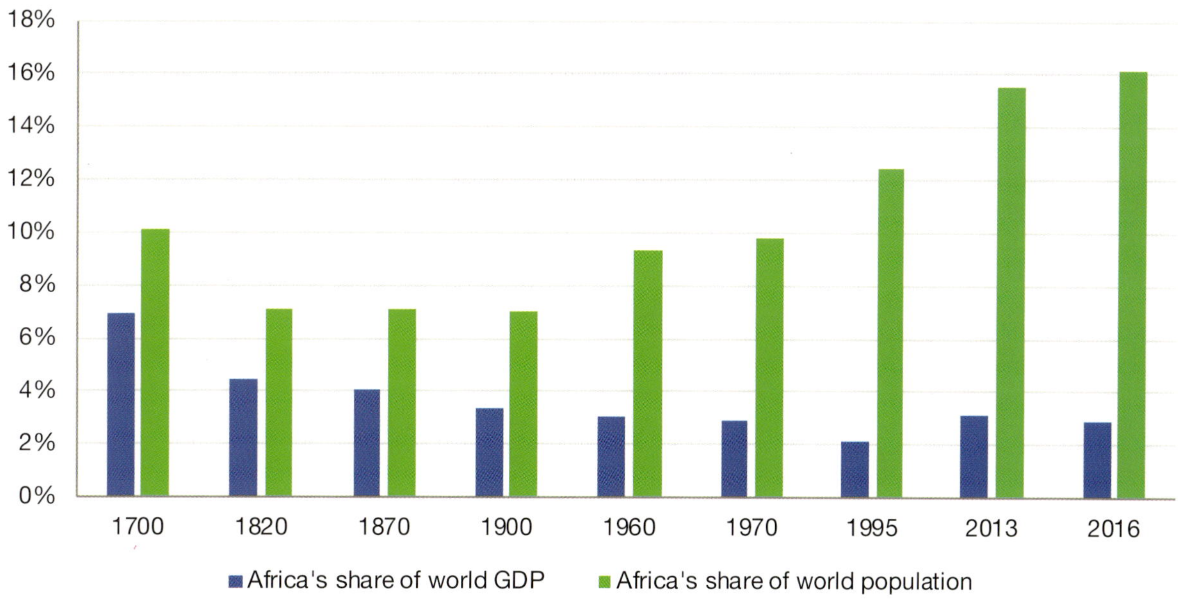

Source: Maddison (2013) for 1700-1900; Centennial Group International (2017) for 1960–2016

For the first time in 20 years, per capita income in Africa declined in 2016, and it is rebounding only weakly in 2017.

of world GDP (at market exchange rates) grew rapidly for some 15 years, reaching 3 percent in 2013: Africans were catching up with the rest of the world. That growth stalled at the beginning of this decade and has not resumed. As a result, Africa's share of world GDP in 2016 was still only 3 percent.

Africa has been growing and many of its socioeconomic indicators continue to improve, but it is no longer catching up with the rest of the world as measured by per capita incomes. Economic growth has slowed around the world since 2010 but more so in Africa than elsewhere. GDP growth in Africa in 2016 and 2017 will be well below global GDP growth.[4] For the first time in more than a decade, Africa's share of global GDP will shrink, in striking contrast to 2000-10 when Africa's share of global GDP grew. Throughout this period, Africa's share of global population has steadily risen, as its population growth rate has continued to outpace that of the rest of the world.

Africa is now again diverging with the rest of the world. Per capita incomes in Africa have been falling relative to the rest of the world throughout the current decade (Figure 8). Africa's per capita incomes have continued to grow since 2010 (1.2 percent a year), but global per capita incomes have grown twice as fast (2.3 percent) and those in emerging and developing economies, three times as fast (3.5 percent). The gap has, moreover, been growing. For the first time in 20 years, per capita income in Africa declined in 2016, and it is rebounding only weakly in 2017. This performance should be a wake-up call to all African leaders and institutions.

Policies rather than endowments determine performance

African averages conceal enormous differences between countries, and this divergence tells a more revealing story than the continent-wide average. First is the difference between countries highly dependent on oil

4. IMF. (2017). *World Economic Outlook*.

Figure 8: Per capita GDP growth has slowed more in Africa than elsewhere

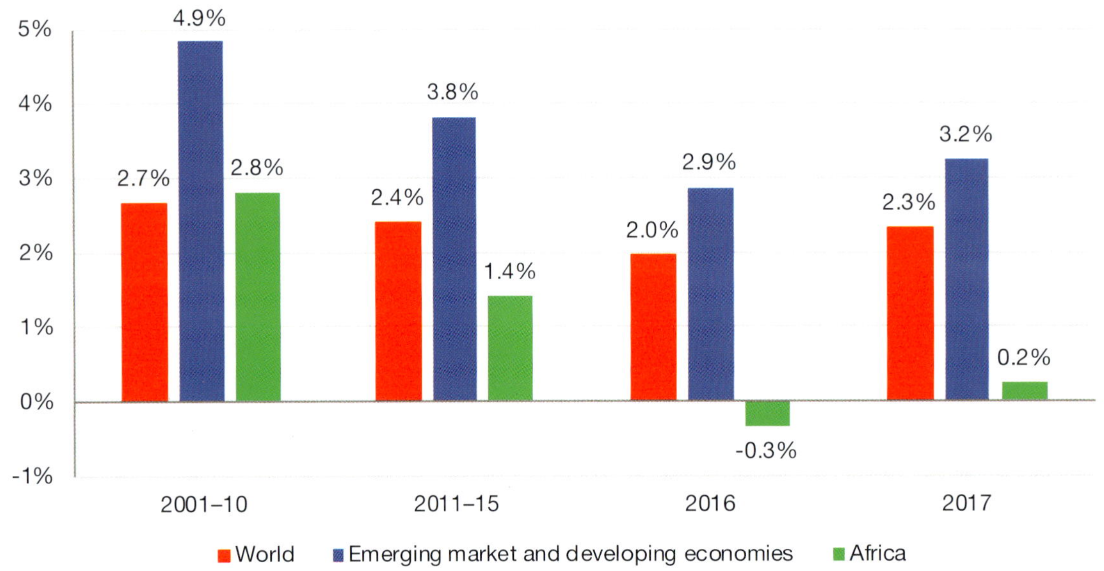

Note: Data for Libya are excluded because of very large (>50%) annual swings in GDP related to the effect of the ongoing conflict on oil production.
Source: Author's calculations based on IMF (2017)

The divergence among countries shows that policies rather than natural resource endowments determined performance.

or mineral exports and those not. Second is the difference between strong and weak performers in these groups. In the first decade of the century, per capita incomes in Africa's oil exporters grew very rapidly (4.1 percent a year) driven by the income gains from high and rising oil prices (Figure 9). But their per capita income growth fell by 70 percent in 2011-15 (to 1.2 percent a year) and turned negative in 2016 and 2017 (-1.0 and -0.5 percent). Per capita income growth in the other resource-intensive economies has been much lower but followed a similar downward trend. For the non-resource-intensive economies, per capita income growth has been modest, but it has been accelerating since 2000 and far above that for the oil or other resource-intensive economies throughout the current decade.

The divergence among countries shows that policies rather than natural resource endowments determined performance. Since 2010, 12 countries in Africa have achieved average per capita GDP growth rates above 3 percent a year.[5] This very diverse group of high performers includes countries large and small; landlocked and coastal; resource-intensive and non-resource-intensive; and with low-, lower-middle, and upper-middle incomes. None of these characteristics determine performance. Instead, it is what countries do—the policies of their governments, the responsiveness of their entrepreneurs, the integrity of their institutions and the political will of their leaders—that makes the difference. This is good news for the continent. Many countries show that convergence is possible, even with less auspicious global conditions. If this African best practice were generalized, the continent would be transformed.

Act now....or accept marginalization

Which Africa emerges by 2060 depends most on what governments, firms and entrepreneurs, and civil society do now. Global economic conditions may be tougher and new

5. Botswana, Côte d'Ivoire, Democratic Republic of the Congo, Djibouti, Ethiopia, Ghana, Lesotho, Mauritius, Mozambique, Rwanda, Seychelles, and Tanzania.

Figure 9: And it slowed most for oil exporters, 2001–17 (%)

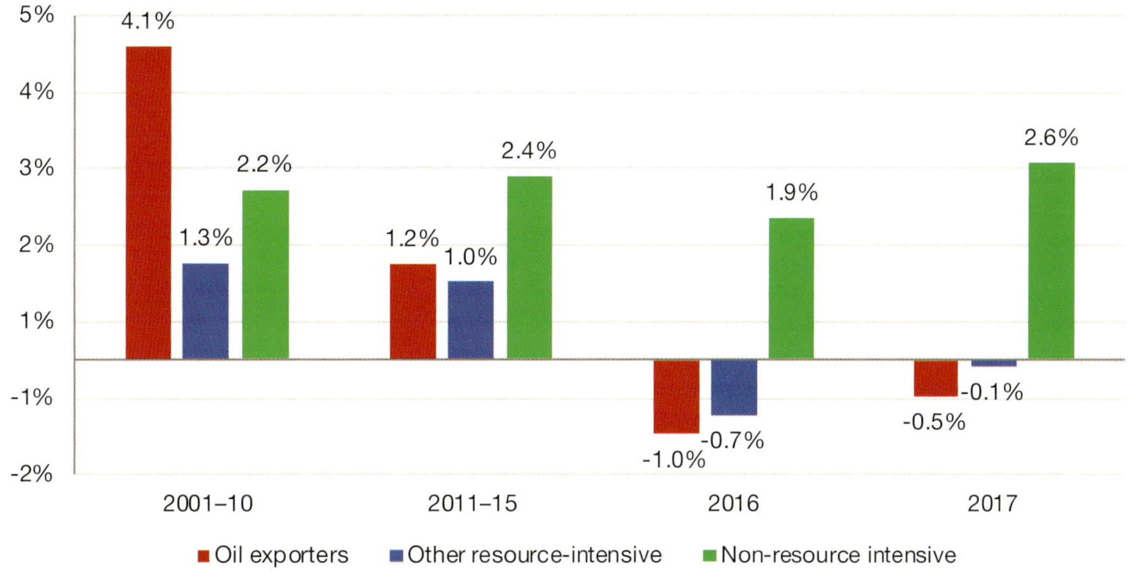

Note: Data for Libya are excluded because of very large (>50%) annual swings in GDP related to the effect of the ongoing conflict on oil production.
Source: Author's calculations based on IMF (2017)

If African best practice were generalized across the continent, Africa would be transformed. And the Africa of 2060 would indeed meet the aspirations of its people.

challenges have arisen but a number of countries continue to do well. These countries have shown what needs to be done and had the political leadership to do it. Elsewhere, political will to reform is often the missing ingredient. Again, if African best practice were generalized across the continent, Africa would be transformed. And the Africa of 2060 would indeed meet the aspirations of its people.

Tougher world demands tougher action

Slower global growth, lower commodity prices, and tighter capital markets make the world a tougher place—and demand tougher reforms if Africa is to converge with the rest of the world. First, global growth in 2016-17 is down by nearly 20 percent compared to a decade earlier (Figure 10). Having averaged more than 4 percent over 2000-10, global growth has been on a downward trend since 2011 and fell to just 3.3 percent in 2016-17. It is, moreover, projected to remain below 4 percent over the next decade, with many downside risks. Among other things, this means that markets for African exports will grow more slowly.

Second, the super-cycle of commodity price increases has ended. Commodity prices tripled between the late 1990s and 2011 (Figure 11). As a result, Africa's terms of trade rose dramatically, much more than in other regions such as Asia, with an accompanying increase in income. Commodity prices have since fallen by half. They are still higher than they were in 2000 but are not projected to return to the levels of 2006-13 in the next decade.

Finally, capital markets have tightened and the very low interest rates and high liquidity of recent years that facilitated a surge in African sovereign debt issuance are gone. The Africa frontier markets (NEXGEM)[6] spread was less than 350 basis points two years ago, but has now increased by 75 percent to around 600 basis points (Figure 12). In addition, the spread between the Emerging Markets Bond Index (EMBIG) and that for African frontier markets

6. The J.P. Morgan Next Generation Markets index (NEXGEM) includes the smaller, less liquid emerging market economies where investment opportunities in external debt markets are limited relative to the larger BRIC countries and other emerging economies where external debt issuance is frequent and large. NEXGEM Africa includes Côte d'Ivoire, Kenya, Ghana, Zambia, Egypt, Nigeria, Gabon, Senegal, Angola, Ethiopia, Mozambique, and Tanzania.

Figure 10: Average world GDP growth

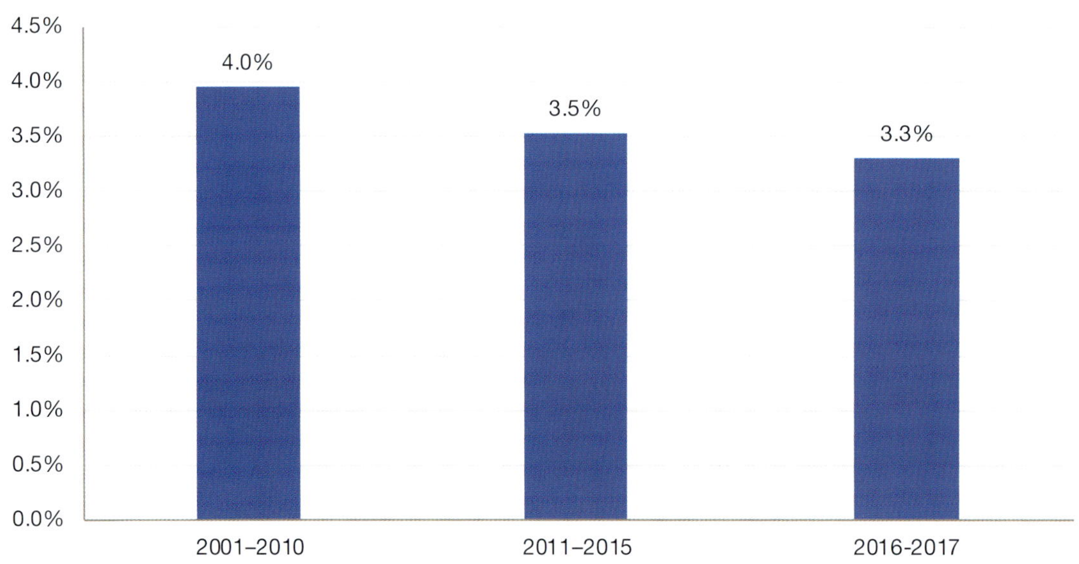

Source: Centennial Group (2017)

To realize its potential and avoid future social conflict Africa needs to re-start convergence.

Figure 11: Terms of trade for selected regions (2000 = 100)

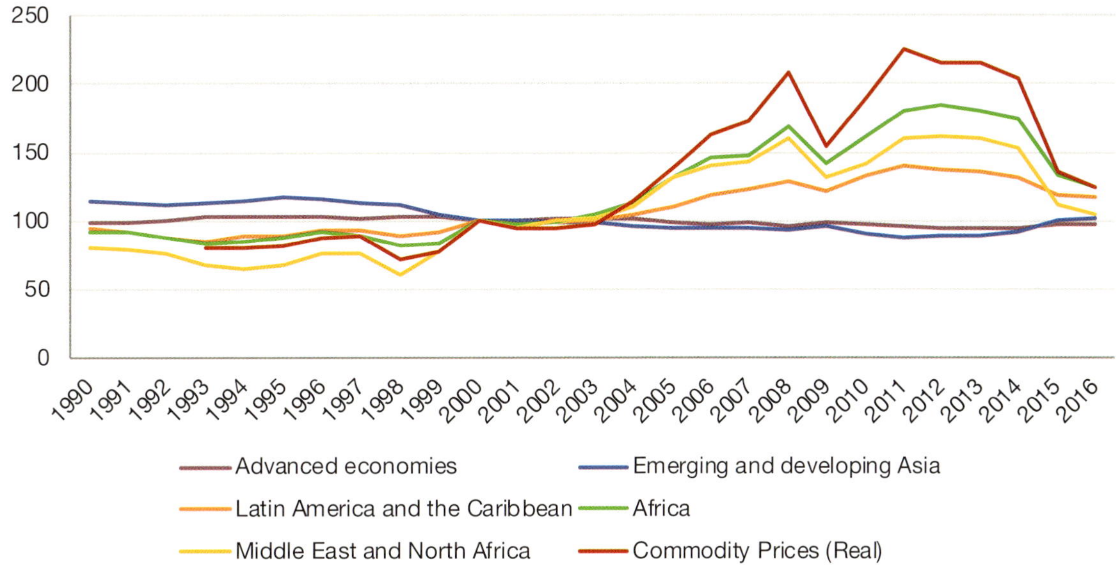

Source: IMF (2016, 2017)

has more than tripled moving from around 70 basis points to around 250.[7] Global rates have risen and the appetite for risk has declined.

Africa also has many opportunities. If these opportunities are seized, the continent can be transformed. Africa has good scope to catch up with global best practice—as Asia did over the past half century—to converge with advanced economies and realize higher incomes for its people. If fertility rates are reduced, Africa's demographics could become its greatest long-term comparative advantage, since by 2050 it will be the only region with a young and growing work force. Urbanization and a rapidly growing middle class could drive productivity growth throughout the continent. Technological advances could increase productivity and alleviate many challenges facing the region. The shift of the global economic center of gravity toward Asia offers new market opportunities. And the continent's strong natural resource base can, if managed well, fuel growth.

Restarting convergence—seven priority areas for action

To realize its potential and avoid future social conflict Africa needs to re-start convergence. The changes in the external environment discussed above are not a surprise—what counts is what countries do, beginning now. The important questions now are how effectively countries invest in physical and human capital for future growth and to increase their resiliency and how quickly they adjust to the new circumstances. Country performance on these points is highly variable across Africa but is, in the aggregate, weak. If countries do not respond rapidly to the new circumstances, the gains of the last decade will be lost. Action on seven fronts is particularly important to enable a return to a convergence path: accelerating the demographic transition; reducing commodity dependence; increasing savings and investment and unleashing the

7. The J.P. Morgan Emerging Market Bond Index Global Diversified (EMBIG index) is a uniquely weighted US-$-denominated emerging markets sovereign index and is the most widely followed benchmark in its class.

Africa's transition to a modern demographic profile of low fertility and low infant mortality is proceeding even more slowly than previously foreseen.

Figure 12: Emerging market and Africa sovereign spreads, September 2014–September 2016

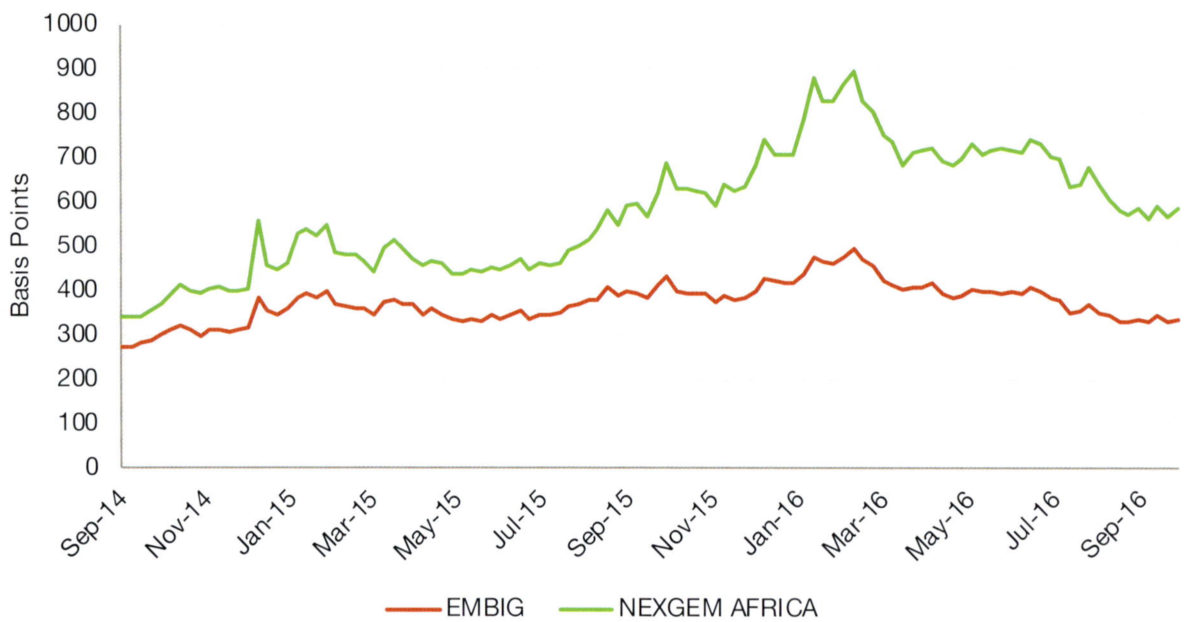

Source: Bloomberg. (2016)

private sector; accelerating productivity growth; reducing conflict and fragility; adapting to climate change; and reducing disparities.

Accelerate the demographic transition

According to the latest UN projections, Africa's transition to a modern demographic profile of low fertility and low infant mortality is proceeding even more slowly than previously foreseen. The variation in the evolution of fertility rates across countries is remarkable. Figure 13 shows fertility over the last 50 years for 13 countries that span the current variation in fertility levels. Three things are particularly striking: (i) 50 years ago, all the countries had fertility rates above 6; (ii) many countries have demonstrated that rapid declines are possible over a decade or two, such as Mauritius and Tunisia in the 60s and 70s, Botswana and South Africa in the 80s and 90s, and Ethiopia and Rwanda over the last twenty years; and (iii) at the same time, fertility levels in a number of countries have not changed at all in 50 years. The result is that fertility now varies from around 2 to more than 7.

The slow demographic transition in Africa has a very large cumulative effect and big implications for the jobs challenge. Africa's dependency ratio is projected to decline through 2050 creating the possibility of a large demographic dividend. The slow demographic transition, however, makes both the human capital formation and job creation challenges, and hence realization of a demographic dividend, orders of magnitude more challenging in Africa than elsewhere.

Good jobs require skilled people—providing quality education for all will be possible only with slower population growth. Given the challenges of providing access to a quality education to today's school-age population in Africa,[8] the speed at which that population increases is

8. See Chapter 4, "Building Human Capital: Improving Education Quality."

The slow demographic transition in Africa has a very large cumulative effect and big implications for the jobs challenge.

Figure 13: Fertility rates by country, 1965–2050

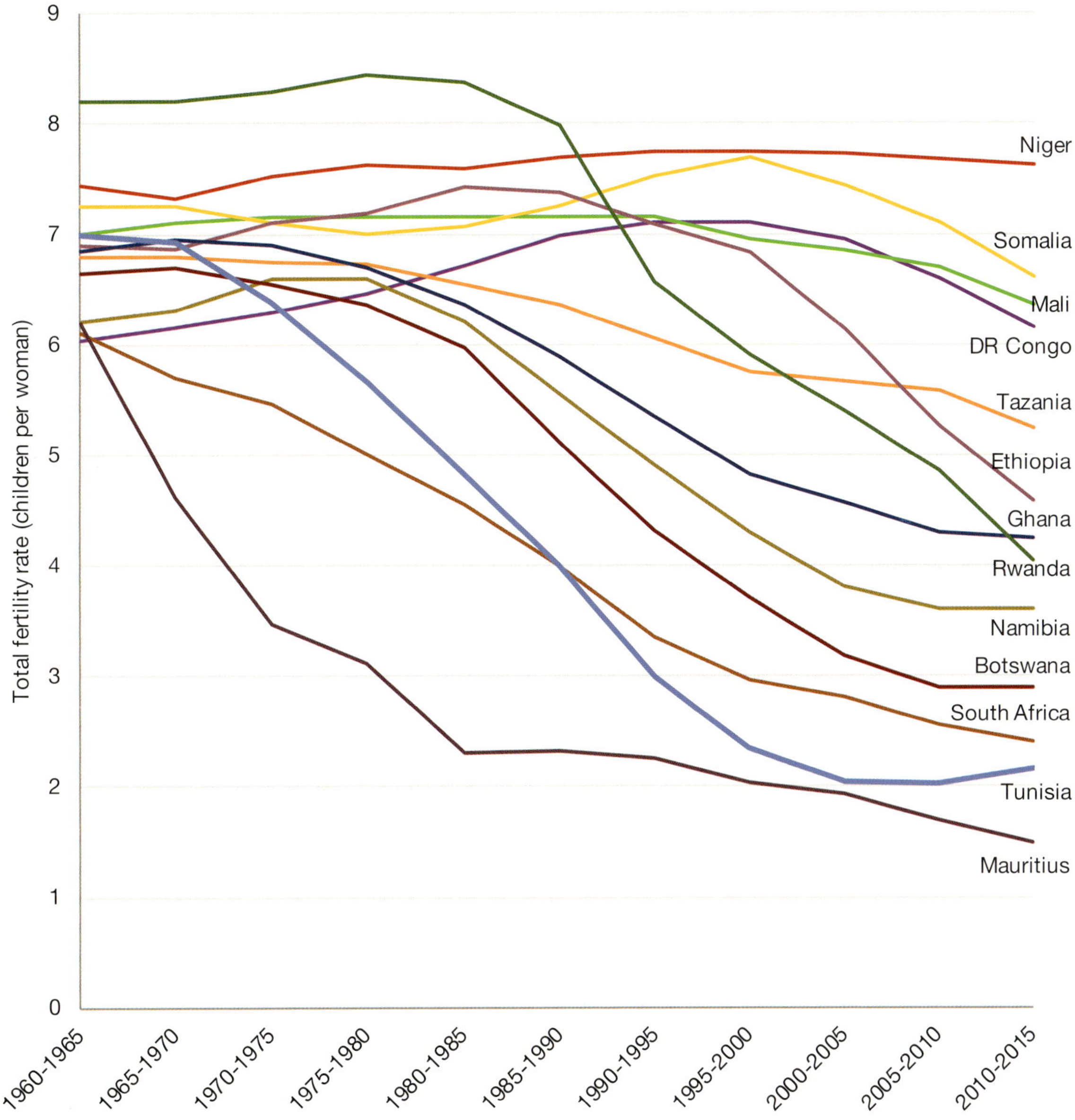

Source: United Nations (2015)

The impact of the slow demographic transition on the jobs agenda is dramatic.

critically important. Today there are some 420 million children aged 5-19 in Africa. Under the UN's "medium fertility" scenario, their number would almost double to 830 million by 2060, which is 34 million more than foreseen just three years ago. Under the "high fertility" scenario, the increase would be 600 million and at current fertility levels would be a staggering 1.1 billion. The institutional, as well as fiscal, capacity to provide quality education to such increased numbers of students is at best questionable.

The impact of the slow demographic transition on the jobs agenda is dramatic (Figure 14). Africa's working-age population has grown by more than 10 percent a year for the last 60 years and will do so for another 35 years. This is in sharp contrast to the experience in Asia, for example, where the working-age population grew by more than 10 percent for only 30 years and in China for only 25 years. Put differently, Asia needed rapid job creation over a generation to absorb the increase in its working-age population but Africa would need a century of rapid job creation to do the same.

These demographic prospects have three important implications for African governments and policy makers. First, it is even more urgent to accelerate Africa's move to a modern demographic profile of low infant mortality and low fertility. The highly heterogeneous experience of African countries in reducing fertility (Figure 13) reveals the importance of making modern contraceptives available to all, educating girls, and getting political and civil society leaders to speak openly about the issue. The important message is that many African countries have shown that it can be done and there is an urgent need for the others to follow their lead.

The second implication is that, even with a heightened effort to reduce fertility, the job creation challenge in Africa is structurally different than in other regions (see Figure 14). For Africa, it is not a question of rapid job creation for one generation to reap a demographic dividend. It is

Figure 14: Working-age population growth rates, 1965–2050

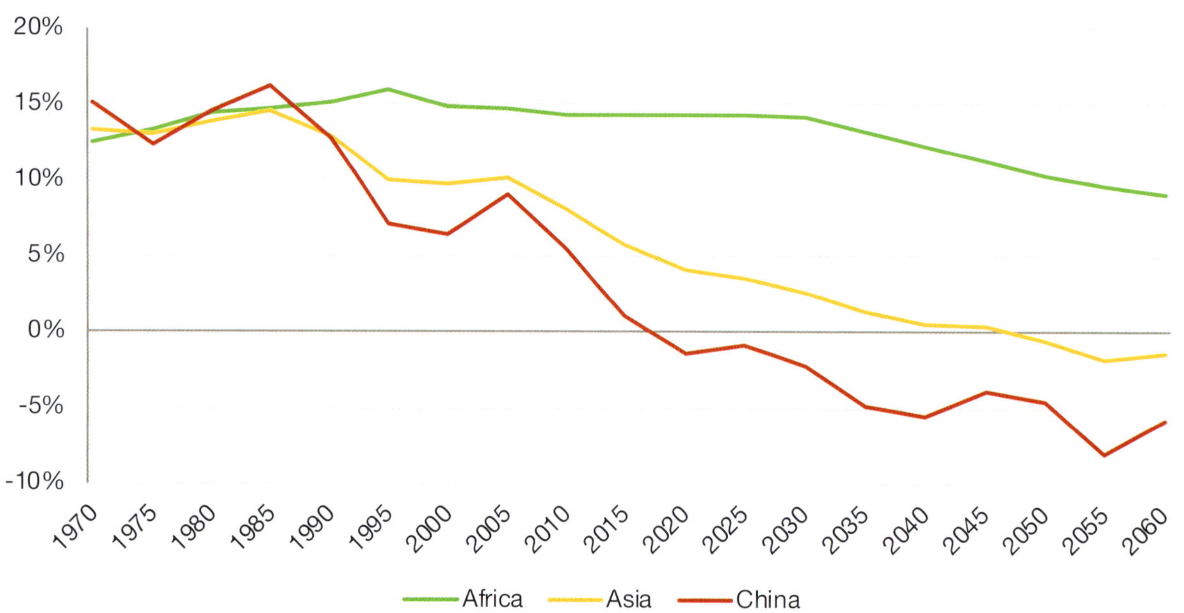

Source: United Nations (2015)

Recognizing that only private firms, rather than governments, can possibly create the needed jobs, implies a much more ambitious agenda across the continent to create the conditions for firms to be competitive and to grow.

a question of keeping ahead of a century of extraordinary growth in the working-age population. Recognizing that only private firms, rather than governments, can possibly create the needed jobs, implies a much more ambitious agenda across the continent to create the conditions for firms to be competitive and to grow.[9]

The third implication is that employment in agriculture and in traditional services will grow, and increased attention needs to be put on raising the productivity of workers in the informal sector.[10] Given the prospect of another 35 years of extraordinary growth of the working-age population and the current low share of formal wage employment, even if such employment were to grow spectacularly it could not absorb today's underemployed and the inevitable increase in the labor force. As noted above, firms, not governments, create jobs but the modal size of a firm in Africa is one person (frequently self-employed in agriculture or services). These "firms" will grow in number and their productivity must increase for incomes to rise.

Reduce commodity price vulnerability

Africa's commodity dependence and hence vulnerability to commodity price swings has increased over the last 20 years. The acceleration in per capita income growth through 2012, and the subsequent fall, is due to many factors but remains very closely linked to commodity prices, as shown in Figure 15. Some countries have made progress but, as a continent, Africa has not reduced its vulnerability to commodity price swings. The share of commodities in African exports increased from around 71 percent in 1995 to 76 percent in 2014. As a result, the substantial decline in commodity prices since 2013-14 has, and will continue to have, substantial repercussions on African economies,

9. See Chapter 7, "Economic diversification of African economies."
10. See Chapter 3, "Africa's inclusive growth challenge: Reducing deprivation and creating jobs."

Figure 15: Per capita income growth rate and commodity price index growth rate, 1965–2050

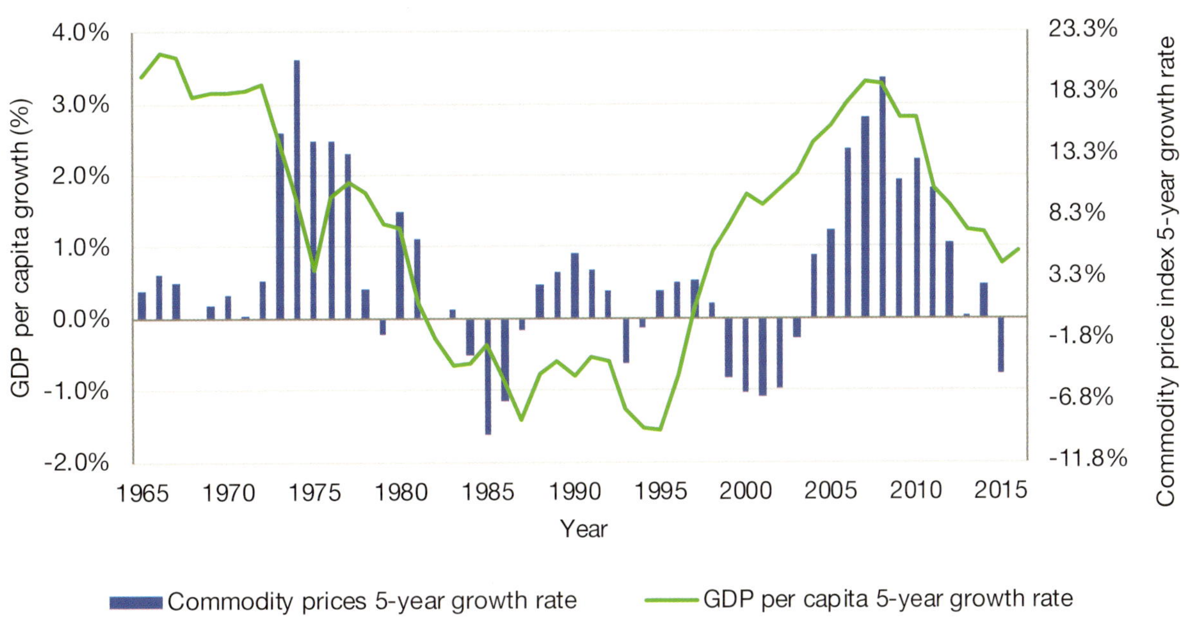

Source: IMF (2016, 2017)

The substantial decline in commodity prices since 2013-14 has, and will continue to have, substantial repercussions on African economies, particularly among countries with a high concentration of oil and mineral exports.

particularly among countries with a high concentration of oil and mineral exports.[11]

More than a quarter of Africa's real GDP growth from 2000 to 2013 can be attributed to rising commodity prices. Commodity prices more than doubled from 2000 to 2012 and even with the subsequent fall are still more than one third higher than they were in 2000. The high concentration of commodities in African exports means that Africa's terms of trade also increased substantially after 2000 and the increase was greater than that in any other region. As a result of these large terms-of-trade gains, the annual increase in real disposable income (6.3 percent), or gross domestic income, was much greater in 2000-12 than the increase in GDP (5 percent). In addition to the direct increase in income from the terms-of-trade improvement from 2000 to 2013, the expected multiplier effect also led to an estimated annual increase of GDP of 1.3 percent. If the terms of trade were to stabilize at current levels, then future trend GDP growth in Africa would be only around 3.6 percent of GDP.

In the aggregate, African economies not only did not reduce their commodity dependence (admittedly difficult) but, for the most part, neither created buffers to commodity price shocks nor adjusted to the new circumstances. Individual country performance is again highly variable but, in the aggregate, Africa has responded to the decline in the terms of trade, which most projections suggest will be long-lived, by drawing down reserves and increasing borrowing rather than adjusting. This response creates an urgent need to steer economies to a sustainable path if the high economic and social cost of disorderly adjustment is to be avoided.

Three types of policy response are urgently needed. First, countries need to adjust to the income loss from lower commodity prices and avoid excessive borrowing to delay adjustment. Broadly, orderly, managed adjustment requires fiscal and monetary policies that are consistent with debt and balance-of-payments sustainability. Ideally, these policies would be supported by a flexible exchange rate regime, which would allow for an independent monetary policy and would provide countries with a critical policy instrument to help absorb external shocks.

Second, they need to reduce future vulnerability by establishing mechanisms, such as fiscal rules and stabilization funds, to smooth expenditure over boom-and-bust cycles.[12] A structural fiscal rule would smooth public spending patterns over time to reduce the pro-cyclicality of public expenditures observed at present as governments increase expenditure when commodity prices rise and are forced to cut them when prices fall. A commodity stabilization fund similar to the Copper Stabilization Fund of Chile together with structural fiscal targets, namely a budget based on long-term trends and not only on current developments, would be optimal for these purposes.

Finally, and most importantly in the long run, they need to diversify their asset base by transforming resource rents from extracting natural resources into human and physical capital. Diversification of their asset base is a key step towards eventual diversification of income flows.[13] Diversification is frequently thought of in reference to economic activities, e.g., manufacturing or services, but diversification of assets is even more important. Rich countries hold the vast bulk of their assets in the form of intangible capital (human and institutional capital) rather than natural resources or produced capital (e.g., roads, power systems, factories). From a continental perspective, one of Africa's biggest challenges is to transform its natural resource wealth into human capital, produced capital, and financial assets, i.e., to diversify its asset base. Only with a diversified asset base can incomes be de-linked from commodity price fluctuations.

11. See Chapter 6, "The Impact of Commodity Terms of Trade in Africa: Curse, Blessing, or Manageable Reality?"

12. See Chapter 6 of this volume, "The Impact of Commodity Terms of Trade in Africa: Curse, Blessing, or Manageable Reality?," and the macroeconomic (Chapter 9) and natural resource (Chapter 12) chapters in Ahlers et al. (2014).

13. See Chapter 7, "Economic Diversification of African Economies."

Beyond confidence and rule of law issues, development of financial systems that offer savings instruments to all potential savers is key.

Increase savings and investment—Unleash the private sector

Savings in Africa increased somewhat during the boom years but have since fallen back to just 17 percent of GDP—the same level as 30 years ago (Figure 16). Country performance varies and solutions need to be country-specific, but Africa will not converge with the rest of the world with such low savings rates. By comparison, savings rates in Asian low- and middle-income countries increased steadily over the same period. As a result, the gap between African and Asian savings rates is twice as high today as it was in 2000.

Low domestic savings are the result of both low public and private savings. Low public savings have, for the most part, been driven by rapid increases in current expenditure and poor domestic resource mobilization. Low private savings reflect many issues but, perhaps most fundamentally, a question of citizens' confidence in their country and in the rule of law. issues, development of financial systems that offer savings instruments to all potential savers is key.

The investment gap between Africa and Asia has also increased. Despite low savings, investment in Africa has increased slightly from around 20 percent of GDP at the beginning of the century to 23 percent in 2016. But Asian investment rates have increased much faster so that the gap in investment rates is 50 percent higher than in 2000. Low public investment is largely an issue of the composition of public expenditure, where current expenditures have grown at the expense of public investment. A particular challenge for the coming decade will be to protect the level of public investment, as governments may find it easier to squeeze public investment further (rather than raise revenue or cut current expenditure) in a less favorable economic environment. Low domestic private investment is largely a reflection of a poor investment climate. The investment challenges are more fundamental than just poor "Doing Business" indicators in that they reflect

Figure 16: Savings and investment rates, 1995–2050 (% of GDP)

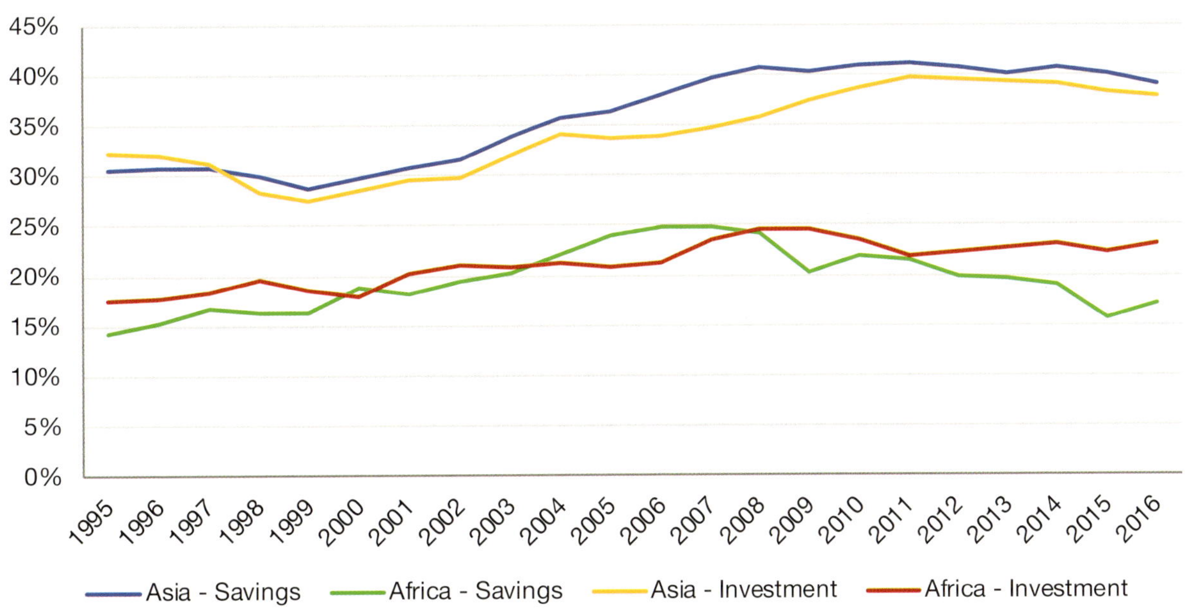

Source: IMF (2017)

The bulk of any increase in investment in Africa must come from private sources. This is not happening today.

citizens' appreciation of opportunity (are there profitable investments to be made?) and the rule of law (if successful, can they reap the rewards or will the profits be lost to well-connected special interests?). A more pragmatic and business-oriented approach to regional integration could also foster increased investment by creating larger markets.[14]

Massive outflows of both human and financial capital are the most telling indicator of citizens' confidence in their country. A recent International Labour Organization (ILO) survey found that an astounding 38 percent of African youth wished to migrate.[15] Massive capital outflows are a further reflection of this lack of confidence. Over the last five years, annual illicit outflows have ranged from $50 billion to almost $200 billion depending on the methodology used for measurement. This implies annual illicit outflows on the order of 4½ to 7 percent of GDP.

The low level of investment is manifested in the real problems of poor infrastructure and weak human capital. Infrastructure investment requirements in Africa are estimated to be in the range of $100-$150 billion (2015 US$) annually compared with current levels of around $75 billion.[16] The resulting poor infrastructure is widely recognized as a constraint for faster growth.[17] Human capital investment is similarly deficient. Despite recent increases in enrollment rates, education outcomes seriously lag those in other regions.

Given its high population growth, Africa needs GDP growth of around 6 percent to rapidly converge with the rest of the world. Such growth is highly unlikely with investment rates hovering just above 20 percent of GDP. Public savings should be a key part of raising national savings rates. Unfortunately, in the aggregate, African countries have used the boom times to increase current expenditure even more than revenue, so that savings as a share of GDP have fallen. Part of the macroeconomic adjustment will require in many countries reduced, but more effective, current expenditure to generate the savings for increased investment.

Public investment is an important but small part of the solution. Countries undoubtedly need to increase domestic resource mobilization, as discussed in the 2015 Addis Summit on Financing for Development. Under the best of circumstances, however, given tighter capital markets and fiscal sustainability concerns, even with better managed current spending, increases in public investment will be small relative to the need. The most critical use of public funds may be, in combination with policy reforms, the reduction of risk for private sector investors in order to mobilize much larger private investment from both domestic and foreign sources.

The bulk of any increase in investment in Africa must come from private sources. This is not happening today. The reasons are broadly two. First, investors, in general, recognize the potential in African countries but neither domestic nor external investors have the confidence to invest because of concerns about macro stability, the rule of law, the stability of the policy framework, or the power of insiders and vested interests. Whatever the cause, until countries identify, debate, and resolve the reasons for low investor confidence, including by their own citizens, private investment is unlikely to increase significantly. Second, and relatedly, many countries in Africa have self-contradictory views of the private sector. On the one hand, they acknowledge in principle that job creation and growth will only come from private sector investment. On the other hand, they view the private sector as almost predatory, interested only in extracting rents and exploiting workers, or as a source for financing party or ethnic politics. The latter view is probably related to the crony capitalism found in many countries. Whatever their origins, these views are incompatible. Governments (and societies) need to have a much clearer view of what they want. If it is a dynamic, competitive, job-creating private sector, then the de facto

14. See Chapter 10, "Regional Economic Integration in Africa."
15. ILO. (2016). *World Employment and Social Outlook 2016: Trends for youth*. Geneva: ILO.
16. See Chapter 8, "Africa's Infrastructure Deficit: Closing the Gap."
17. See Chapter 8, "Africa's Infrastructure Deficit: Closing the Gap."

Raising per capita incomes in Africa on a sustained basis will ultimately require raising productivity.

policies of the recent past will not do. It is not simply a question of fixing a regulation here and there, however necessary that may be, but of changing mentalities.

Accelerate productivity growth

Raising per capita incomes in Africa on a sustained basis will ultimately require raising productivity. Given Africa's low level of capital, per capita incomes in many countries can still grow by increasing the stock of capital, i.e., by investment. However, sustained per capita income increases will increasingly depend on productivity increases. African total factor productivity (TFP) growth has been dramatically below that of emerging market and developing countries in Asia for the last twenty years (Figure 17).

Improvements in human and institutional capital are key to raising productivity. As discussed above, rich countries hold the vast bulk of their wealth as human and institutional capital, which is key to their high productivity and hence incomes. One aspect of human capital development in Africa requires urgent attention: the quality of education.[18] New evidence suggests that a majority of African students have not mastered beginning-level skills even after 6 years of schooling. Moreover, most students spend only 2-3 hours a day in learning activities even while in school, and teachers spend relatively little time teaching. Basic skills are the foundation for all future learning and cannot be leapfrogged. The waste—students in school but not learning, graduates condemned to low-productivity jobs, and large public expenditure on education with no results—is staggering. Fortunately, the variation across schools and across countries shows that learning outcomes are largely determined by how money is spent rather than how much money is spent. All African leaders (and societies) need to focus on learning outcomes, rather than numbers

18. See Chapter 4, "Building Human Capital: Improving Education Quality."

Figure 17: Total factor productivity growth, 1995–2016 (%)

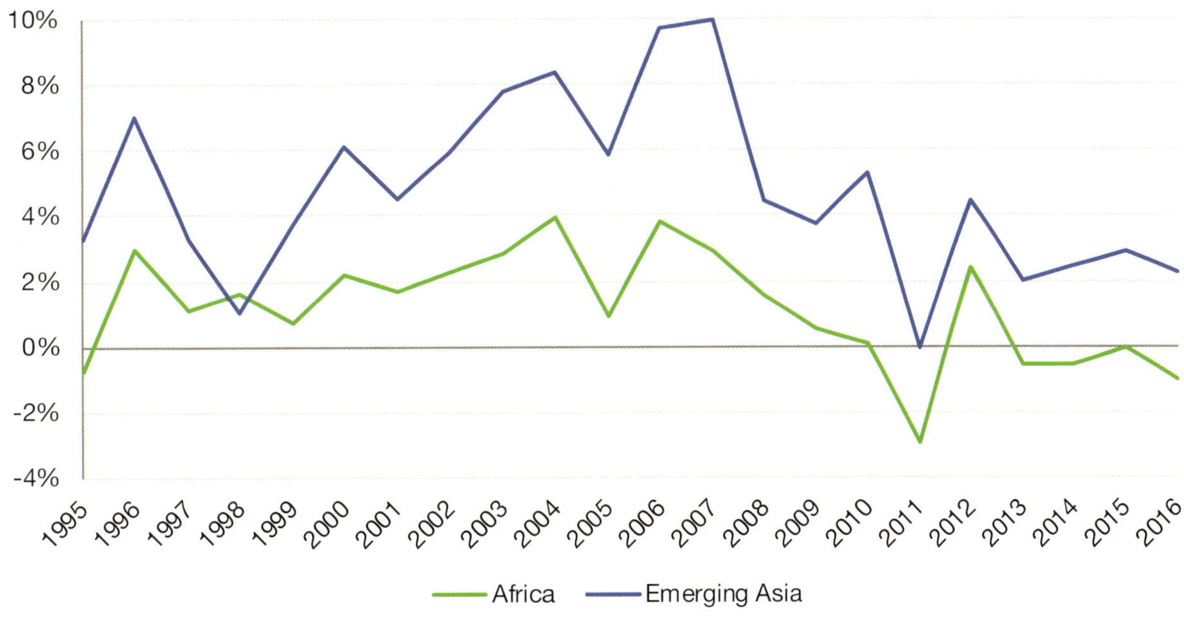

Source: Centennial Group (2017)

It is urgent for African leaders and the international community to invest now to foster adaptation to climate change, including in agricultural research, urban infrastructure, and improved water management.

of buildings built, and on what teachers know and do, rather than just numbers of teachers or the politics of teacher unions.

Raising productivity will require not only faster adoption of new technologies but also strengthening the institutions (from rule of law to labor market flexibility) that allow businesses, from family farms to conglomerates, to combine inputs in more productive ways. In a very practical way, this is where the inclusion agenda meets the growth agenda. African entrepreneurs succeed around the world, including surviving very tough environments. They prosper, however, where initiative by all members of society is encouraged and where the fruits of that initiative are not stolen.

Reduce conflict and fragility

Countries involved in armed conflict or so fragile that they cannot provide security and other basic services to their populations present a special challenge and a special risk to their neighbors. More than one in three African countries (20 of 54) are classified as fragile on the harmonized list established by the AfDB and the World Bank. Almost 290 million people, a quarter of the continent's total, live in these countries. Unfortunately, the situation has improved little since the harmonized list was first produced in 2010; 16 of the 20 countries have been on the list since it was created, the share of Africa's population living in fragile countries has not changed, and the absolute number of people in fragile states has increased by about 150 million. The situation in the Sahel—which combines arms from Libya, extremist religious expansion, and persistent poverty—is particularly worrisome.[19]

Ending conflict and building capable states from fragile ones is clearly a long-term undertaking but three things may help in the short run. First, more aggressive mediation by regional bodies and the African Union when internal conflicts are brewing may reduce the dangerous and hard-to-reverse slide into open conflict. Second, when mediation efforts fail, greater regional military capacity to intervene quickly may prevent further deterioration. Finally, it is urgent that the international community recognize that security is a global public good, and that weak states in the Sahel, for example, cannot finance the required level of security expenditure without increased international support.

Adapt to climate change

The economic impact of climate change at the country level is difficult to quantify, but most climate models indicate that throughout Africa temperatures will rise, rainfall will become more variable, and severe weather events will become more common. From a continental perspective, the biggest climate issue for Africa is not reducing emissions (however laudable) but adapting to coming climate change. Green (i.e., emission-reducing) investments may have high returns, foster broader green growth, and generate favorable financing but they will have little impact on global emissions. The climate change already underway will, however, have dramatic effects on agriculture, the largest source of employment on the continent, and on coastal cities, home to a rapidly increasing share of the population.[20] Although the specifics are beyond the scope of this paper, it is urgent for African leaders and the international community to invest now to foster adaptation, including in agricultural research, urban infrastructure, and improved water management.

Reduce inequality and disparities

The combination of large and growing disparities between the rich and poor; unequal access to education, health, and other social services; and a large share of the population still living in poverty constitutes a social time bomb for much of Africa. Unfortunately, these disparities continue to grow at the national and regional levels and with respect to the rest of the world. The combination of growing inequality with high levels of corruption also leads

19. See Chapter 11, "New Threats to Africa's Stability and Growth."

20. See Chapter 9, "Urbanization and Demographics: Planning Cities That Work."

Continental inequality will only fall if African best practice—whether in demographic, macroeconomic, or structural policies—is generalized across the continent.

to the widespread perception of "unfair" societies which has sparked political unrest in numerous countries.

From a continental perspective, the largest part of inequality is within countries. At the national level, Gini coefficients are relatively high in Africa, ranging from 32 to 63, but have not shown any consistent trend either up or down over the last decade. Of the 36 countries for which data is available, the Gini coefficient rose in 18 countries and fell in another 18 countries.

The biggest increase in inequality, however, has come from an increase in the differences between countries.[21] Per capita incomes in the five richest African countries are 24 times larger than those of the poorest five countries today, compared to 16 times larger 20 years ago.

Reducing continental inequality requires poorly performing countries to catch up with their better-performing neighbors. The combined effect of national and inter-country inequality is a continental Gini coefficient of 56, which is higher than that of any other region except Latin America. In Latin America, however, the Gini coefficient is falling while in Africa it is rising. Continental inequality will only fall if African best practice—whether in demographic, macroeconomic, or structural policies—is generalized across the continent.

Conclusion—Capable states and pragmatic leadership

Africa's advantages—strong resource base, growing labor force, growing consumer base—remain but convergence has stalled. In the changed global environment, this combination naturally calls for more concerted action to address the above-mentioned seven challenges. Fortunately, there is considerable technical consensus on what needs to be done, and a number of African countries continue to show how to do it. If these African best-practice policies were generalized, the continent would be converging with the rest of the world.

Politics will affect outcomes more than technical economics because political will to address the tough issues is frequently the missing ingredient for concerted action. In many countries, both in Africa and elsewhere, dysfunctional politics constrain policy choice and implementation. Political leaders often face incentives to focus on private (family, party, region, ethnic group) gain rather than to provide public goods. Outcomes will be dependent on how political systems evolve. Citizen engagement and greater transparency may contribute both to creating capable states that deliver security, rule of law, and services to all citizens, and to the emergence of strong, pragmatic leaders who focus on results not ideology and who are accountable to citizens. Capability is largely a question of governance--of how institutions work and work together. Capable states are not created overnight but are the result of sustained efforts to strengthen capacity and build credibility and accountability. Capable states can encompass a wide variety of political systems but ultimately, they need to be accountable to their citizens for delivering results. Strong, pragmatic political leadership could accelerate change in the short term and lay the basis for sustained strengthening of institutions, including political ones. The biggest threats to success are complacency and a lack of political will to tackle the big problems. The challenge is less what to do than how to implement the chosen course of action and how to sustain a "do whatever it takes" mentality to get results.

The agenda summarized above emphasizes issues and approaches rather than detailed measures for two reasons. The first is simply that, as often observed, Africa is very diverse and detailed action plans must be country-specific. The second, and more important, reason is that solutions that do not emerge from some form of national debate about what exactly is the problem to be solved and what needs to be done are very unlikely to succeed. Countries can benefit enormously from the experience of others but they need to develop a minimum societal consensus on

21. See Chapter 9, "Urbanization and Demographics: Planning Cities That Work."

The stalled performance of recent years is an urgent call to action for all who want a prosperous, rather than marginalized, Africa in 40 years.

what needs to be done if they are to sustain the concerted action necessary for success.

Such a societal consensus on the reform agenda, and the political leadership to forge it, while present in a few countries, is missing in most. The stalled performance of recent years is an urgent call to action for all who want a prosperous, rather than marginalized, Africa in 40 years.

Africa's Inclusive Growth Challenge: Reducing Deprivation and Creating jobs

Chapter 3

Louise Fox

Introduction[1]

Poverty and inequality remain high in Africa despite a decade and a half of sustained economic growth on the continent. The share of the poor in absolute poverty ($1.90 per day in current prices) has fallen by about 1 percent a year since 1990 in Sub-Saharan Africa (SSA), but absolute numbers of poor are still growing (Beegle et al. 2016).[2] Multidimensional poverty measurements suggest high levels of deprivation, especially in rural areas (Alkire and Housseini 2014).[3] In North Africa, political and security developments have stalled growth for the past several years, halting and in some cases reversing progress in reducing poverty.

The demographic transition is uneven in SSA. While the demographic transition is now well on its way in Northern Africa and in the richer countries of Southern Africa, the demographic profile of most low- and lower-middle-income countries is changing slowly. This is one reason for slower poverty reduction despite high economic growth. When the poverty level is high and population is increasing at 3 percent per annum, there is a need for even higher levels of GDP growth to achieve a significant poverty reduction.

High fertility is creating a big youth bulge, concentrated in the poorest countries. About 2.5 million youth will enter the labor force every year from 2015 to 2025. Although the generation now entering the labor force in Africa is the continent's most educated one to date, in the low- and lower-middle-income countries overall education levels remain low compared to global competitors. Additionally, quality issues within schools mean that years of education do not guarantee that students achieve employable knowledge and skills.

This is an economic, social and political issue. In poorer countries, youth work in the same jobs as their parents did – in agriculture or nonfarm household enterprises, as they cannot afford to be unemployed. Low productivity in these activities results in low earnings and underemployment. In richer countries, youth unemployment is high. The North African region and the Republic of South Africa have the highest youth unemployment rates in the world, at more than 30 percent. In all countries well-educated urban youth are more likely to be unemployed, indicating that the school-to-work transition is problematic. Employment opportunities in urban areas are scarce and the cost of living is high, so even as urban poverty is declining and an urban middle class is growing the absolute number of urban poor remains stubbornly high.

Meanwhile, access to media revealing lifestyles enjoyed by the African elite as well as by middle and upper classes in other wealthy regions is creating high expectations among poorer young people, who are increasingly dissatisfied with their limited opportunities. In North Africa, young people had hoped that political change would improve these opportunities, but weak economies have dashed these hopes. In SSA, the majority of youth still live in rural areas, but want to leave because of lack of services and low opportunities to earn income. But opportunities for less educated youth are scarce in urban areas, so the majority remain in rural areas.

The sense of exclusion is not just economic. A perceived lack of space for political participation and disappointment with/distrust of the political process among young people add to dissatisfaction with economic opportunities and fuels some radicalization. Violence has flared up, especially in areas where the influence of a more conservative and militant brand of Islam has grown (Ismail 2016) but also in countries such as Kenya (2008) and Burundi (2016).[4]

The action agenda varies by country situation. In the low- and lower-middle-income countries of SSA, prospects for

1. Please note that this chapter is based on research done prior to Fox taking her current position at USAID and does not represent the views of USAID or the United States government.

2. Beegle, K., Christiansen, L., Dabalen, A., & Gaddis, I. (2016). *Poverty in a Rising Africa*. Washington: World Bank.

3. The Multidimensional Poverty Indicator (MDPI) is an aggregate indicator which measures household deprivation across several dimensions, including: (i) access to education; (ii) nutrition and health status; (iii) housing conditions and access to safe water; and (iv) ownership of basic consumer goods (as a measure of wealth). It is broader than monetary poverty and easier to measure. See Alkire, S., and Housseini,B. (2014). Multidimensional Poverty in Sub-Saharan Africa Levels and Trends. Oxford: Oxford Poverty & Human Development Initiative.

4. Ismail, O. (2016). What Is in a Job? The Social Context of Youth Employment Issues in Africa. Journal of African Economies 25(suppl_1): i37–60.

> *As the youngest continent, almost all countries face a challenge now and in the future to develop an inclusive growth path that provides opportunities for all labor force participants to find a sustainable, remunerative livelihood, ensuring that the next generation has a higher level of welfare than the previous one.*

continued improvements in livelihoods and living standards are good, especially if broad-based growth is enabled and social infrastructure policy is refocused on efficiency and outcomes. In resource-rich countries, a policy reset is needed to adjust to the collapse in public revenues from mineral exports. This reset needs to address the high levels of poverty and deprivation, especially in neglected rural areas. Conflict-affected countries need a political settlement to create the enabling conditions for more public and private investment. If this settlement occurs, bounce-back growth could reduce monetary poverty and allow governments to focus on reducing the very high levels of deprivation that currently exist. In upper-middle-income countries, the inclusive growth agenda is more complex, requiring both a more competitive environment for private sector investment and productivity growth as well as an intensive focus by governments on improving the institutions underpinning markets and social welfare.

Recent developments

Although Africa constitutes a single land mass, the continent is a mix of countries with diverse histories, cultures, ethnicities, ecosystems, political and economic systems, and levels of poverty and wealth. Yet as the youngest continent, almost all countries there face a challenge now and in the future to develop an inclusive growth path that provides opportunities for all labor force participants to find a sustainable, remunerative livelihood, ensuring that the next generation has a higher level of welfare than the previous one. While each country will necessarily need its own diagnosis and strategy, both progress to date and challenges ahead depend on starting point (endowments) as well as opportunities in the globalized economy.

The recent experience and potential of the economy for inclusive growth is used to organize African countries into five country types: upper-middle income, lower-middle income, low income, and two special categories, fragile states and resource rich countries (see Annex for list of country groups and criteria) (Figure 1).

1. The upper- and upper-middle-income countries: While many in this group started their development process from a natural resource base (e.g. South Africa, Namibia, Gabon) they achieved upper-middle-income status through economic transformation and diversification. The service sector commands the largest share of employment and agriculture the lowest share. Urbanization rates are high. Although well along in the demographic transition, their key labor force challenge is an educated but unemployed youth population. Public financing for key social services and a stronger safety net keep serious poverty and deprivation low (measured by the Multi-Dimensional Poverty Index, or MDPI), but inequality is high, especially in Southern Africa. Only 6 percent of Africa's population is found in this group. In terms of population and size of economy, South Africa and Tunisia account for 90 percent of this group.
2. The resource rich countries: By per capita income the second richest category, these countries have achieved their economic growth primarily through mineral exports, not transformation. They have recently enjoyed high growth because of higher commodity prices, but as that cycle dips their inclusive growth challenges are being exposed. Their economies tend to be dualistic, with urban employment dominated by the public sector but still a high share employed on family farms, mostly subsistence production in rural areas. Private investment is low because there are few opportunities outside the mineral sector. Resource rents have financed some service delivery improvements in urban areas, but in rural areas poverty and deprivation remain high, the latter much higher than would be expected given income level. Inequality is also high. Fertility tends to be high as well. So this group has a young labor force, which is well-educated in urban areas but poorly educated

Open unemployment is emerging in urban areas, especially for educated youth, but remains unaffordable for most households owing to the lack of a safety net.

Figure 1: Basic indicators for country groups

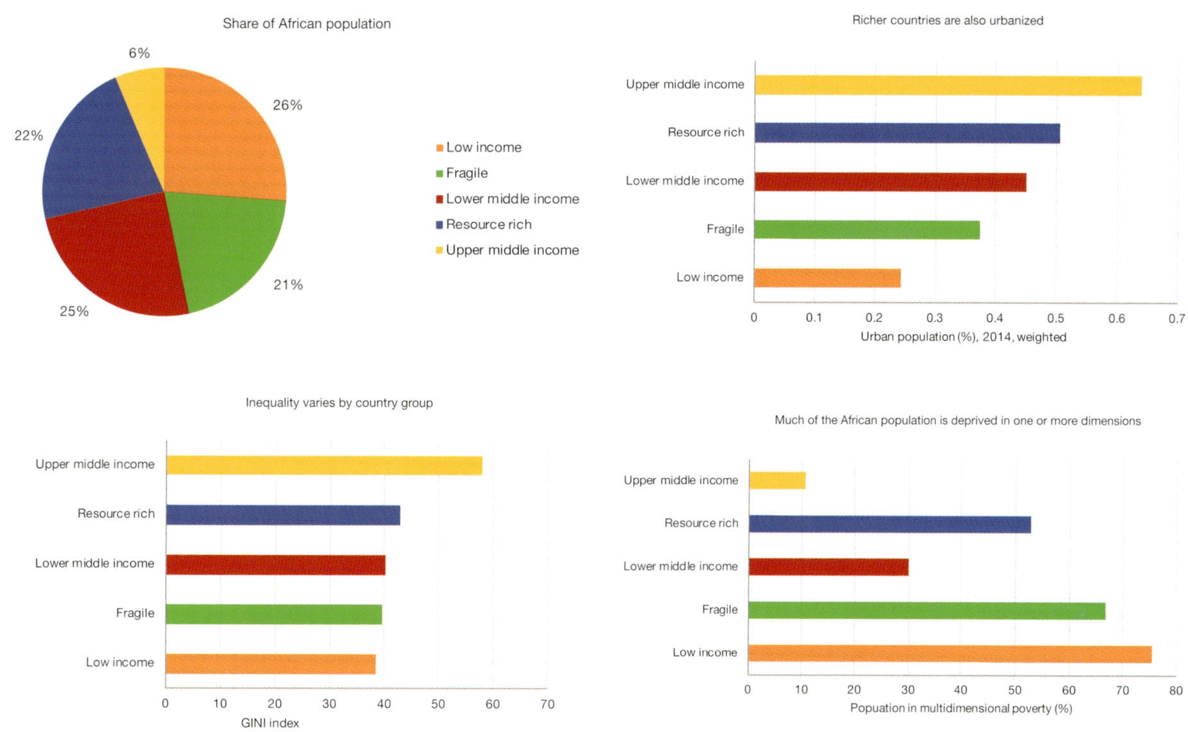

Note: All graphs in this chapter have been weighted by population.
Source: World Bank (2016d).

in rural areas, increasing the challenges to inclusive growth. In terms of population and size of economy, Nigeria and Algeria account for 88 percent of this group.

3. The lower-middle-income countries: Poorer and less diverse than the upper-middle-income group, these countries have nonetheless posted solid GDP growth rates over the past decade and have been diversifying their economies beyond agriculture. This diversification has been accompanied by increased private investment and labor productivity growth, especially in the non-agricultural sectors. Yet half the population still resides in areas classified as rural, and agriculture still employs the majority of the labor force in these countries, with the service sector second. Open unemployment is emerging in urban areas, especially for educated youth (Fox, Senbet, & Simbanegavi, 2016), but remains unaffordable for most households owing to the lack of a safety net.[5] Education levels of youth entering the labor force are rising rapidly (see Figure 3), and fertility is falling (slowly) in many countries, reducing the dependency burden in the future but ensuring a large youth bulge for the next 20 years. Extreme poverty has declined, but deprivation remains high as governments struggle to improve access to housing, education, and water

5. Fox, L., Senbet, L., & Simbanegavi, W. (2016). Youth Employment in Sub-Saharan Africa: Challenges, Constraints and Opportunities. Journal of African Economies 25(suppl_1): i3–15.

The last decade has seen both healthy per capita growth and reduction in extreme poverty in all country groups.

supply, especially in rural areas. A large and diverse group, typical countries include Egypt, Côte d'Ivoire, Senegal, Ghana and Kenya.

4. The low-income countries: Among the poorest countries in the world, these countries have also been posting solid growth rates and modest poverty reduction. But they are still plagued by low human capital, high dependency ratios, high levels of deprivation in both urban and rural areas, and often-ineffective institutions. Poverty levels sharply limit unemployment, but underemployment is chronic. Both economic transformation and demographic transition are at a nascent stage. High population growth and high dependency ratios are a challenge now and in the future, affecting the potential for human capital development, labor productivity growth, and sustainable livelihoods. All are in Sub-Saharan Africa; as much as 70-80 percent of their population resides in rural areas. Typical countries include Ethiopia, Malawi, Mozambique, Burkina Faso, and Uganda.
5. Fragile states: These countries are weakened by conflict, which has prevented them from realizing their potential. Once the conflict settles opportunities will be abundant for bounce-back growth. But conflict or the threat of conflict has hindered infrastructure and human capital development. These countries tend to be aid dependent. Typical examples include Somalia, Mali, Burundi, Comoros and Liberia.

For exposition purposes, we have assigned each country to one group, but the categories are not mutually exclusive. For example, Libya is in the fragile-states group, but it is also resource rich; Gabon is still quite resource rich but shares many other characteristics with the upper-middle-income countries (such as high open unemployment). However, focusing on the dominant features associated with each country type helps distinguish and organize the employment and inclusive growth challenges, opportunities and action agendas within the continent.

Inclusive growth achievements

The last decade has seen both healthy per capita growth and reduction in extreme poverty in all country groups (Figure 2). Not surprisingly, per capita growth has been highest in the low-income countries—where opportunities abound for diversification and productivity increases simply through using existing technologies and adding capital to raise productivity. At the other end of the spectrum, growth has been lowest in the richer countries, where the scope for "quick wins" is lower. Growth in these environments is more dependent on continued innovation, which is often spurred by competition (domestically and internationally) and low transaction costs created by the efficient functioning of financial, land, labor and goods markets. Growth needs to be enabled by the effective provision of public goods such as basic research, regulation to ensure competition, information provision and dissemination, and contract enforcement mechanisms. These institutional preconditions are hard to achieve, which is why countries can get stuck in a "middle-income trap." In between is the growth performance of the lower-middle-income countries where gains in agricultural productivity as well as urbanization and the development of a private industrial and service sector have created opportunities for diversification. Conflict—the defining feature of the fragile states—has interrupted growth in this group, although on average progress has been registered. Growth in resource rich countries has been achieved primarily through high mineral prices.

All country groups have seen a reduction in extreme poverty rates, according to the World Bank's international poverty line. In the low-income countries, where statistics on monetary poverty are weak, the reduction in monetary poverty for Sub-Saharan Africa is estimated to be even higher than shown in the data above—by about 5 to 6 percent if Nigeria is excluded—according a recent study

Economic transformation and diversification is important for sustained and inclusive growth.

Figure 2: Trends in growth, poverty reduction, and employment

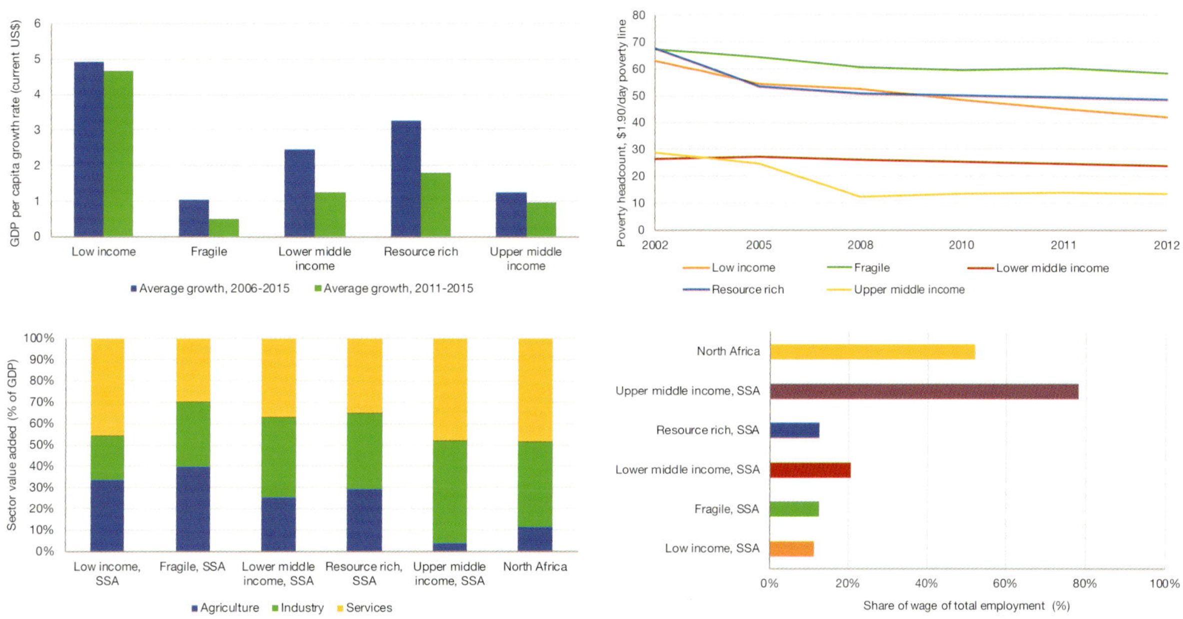

Source: World Bank (2016d); Fox, L. & Thomas, A. (2016) for SSA employment data

(Beegle et al. 2016).[6] Yet even with this progress about half of the population in Africa still lives on US$2/a day or less.[7] In all but the richest countries the vast majority of the population lives on less than US$4 per day, and even fewer households reach the international middle-class definition of US$10 per day used in *Africa 2050* (Ahlers et al. 2014). This means that while economic growth brought many households out of extreme poverty, they still have a precarious living standard. Of the 6 percent of the population estimated by the Pew Research Center to be in the international middle class in 2011, the majority lived in the Republic of South Africa and in North Africa countries (e.g. Tunisia, Morocco and Egypt) (Kochhar, 2015).[8]

Economic transformation and diversification is important for sustained and inclusive growth. The movement of factors of production out of low-productivity sectors such as agriculture into high-productivity enterprises, especially labor-intensive ones in sectors such as manufacturing, can be an escalator towards employment transformation. In Figure 2, the extent of transformation in value added and employment is shown. In this case, the countries of North Africa are shown separately, as they have been more successful at developing a manufacturing sector than most of SSA. In all countries in Africa, higher value-added sectors have been expanding, but only in the upper-middle-income countries in SSA and in the North African countries is the share of the labor force engaged in agriculture below 10 percent.

The picture is similar for employment transformation. In SSA, in all except the richest countries, the majority of the labor force does not have any type of wage/salary job as their main economic activity (not even a causal wage

6. Developments in Nigeria, with the continent's largest population and economy, have a major effect on aggregate African statistics. However, the household survey data (multiple sources) present a contradictory and confusing trend owing to poor quality of some surveys. As a result, Beegle et al. (2016) exclude them from a number of regional analyses.
7. Measured in US$ PPP. See, for example, Beegle et al. (2016) for a discussion.
8. Kochhar, R. (2015). A Global Middle Class Is More Promise than Reality. Washington: Pew Research Centre.

While a young labor force can be an advantage, in many African countries it is slowing down both poverty reduction and the employment transformation.

job such as construction labor). In resource rich countries, the problem is most severe. Although 30 percent of the labor force has a wage/salary job in the resource rich countries, over two-thirds of these were in the public sector, a difficult trend to sustain (Fox & Thomas 2016).[9] In contrast, about two-thirds of the wage/salary jobs in the low- and lower-middle-income countries are in the private sector. The high private-sector wage job growth after 2000 in the low- and lower-middle-income countries is a major achievement; in countries such as Tanzania, Uganda and Ghana this segment grew three times faster than the labor force. But because it started from a very low base, this segment remains small, as a share of employment. The majority of employment in these countries is in household farms and firms.

North African countries have been able to achieve more employment transformation owing in part to a larger share of manufacturing in GDP (about 16 percent compared with 8 to 12 percent for middle-income SSA countries). Labor intensive manufacturing rapidly creates wage and salary jobs; this has been one of the major achievements of the East Asian export miracle. But North African countries also have a higher share of public sector employment in total employment than the middle-income SSA countries, helping to boost the share of wage jobs in total employment. Wage job creation has stalled recently, not only because of slower growth but also because of the inability of the public sector to keep increasing employment, as well as security concerns (Keefer. 2015). Economic policy has played a key role in this process (Box 1).[10]

In addition to the low starting point there are two other reasons why the strong economic growth since 2000 did not result in employment transformation in SSA. The first is the high share of services in the nonagricultural economy and the nature of this service sector. The majority of the private sector service employment is in household enterprises (HEs), including: wholesale and retail trade, repair of consumer items, manufacturing and sale of prepared foods (e.g. milled grain or cassava flour, brewed beer, homemade bakery items), hair dressing, informal transportation (motorcycles or bicycles), informal bars or restaurants and the like (Fox & Thomas 2016). Although about 75 percent of total wage employment on the continent is in services (including public sector employment), the majority of service employment is still in household enterprises.

A second reason for the sluggish employment transformation is the fast labor force growth. In most low-income, lower-middle income, and resource rich countries in SSA, the demographic transition has barely started (or not started at all). In North Africa, improved reproductive health services and efforts to delay marriage and childbirth among teen-aged girls have resulted in a significant fertility decline. For example, in Morocco, fertility is approaching replacement rate while in Egypt it has been at about 3.3 children per female for more than 20 years.[11] But in Ghana and Kenya, fertility is only now approaching 4 births per female, while in Côte per female at 5 or more (and child mortality declining rapidly), about 2.5 million young people will enter the labor force every year between 2015 and 2025 – mostly in SSA. Sub-Saharan Africa is the youngest region, and will remain young for most of this century. While a young labor force can be an advantage, in many African countries it is slowing down both poverty reduction and the employment transformation.[12]

9. Fox, L. & Thomas, A. (2016). Africa's Got Work to Do: A Diagnostic of Youth Employment Challenges in Sub-Saharan Africa. *Journal of African Economies 25*(suppl_1): i16–36.
10. Keefer, P., Sahnoun, H., Sy, A., Hussain, S., & Schiffbauer, M. (2015). *Jobs or Privileges: Unleashing the Employment Potential of the Middle East and North Africa*. Washington: World Bank.

11. These two countries account for 45 percent of the population in the lower-middle-income group, which pulls down the average number of children. For SSA alone, the estimate is almost 5 children per female.
12. Many authors have argued that Africa's young population will bring a "demographic dividend" in terms of higher growth and welfare. It is true that East Asia did benefit from a rapid drop in fertility through an increase in savings and economic policies that created massive employment opportunities for youth. Other regions have not been able to realize this result, however, including Latin America in the past and North Africa today. In SSA, fertility rates are falling very slowly, so a dividend is unlikely to occur. For further discussion of the demographic dividend and Africa's progress, see Yazbeck, A., Raja, S., & Canning, D. (2015). *Africa's Demographic Transition*. Washington: World Bank; Paris: Agence Française de Développement.

Most HEs in Africa today are pure self-employment, and only 10 percent have hired someone outside of the family.

Box 1: What is a household enterprise?

Household enterprises (HEs) are unincorporated, nonfarm businesses owned by households. From an employment perspective, they include self-employed people running unincorporated businesses (which may or may not employ family or other workers) and family members working in those businesses. When employment in the HE sector is tabulated, employees from outside the family are not included in this category; they constitute wage workers. The owners account for most of the employment in the sector. Family helpers make up only 11 percent of employment in the sector (not counting wage workers). The enterprise perspective shows the same pattern. Most HEs in Africa today are pure self-employment, and only 10 percent have hired someone outside of the family. Therefore, employment in the sector primarily grows through the creation of new enterprises.

HEs may also be referred to as "own-account workers" (another term for "self-employed"); and "contributing" or "unpaid" family workers, indicating that the family members work in the enterprise but receive no cash payment based on hours worked or output, although they may share in the profits. Some call these enterprises "microenterprises," but the term is not used uniformly. For example, some authors categorize both self-employment and larger, more substantial businesses as microenterprises (and may include in this group partnerships and firms that employ a number of workers regularly). From a policy perspective grouping these two activities together is not desirable as research has shown that HEs have different characteristics from larger business, behave differently and face different constraints.

Figure B1: Most enterprises are family operations

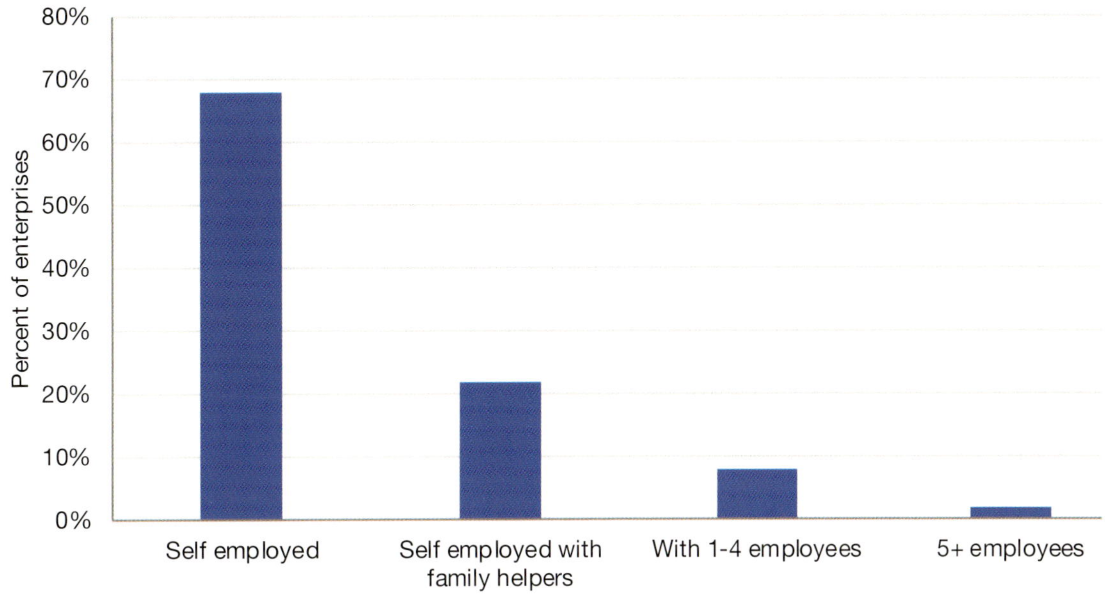

Source: Filmer & Fox (2014)

Concern has been rising in the continent over the quality of education provided by the public sector, as international testing data have become available.

Human development

African countries have realized tremendous progress in human capital development, as measured by a number of indicators (Figure 3). The lowest-income countries, which started at very high levels of deprivation, have made substantial gains in life expectancy and child mortality. Progress on these two indicators is noteworthy as they are affected by a combination of social-economic conditions and access to health services. Meanwhile the poor progress of the resource rich countries stands out. South Africa's delay in effectively addressing the HIV/AIDS epidemic resulted in a 10-year decline in life expectancy between 1990 and 2005, which drags down the average of the high income group. The HIV/AIDS epidemic also drove down life expectancy in the rest of Eastern and Southern Africa in the 1990s and 2000s.

Education levels have also improved, especially among the youth population, where the improvements of the past decade are evident. In low-income countries, the youngest age group is as educated as the next group, but in other countries, the peak education level is in the age group 20-24, reflecting an increasing tendency to attend secondary school, meaning that youth stay in school well beyond age 15. In lower-middle-income countries, average years of education of the labor force in their 20s is nearly 8 years, indicating that Africa is starting to produce the skilled labor force required for 21st century economic activities. In all country groups, females are gaining access to secondary education at the same rate as males, another important achievement, although these averages hide significant within-group differences.[13] Concern has been rising in the continent over the quality of education provided by the public sector, as international testing data have become available (Filmer & Fox 2014; see also Chapter 4 of this volume, "Building Human Capital: Improving Education Quality").[14] This means that data on years of education may be deceptively optimistic about the state of human capital development in the region.

In sum, recent trends reveal an overall picture of major improvement in living standards, especially in the poorest countries that have not been affected by conflict. However, they also reveal a number of challenges:

- High fertility in SSA means that dependency ratios will remain high for the foreseeable future. It also means that the population will double in 25 years. This is a challenge for public services provision. It is difficult to increase quality when the number of children needing services is increasing exponentially. Expenditures on health and education services for the rapidly growing population crowd out other needed public investments. Large families and high dependency ratios reduce private savings. As a result, growth may be lower (Yazbeck, Raja, & Canning 2015).[15] Differential fertility rates in rural vs. urban areas and rich vs. poor families widen income inequality.
- Some of the world's most unequal countries are in Southern Africa. Other regions do not show such high inequality, although inequality and fragility appear to be linked (Beegle et al. 2016). Inequality is a result of both history and recent economic policy, but rising inequality makes poverty reduction more difficult and may reduce growth (Keefer & Knack 2002).[16]
- Rapidly urbanizing countries grow faster and tend to increase welfare faster, owing to the lower cost of providing social services in urban areas (Buckley, Annez, & Spence 2008).[17] However, managing urban environments and ensuring the delivery of public goods necessary to reap the benefits of urbanization is a complex task. This is reflected

13. A few key countries have missing data on secondary education enrollment in this series, including Ethiopia, the largest country in the low income group.

14. Filmer, D. & Fox, L. (2014). *Youth Employment in Sub-Saharan Africa.* Washington: World Bank.

15. Yazbeck, A., Raja, S., & Canning, D. (2015)

16. Keefer, P. & Knack, S. (2002). Polarization, Politics and Property Rights: Links between Inequality and Growth. *Public Choice 111*(1–2): 127–154.

17. Buckley, R., Clarke Annez, P., & Spence, M. (eds.). (2008). *Urbanization and Growth.* Washington: World Bank.

High fertility in SSA means that dependency ratios will remain high for the foreseeable future. It also means that the population will double in 25 years.

Figure 3: Trends in human development

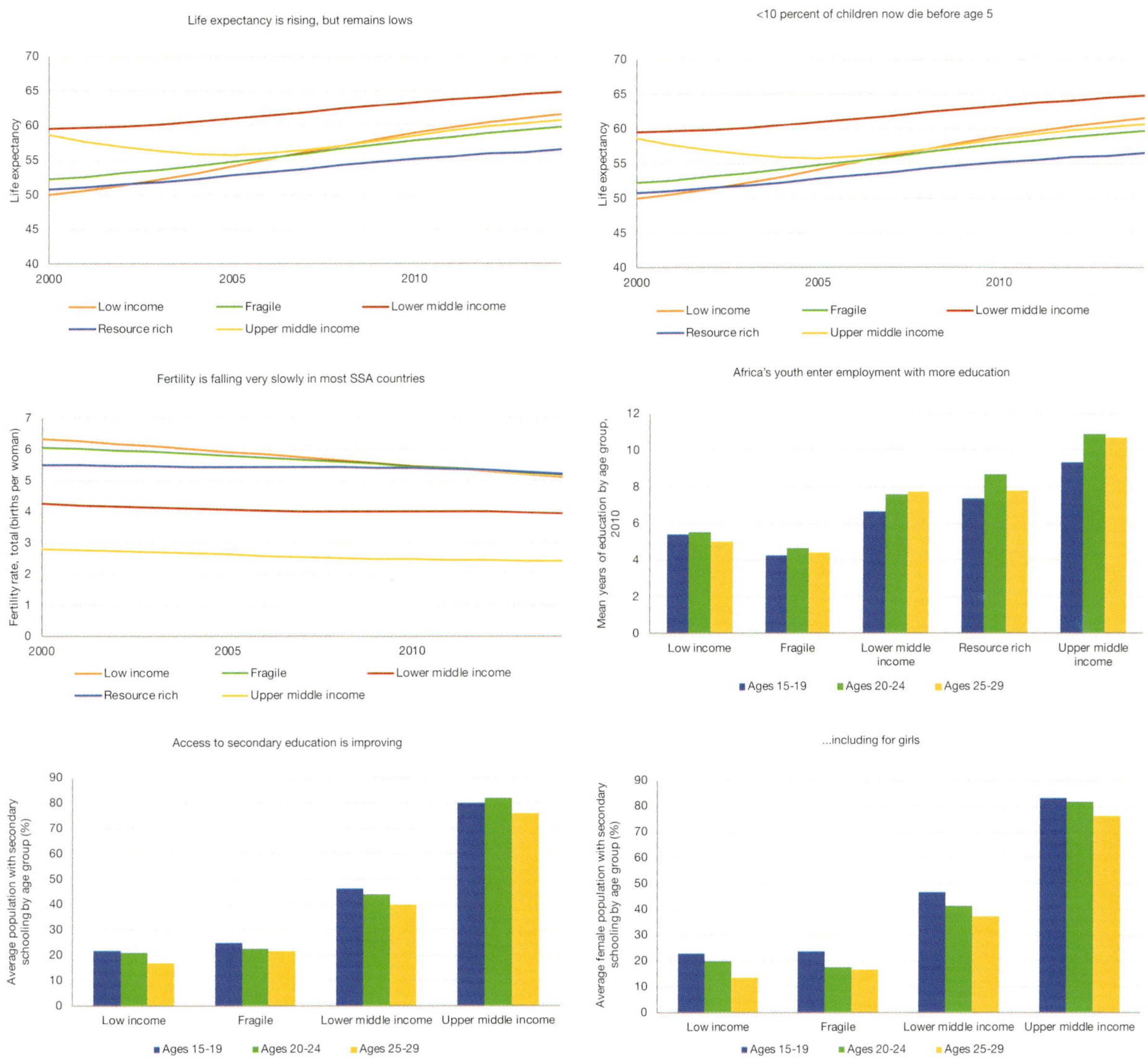

Note: Coverage of African resource rich countries in the EdStats database is limited, so these countries are excluded
Source: World Bank (2016d); World Bank EdStats database

In most African countries, households will still have to work their way out of poverty through higher earnings from economic activity.

in the high levels of multi-dimensional poverty, as this index includes housing conditions and access to safe water and sanitation. SSA has the highest share of the population in urban areas living in slums (Marx, Stoker, & Suri, 2013).[18] Addressing the housing challenge will require addressing underlying land market issues in SSA (Duranton 2015).[19]

- Countries dependent on mineral exports face additional challenges in realizing inclusive growth. Human development indicators lag, as does non-farm employment.
- For middle-income countries, narrow elites that control the economy may be holding back productivity growth and the creation of good jobs for youth (see Box 2). At the same time, education systems' narrow focus on traditional cognitive learning at the expense of problem-solving and socio-emotional skills contributes to high unemployment among the most educated youth (Filmer & Fox 2014; Glick, Huang, & Mejia 2015).[20]
- Even in African countries with a relatively stable political situation (e.g. Tunisia), increasing insecurity caused by rising local and international terrorism threats is deterring private investment; countries with more political turbulence such as Egypt are paying a high price in growth, including declining tourism revenues. This situation is not easily resolved and will continue to challenge the region.

African countries will be confronting these challenges during a period of continuing slow growth in Organisation for Economic Co-operation and development (OECD) countries and worrisome headwinds coming from China. Mineral-exporting countries will face major stabilization issues, which may affect growth in their neighbors as well. Can African countries build on the gains of the past decade and continue to reduce poverty and deprivation? Two key areas are critical for public sector action: (i) policies to ensure economic growth continues in the sectors where most households earn income; and (ii) policies to increase the efficiency of public sector expenditures, especially investments in people.

Action agenda for inclusive growth

In most African countries, households will still have to work their way out of poverty through higher earnings from economic activity. Efficient social service delivery by the public sector plays a key role in reducing deprivation and improving living standards, especially in poorer countries where there are few affordable private sector alternatives. But better service delivery will not be enough. The action agenda for all countries on inclusion has to include policies to enable productivity improvements in all segments of the economy.

Action agendas for common challenges

Youth

The youth employment challenge has become a major concern for governments and stakeholders. This issue is a really subset of the overall employment challenge in Africa. While youth can be expected to be in the forefront of the employment transformation, given where SSA starts today and the sheer numbers of projected new entrants to the labor force, the employment transformation will be slow. All stakeholders, especially youth and their families, need to recognize this. Research has shown that policies that improve opportunities in the sectors where most people work will benefit youth (Filmer & Fox 2014).

Private investment is needed to create more wage employment in all countries. The obstacles to achieving this will differ by country. Increasing private investment in new and existing firms at levels needed to employ these

18. Marx, B., Stoker, T., & Suri, T. (2013). The Economics of Slums in the Developing World. *Journal of Economic Perspectives 27*(4): 187–210.
19. Duranton, G. (2015). Growing through Cities in Developing Countries. *World Bank Research Observer 30*(1): 39–73.
20. Glick, P., Huang, C., & Mejia, N. (2015). The Private Sector and Youth Skills and Employment Programs in Low-and Middle-Income Countries. Washington: World Bank.

It is obvious why older and less productive firms would want governments to stifle competition, and why some governments would find it hard to resist this pressure. What is less visible is the cost to youth and the broader society of these job-killing policies.

Box 2: Tradeoffs between objectives: The political economy of job creation in North Africa

Most African government have signed a number of regional declarations promising to create more jobs for youth. Most have employment strategies with job targets and claim that youth employment is a high priority. But do they really want to undertake the measures needed to reach their targets? Or do they recognize that many of the measures needed to create new firms and increase investment in labor intensive industries could negatively affect the profits of the most politically-connected firms in the country? Evidence in a recent study by the World Bank on job creation in the Middle East and North Africa suggests the latter—that current industrial policies favor a few politically connected firms, insulating them from domestic and international competition and discouraging new firms from entering key sectors.

In most countries, the private sector creates the majority of new jobs. The quality of these jobs—earnings, stability and working conditions—tends to be highest in large, modern firms. As a result, an important element of an employment strategy is to encourage the development of firms that create more and more stable jobs: younger more productive firms. But these firms have to be able to enter the marketplace and compete on a level playing field. This means implementing policies that discourage a few large firms from "cornering the market" and keeping other firms out; put more positively, it means policies that encourage competition.

Competition policies support increasing productivity because the firm owners know that if they don't keep improving, others will take their place. They also support job creation because owners know that if they are successful they will be able to invest more, generate more output and ultimately more profits. But these same policies will threaten the market share and profits of existing firms that do not innovate, do not invest and therefore do not keep up with changing marketplace. As a result, existing firms try to get governments to enact policies that protect them from new entrants. In North Africa, these policies were adopted, including requiring licenses for new firms to enter (which were then rarely granted), limiting foreign competition through limits on foreign direct investment (FDI) and imports, and using government discretion to harass firms that are not politically connected. Governments also subsidized energy-intensive sectors, which create fewer jobs.

The cost of these policies has been high. The World Bank report estimates that in Egypt, economy-wide employment growth slows by almost 1.5 percent annually when politically connected firms enter a sector where they had not previously been present. This employment growth slowdown amounts to about two-thirds of total labor force growth, meaning a large majority of new entrants do not get jobs because of these policies. In Morocco, firms that operate in sectors with high administrative burdens create fewer jobs. Issues such as long wait times for construction permits especially constrain new firm growth and firm expansion.

Countries often limit FDI in order to encourage job growth in domestic firms, another anti-competitive mistake. According to the report, while increased FDI in Jordan did indeed lead to a loss of market share in some older firms operating in the same sector, it created a lot of new jobs in domestic service provider firms and in young firms in the same sector, who learned from their new competitors. Meanwhile, aggregate productivity in the economy rose.

It is obvious why older and less productive firms would want governments to stifle competition, and why some governments would find it hard to resist this pressure. What is less visible is the cost to youth and the broader society of these job-killing policies.

Source: Keefer, Sahnoun, Sy, Hussain, & Schiffbauer (2015)

youth requires an improvement in the business environment (Filmer & Fox 2014; Keefer et al. 2015). While there is some evidence that industrial labor costs are higher in Africa than in Asia, overall, labor costs are a low share of total value added in industry, especially in low- and lower-middle- income countries (Gelb, Meyer, & Ramachandran, 2013).[21] High energy costs (caused in part by the need to use back-up generators), transportation and logistics costs (which drive up both input and ex-factory costs), and

21. Gelb, A., Meyer, C., & Ramachandran, V. (2013). Does Poor Mean Cheap? A Comparative Look at Africa's Industrial Labor Costs. SSRN Electronic Journal.

The youth element in the employment challenge is the school-to-work transition.

interest rates are more important as a share of total cost. Improvements that could make a difference in non-labor costs would be: more reliable electricity; better functioning ports and logistics infrastructure; cheaper finance through a deeper, more competitive banking sector; and fewer restrictions and red tape associated with starting or expanding a business. Labor costs cannot be ignored however; in a globalized world, competitive labor costs have provided an important edge to Asian countries in developing a manufacturing industry.

New research is showing that management plays a large role in firm productivity and growth (Bloom et al. 2013).[22] Previous research on firm constraints may have underestimated the importance of these skills in East Asia's success relative to Africa. Management skills are in short supply in Africa (Dinh et al. 2012), and this shortage is not easily remedied.[23] A number of programs have been developed to teach entrepreneurship and management, but evidence on their success is lacking. Evaluations of comprehensive Business Development Services (BDS) programs suggest that while they are expensive, if carefully targeted at established, growth-oriented businesses, they can help business expand and increase employment (Grimm & Paffhausen 2015).[24]

The youth element in the employment challenge is the school-to-work transition. The most common intervention offered by governments, donors, NGOs and other actors to youth seeking to establish a livelihood is training, especially vocational training (Fox, Senbet, and Simbanegavi, 2016; Fox 2016).[25] Unfortunately, this intervention has a poor track record. A recent rigorous evaluation of vocational training in Kenya provided vouchers to a random selection of potential youth participants and let them choose the type of training and the provider (public or private). Results showed no subsequent earnings effect either for wage earners or self-employed participants compared to those who did not participate, nor was there an effect on overall participation or employment (Hicks et al. 2015).[26] This result has been found in several other evaluations of training programs (Hirshleifer et al. 2015; Tripney et al., 2013; Filmer & Fox 2014).[27]

Some results are emerging on programs that work with youth before they leave school, stressing "employability" skills. Countries can try to rebalance the curriculum, especially in secondary school and in higher education, to include "employability" skills such as life and business skills. Promising approaches include bringing in staff from private firms to provide information about job requirements, role models, mentoring etc., exposing adolescents to the culture of a modern firm at an early age. Apprenticeships also have a good track record at helping youth transition into self-employment and, in richer countries, wage employment. It is not clear if this is because they teach skills in an applied setting, or if they primarily succeed by teaching employability skills, or both. More evaluations are needed to identify cost-effective approaches that scale up.

Policy is best informed by data. Yet data on what youth are actually doing and how they manage the transition are still not widely available. One problem is that national survey data provide a poor picture of what the labor force is actually doing. A large share of the labor force in low-income countries undertakes a number of activities over the year. Nonetheless, surveys tend to focus on activities over the past seven days (in order to measure unemployment) or to

22. Bloom, N., Eifert, B., Mahajan, A., McKenzie, D., & Roberts, J. (2013). Does Management Matter? Evidence from India. *The Quarterly Journal of Economics 128*(1): 1–51.
23. Dinh, H., Palmade, V., Chandra, V., Cossar. F. (2012). *Light Manufacturing in Africa: Targeted Policies to Enhance Private Investment and Create Jobs*. Washington: World Bank.
24. Grimm, M. & Paffhausen, A. (2015). Do Interventions Targeted at Micro-Entrepreneurs and Small and Medium-Sized Firms Create Jobs? A Systematic Review of the Evidence for Low and Middle Income Countries. *Labour Economics 32*: 67–85.
25. Fox, L. (2016). What Will It Take to Meet the Youth Employment Challenge in Sub-Saharan Africa?. GLM | LIC Working Paper (10).
26. Hicks, J., Kremer, M., Mbiti, I., & Miguel, E. (2015). Vocational Education in Kenya-A Randomized Evaluation.
27. Hirshleifer, S., McKenzie, D., Almeida, R., & Ridao-Cano, C. (2015). The Impact of Vocational Training for the Unemployed: Experimental Evidence from Turkey. *The Economic Journal.*; Tripney, J., Hombrados, J., Newman, M., Hovish, K., Brown, C., Steinka-Fry, K., Wilkey, E. (2013). Technical and Vocational Education and Training (TVET) Interventions to Improve Employability and Employment of Young People in Low-and Middle-Income Countries: A Systematic Review.

The sluggish employment transition, especially in countries where the labor force is growing rapidly relative to wage employment opportunities, means that most new employment opportunities will continue to be found in household farms and firms (HEs).

measure the main activity only, not any second job (regardless of recall period). An important characteristic of youth, especially low-income youth, is that they move between activities during their search (Filmer & Fox 2014; Fox & Pimhidzai 2013).[28] More survey research is needed on how to collect such data efficiently in low-income settings.

Informality

Closely related to the youth employment agenda is the informality agenda. Today, in low- and lower- middle-income African countries, only 10 to 20 percent of employment is in wage and salary jobs, and only about half of that is formal (permanent, with a contract, covered by social protection scheme). These ratios are not likely to change much over the next 10 to 15 years (Filmer & Fox 2014). The sluggish employment transition, especially in countries where the labor force is growing rapidly relative to wage employment opportunities, means that most new employment opportunities will continue to be found in household farms and firms (HEs). Together, this type of small scale economic activity is commonly called the informal sector. Additional employment will also be created in casual wage jobs (known as informal employment).

While governments and other development actors include the goal of raising earnings on family farms in policies and projects, they are often not supportive of HEs. Employment policy frameworks rarely mention them as an important source of employment for youth (or anyone). Instead policy proposals seem to have one of two objectives: (i) to turn them into medium-sized businesses through "formalization policies"; or (ii) to eliminate them. Neither approach actually solves the problems facing owners of the HE and their families. As has often been reported, HEs and growth-oriented business are different entities. In the words of Berner et al. (2012), HEs and growth-oriented small businesses operate under a "different logic."[29] HEs tend to operate in business segments characterized by easy entry, low capital requirements, embedded in kin and family networks for survival. They are part of a household portfolio of activities, selected to reduce overall household economic risk. According to sociological studies, business growth is rarely the focus of the owner. Available evidence confirms that employment doesn't grow beyond the household (Filmer & Fox 2014). Indeed, as Berner et al. (2012) note, the specialization and risk-taking needed to develop larger scale enterprises are not what poorer households are looking for from an economic activity.

The sector does expand, however, as more businesses are created in more households. This is how youth will enter the sector. Even without hiring employees, HEs can survive, provide a good livelihood and increase household income. As with any other economic activity, they need a good business environment. This can be created by governments, and was done during the East Asia employment transition. Currently, most African governments are predatory or negligent with respect to this sector. Police tend to harass them; local authorities do not include them in local development plans. They are seen as a source of revenue for local or national governments, even though their income falls below national tax thresholds. This sector does not need "formalization policies" unless such policies add value to their livelihood. If registration of their business adds value, they will seek it out. Government should not add burdens to this livelihood.[30]

A positive agenda for this sector would include: (i) increasing secure space to work and sell goods and services, in areas with foot traffic where their clients will easily find them (with urban services such as water and waste disposal); (ii) increasing access to financial services, through mobile banking, microfinance and other approaches designed for this client base; and (iii) increasing channels

28. Fox, L. & Pimhidzai, O. (2013). *Different Dreams, Same Bed: Collecting, Using, and Interpreting Employment Statistics in Sub-Saharan Africa—The Case of Uganda*. Washington: World Bank.

29. Berner, E., Gomez, G., & Knorringa, P. (2012). Helping a Large Number of People Become a Little Less Poor': The Logic of Survival Entrepreneurs. European *Journal of Development Research 24*(3): 382.

30. An alternative to a "registration" agenda is to permit HEs to do business in the name of the owner. This is common in Ghana, for example. HEs register when their revenues and profits are large enough and stable enough to justify the paperwork.

While there is much heterogeneity within gender categories, most countries have a set of norms and expectations that affect, and usually constrain, women's opportunities in employment, in other aspects of economic life, and in civic participation.

of voice within communities and government to make sure policies and programs meet their needs.[31] Recent evaluation research suggests that youth training programs are not particularly effective at helping youth enter this sector, although some business training or apprenticeship plus cash grant or loan programs have shown some success. The cost of these programs has been high, so scale up has not been possible (Filmer & Fox 2014). Lower cost models are needed. Informal or semi-formal financial services targeted at youth can help them overcome financing obstacles; this is one area where microfinance has shown success (Banerjee, Duflo, & Hornbeck 2014).[32]

Informal employment (where a firm hires someone without a permanent contract and does not pay labor taxes earmarked for public social security schemes) requires a different policy approach. Firms should not be allowed to violate labor laws. But governments may wish to examine why firms hire informally. Small firms may not be able to provide regular employment owing to uncertainties or seasonality in demand for their product, or they may not be able to realize the productivity needed to pay adequate wages and pay the cost of an extensive social protection program. Where informal employment (in violation of the labor laws) is expanding rapidly, it may be necessary to review policy frameworks, seeking ways to provide additional flexibility in hiring and firing rules and/or lowering the cost of a minimum social protection package. Initiatives to address this problem should avoid destroying the opportunities that labor market participants are clearly seeking out.[33] Temporary agencies could address the flexibility problem in urban areas if they are permitted to operate efficiently.

Over time, two factors have been shown to reduce both informal HE activity and informal wage activity as a share of total employment: increasing incomes through higher productivity and slower growth of the labor force. These two features tend to occur together, as a result of a long period of socio-economic development. Indeed, value added rises because agglomeration and scale economies usually found in the formal sector start to take hold in broader swaths of the economy. Workers are gradually drawn into the formal sector. Africa is not at this point yet, but upper-income countries have reached a turning point and middle-income countries may reach such a turning point in a few decades, if economic progress continues.

Gender

It almost goes without saying that within an inclusive growth agenda, the gender dimension needs to be addressed explicitly. While there is much heterogeneity within gender categories, most countries have a set of norms and expectations that affect, and usually constrain, women's opportunities in employment, in other aspects of economic life, and in civic participation. These include norms and customs around acceptable behavior in public, laws, norms and traditions about what jobs women can do (or are "suitable" for women) that result in occupational segregation, norms around housework and other forms of unpaid work, norms around women's participation in household decisions, laws that prevent women from exercising economic power including owning assets in their own name, and policies and practices that may infringe on women's safety and security. Aspirations and socio-emotional skills to act upon them are formed early on in the life of females in Africa and enforce adherence to customs and norms.

The economic case for expanding women's economic opportunities is powerful. There is ample and growing evidence that when women are able to develop their full

---

31. See Filmer & Fox, (2014), and the references therein for further discussion of this policy agenda.
32. Banerjee, A., Duflo, E., & Hornbeck, R. (2014). (Measured) Profit Is Not Welfare: Evidence from an Experiment on Bundling Microcredit and Insurance. *NBER Working Paper* (20477).
33. See Maloney, W. (2004). Informality Revisited. *World Development 32*(7): 1159–78, for a discussion of policy tradeoffs with application to Latin America. While pointing out that the vast majority of informality is in farms and HEs, he argues that flexibility in hiring and firing benefits both workers and firms, and that labor legislation should take these preferences into account. He also argues that expensive, "bundled" social protection programs exclude workers who would be satisfied with a more minimalist package, taking most of their compensation in wages.

The economic case for expanding women's economic opportunities is powerful. There is ample and growing evidence that when women are able to develop their full economic potential there can be substantial overall economic gains.

economic potential there can be substantial overall economic gains. A key action agenda item is eliminating legal barriers and enforcing the right to equality. According to the World Bank, legal gender differences are widespread: 155 of the 173 economies covered have at least one law impeding women's economic opportunities; across 173 economies, 100 restrict women's work in certain jobs; and in 18 countries women cannot even get a job without their husband's permission (World Bank 2015).[34] Discrimination in family law is often a source of economic hardship for women, especially as concerns access to land in rural areas.

The other parts of the action agenda on gender equity are country specific. A general point is that increasing female empowerment at a young age—e.g. during adolescence—can support many of the other agenda items, including lower fertility, higher human capital, and increases in earnings and productivity. Effective programs are still being tested; few have scaled up in Africa. Rural females of all ages spend many hours per week performing household chores, limiting their labor force participation or progress in school. Infrastructure investments that reduce the burden of housework for women and girls (e.g. water supply, transportation) can provide an inclusive growth boost as well, especially in rural areas (Agénor & Canuto, 2012).[35]

Service delivery reform

African countries need to continue to expand and improve social and economic infrastructure services. In most countries, this means more domestic resource mobilization. It may mean new financing models. But it also means more efficiency and effectiveness in the public sector, especially in lower-middle-income countries where the number of children is still growing dramatically even as adult diseases such as hypertension, heart disease and cancer are growing as a cause of death and disability. African countries are experimenting with new approaches such as result-based financing in health and education, with putting in place multi-sectoral early childhood development programs (a proven intervention in OECD countries), with finding new ways to source and deliver inputs such as drugs and supplies, and with low-cost basic health insurance plans to help households deal with the financial challenges of health care for chronic and non-communicable diseases.

Countries recognize that they have to up their game on outcome measurement and on incorporating lessons into practice. For example, Uganda has had a "value for money" expenditure evaluation program in the Ministry of Finance for nearly a decade. Other countries are developing similar units. Kenya and many other African countries are using impact evaluation methodologies to discover what is working and what is not. While many impact evaluations in Africa have been performed by academics on pilot NGO-run programs (limiting their applicability to large-scale government efforts), governments are now running them on their own programs. They are sharing the results in South-South learning events and through informal contacts between national researchers. These are all positive trends in the face of huge challenges.

Action agendas for inclusive growth by type of country

Low-income countries need balanced growth to continue the progress of the past 15 years. They have 70 percent of primary employment in the agricultural sector and a large rural population; neither of these two characteristics is expected to change rapidly in the next 20 years, owing to high population growth. These countries cannot neglect the agricultural sector. One key area for action is land policy, which is crucial to encouraging commercialization (medium and large farms) while protecting small holders' land for subsistence. It is also an important youth employment policy. Under traditional land tenure systems,

34. World Bank. (2015). *Women, Business and the Law 2016: Getting to Equal*. Washington: World Bank.
35. Agénor, P. & Canuto, O. (2012). Access to Infrastructure and Women's Time Allocation: Evidence and a Framework for Policy Analysis. *Policy Paper* (45).

In urban areas, the demand for wage employees is too low relative to the supply of youth looking for work, so most urban youth will have to create their own employment by starting a household enterprise.

youth have trouble getting access to land, even though they have more education and energy. Youth could lead the commercialization process, for example, by interacting with contract growers and other private sector actors aiding commercialization by bringing technology and reducing financing constraints. But they need land to do this. Rural policy also needs to support rural farm and nonfarm diversification opportunities (e.g. livestock, dairy, agroprocessing, services) to create higher income earning opportunities for rural households.

In urban areas, the demand for wage employees is too low relative to the supply of youth looking for work, so most urban youth will have to create their own employment by starting a household enterprise. As noted above, urban policy needs to plan for the growth of this sector and create the necessary infrastructure. In both rural and urban areas, access to education, health and safe water remain a challenge. This is not only an investment problem; service delivery needs to improve, through reform in current delivery models focusing on outcomes not only on infrastructure.

Lower-middle-income countries need improved agricultural productivity, which will continue to be important for inclusive growth. As in the low-income countries, this should be possible as land and labor productivity are still low and countries continue to import food. Commercialization is increasing in the sector through private investments in higher value crops and more productive technology for food crops. Demand for processed food is increasing as incomes rise; development of the agribusiness sector offers opportunities for stable employment in towns and peri-urban areas. Private investment will enter agricultural processing sector if the enabling environment improves (e.g. better veterinary services for livestock, public investment in storage facilities and transport networks as well as less government intervention in grain and food markets). A sizable share of youth will stay in rural areas and can be part of the increased commercialization of agriculture; they have education but they need access to land, technology and markets. A minority of youth can be expected to leave rural areas and migrate to towns and secondary cities looking for better opportunities however. For urban populations, the action agenda includes the two topics discussed in the previous section: more wage jobs and higher productivity in HEs.

Most lower-middle-income countries are getting an income improvement from declining energy prices. But they still face stabilization challenges—domestic debt has been rising, as has interest rates on sovereign bonds. Yet much more public investment is needed in transportation and electrical infrastructure, in education and health services, and in urban service delivery (such as water, sanitation, solid waste management, traffic management and flood control). This implies a focus on cost-effectiveness and domestic resource mobilization in order for the public sector to play its part in enabling inclusive growth. While private education is providing a quality alternative to the public system in urban areas, the public sector remains the only option for low-income urban and almost all rural households. Some advisors have suggested just giving households cash and letting them buy the services they need, but a recent study in Tanzania shows that this is an unpopular option (Sandefur, Birdsall, & Moyo 2016).[36] Voters want the government to deliver public social services, and they want the quality to improve. Efficiency will have to increase in these systems for this to happen. Meanwhile, pilots have shown that cash transfers are an effective social protection program, in many cases even allowing households to undertake the investments needed to raise their incomes (Evans & Popova 2014).[37] These programs may work as a platform to support disadvantaged youth to effectively enter employment.

Upper-middle-income countries face more complex growth challenges in order to emerge from the

36. Sandefur, J., Birdsall, N., & Moyo, M. (2016). The Political Paradox of Cash Transfers. Washington: Center for Global Development.
37. Evans, D. & Popova, A. (2014). Cash Transfers and Temptation Goods: A Review of Global Evidence. *World Bank Policy Research Working Paper* (6886).

In fragile states, reduction of conflict and improved security is obviously a prerequisite for inclusive growth.

middle-income trap. They need new firms as well as continuous productivity gains in older ones. The enabling environment needs to include appropriate competition policies to ensure that less dynamic firms go out of business while more dynamic ones expand. This means both job creation and job destruction. Labor mobility can be enabled through a mixture of safety nets to support those who lose their jobs, transportation networks to help workers reach new jobs, and information about rising sectors and occupations for those in transition. Most upper income countries now have social entrepreneurs who have created digital platforms to increase the flow of information, letting governments get out of the job-matching business.

Digital platforms are not enough to meet the youth employment challenge in upper-income countries. Without an increase in demand for labor, policies on the supply side will not be effective enough and youth unemployment will continue. With a more robust and dynamic private sector there may be scope for programs to help youth transition into employment. In some countries, youth are educated, but employers complain that they are not "job-ready." This may be a reflection of outdated curricula that lacks a focus on problem-solving and social skills. Curriculum reform takes time, but some short modules could be added to secondary and post-secondary programs, with appropriate evaluations. Governments may wish to encourage post-secondary institutions to expand programs in sectors where domestic and international demand is likely to increase, such as health services and business and management skills, while reducing programs designed to help youth enter the civil service (such as legal studies programs).

Most upper-income countries have public post-school programs to help youth develop skills for job. These programs have low success rates, although outstanding models exist in some localities. Successful programs need to be short, involve on-the-job training and be implemented jointly with the private sector so that they focus on developing the type of skills employers need. NGOs tend to have more success developing and implementing such programs (Fox 2016). In some North African countries, there may be scope for relaxing some parts of the labor code related to hiring and firing workers in order to increase employers willingness to hire less experienced youth (Glick, Huang & Mejia 2015).

In fragile states, reduction of conflict and improved security is obviously a prerequisite for inclusive growth. While better governance, which would enable the provision of more public goods and social services to the majority of the population, is also desirable to restart inclusive growth, it is not always achievable (Levy 2014).[38] One lesson from countries such as Mozambique, Rwanda and Uganda, which have successfully emerged from fragility through inclusive growth, is the key role of agriculture in a bounce-back growth path. Increased incomes in rural areas, combined with modest improvements in education and health services, were responsible for much of the poverty reduction in the immediate post-conflict period in these countries. Richer, mineral-exporting fragile countries such as Libya or Chad will have to find a political settlement that provides an acceptable distribution of resources to all sides. Cash transfer social-protection programs, which can be easily monitored, could be one tool to achieve this. These programs have been shown to improve agricultural incomes in low-income countries, so they may the most cost-effective approach to rural employment and poverty alleviation, at least in the initial years (Brune et al. 2015).[39] Finally, in cases such as South Sudan, where many have entered the labor force without the chance to go to school, "second chance" education programs for teens and literacy programs for adults may be considered to enhance the basic skills of the labor force.

Resource rich countries need a policy reset. These countries face a big challenge on the macroeconomic

38. Levy, B. (2014). *Working with the Grain: Integrating Governance and Growth in Development Strategies*. Oxford: Oxford University Press.
39. Brune, L., Giné, X., Goldberg, J., & Yang, D. (2015). Facilitating Savings for Agriculture: Field Experimental Evidence from Malawi. *NBER Working Paper* (20946).

All countries need to create more wage employment. The fastest way to do this is by creating and growing labor intensive non-agricultural medium and large enterprises.

and growth fronts. There is an opportunity to reverse the "resource curse" of poverty, inequality and weak private-sector wage job growth, by diversifying the economy and creating more income earning opportunities for the bottom 60 percent in agriculture and informal services, thus producing goods and services demanded by wage earners. Countries such as Indonesia were able to achieve this. African countries must seize the opportunity that the current crisis brings or they will stay behind the curve, trapped in a cycle of failed fiscal retrenchment for multiple years, as has happened in the past. The challenge for these countries is to spend public money more effectively, providing more public goods. Meanwhile, the public sector will not have the resources to satisfy the employment aspirations of urban youth for the foreseeable future. This means that policies designed to drastically increase private investment in industry outside the mineral sector in order to create the wage jobs are critically important.

Conclusion

From an inclusive growth viewpoint, Africa has had a good start to this century. Most people in most countries realized tangible improvements in economic well-being. The main exceptions were the fragile states. Except for the upper-income countries, households escaped poverty through raising the productivity of their livelihoods – in other words, by earning more in cash and kind from economic activities. In South Africa, non-labor income (transfers to poor households) played a big role in poverty reduction as unemployment remained high.

Expansion in social infrastructure complemented other growth policies, raising human capital and non-monetary living standards. Most of the gains came through investments in quantity – more schools and health clinics, more teachers and health workers, more books, more vaccinations, more supplies. While access problems persist in low-income countries, in middle-income countries access to primary education, water, and basic health care services are assured. But social indicators also reveal quality problems. Many more mothers are getting prenatal care and giving birth with the assistance of trained staff, but maternal, infant and child mortality are still high. Housing remains a challenge in rapidly growing urban areas. Education indicators reveal that classroom time is not used effectively for learning. The good news is that countries are starting to face up to these challenges.

Growth has to continue for poverty reduction to continue, and it has to occur in the sectors where the poor work. In all but the upper-middle countries, this means improving productivity in agriculture (family farms as well as large commercial farms), and in household enterprises. All countries need to create more wage employment. The fastest way to do this is by creating and growing labor intensive non-agricultural medium and large enterprises. Employment policy in Africa, therefore, needs to address twin goals: (i) higher earnings and more secure livelihoods in the agriculture and HEs segments of the economy; and (ii) creating more wage jobs in modern enterprises. Youth will enter all three sectors when opportunities are available; the objective of youth employment policy should be to ensure that they can earn an acceptable living.

Annex 1

Table A1: Country classification

Resource-rich	Fragile	Upper middle income	Lower middle income	Low income
Algeria[1]	Burundi[3]	Botswana	Cameroon	Benin
Angola[1]	Central African Republic[3]	Gabon	Cape Verde	Burkina Faso
Congo[2]	Chad[3,4]	Mauritius	Côte d'Ivoire	Ethiopia
Equatorial Guinea[1]	Comoros[3]	Namibia	Egypt	Gambia
Nigeria[2]	Djibouti[2]	South Africa	Ghana	Guinea
	DR Congo[3,4]	Tunisia	Kenya	Malawi
	Eritrea[3]		Lesotho	Mozambique
	Guinea-Bissau[3]		Mauritania	Niger
	Liberia[3]		Morocco	Rwanda
	Libya[1,4]		São Tomé & Principe	Tanzania
	Madagascar[3]		Senegal	Uganda
	Mali[3]		Swaziland	
	Sierra Leone[3]		Zambia	
	Somalia[3]			
	South Sudan[3]			
	Sudan[2]			
	Togo[3]			
	Zimbabwe[3]			

1 Upper middle income
2 Lower middle income
3 Low income
4 Resource-rich

Criteria

Resource rich: Oil, gas, and mineral exports greater than 90 percent of total exports in 2014

Fragile: Derived from the harmonized list between the World Bank and AfDB fragile country designations.

Income categories: As defined by the WB FY2016 income classifications based on GNI (Atlas method, 2014), low-income is $1,045 or below, lower-middle income in $1,045 to $4,125, and upper-middle income is $4,125 to $12,736.

Building Human Capital: Improving Education Quality

Chapter **4**

Kaisa Alavuotunki and Ritva Reinikka

Imagining Africa in 40 years—The role of education

A skilled and productive labor force is one of the key elements of the Africa convergence scenario presented in Chapter 2, including its five-fold increase in per capita incomes over the next 40 years. In the underlying vision, basic education would be universal and free for the first nine years, and enrollment would exceed 80 percent in secondary and 35 percent in tertiary education. African universities would have emerged as leading global research centers of excellence in areas such as extractive industries, agribusiness, and biotechnology.

This chapter has two broad objectives. First, it examines whether key education targets are on track to make the vision a reality. Second, it deepens the analysis of quality of education in Africa, especially in Sub-Saharan Africa (SSA), by analyzing new and unique school-level data—and suggests an action agenda based on the analysis.

Specifically, this section first summarizes the quantitative targets set for education. Second, it makes a case for quality of education and learning to become top priorities in Africa. Third, it highlights the role of teachers as the most important school-specific element for quality and argues that, therefore, any quality improvement program must focus on the teacher.

Quantitative targets

Using 2010 as the base year, quantitative targets were developed for the education sector in the initial vision 2050 for Africa.[1] These targets include doubling of the completion rate for an eight- or nine-year basic cycle, a five-fold increase in enrollment in both early childhood education and tertiary education, and a three-fold increase at the upper secondary level. To be sure, reaching these targets represents a major challenge. But the required annual growth rates for 2010-2050 are not as high as those African countries have actually achieved in the past four decades. Specifically, during the period 1970-2009 tertiary education in Africa experienced a 20-fold, secondary a 12-fold, and primary a 3.5-fold expansion.

There are factors that add to the challenge because the education systems are becoming much larger and more complex due to population increase and because under-served populations are typically more difficult and more costly to reach. Africa's population aged 5-14 is expected to expand 71 percent between 2010 and 2050. North Africa and SSA will, however, have very different trajectories: population projections indicate an increase of 83 percent in the aged 5-14 cohort in SSA but only a 6 percent increase in North Africa. A slow demographic transition means that countries in SSA will need to continue massively to expand their school systems to educate new cohorts that are larger than the previous ones.

To reach the targets by 2030, SSA must almost double the teaching force in place in 2010 in primary and lower secondary education even at current pupil-teacher ratios.[2] In addition to the near doubling of the population aged 5-14 in SSA between 2010 and 2050 mentioned above, 24 percent of SSA's school-aged children were out of school in 2010; all children need to go to school and so should be included in the student population. Assuming constant prices and salaries, the required annual increase in the salary budget to achieve the necessary teaching force is estimated at 3.3 percent.

However, in order to allow for some reduction in the pupil-teacher ratio and the needs in post-basic education, the annual salary budget should increase between 4 and 6 percent. Indeed, there is growing pressure for post-primary education—secondary schools and tertiary education—arising from the success of rapid primary school enrollment growth over the last two decades.[3]

Teachers' salaries account for the largest single item in education expenditures in most countries. In Africa,

1. Fredriksen, B. & Kagia, R. (2014). "Breaking the Human Capital Barrier" in Ahlers et al. (2014).

2. Fredriksen & Kagia (2014)

3. These figures do not include any increase in public funding for early childhood teachers even if it is now clearly understood by most that early years are critically important for human capital development.

Historically, public policy to advance basic literacy and numeracy has done more to advance human conditions than perhaps any other single policy.

salaries for teachers and education officials account for more than 70 percent of the expenditure in education, approximately 12 percent of total public expenditure. In the decade preceding 2010, the annual increase in public spending on education was 5 percent. Hence, in light of the recent past the required increase should be feasible—if economic growth can be maintained above 6 percent as foreseen in the convergence scenario.

Quality of education is key for the future

Historically, public policy to advance basic literacy and numeracy has done more to advance human conditions than perhaps any other single policy. Literacy and numeracy are not only core competencies but are also the foundation and prerequisites for higher and lifelong learning, as well as for innovation and adoption of new technologies. Laying this foundation cannot be leapfrogged.[4] Fundamental skills of literacy and numeracy must be learned—there are no shortcuts. Hence, basic education for all is critical—basic education where children actually learn while in school.

Literacy statistics reflect current and past learning outcomes. In the 15-24 age-group, the illiteracy rate in Africa is 28 percent today, with negative impact on labor productivity, family welfare, and demographic transition. In the past, illiteracy was most often an issue of lack of access to education—today it is increasingly due to children not learning even if in school. This chapter argues that the illiteracy rate risks stagnating, or even worsening, if the quality of basic education does not drastically improve from the current situation.

... and teachers are key for quality

Several different factors contribute to student learning, including individual characteristics (ability) and family circumstances (such as income and parents' education). But research suggests that, among school-related factors, teachers matter most.[5] When it comes to student performance on reading and math tests, a teacher is estimated to have two to three times the impact of any other school factor, including facilities and leadership.

Despite common perceptions, effective teachers cannot reliably be identified based on their place or level of education or their experience (i.e., years they have been teaching). The best way to assess teachers' effectiveness is to look at their on-the-job performance, including what they do in the classroom and how much progress their students make on achievement tests. Recent evidence suggests that a teacher's impact on student achievement remains reasonably consistent, even if the teacher changes schools and regardless of whether the new school is more or less advantaged than the old one.

Training, recruiting, and deploying teachers hence must be one of the most important preoccupations of the education systems in Africa if quality of education is to make the needed leap in performance. The teaching force has grown vastly in the past decades and, in 2010, it stood at 3.1 million primary and 1 million lower secondary teachers in SSA. Still, a doubling of the stock of teachers is needed by 2030. What these large numbers of teachers—both existing and new—do and know matters a great deal for quality of education.

The rest of the paper is organized as follows. The second section explores recent trends in public spending on education. The third section focuses on quality of education by examining results from global and Africa-specific student learning assessments. The quality of existing teachers is highlighted in the fourth section, which investigates what teachers do, what teachers know, and how this affects student learning. The final section concludes and suggests an action agenda.

4. Fredriksen and Kagia (2014)

5. Rand Corporation. (2012). Teachers matter: Understanding teachers' impact in student achievement. (CP-693/1).

African countries already devote relatively large shares of their public spending to education—in many countries education expenditure is on par with or higher than OECD countries.

Recent trends in public spending on education

Is public spending on track to meet future needs?

African countries already devote relatively large shares of their public spending to education—in many countries education expenditure is on par with or higher than OECD countries. OECD countries spend an average of 5.2 percent of their GDP on education and 11.3 percent of their total public spending;[6] in comparison, African countries devoted 4.8 percent of their GDP and 17.2 percent of their total government expenditure to education in 2015.[7]

Figures 1 and 2 illustrate education spending as a share of GDP and as a share of total government expenditure, respectively, for 41 African countries. Variation across countries is considerable. Zambia and Central African Republic devoted only a little over 1 percent of their GDP and around 6 percent of their total government expenditure to education; at the other end, for example, Botswana devoted 9.6 percent of its GDP and Ethiopia 27.0 percent of its total government expenditure to education.

Economic growth and the proportion of GDP that a country devotes to education spending jointly determine the incremental funding that is available for expanding the education system. Have countries managed to turn their economic growth into incremental spending on education? Figure 3 shows average annual changes in government education expenditures (constant prices) since 2010 for 29 African countries. Indeed, public spending on education has increased in most countries, at an average annual growth rate of 8 percent. In four countries—Sierra Leone, Malawi, Democratic Republic of the Congo, and Niger—education spending has increased 15 percent or more annually.

Figure 4 shows how annual changes in education spending at primary and secondary levels vary by country, revealing large differences across countries. In Mali, the total spending on education increased annually by 13 percent, but primary education funding grew by 39 percent while spending on secondary education fell. Rwanda, on

6. OECD. (2016b). Education at a Glance. OECD Indicators.
7. UNESCO. (2016). UNESCO Institute for Statistics. in 2015 or the most recent year available.

Figure 1: Public spending on education as a percentage of GDP, selected African countries

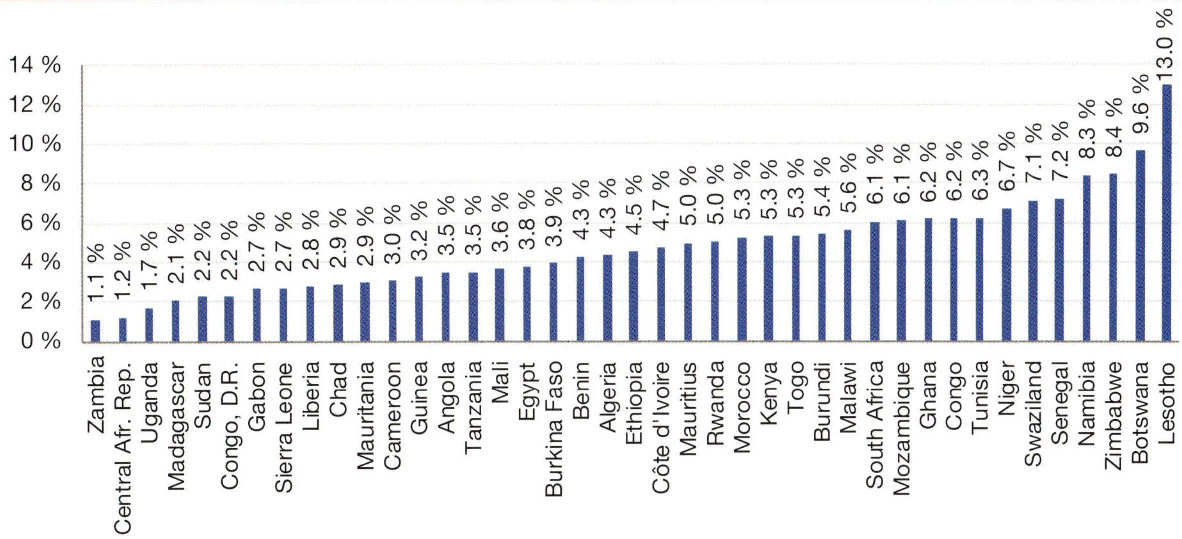

Note: 2015 or most recent year available
Source: UNESCO (2016)

Public spending on education has grown at 8 percent annually on average.

Figure 2: Share of education of total public spending, selected African countries

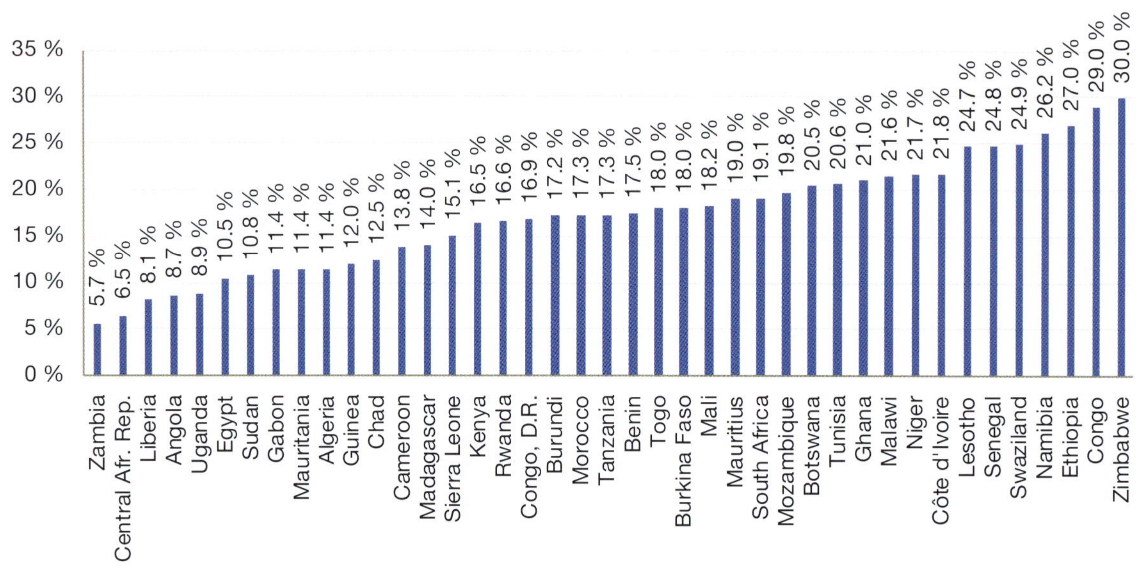

Note: 2015 or most recent year available
Source: UNESCO (2016)

Figure 3: Average annual change in public spending on education since 2010, selected African countries

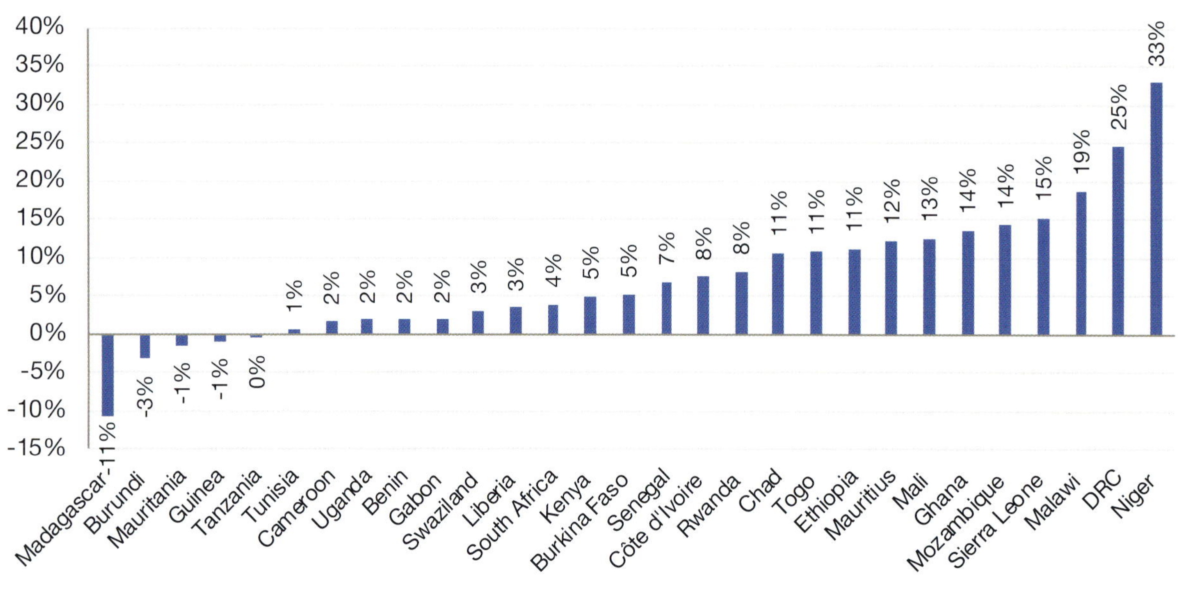

Note: Most recent year available since 2010. Change in constant local currency unit.
Source: UNESCO (2016)

Financial resources are a necessary condition for quality education, but they are by no means sufficient.

Figure 4: Average annual change in public spending on primary and secondary education since 2010, selected African countries

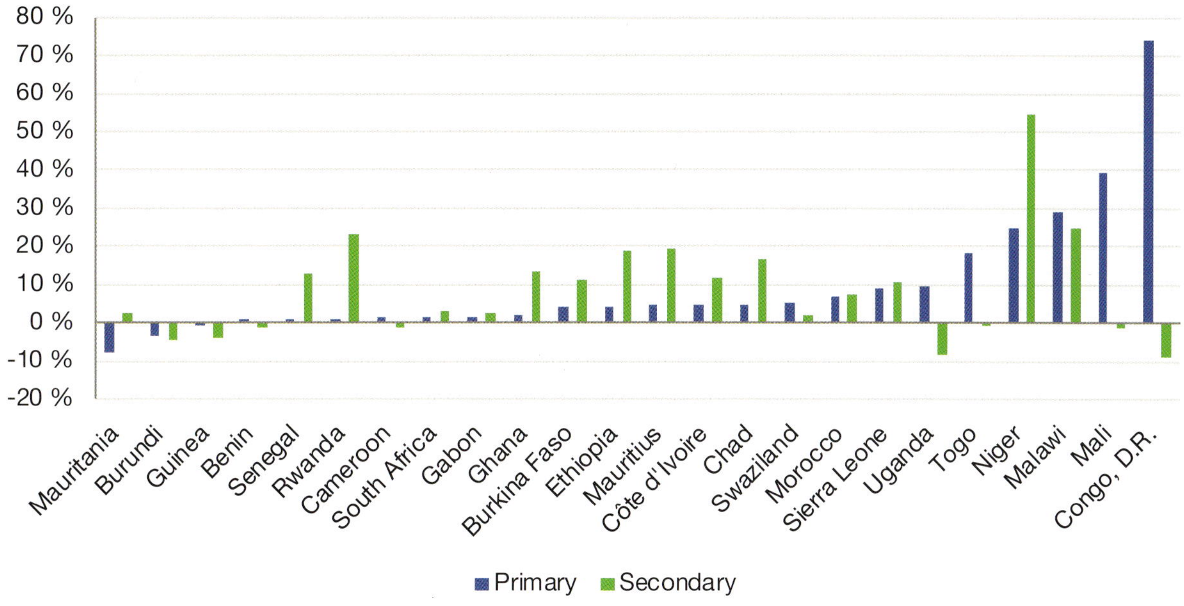

Note: Most recent year available since 2010. Change in constant local currency unit
Source: UNESCO (2016)

the other hand, has increased spending mainly on secondary education. Two countries, Niger and Malawi, have managed to increase spending on both primary and secondary education by over 20 percent annually.

The above brief analysis shows that considerable public resources are already being spent on education in most African countries. Furthermore, public spending on education has grown at 8 percent annually on average.[8] This respectable growth in spending is more than adequate for expanding the teaching force—and it leaves considerable additional resources for other expenditure items as well.

The high pupil-teacher ratio in SSA, however, has not budged much in recent years. It was 42 pupils to 1 teacher in 2016[9] compared to 43 pupils to 1 teacher in 2010.[10]

Weak link between spending and outcomes

Financial resources are a necessary condition for quality education, but they are by no means sufficient. Indeed, researchers have documented a weak correlation between spending and results in education from both cross-country and within-country analysis—whether measured in terms of aggregate spending as a share of GDP, spending per student, or trends over time.[11] The lack of correlation holds whether spending is compared to outputs (education

8. Private expenditure on education is also substantial in many countries but data on these trends are not readily available.

9. World Bank. (2013a). Service Delivery Indicators. http://datatopics.worldbank.org/sdi/. Washington: World Bank.
10. Fredriksen and Kagia (2014)
11. World Bank. (2003). *World Development Report 2004: Making Services Work for Poor People*. Washington: World Bank.

A total of 72 countries participated in the most recent PISA round in 2015; the only African countries to participate in this round were Algeria and Tunisia.

Figure 5: Malawi primary school leaving exam pass rate vs. per-student spending

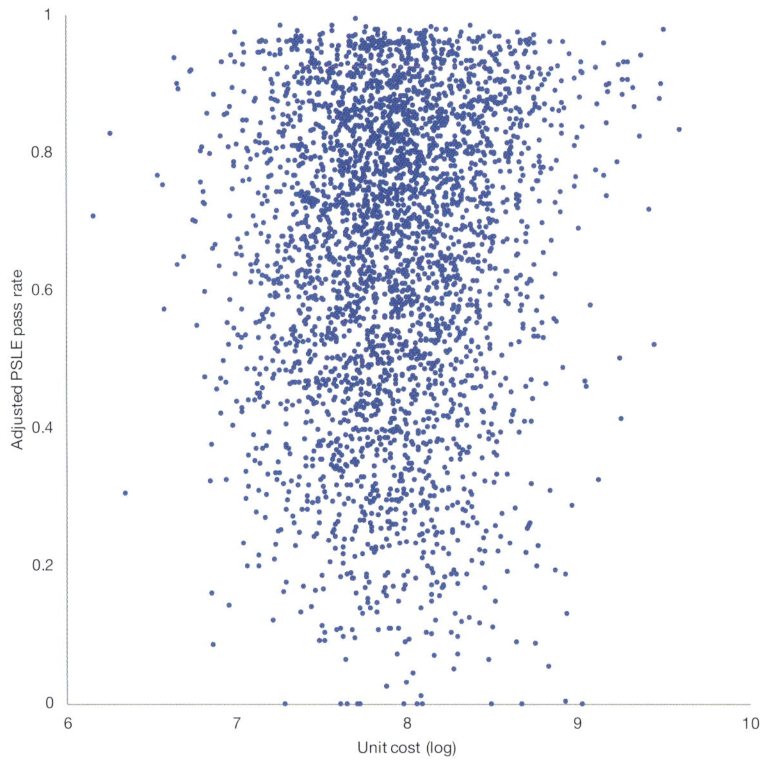

Source: Bruns, Filmer & Patrinos (2011)

attainment) or outcomes (learning), and it holds after controlling for other variables, such as income.

Figure 5 depicts an example of school-level data from the Malawi Primary School Leaving Exam pass rate and per-student spending—the unit cost includes teacher- and school book-related expenses—in government-funded schools. It is obvious that the link between spending and outcomes is at best weak—or rather non-existent. Unfortunately, Malawi is not an unusual example in this regard.

What learning assessments tell us about quality of education

Evidence from global assessments

The Program for International Student Assessment (PISA) is a worldwide learning assessment conducted by the OECD in member and non-member countries.[12] It assesses 15-year-old pupils' performance on mathematics, science, and reading, with a specific focus on the application of knowledge rather than on the curriculum alone. A total of 72 countries participated in the most recent PISA round in 2015; the only African countries to participate in this round were Algeria and Tunisia. They ranked among the bottom five out of the 72 countries. Hence, while

12. OECD. (2016c). Program for International Student Assessment (PISA).

Overall, African countries demonstrate low performance on TIMSS, all ranking among the bottom 10 among the 57 participating countries in 2015.

globally important, given that only two African countries participate, PISA is not a very useful source of information on learning from the African perspective.

Another global learning assessment is the Trends in International Mathematics and Science Study (TIMSS),[13] which is a series of assessments of pupils' mathematics and science knowledge carried out once every four years. During the past two decades, TIMSS has reported on mathematics and science achievement trends at the fourth and eighth grades, providing insights into how educational systems are functioning as well as critical intelligence about the possibilities for educational reform and improvement.

The most recent TIMSS results are available for 2015. Four African countries—Botswana, Egypt, Morocco, and South Africa—participated in this round. Ghana and Tunisia participated in the 2011 assessment. Figure 6 summarizes the results in the TIMSS math assessment for these six countries and shows a number of international comparators.

Singapore and the Republic of Korea are among the world leaders in math results according to TIMSS. Tunisia was the best performer among participating African countries, on par with Chile. Overall, African countries demonstrate low performance on TIMSS, all ranking among the bottom 10 among the 57 participating countries in 2015.[14] South Africa and Morocco managed to improve their results slightly between 2011 and 2015 by increasing the proportion of students who passed "low" (benchmark 400) and "high/intermediate" (benchmarks 550 and 475, respectively). However, in Botswana, the proportion of students who did not even reach "low" in fact increased from 50 percent to 53 percent.

13. TIMSS is carried out by the International Association for the Evaluation of Educational Achievement, a non-profit international scientific cooperative that has been active since 1958.

14. In 2015, 57 countries and 7 benchmarking entities (regional jurisdictions of countries such as states or provinces) participated in the fourth grade assessment, the eighth grade assessment, or both. In total, more than 580,000 students were tested in TIMSS 2015.

Figure 6: TIMSS Grade 8 assessment results in mathematics, 2015

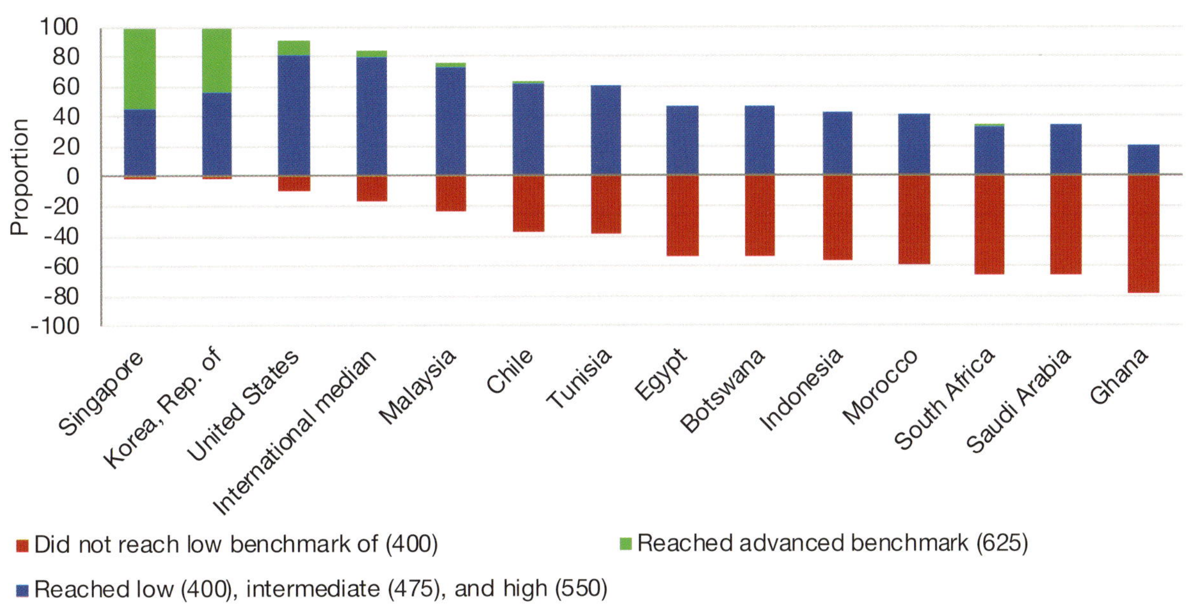

Note: Botswana and South Africa tested ninth graders; Ghana, Tunisia, and Indonesia results are from 2011.
Source: Authors' calculations based on Trends in International Mathematics and Science Study (TIMSS) (2015).

The TIMSS results indicate that a large proportion of pupils are spending eight years in school without learning the basic math skills.

Even more important than the rankings is the length of the red bar labeled "Did not reach low benchmark of 400" in Figure 6. The bar shows the share of eighth graders[15] who did not get "beyond elementary understanding of whole numbers and basic graphs." The longer the red bar, the larger is the share of eighth graders who did not possess basic knowledge in math. In other words, they have learned little math during their eight years in school. In Tunisia, this share was the smallest at 39 percent; in South Africa, it was 66 percent, while in Ghana, as high as 79 percent.

In sum, the TIMSS results indicate that a large proportion of pupils are spending eight years in school without learning the basic math skills. This does not bode well for increased productivity and earnings—or for the economic catch-up with the rest of the world as articulated in the Africa convergence scenario. To be sure, the TIMSS results are a call for urgent action for policymakers.

15. In Botswana and South Africa, ninth graders were tested instead.

Evidence from African assessments

There are two major school-based learning assessments in Africa, one in southern and eastern Africa (SACMEQ) and the other in francophone Africa (PASEC). In addition, in East Africa, a nongovernmental organization, Uwezo, carries out household-based learning tests of children between ages 6 to 16.

The Southern and Eastern Africa Consortium for Monitoring Educational Quality (SACMEQ) carries out large-scale cross-national research studies in the Southern and Eastern Africa region (Figure 7 for member countries).

Figure 7: SACMEQ member countries

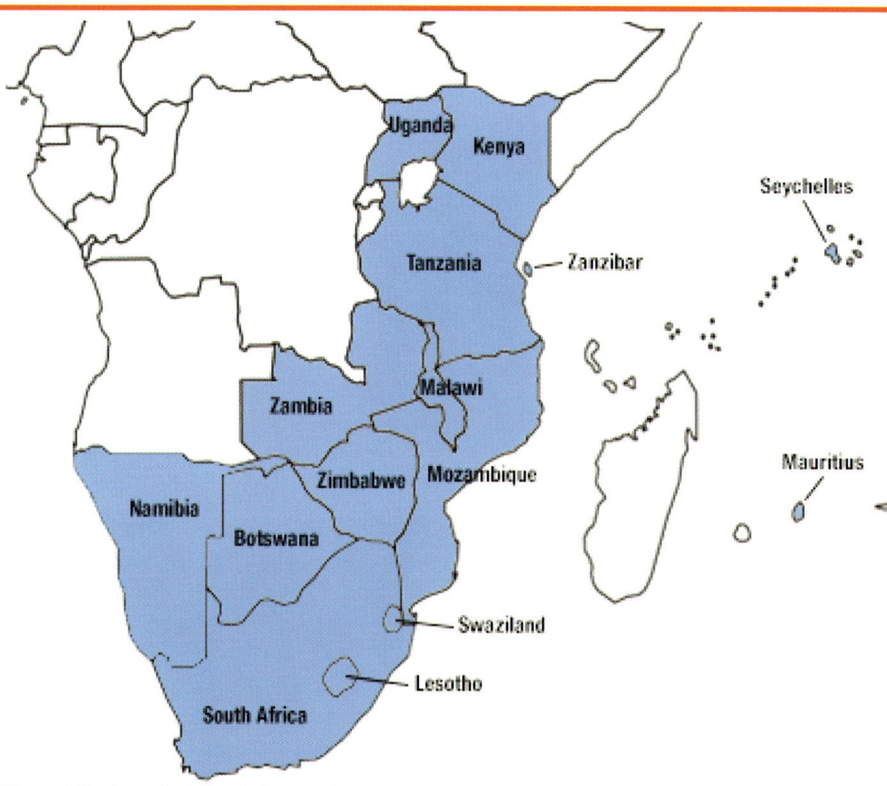

Source: Southern and Eastern Africa Consortium for Monitoring Educational Quality (SACMEQ) (2016)

For most young people in Africa primary school is the only formal skill training they receive—and yet it is such poor quality.

Figure 8: SACMEQ Grade 6 assessment results in mathematics, 2007

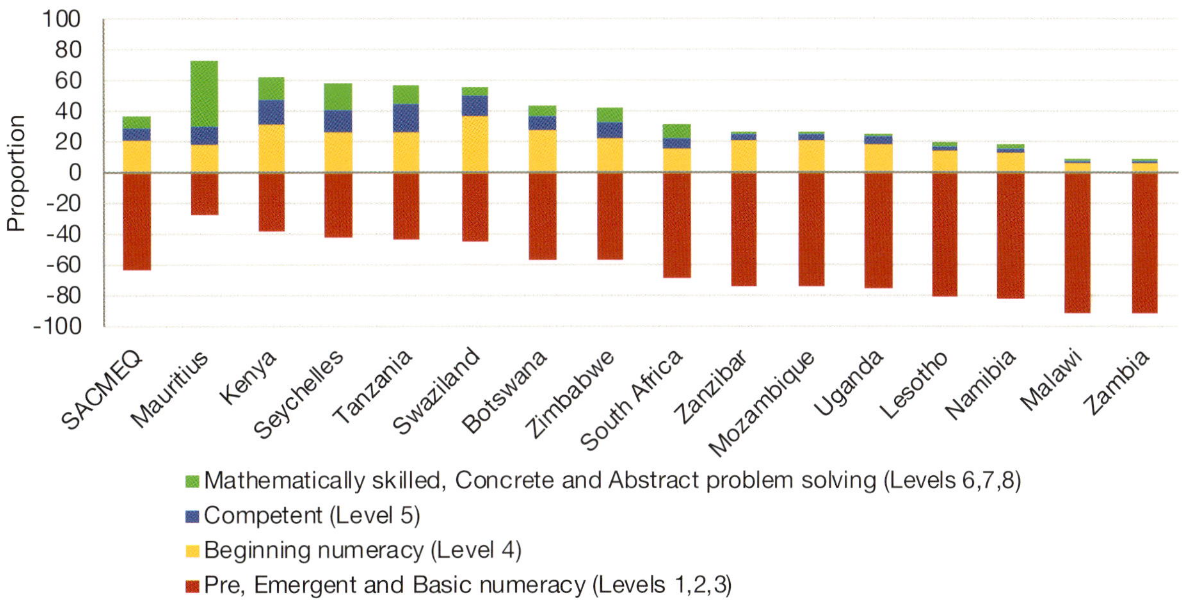

Source: Southern and Eastern Africa Consortium for Monitoring Educational Quality (SACMEQ) (2016)

It aims to assess the conditions of schooling and performance levels of learners and teachers in the areas of literacy and numeracy.[16] SACMEQ is like PISA, but is conducted at the regional level.

SACMEQ is a regionally benchmarked set of student assessments at Grade 6. SACMEQ results from the latest round (2007) suggest substantial shortcomings in learning achievement (Figure 8). The red bars in the chart show the proportion of test-takers in each country that does no better than basic numeracy in the SACMEQ math test. Sixth-grade pupils can recognize numbers, but they cannot do much with them—yet, these students have spent six years in school. The average proportion scoring "pre, emergent, and basic numeracy" is 60 percent of pupils, ranging from 27 percent in Mauritius to 92 percent in Zambia. Consider the ineffective use of resources, both on the household and the government sides, that results in such an unsatisfactory outcome. For most young people in Africa primary school is the only formal skill training they receive—and yet it is such poor quality. As a result, young southern and eastern Africans are coming into the labor market unprepared.

What about learning outcomes in Central and West Africa? La Conférence des Ministres de l'Éducation de pays ayant le français en partage (CONFEMEN) has managed learning assessments in francophone Africa since 1993. The participating countries are shown in Figure 9. This learning assessment is called PASEC, or *programme d'analyse des systèmes éducatifs de la CONFEMEN*, and is administered in different years in different countries to students in various grades at the beginning and at the end of the same school year.

Among sixth-grade students who were tested as a part of the PASEC regional assessment in 10 francophone countries in West and Central Africa in 2014, less

16. SACMEQ has completed three cross-national education assessments so far at five- to six-year intervals (SACMEQ I, 1995-1999; SACMEQ II, 1998-2004; and SACMEQ III, 2005-2010).

As evident from both the international and regional learning assessments, pupils in African primary schools are not acquiring foundational skills of literacy and numeracy consistent with the official curricular requirements in their countries.

Figure 9: PASEC member countries

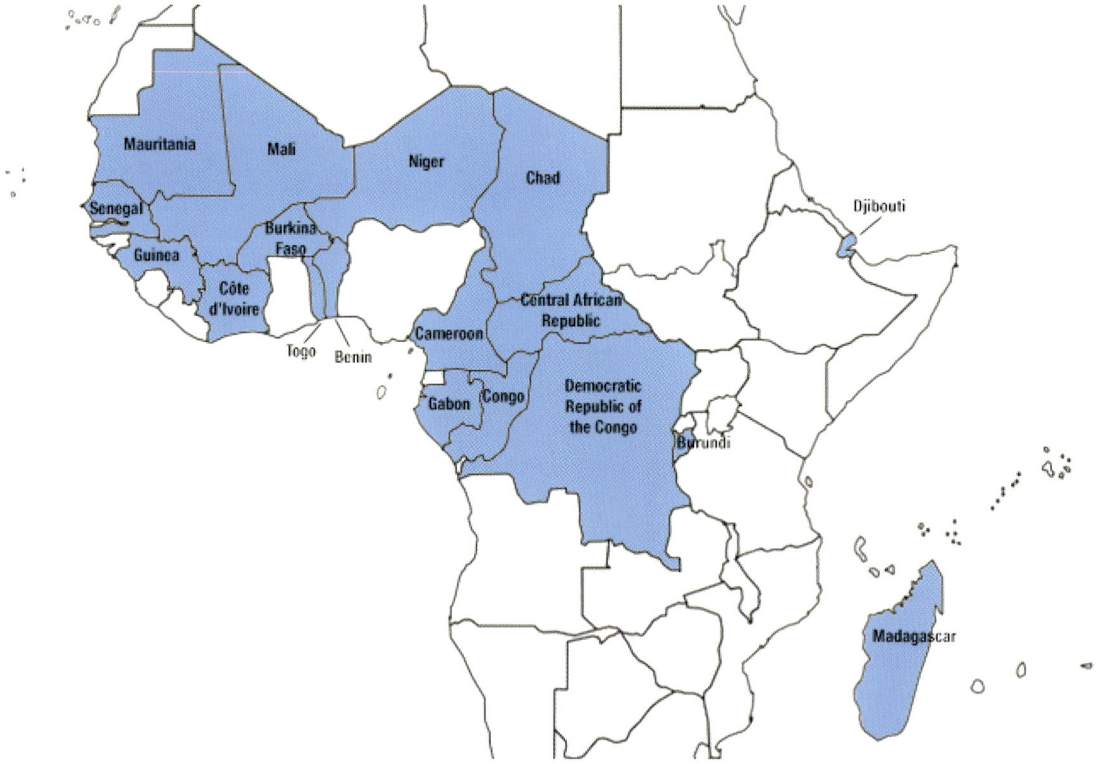

Source: Malpel (2016)

than 45 percent of students attained the competency level in reading or mathematics deemed "sufficient" to successfully continue their schooling.[17] The mathematics assessment results are summarized in Figure 10. On average, 40 percent of students attained the competency level in mathematics considered "sufficient," ranging from 87 percent in Burundi to 8 percent in Niger.

Lastly, Uwezo (which means "capability" in Kiswahili) is an initiative that aims to improve competencies in literacy and numeracy among 6 to 16 year old children in Kenya, Tanzania, and Uganda. The idea of Uwezo is very simple. Instead of focusing on numbers of classrooms built, teachers recruited, and books supplied, Uwezo asks the question "are children learning?"[18]

Like SACMEQ and PASEC, Uwezo (2013) finds that many children across East Africa are not learning basic literacy and numeracy skills. Only two out of ten pupils (20 percent) in the third year of primary school can read and do basic mathematics at Grade 2 level. By the time they reach the last year of primary school, one out of four East African children (24 percent) still have not acquired these skills.

For children aged 10 to 16, whether in or out of school, results suggest much room for improvement. In Kenya, 64 percent passed both one literacy and a numeracy test;

17. Malpel, J. (2016). PASEC 2014: Education System Performance in Francophone Sub-Saharan Africa. *Programme d'Analyse des Systèmes Educatifs de la CONFEMEN*. Dakar: PASEC.

18. Data on learning outcomes, school conditions and households were collected in 2013 in every district across the region through citizen-led household based assessments. Learning outcomes were assessed among children aged 6 to 16 through tests set at Grade 2 level.

In this regard, there really is what UNESCO calls a "learning crisis" in Africa.

Figure 10: PASEC Grade 6 assessment results in mathematics, 2014

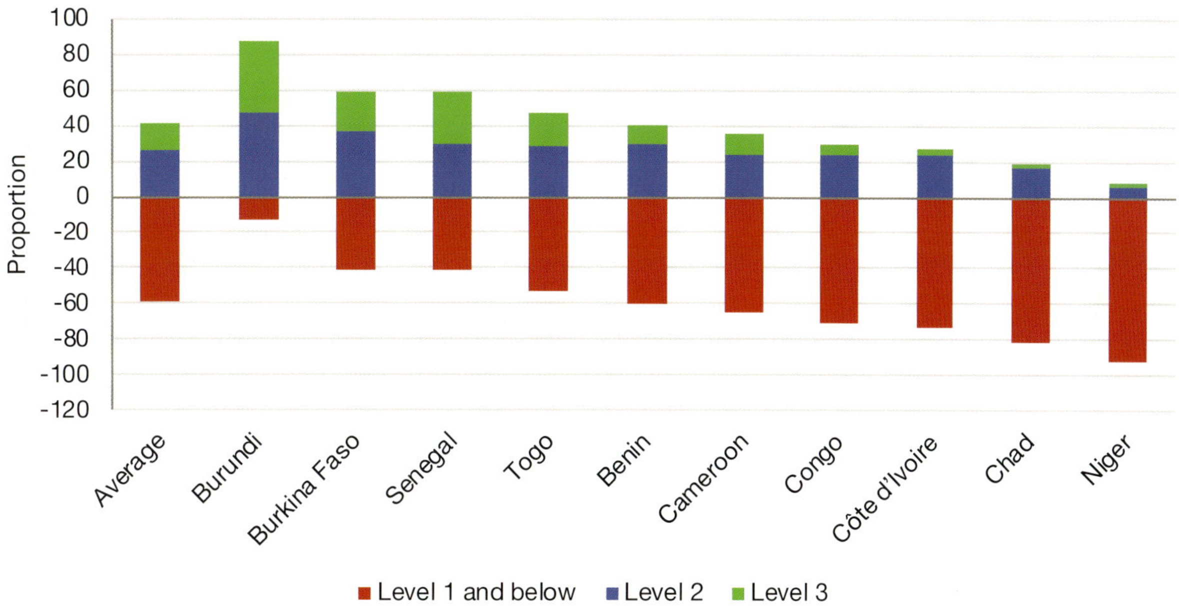

Note: "Level 1 and below" is lower than "sufficient" competency threshold to successfully continue schooling.
Source: Malpel (2016)

Figure 11: Grade 2 literacy and numeracy test pass rates for children aged 10 to 16, East Africa

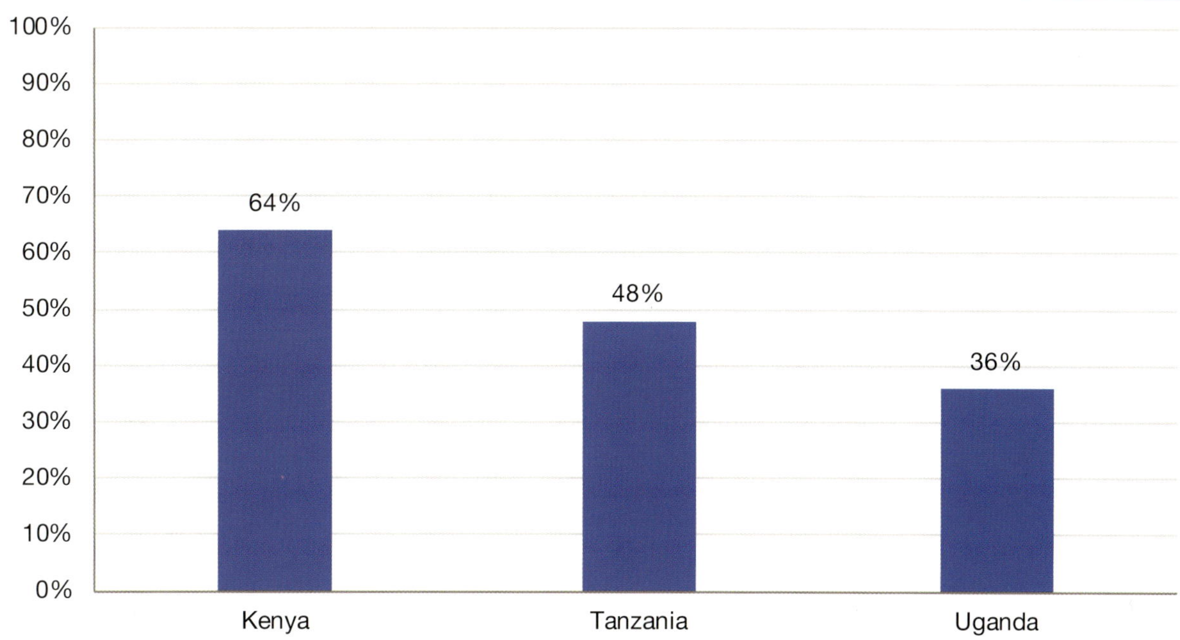

Source: Uwezo (2013)

The quality agenda is not just about money—and, in most cases, the money is already being spent. Instead, it is about the systems of education and their reform, with emphasis on learning.

in Tanzania the share was 48 percent and in Uganda, 36 percent. This means that, even in Kenya, the best performing country, fewer than 7 out of 10 of children aged 10 to 16 have mastered Grade 2 literacy and numeracy skills (Figure 11).

In short, as evident from both the international and regional learning assessments, pupils in African primary schools are not acquiring foundational skills of literacy and numeracy consistent with the official curricular requirements in their countries. They learn far too little. Indeed, in this regard, there really is what UNESCO calls a "learning crisis" in Africa.[19]

Recall that basic skills cannot be leapfrogged; they must be learned. Therefore, Africa's education agenda needs to shift decisively from quantity to quality and learning. African countries have been investing heavily in education and have achieved a vast expansion in access to schooling in a record time. Public spending continues to increase rapidly as education systems are growing, class sizes are being reduced, and post-basic education expands. But quality is severely lacking. Importantly, the quality agenda is not just about money—and, in most cases, the money is already being spent. Instead, it is about the systems of education and their reform, with emphasis on learning.

Service Delivery Indicators—Focus on teachers

The empirical evidence in this section comes from the new Service Delivery Indicators (SDI), which are currently available only for SSA countries.[20] The SDI is an ongoing Africa-wide program to collect informative and

19. UNESCO. (2013). *The Global Learning Crisis: Why Every Child Deserves a Quality Education*. Paris.

20. Morocco has also carried out an SDI-inspired survey in education but the results have not yet been finalized.

Figure 12: What Service Delivery Indicators (SDI) measure

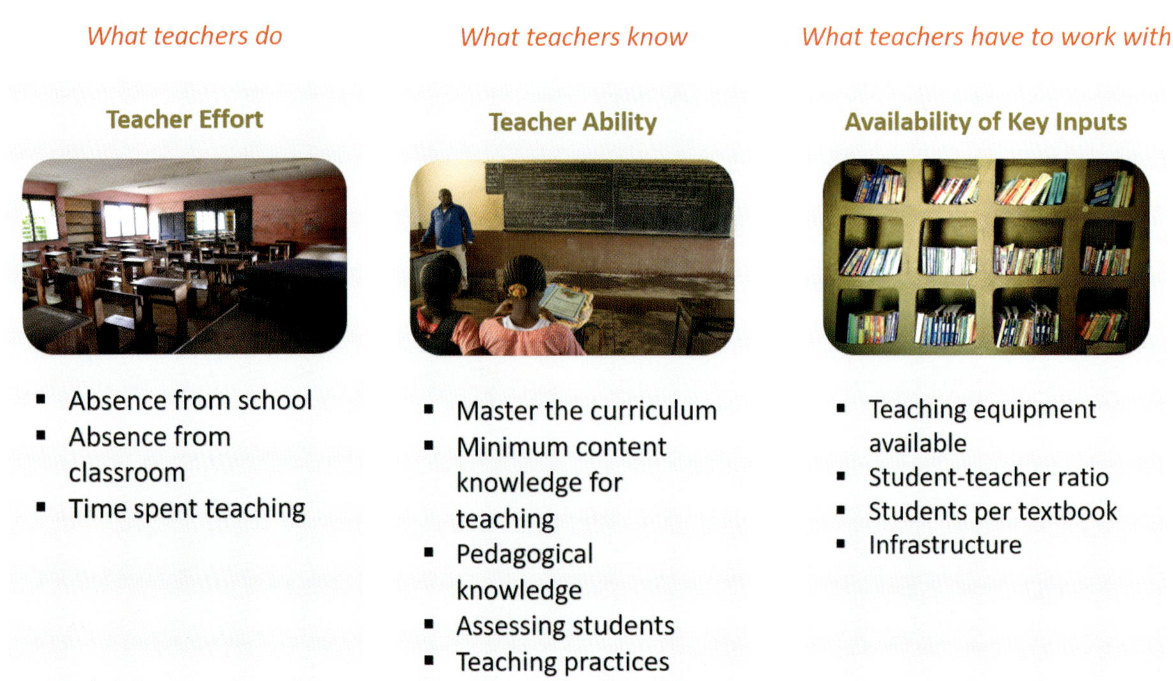

Source: World Bank (2013a)

To date the SDI—or SDI-inspired nationally representative surveys—have been implemented in 11 countries.

standardized measures of what primary school teachers do, what they know, and what they have to work with (Figure 12).[21] It is a unique source of new information on the most important school-specific factor, the teacher.

The SDI program grew out of concern about poor learning outcomes observed in the various student assessments, as well as shortcomings in the fast-expanding systems of education. These shortcomings are most distinctly manifested at the school level, hence the SDI focuses on schools. Despite the focus on schools, the "learning crisis" cannot be tackled at the school level alone. Educational achievement is not about schools or teachers alone but the entire system of education—and society.

The SDI provides a set of metrics for benchmarking service delivery performance in education (and in health care). The indicators enable identification of gaps and tracking of progress over time and across countries. It is envisaged that the broad availability, high public awareness, and persistent focus on these indicators will mobilize policymakers, citizens, service providers, donors, and other stakeholders for action to improve the quality of services and ultimately to improve learning outcomes.

To date the SDI—or SDI-inspired nationally representative surveys—have been implemented in 11 countries in Africa, representing the service delivery experience of over 450 million people. The countries for which SDI data are available are Kenya, Madagascar, Mozambique, Niger,

21. The SDI program is implemented in partnership with the African Economic Research Consortium (AERC), AfDB, and the World Bank. Funding is provided by the participating African countries, the William and Flora Hewlett Foundation, the UK Department for International Development, and the World Bank.

Figure 13: Service Delivery Indicators in Africa

Source: World Bank (2013a)

When examining absence from classroom, we find that, 42 percent of teachers, on average, are not teaching. They are either absent from school or, even if at school, absent from the classroom.

Nigeria, Senegal, Tanzania, Togo, and Uganda.[22] In the SDI pipeline for 2017 are Benin, Burkina Faso, Cameroon, Democratic Republic of the Congo, and the Republic of the Congo (Figure 13).

The surveys collect a broad set of school-, teacher-, and student-specific information, with an approach that relies as much as possible on direct observation rather than on respondent interviews. Data are also collected through visual inspections of fourth-grade classrooms and the school premises, direct physical verification by unannounced visits (absence rate), and teacher and student tests. The SDI is the only available survey where both student performance and teacher effort and knowledge are measured in considerable detail and linked so that they can be analyzed together. Table A1 in the annex contains, in a summary format, a comparison of SDI results for public schools across 9 countries.

What do teachers do?

The SDI measures teacher effort using three principal statistics: absence from school,[23] absence from classroom,[24] and time on task or actual teaching time. As shown in Figure 14, teacher absence at the time of an unannounced visit is high in Africa. This includes teachers absent from the school, as well as teachers who are

22. As shown in Figure 13, Ethiopia and Zambia have implemented SDI-inspired surveys, while Morocco is in the pipeline as its results are currently being finalized. Mozambique will soon initiate a second round in education, while Tanzania is currently implementing a third SDI education round.

23. School absence rate is measured as the share of teachers who are absent from school at the time of an unannounced visit. During the first announced visit, a maximum of ten teachers are randomly selected from the list of all teachers who are on the school roster. The whereabouts of these ten teachers are then verified in the second, unannounced, visit. Teachers found anywhere on the school premises are marked as present.

24. Classroom absence rate is measured as the share of teachers not in the classroom at the time of an unannounced visit. The indicator is constructed in the same way as the school absence rate indicator, with the exception that the numerator now is the number of teachers who are either absent from school or present at school but absent from the classroom when they should be teaching.

Figure 14: Absence rates in public schools, selected SSA countries

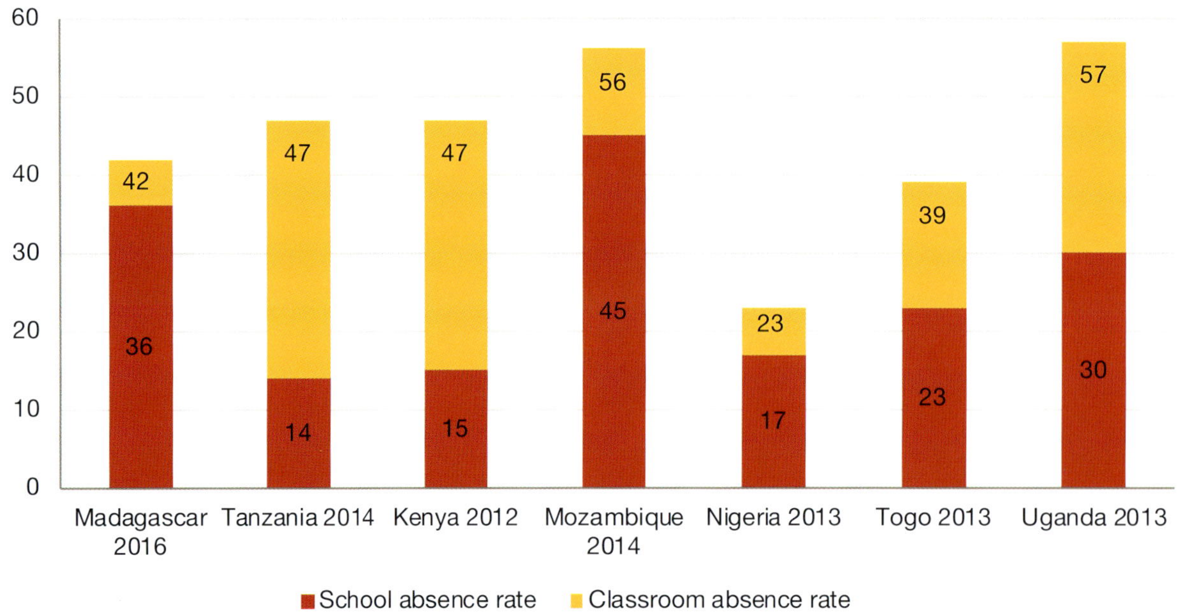

Source: World Bank (2013a)

The result of absenteeism is that the actual number of hours that students are being taught is low; on average, 2 hours 53 minutes a day as compared with the average scheduled teaching time of 5 hours 31 minutes.

at the school but not in the classroom when they should be teaching.

On average, the absence rate from school is 20 percent, ranging from 14 percent in Tanzania to 45 percent in Mozambique. At any given time, on average, every fifth teacher is absent from school in Sub-Saharan Africa. When examining absence from classroom, we find that, 42 percent of teachers, on average, are not teaching. They are either absent from school or, even if at school, absent from the classroom. The classroom absence rate ranges from 23 percent in Nigeria to 56 percent in Mozambique and 57 percent in Uganda.

The result of absenteeism is that the actual number of hours that students are being taught is low; on average, 2 hours 53 minutes a day as compared with the average scheduled teaching time of 5 hours 31 minutes (Figure 15). The time on task is, hence, only about a half of what the statutes of education policy require.[25]

When a large share of teachers are not teaching, unsurprisingly, a large share of classrooms are occupied by only pupils. Consistent with the findings on absence from classroom (conditional on teacher being at school), averaging across countries, one third of the classrooms were "orphaned," i.e., classrooms where students were present but there was no teacher.

What do teachers know?

For teachers to be effective, they must have the necessary content knowledge for good teaching. To assess content knowledge, the SDI survey asked language teachers to mark mock student exams in language (English, French, or Portuguese)[26] and math teachers

25. Teaching is defined very broadly, including actively interacting with pupils, correcting or grading pupil's work, asking questions, testing, using the blackboard, or having pupils working on a specific task, drilling, or memorization. Non-teaching activities include working on private matters, maintaining discipline in class, or doing nothing and thus leaving pupils not paying attention.

26. Possessing knowledge equivalent to the fourth-grade curriculum is not sufficient to teach language in lower primary, because it is difficult to teach a student how to compose even a simple text without having knowledge

Figure 15: Scheduled teaching time and actual time spent teaching, selected SSA countries

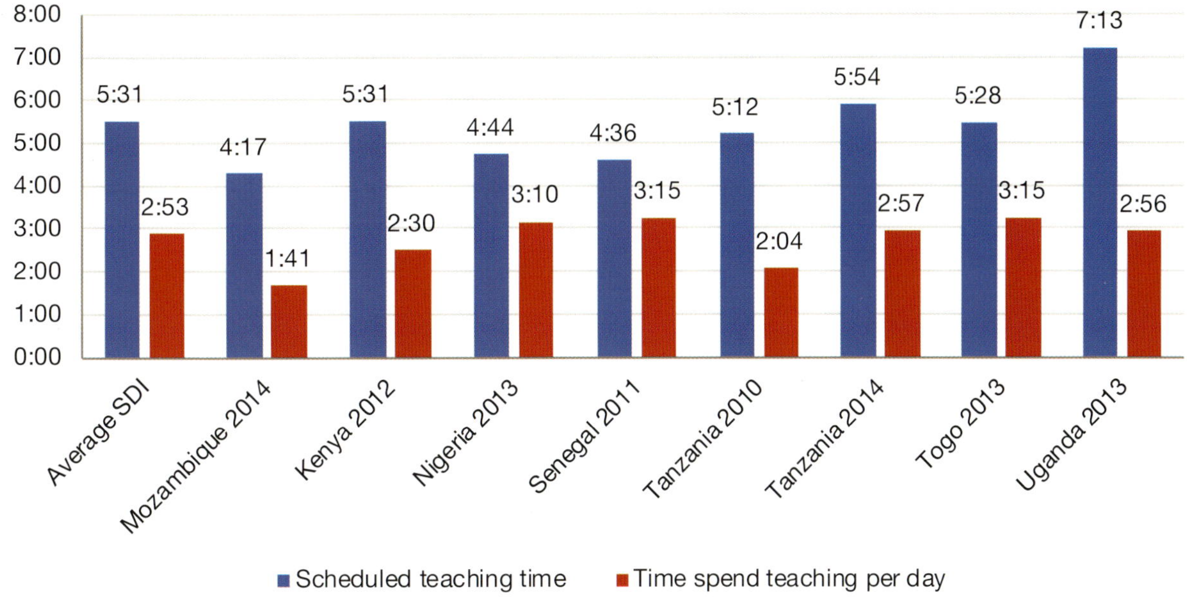

Source: World Bank (2013a)

It is evident that teacher knowledge in SSA is far below what it should be—and what is expected by policymakers, employers, and parents.

in mathematics.[27] The mock student exam was based on the fourth-grade curriculum and consistent with the teachers' normal activities—marking student work. This approach—a mock student exam paper—also recognizes teachers as professionals in the assessment situation.

The SDI found that, in the seven countries where the survey data have been analyzed to-date, only 13 percent of language and math teachers possessed what can be considered minimum knowledge to teach the curriculum they were teaching. As depicted in Figure 16, only 0.1 percent of Grade 4 teachers in Madagascar scored more than 80 percent on the language and mathematics curriculum compared to 40 percent in Kenya.

Teachers' test scores of language, mathematics, and pedagogy combined are shown in Figure 17. Average score is 42 percent, while the test results range from 57 percent in Kenya to 27 percent in Mozambique. The weakest area is pedagogy.

It is evident that teacher knowledge in SSA is far below what it should be—and what is expected by policymakers, employers, and parents. While systematic teacher test results do not exist from the past, it seems that the mass expansion of the teaching force during the last two decades have come at the cost of teacher quality.

that goes well beyond the curriculum. The SDI, therefore, considers a language teacher in Grade 4 to have minimum subject content knowledge if he or she can confidently correct children's work in such aspects of literacy as reading comprehension, vocabulary, and formal correctness (grammar, spelling, syntax, and punctuation), all of which are competencies a teacher in lower primary would routinely be required to teach. To this end, the language test contained (in addition to the spelling and grammar exercises) Cloze passages to assess vocabulary and reading comprehension, and a letter written to a friend describing their school, which the teacher had to mark and correct. The SDI defines "minimum knowledge in language" as marking at least 80 percent of the items on the language test correctly.

27. In mathematics, a teacher has minimum subject content knowledge if he or she can accurately correct pupils' work in such aspects of numeracy as manipulating numbers using whole number operations. This requirement amounts to correctly scoring 80 percent or more of the questions on the lower primary portion of the mathematics test. In essence, the test measures whether the math teacher masters his or her students' curriculum, allowing for 20 percent points margin of error.

Figure 16: Teacher knowledge in public schools: Minimum knowledge in language and math

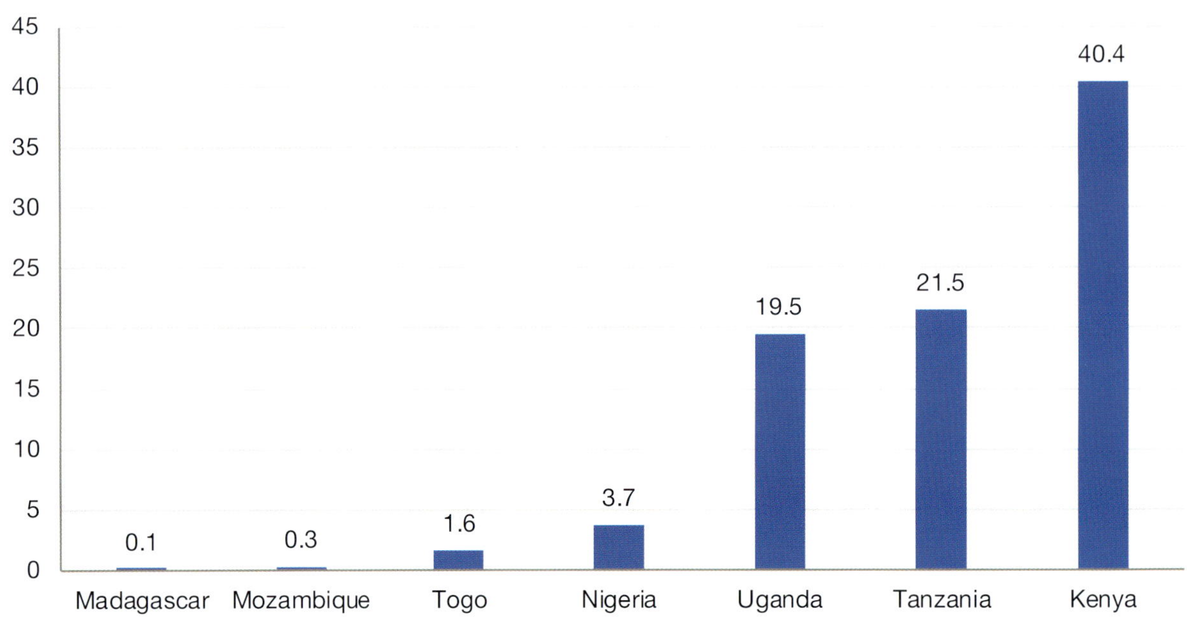

Source: World Bank (2013a)

Reforms that create a situation where students are taught by teachers with at least minimum subject (content) knowledge and minimum pedagogical knowledge and skills would make it possible to take a quantum leap and considerably improve student learning in Africa.

Figure 17: Teacher test scores: Language, mathematics, and pedagogy combined

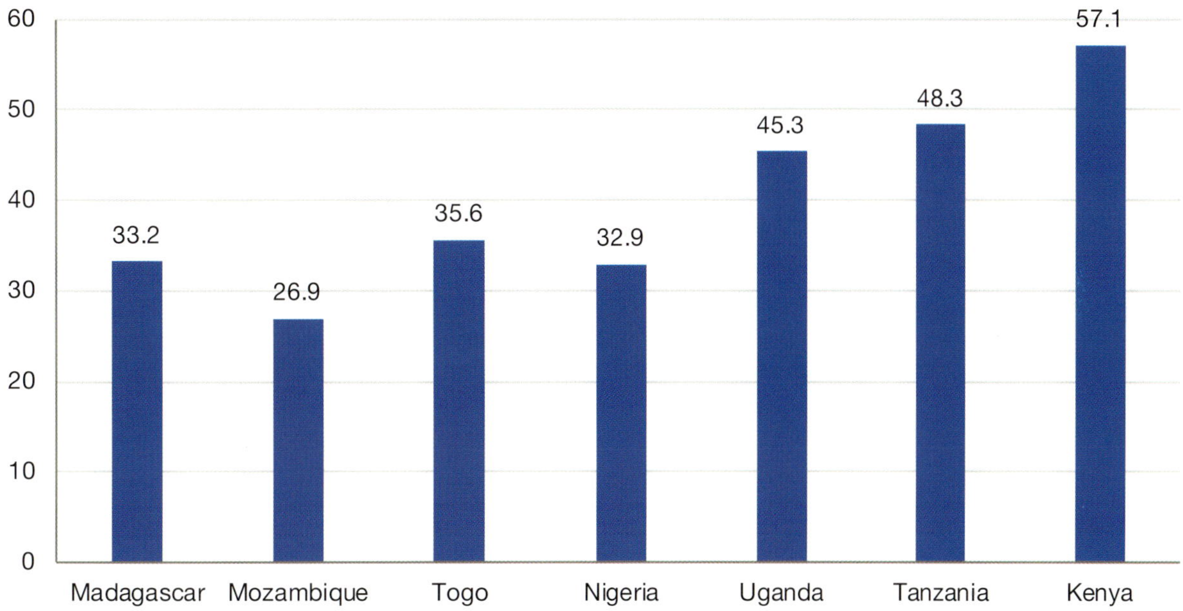

Source: World Bank (2013a)

How much do teachers matter for learning?

The SDI is unique in that it collects both student and teacher test data and thus allows empirical examination of the extent to which teacher quality matters for student learning in Africa. In other words, one can ask whether—and to what extent—students' academic performance would increase if they were taught by better teachers, specifically, by those with higher content knowledge and greater pedagogical knowledge and skills.

Analysis of the SDI data finds large positive effects of teacher's good content knowledge and pedagogical knowledge and skills on student learning.[28] Specifically, moving a student from a teacher with little content or pedagogical knowledge and few pedagogical skills to a teacher with high scores on these three dimensions would raise student test scores by 1.1 standard deviation. This is a very large increase and would make a big difference for learning—more or less the quantum leap that the learning assessments suggest is needed. In comparison, in randomized controlled trials, which have been carried out on numerous education interventions, an impact 0.1 to 0.2 standard deviations is often considered a large impact.

These findings strongly suggest that reforms that create a situation where students are taught by teachers with at least minimum subject (content) knowledge and minimum pedagogical knowledge and skills would make it possible to take a quantum leap and considerably improve student learning in Africa.

How do private schools compare to public schools?

Private schools account for around 20 percent of total primary school enrollment in low-income countries.[29] Con-

28. Bold, T., Filmer, D., Martin, G., Molina, E., Stacy, B., Rockmore, C., Svensson, J. & Wane, W.. (2017 January). What Do Teachers Know and Do? Does It Matter? Evidence from Primary Schools in Africa. *Policy Research Working Paper* (7956). Washington: The World Bank Group.

29. Baum, D., Lewis, L., Lusk-Stover, O. & Patrinos, H. (2014). What Matters Most of Engaging the Private Sector in Education: A Framework Paper. *Systems Approach for Better Education Results (SABER) Working Paper Series* (8). Washington: The World Bank.

> *Private schools are not able to overcome many of the same problems faced by public schools—these problems seem to be systemic.*

trary to common perception, most of these private schools are informal and low-cost. According to the SDI data, African private schools tend to perform better than public schools.[30] Their teachers tend to exert more effort, show more knowledge, and exhibit better teaching practices than their public sector counterparts (Table 1).

Yet, private schools are not able to overcome many of the same problems faced by public schools—these problems seem to be systemic. Indeed, even in the private sector, close to one third of teachers are absent from the classroom. While teachers' time on task—i.e., the length of the actual school day—is four hours, on average (rather than the 2 hours and 53 minutes in public schools), it is still two hours shorter than the scheduled time. In addition, while teachers in private schools have significantly higher test scores, their pedagogical knowledge is almost as weak as that of public school teachers.

Analysis shows that the better performance of private school teachers is reflected in learning outcomes.[31] The student score in mathematics and language is between one-third and two-thirds higher in private schools. The reading comprehension score of a private school student is three times as high as those of public school students. However, at least some of the better performance may be due to sorting of more capable students to private schools and not only because of better-performing teachers.

30. Bold et al. (2016)
31. Bold et al. (2016)

A comparison of student test scores in the SDI

Lastly, we compare student test scores in mathematics in the best, average, and worst schools in three countries where the SDI survey has been implemented: Kenya, Nigeria, and Uganda. The best schools are defined as belonging to the top decile of teacher presence and subject (content) knowledge and in the bottom decile of pupil-teacher ratio. Average schools are in the middle of the distribution, while the worst schools are at the opposite end from the best schools.

Comparison of SDI results across Kenya, Nigeria, and Uganda reveals large differences (Figure 18). While Ugandan top schools fare better than the best schools in the other two countries, within-country differences in test scores between Uganda's best and worst performing

Table 1: Comparison of public and private schools

	Public	Private
Teachers		
Absence from class (%)	48	28
Time spent teaching	2h 48m	4h 2m
Score Language	49	55
Score Mathematics	50	58
Score Pedagogy	23	25
Good practice in the classroom	9	12
Students		
Score Language	44	73
Score Maths	42	56
Score NVR	54	61

Note: Data covers Kenya, Nigeria, Togo and Uganda where private school samples are available. Therefore, averages differ slightly from other tables and figures presented in this paper.
Source: Bold et al. (2016)

The next priority is improving the quality of learning in school so that children emerge equipped with the education they need to address the challenges of the complex economic, social, and political world they face.

Figure 18: Student test scores in best, average, and worst schools in mathematics

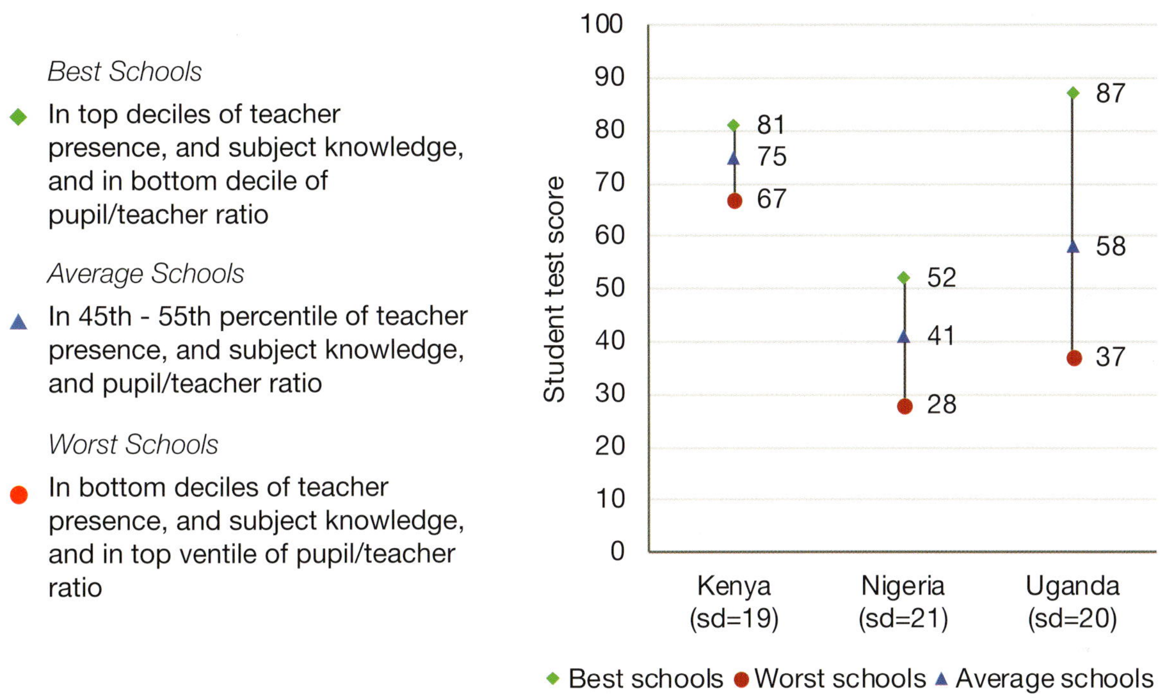

Source: World Bank (2013a)

schools are much larger (50 points out of 100) than those in Kenya (14 points) or Nigeria (24 points). Looking across the three countries, it is remarkable that student test scores in mathematics in Nigeria's best schools are lower than Kenya's worst schools.

Conclusions and an action agenda

Africa has largely accomplished the goal of universal enrollment of children in primary school, although significant regional and social pockets of disadvantage remain and completion rates need to improve. The next priority is improving the quality of learning in school so that children emerge equipped with the education they need to address the challenges of the complex economic, social, and political world they face. This is also what was agreed in the United Nations for the sustainable development goal number four.

This chapter emphasizes the centrality of quality. Until recently, attention has been mostly on increasing access to education. In the past two decades, most countries in Africa have effectively used increased financial resources—both domestic and external—to expand school participation for all. Today Africa spends a similar share of its GDP and public spending on education as OECD countries. A fast-growing population and new demands for post-primary education will continue to require increasing resources in the future, too. In order to achieve this, both continued economic growth and selectivity are critical.

Improving quality is not just a question of money. Rather, it is about putting the focus squarely on learning. How can this be done? First, one must start with measurement. Regular learning assessments—either international or regional—should become the norm. Currently, learning is measured at best sporadically. For example, SACMEQ

Education systems need to develop and support good teachers in a much more comprehensive and effective way than is the case today.

in Southern and Eastern Africa was last carried out in 2007. Few African countries participate in international learning assessments, such as TIMSS or PISA. This state of affairs should change, and relevant quality targets should be developed.

Second, improvement in learning requires reforming the entire system of education. Such reform needs to go well beyond the education ministries and those reporting to them—it is a project for the whole of society. There is, unfortunately, no silver bullet, technical fix or intervention that will do it. Instead, such a reform needs to strengthen the relationships of accountability between national and local politicians, education service providers, and parents. It is about politics, incentives, and empowering parents and other stakeholders, all with the focus on quality and learning.

While student learning assessments and the SDI data on teachers provide a detailed nationally representative diagnosis of the problem at the school level, finding solutions will require national dialogue, consensus building, and continued monitoring of progress. Just calling for more funding for education will no longer do.

Third, it is important that education is broad-based with universal basic education and at least 80 percent secondary and 35 percent tertiary enrollment. In order to achieve broad-based learning, countries cannot ignore the systemic failures and focus on, say, science, technology, engineering, and mathematics—the so-called STEM subjects—for the elite group of students. It is not sufficient just to have a group of well-educated students who will take the country forward. Without broad-based education, much talent would be lost if poorer children did not get an opportunity to learn basic skills and beyond. The same would be the case if girls were not able to access good education. This large talent pool could not be harnessed for national productivity—and many would be condemned to the cycle of poverty. Empirical evidence supports this argument. Namely, it is not just the average test scores—or the top test scores—that matter for economic growth but also the bottom scores.[32]

This chapter emphasized two other related aspects, or basic premises. First, that basic skills cannot be leapfrogged, they must be learned. Learning assessments reviewed in this paper demonstrate unequivocally that students are not learning anywhere near what they should be learning according to countries' education policies and plans.

Second, the teacher is the most important school-related factor in education. It is evident from the new SDI data that teacher effort and knowledge in SSA is far below what it should be—and what is expected by the continent's policymakers, employers, and parents. The SDI surveys provide unique and policy-relevant evidence on what teachers do and know—such test results have not been available in the past. It seems clear that the mass expansion of the teaching force during the last two decades in Africa has come at a high cost of teacher quality.

The SDI data also show that, when taught by teachers with at least minimum subject knowledge and pedagogical knowledge and skills, student test scores are vastly better. Thus, it is indeed possible to take a giant leap in quality of education and greatly improve student learning in Africa.

Lastly, while we have explored the problem of poor learning with the focus on teachers, it is important to point out that the issues raised in this paper reflect system-wide problems, not just teacher-specific ones. Solving them calls for system-wide solutions. Most teachers enter their profession with intrinsic motivation and desire to help students learn. An important message is, therefore, that the education systems need to develop and support good teachers in a much more comprehensive and effective way than is the case today.

32. Hanushek, E. & Woessmann, L. (2015). *The Knowledge Capital of Nations. Education and the Economics of Growth*. CESifo Book Series. Cambridge, MA: The MIT Press.

Annex 1

Table A1: Comparison of SDI results across countries (public schools)

	Madagascar 2016	Tanzania 2014	Average SDI	Kenya 2012	Mozambique 2014	Nigeria* 2013	Senegal 2011	Tanzania 2011	Togo 2013	Uganda 2013
Teacher Ability										
Minimum knowledge (At least 80% in language and mathematics)	0	21.5	12.7	34.8	0.3	2.4	Not comparable	Not comparable	0.9	19.4
Test score (language, mathematics, and pedagogy)	32.1	48.3	42	55.6	26.9	30.5	Not comparable	Not comparable	33.9	45.5
Teacher Effort										
School absence rate	35.9	14.4	20.1	15.2	44.8	16.9	18	23	22.6	29.9
Classroom absence rate	42.2	46.7	42.1	47.3	56.2	22.8	29	53	39.3	56.9
Scheduled teaching time	5h 03min	5h 54min	5h 31min	5h 31min	4h 17min	4h 44min	4h 36min	5h 12min	5h 28min	7h 13min
Time spent teaching per day	2h 56min	2h 46min	2h 53min	2h 30min	1h 41 min	3h 10min	3h 15min	2h 04min	3h 15min	2h 56min
Availability of Inputs										
Observed pupil-teacher ratio	16.9	43.5	42.1	39.3	21.4	21.5	27.2	52	31.4	53.9
Share of pupils with textbooks	6.8	25.3	37.2	44.5	68.1	33.7	18	19.7	76	6
Minimum equipment availability (90% with pencils and notebooks)	65.1	61.4	57.8	74.3	76.8	48.2	Not comparable	Not comparable	24.3	79.5
Minimum infrastructure availability	16	40.4	36.2	60.2	29.1	13.4	Not comparable	Not comparable	14.4	57.2
Pupil Learning										
Test Score (out of 100) (language, mathematics)	46.6	40.1+*	45.4	69.4	20.8	25.1	Not comparable	Not comparable	38.1	45.3
Language test score	39.7	36.5+*	44.8	72.5	18.7	23.3	Not comparable	Not comparable	36.9	43.4
Mathematics test score	53.5	58.2	45.2	57.4	25.1	28.2	Not comparable	Not comparable	41.3	41.7

Note: Values for Nigeria are the weighted average of the four states surveyed, namely Anambra, Bauchi, Ekiti, and Niger.
Source: World Bank (2013a)

Transforming Rural Africa: Growing a Productive Agriculture Sector

Chapter 5

Kevin Cleaver

Why is African agriculture important?

A special look at African agriculture, as opposed to many other sectors of economic activity, is justified due to the large number of Africans dependent on agriculture and living in rural areas (about 59% of Africa's population). About 25% of African gross domestic product is currently derived from agriculture (with a range of 3-50%),[1] and much of its industry is agro-based (about 20% of African GDP is produced by agribusiness input supply, processing, marketing, and retailing).[2] 60% of African employment is in agriculture.[3] In order for African economies to grow rapidly and to provide employment for increasing numbers of people, African agriculture needs to grow rapidly and absorb increasing numbers of people entering the labor force.

Over the longer term, agriculture's share in African economies and in employment will decrease, as it has done in middle income countries in Asia and Latin America, as well as in industrialized economies. This process, however, is not instantaneous, and for the next several decades, rapid agricultural and agro-industrial growth are needed to stimulate more rapid economic growth and employment creation. The UN's International Fund for Agricultural Development (IFAD) estimates that most young Africans will be living in rural areas until about 2035, after which urbanization and natural growth will shift the balance towards towns and cities.[4] Population growth will add an estimated 350 million entrants to the labor force between 2015 and 2030. About 65% of young people now work in agriculture and another 25% in informal household enterprises.[5] So many of these new entrants must find employment in agriculture and rural enterprise.

A second reason for concentrating on agriculture is that so many of Africa's poor live in rural areas (about 70%) and are directly or indirectly dependent on agriculture and agro-industry. (This is greater than the number of people employed in agriculture.) Because they are directly or indirectly dependent on agriculture, stimulating agricultural development would provide them additional income, which in turn would help them exit from poverty. There are, of course, other avenues for some of them to exit from poverty including migration to cities or abroad or development of non-agricultural activities in rural areas. These other avenues have in fact been favored, as agriculture has stagnated in most of Africa, as will be shown below. The problem is that migration to the cities often has not provided an exit from poverty, as urban development and non-agricultural growth have not been sufficient to provide jobs and incomes for many. Instead, many migrants simply go from being rural poor to urban poor. Migration abroad, particularly to Europe, has been an outlet for some, but for many migrants this has also been disappointing, and for some it has resulted in death as migratory routes are dangerous and migrants are often not welcome.[6]

A third reason relates to food availability and nutrition. It is well established that food security and nutrition status are largely related to income levels, information availability, and education, rather than agricultural production per se. People who understand nutrition and have the incomes necessary to buy food tend to have better nutritional status, regardless of a country's level of agricultural production. This is because they ordinarily can buy food, including imported food, if there are national food production deficits. International agricultural markets are now sufficiently globalized that importing foodstuffs is relatively easy if the importers, and their customers, have income. There is a

1. AfDB. (2016). *Strategy for Agricultural Transformation in Africa, 2016-2025*, Abidjan: AfDB, p. 3; IFAD. (September 2016). *Rural Development Report 2016: Fostering Inclusive Rural Transformation*, Rome: IFAD, p. 133 cites similar figures.
2. IFAD (2016).
3. IFAD (2016).
4. IFAD (2016), p. 143.
5. IFAD (2016).

6. The World Bank's 2008 World Development Report, *Agriculture for Development* (World Bank 2008), provided evidence from China and India showing that growth originating in agriculture was three times more effective in reducing poverty than growth originating in other sectors (p. 26, p.30, p. 46). A comparable careful analysis has not been done for Africa, but the World Development Report came to a similar conclusion for Sub-Saharan Africa (Box 1.2, p. 30).

Despite the importance of African agriculture for economic growth, job creation, food security, and nutrition, it has performed poorly in nearly all countries of the continent for the past 35 years.

problem, however, in some countries in Africa with access to imports, particularly among the poor in rural areas. The poor do not have the income to pay for imported food, and transport constraints often prevent food arriving in poor rural areas where the purchasing power is low. In these cases, expanded local agricultural production is often the best option for addressing nutrition problems because it both raises incomes and increases availability. It is in these places, often suffering from war or drought, that food aid donors concentrate because incomes are low and increasing local food production difficult. It is, therefore, useful to think of ways to expand agricultural production in these difficult areas to help address food security and nutrition issues, as well as to generate jobs and income.[7]

Performance of African agriculture

Despite the importance of African agriculture for economic growth, job creation, food security, and nutrition, it has performed poorly in nearly all countries of the continent for the past 35 years. There have been African countries in which agriculture has performed well for several years, but in most cases these gains have disappeared over time. The traditional way to measure agriculture performance involves several indicators, including quantities produced per hectare of land, value of agriculture produced per hectare of land and per unit of labor, and total factor productivity (value of production compared to the combination of the of land, labor, capital, and material used in its production). These measures establish agricultural productivity, which can be compared across countries and compared with other developing countries and with industrial countries. Data permitting such measurements are notoriously poor in Africa. For this chapter, an extensive effort was undertaken to mobilize such data as exist. Data comes largely from the Food and Agriculture Organization (FAO), the World Bank, the International Food Policy Research Institute (IFPRI), and United Nations Conference on Trade and Development (UNCTAD).[8] The limited number of relatively reliable productivity measures are shown below. They continue to point to low average productivity of African agriculture and low growth of productivity over time in most countries (see Annex Table A1).

Crop yields for major cereals were significantly lower in Africa than the world average in 1990 and remain significantly lower in 2014, which is the latest year for which data are available (Tables 1 and 2). Average African crop yields are lower than in the comparator non-African developing countries selected. The comparator countries were chosen because they are regarded as having maintained a relatively favorable (though far from perfect) policy posture toward agriculture during the past 15 years.

Have African farmers been catching up in yields per hectare over time? Growth rates in crop yields for wheat and sorghum have been slightly higher in Africa than the world average, and about equal to or less than the world average for millet, rice, and maize (Table 3). Comparison with the good developing country agriculture performers shows a mixed picture with Vietnam and India doing relatively well and China performing poorly in terms of the speed of growth of cereal yields.[9]

Growth in crop yields should have been faster in Africa over this 24-year period because initial yields were low and the productivity enhancing techniques needed for faster growth are known (including more fertilizer, irrigation water, and farm mechanization).[10] Scrutiny of the table suggests,

7. The World Bank's 2008 World Development Report also argued that agricultural development is important for nutrition beyond its importance for income growth by increasing access to food in places with low access to imports (World Bank 2008, pp. 94-95).

8. FAO data is drawn from FAOSTAT: http://www.fao.org/faostat/. UNCTAD data is drawn from UNCTADSTAT: http://unctadstat.unctad.org. World Bank data is drawn from the World Development Indicators (2016): http://databank.worldbank.org.

9. It is worth noting that though Table 3 shows crop yield declining for most major staple crops in China, those five crops diminished significantly in importance to Chinese agricultural production (from 32.8% of total value of agricultural production in 1995 to 23.5% in 2013) as production shifted towards higher value meats and vegetables. The result was a rapid growth in agricultural GDP despite declining crop yields for major staples.

10. This idea forms a major part of the argument by the three Rome based agricultural agencies of the UN regarding the possibility of achieving zero hunger: FAO, IFAD, WFP. (2015). *Achieving Zero Hunger.* Rome: FAO, IFAD, WFP. This article pointed out, for example, that wheat yields in Europe are 7 tons per hectare (2015) (p.3), while wheat yields are only 2.6 tons per hectare in Africa. See also Fischer, R.A., Byerlee, D., & Edmeades,

Crop yields for major cereals were significantly lower in Africa than the world average in 1990, and remain significantly lower in 2014.

Table 1: Crop yields (tons/hectare) of major cereal crops, compared to high performing agricultural producers (1990)

	Maize	Millet	Rice	Sorghum	Wheat
Africa	1.5	0.7	2.1	0.7	1.6
World, Average	3.7	0.8	3.5	1.4	2.6
China	9.4	3.7	12.8	7.6	5.9
Mexico	2.0	0.5	3.7	3.3	4.2
Peru	2.0	-	5.2	2.7	1.1
Vietnam	1.6	-	3.2	-	-
India	1.5	0.7	2.6	0.8	2.1

Source: FAO (2016a)

Table 2: Crop yields (tons/hectare) of major cereal crops, compared to high performing agricultural producers (2014)

	Maize	Millet	Rice	Sorghum	Wheat
Africa	2.1	0.6	2.7	1.0	2.6
World, Average	5.6	0.9	4.6	1.5	3.3
China	6.0	2.4	6.7	5.0	5.0
Mexico	3.3	1.0	5.7	4.2	5.2
Peru	3.2	-	7.6	4.4	1.5
Vietnam	4.4	1.3	5.8	-	-
India	2.8	1.3	3.6	0.9	3.0

Source: FAO (2016a)

Table 3: Annual growth in African and comparator crop yields, 1990-2014, (%)

	Maize	Millet	Rice	Sorghum	Wheat
Africa	2.0	-0.7	1.1	1.5	2.8
World, Average	1.9	1.1	1.1	0.8	1.1
China	-0.8	-0.7	-1.8	-1.1	-0.8
Mexico	2.2	6.1	2.1	1.5	1.1
Peru	2.1	-	1.7	6.9	2.2
Vietnam	4.8	-	2.5	-	-
India	3.1	5.7	1.6	1.7	1.6

Source: FAO (2016a)

Mirroring the situation with crop yields, the growth in total factor productivity (land, labor, capital, and materials) in agriculture has been slow, hovering at 1.4 % growth per annum in the period 2000 to the most recent year in which data are available.

however, that except for wheat and sorghum the growth rate of crop yields in Africa has not been more rapid than in the rest of the world. The advantage of being able to apply known technology for maize, rice, and millet is not stimulating a much more rapid increase in the yields of these crops in most of Africa. The crop with the fastest growth in yields in Africa is wheat, which is a relatively minor crop in Africa. (It is a temperate zone crop and thus confined in Africa to highland areas that have temperate climates.)

Mirroring the situation with crop yields, the growth in total factor productivity (land, labor, capital, and materials) in agriculture has been slow, hovering at 1.4 % growth per annum in the period 2000 to the most recent year in which data are available (Figure 1).[11] This is not much different from total productivity growth in the earlier period and is consistent with Africa's poor performance with respect to crop yields per hectare.

However, there is considerable variation within Africa on this measure. Total factor productivity growth in the 2000-2011 period was higher in several African countries (e.g. Niger, Angola, Congo, Sierra Leone, South Africa, Botswana, Morocco, and Cameroon).

IFAD reported similar results in its recent Rural Poverty Report. Although the IFAD analysis covers a somewhat different period, its results are nearly identical to the analysis done by IFPRI. It showed the following results based on its data (Table 4).[12]

E.O. (June 2009). Can Technology Deliver on the Yield Challenge to 2050, *Expert Meeting on How to Feed the World in 2050*, Rome: FAO, 24-26.

11. IFPRI defines its total factor productivity measure as follows: "Total factor productivity (TFP) is the ratio of total output (crop and livestock products) to total production inputs (land, labor, capital and materials). The output values are the FAO-constructed gross agricultural outputs, measured in constant 2004-2006 US dollars and smoothed using the Hodrick-Prescott filter. Each output value is a composite of 190 crop and livestock commodities aggregated using a constant set of global average prices from 2004-2006. Inputs include agricultural land, measured by the sum, in hectares, of cropland and permanent pasture; labor, measured by the number of animals in cattle equivalents; machinery, measured by the total amount of horsepower available from four-wheel tractors, pedestrian-operated tractors, and combine-threshers in use; and fertilizer, measured by tons of fertilizer nutrients used." (IFPRI 2014). See also Annex Table 1.

12. IFAD (2016), p. 139.

Figure 1: Growth in total factor productivity (aggregate of land, labor, capital, and material)

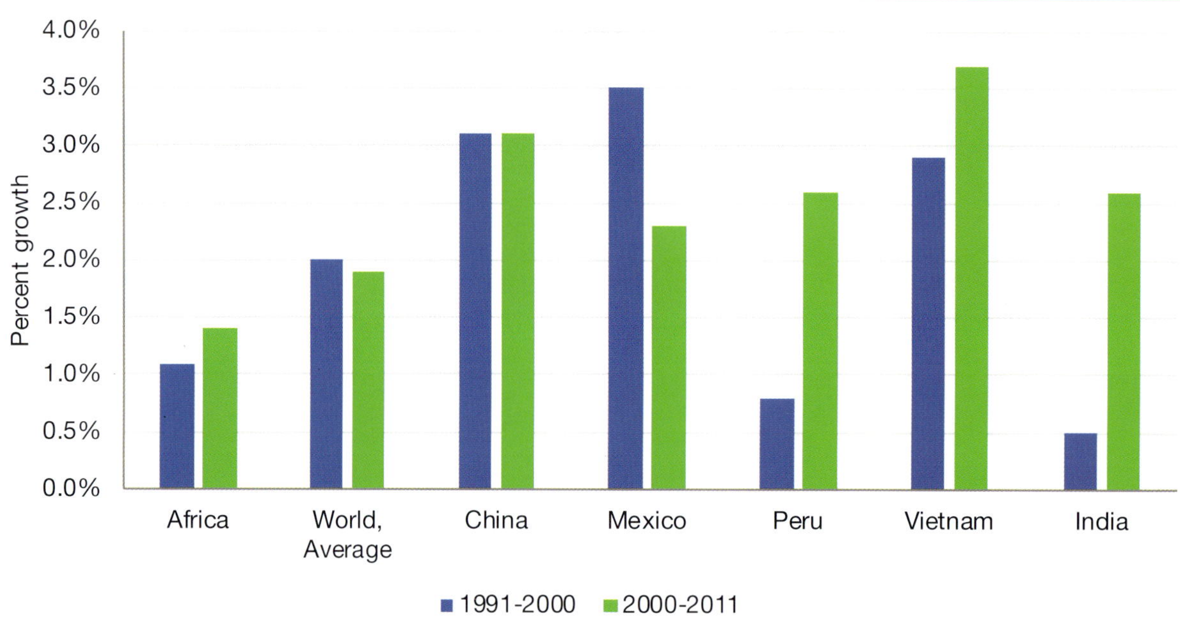

Source: IFPRI (2014)

The rate of per capita agricultural growth has fallen in the most recent period, and is lower than that of other developing countries.

Table 4: Agricultural factor productivity, annual change (%)

	Total factor productivity	Labor productivity	Land productivity
	1992-2012	1990-2014	1990-2012
Sub-Saharan Africa	1.07	1.09	1.06
Rest of World	1.75	2.04	1.76

Source: IFPRI (2014)

Low growth in productivity should translate into low growth of agricultural GDP unless there are large infusions of capital investment, increases in labor use, expanded use of land (for example, by cutting down forests to plant crops), or increased use of inputs such as fertilizer.

The data show African agricultural growth to have been greater than the world average, and at least as good as (and in some cases better than) that in other developing countries over the long term (Figure 2). The average agricultural growth rate in Africa covers considerable variation between African countries with several countries growing faster than the average of the last five years (Mali, 11.7%; Algeria, 7.4%; Congo, 7.0%; Ethiopia, 6.6%; and Togo, 6.4%). Average African population growth has been relatively rapid, however, at about 2.7% p.a. in the 1980-2000 period, falling to about 2.5% p.a. in the period 2000 to the present. Per capita agricultural growth has, therefore, been lower (3.8% p.a. in the 2000-2010 period and 1.1% p.a. in the 2011-2015 period). Additionally, the rate of per capita agricultural growth has fallen in the most recent period, and is lower than that of other developing countries. This is important for comparison with other countries. China's

Figure 2: Growth rate of agriculture value added (constant prices)

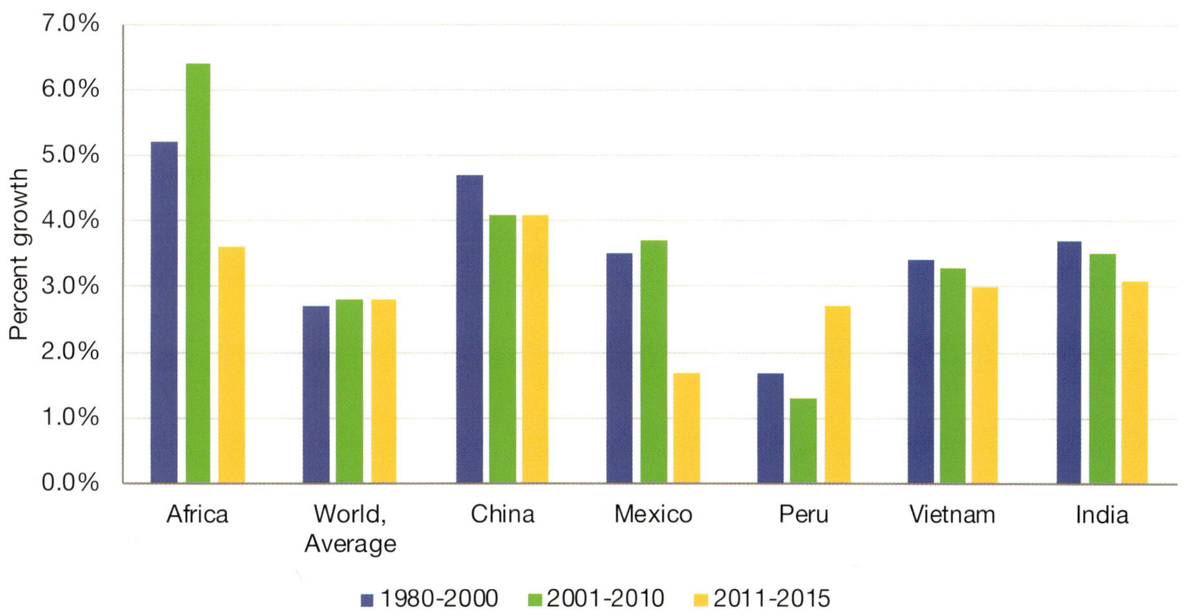

Source: Derived from World Bank (2016d)

Future agricultural growth will need to come increasingly from the combination of faster productivity growth, continued expansion of labor use, and investment.

recent population growth has been close to zero, so that their remarkable agricultural growth rate is relatively close to their per capita agricultural growth rate.[13]

The most recent African agricultural growth rate computed in per capita terms (1% p.a.) is nearly identical to the growth in total factor productivity for the most recent period. However, in the earlier period (2001-2010) agricultural growth was considerably higher than productivity growth. Where was this growth coming from? Africa was, in earlier years, getting some agricultural growth from the application of more labor due to rapid rural population growth. Some additional growth came from expanding area under crops. When these two sources of growth are added to the limited productivity growth, the result was a higher rate of agricultural growth. The IFAD analysis cited above came to the same conclusion: Most agricultural growth in Sub-Saharan Africa has been attributable to expansion of land under cultivation, followed by expansion in agricultural labor, with some increase in agricultural value added due to improved terms of trade effects.[14]

The availability of new crop land appears to be drying up in the more recent period. Thus, although agricultural labor has continued to expand, it is applied to a constrained land base (Table 5). The result is that Africa's rate of agricultural growth has reflected its productivity growth, which has been slow; therefore, the rate of agricultural growth has declined. Future agricultural growth will need to come increasingly from the combination of faster productivity growth, continued expansion of labor use, and investment.

13. As described in footnote 9 above, China's remarkable agricultural growth has been primarily due to a shift to higher value crop and livestock production and not to an increase in yields for staple crops.
14. IFAD (2016), p. 139.

Nutrition and food security

Has the relatively poor agricultural performance in Africa contributed to food insecurity and nutrition problems? The prevalence of undernourishment in Africa is higher than elsewhere in the world, and though it has declined in the past 25 years, the decline has been only from 29% of the African population undernourished to nearly 19% currently (Figure 3).

The impact of this high prevalence of undernourishment in Africa is telling. Some 36% of African children under 5 years of age are stunted due to nutrient deficiencies, and 18% are underweight.[15]

The average incidence of undernourishment in Africa is higher than in the comparator countries, particularly the two Latin American comparators. However, there is considerable variation among African countries. Several Africa countries have a current incidence of malnutrition equal to Mexico's, including Tunisia, South Africa, Algeria, Egypt, Gabon, Ghana, Mali, Morocco, and Mauritius. Several of these countries, but not all, are also relatively good agricultural performers. This supports the finding that good agricultural growth helps to resolve issues of malnourishment but does not alone solve the problem. Other, more important factors are at play including population growth, education levels, income growth, the composition of food

15. Black, RE et al. (2013). Maternal and child undernutrition and overweight in low income and middle income countries. *Lancet 382*: 427-51.

Table 5: Labor and land use in African agriculture

	1995	2000	2005	2011	2015
Labor use (millions)	127.4	179.0	198.1	224.2	243.8
Agricultural land (millions of ha)	1102.8	1123.2	1150.2	1168.7	1172.2*
Agricultural land per laborer (ha/person)	8.7	6.3	5.8	5.2	5.0*

Source: FAO (2016a)
**2013*

Africa was found by FAO to be the only region in the world where the number of hungry grew, from 175 million in the 1980s to 235 million by 2009.

Figure 3: Prevalence of undernourishment

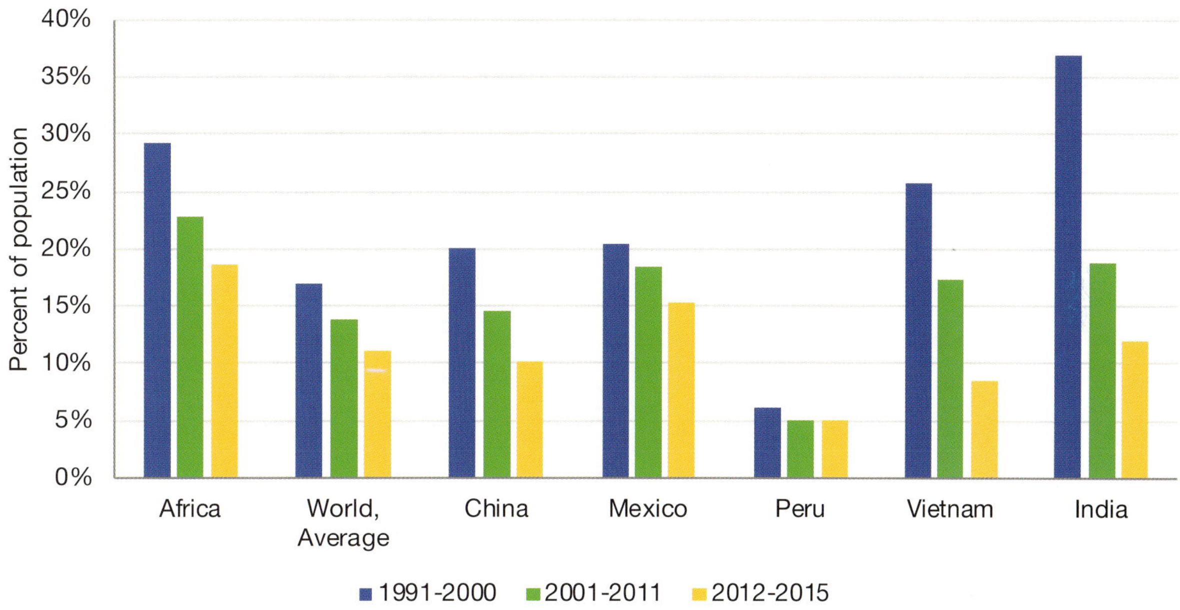

Source: World Bank (2016d)

intake, and diet (some food is more nutritious). Where civil war or civil strife exists, food insecurity and malnutrition are almost always severe. Many African countries continue to have an extraordinarily high prevalence of malnutrition. Those with over double India's rate include Central African Republic, Chad, Congo, Liberia, Namibia, Rwanda, Tanzania, Zambia, Sudan, and Zimbabwe. Most of these have suffered long bouts of civil strife.

Africa was found by FAO to be the only region in the world where the number of hungry grew, from 175 million in the 1980s to 235 million by 2009. According to the FAO, about 23% of Africa's population remained hungry in 2012.[16]

Where indicators of food security and nutrition are better than agricultural performance, it is usually because other sources of income permit food imports. Indeed, the growth in food imports, at 5.6% p.a. in the 1996-2005 period and 10.7% p.a. in the most recent (2006-2015) period, has been extraordinarily rapid in Africa.[17] In 2009, 74% of African wheat consumption and 41% of its rice consumption was imported.

The more rapid rate of increase in food imports in the most recent period mirrors the slower per capita agricultural growth rate in that period. The food import growth rates along with the high rates of undernourishment suggest that there is ample room for expanded agricultural production, both to assist in supplying food and eventually to substitute for imports.

16. Hunger and malnutrition, though closely related concepts, are measured differently, which explains the somewhat different results.

17. UNCTAD data is drawn from UNCTAD. (2017). UNCTADSTAT. Retrieved at http://unctadstat.unctad.org.

> *The first widespread proximate cause is extremely limited fertilizer use. Africa's fertilizer use is much lower than the average in the world, and lower than that in comparator developing countries.*

Conclusions regarding agricultural performance in Africa

Low agricultural productivity in Africa has contributed to low growth in agricultural GDP and, therefore, low growth of incomes derived from agriculture. It has also contributed to widespread gaps in food availability. Although food imports have grown rapidly, there is still a widespread nutrition problem. The nutrition/food security problem cannot be solved by faster agricultural growth alone. Reduction in civil strife, faster overall income growth, and nutrition education, among other factors, are more important. But faster agricultural growth would translate into faster growth in rural and farm incomes, which would contribute to improved nutrition, and in some cases, could make the difference in physical food availability as well.

Proximate causes for low growth of African agriculture

There is an extensive literature identifying the immediate, or proximate, causes for low productivity and slower than desirable growth of African agriculture. The first widespread proximate cause is extremely limited fertilizer use. Africa's fertilizer use is much lower than the average in the world, and lower than that in comparator developing countries.

This situation is not changing. Growth of fertilizer use in Africa has been negligible (in absolute terms), as shown in Figure 4: 2013 fertilizer use is about the same as in 2003. For the world as a whole, and for most of the comparator countries, fertilizer use has increased by much larger absolute amounts.

The causes for low fertilizer use in Africa are several. First has been the frequently limited farmer knowledge about fertilizers. The second relates to negative incentives for the use of fertilizers created by governments in

Figure 4: Fertilizer consumption per hectare of agricultural land

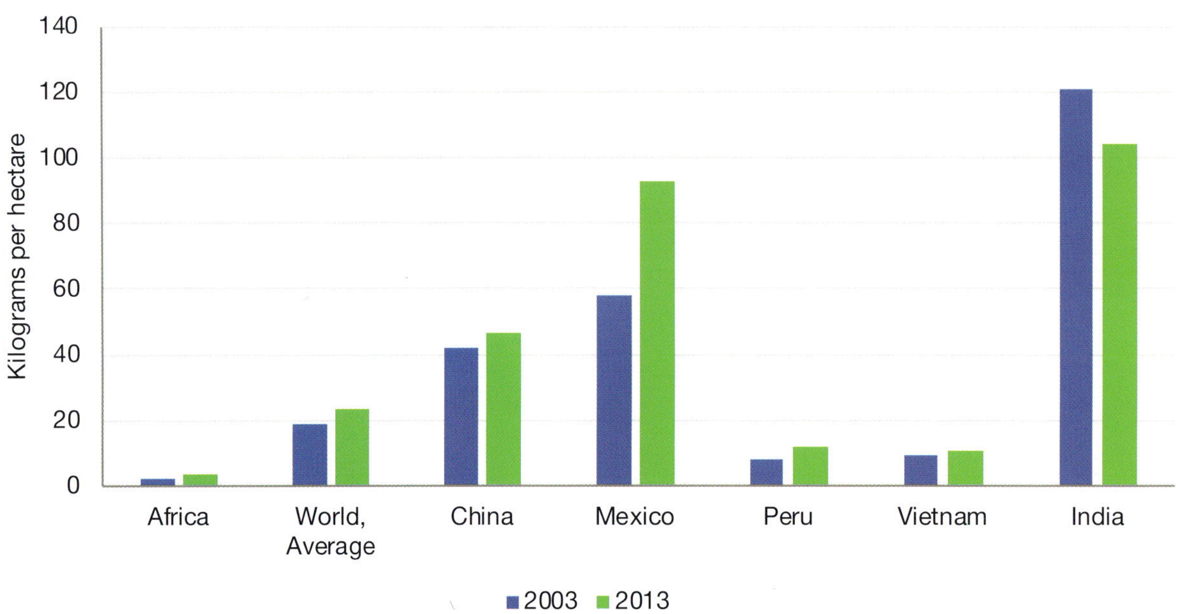

Source: FAO (2016a); World Bank (2016d)

A related cause of low African agricultural growth has been the high cost of transporting agricultural products and inputs due to poor roads, high fuel costs, and weak competition that limits the marketing of agricultural products.

the form of wide-spread price controls. Suppression of prices received by farmers for their crops, which has been common in Africa, reduces the profitability of applying fertilizers. Most governments also suppressed the private marketing of fertilizer, instead maintaining government control of distribution citing the "strategic" nature of fertilizers. The track record of government agencies in distributing fertilizer in Africa is poor. In addition, many governments created barriers to inter-regional trade in fertilizers, usually to protect their own parastatal fertilizer companies. As a result, fertilizer could not move from African countries where fertilizer was available to those where fertilizer was unavailable.[18] Expanded fertilizer use has been instrumental in the expansion of crop production elsewhere in the world, and its absence in Africa has been perhaps the most important proximate cause of low crop yields and low growth in production.

A related cause of low African agricultural growth has been the high cost of transporting agricultural products and inputs due to poor roads, high fuel costs, and weak competition that limits the marketing of agricultural products.[19] High transport cost is also influenced by the poor condition of ports and rail. Poor infrastructure is, in turn, due to poor maintenance and in part to lack of investment. Data show flat infrastructure financing in Africa in current prices, declines in real terms, and large unmet needs (Table 6). Low road density leads to isolation of farmers, which is associated with lower agricultural productivity and more poverty.[20]

Agriculture requires water. Limited or sporadic rainfall in much of Africa is a constraint, as it is in South Asia and much of East Asia. In South Asia and East Asia, this constraint has been addressed by massive investment in irrigation. Currently, 42% of South Asia's arable land is irrigated compared with only 1.3% of Africa's arable land (Table 7). This percentage has not changed in decades, indicating continued low investment in irrigation. The major reason for low investment is the low priority allocated to agriculture by most African governments; another is the high cost of irrigation investment in Africa. The World Bank estimated in its 2008 World Development Report on Agriculture that the cost of investment in Sub-Saharan Africa was $8347 during the years 1995-1999 (the last period for which such an analysis was conducted).[21] The investment cost outside of Africa for the same period was $3506.

Much of the land in Africa is public forest land, parks, and public range land. Governments have historically

18. Good analysis of the African fertilizer situation is provided in World Bank. (2016b). *Enabling the Business of Agriculture*. Washington: World Bank. See also AfDB (2016), p. 17.
19. AfDB (2016), Technical Annexes, Abidjan, Cote D'Ivoire emphasizes the transport hurdles (pp. 18-19).

20. Ahlers et al. 2(014), p. 289, contains the following statement: "Thurlow and Wobst (2004) found rural poverty in Zambia to be higher in remote areas. Stifel and Minten (2003) showed rural poverty to be higher and rice productivity to be lower in more remote places of Madagascar. BBinswanger, H., Khandker, S., & Rosenzweig, M. (1993). How Infrastructure and financial institutions affect agricultural output and investment in India. *Journal of Development Economics 41*(2); 337-366., make this conclusion very broadly across Indian agriculture." See Thurlow, J. & Wobst, P. (2004). The Road to Pro-poor growth in Zambia: Past Lessons and Future Challenges, *Development Strategy and Governance Division Discussion Paper* (16), Washington; IFPRI. See Stifel, D. & Minten, B. (2003). Transactions costs and agricultural productivity: Implications of Isolation for rural poverty in Madagascar. Background paper for the Northeast Universities Development Consortium Conference, Yale University, New Haven, Connecticut, October 17-19. See Binswanger, H., Khandker, S., & Rosenzweig, M. (1993).
21. World Bank (2008), p. 65.

Table 6: Infrastructure financing in Africa

	2012	2013	2014	2015
Total infrastructure financing (billions of current dollars)	89.3	99.6	74.5	83.4
Infrastructure investment required (5.5% of African GDP benchmark) (billions of dollars)	127.2	132.3	136.4	125
Percent unmet	29.8%	24.7%	45.4%	33.3%

Source: ICA (2015); World Bank (2016d)

Climate change may already have begun to contribute to increased water scarcity, increased frequency of severe weather shocks (including droughts), and increased coastal flooding.

Table 7: Land equipped for irrigation in Africa

	1995	2000	2005	2010	2013
Total land equipped for irrigation (millions of ha of land)	12.4	13.2	14.1	14.7	15.0
Total agricultural land (millions of ha of land)	1,102	1,123	1,150	1,163	1,172
Percent of total agricultural land equipped for irrigation	1.1%	1.2%	1.2%	1.3%	1.3%

Source: FAO (2016a)

managed this land poorly. The result has been high rates of deforestation (an annual loss of approximate 0.5% of forest area from 2005-2015), land degradation (about 67% of Africa's land area has become or is becoming highly degraded due to nutrient depleting crop cultivation, fragile soils, overgrazing, and firewood collection),[22] loss of biodiversity, and land conflicts between people. Figure 5 shows the loss in total forest area in Africa during the past 10 years. Forest production is included in agricultural production, so this contributes to the poor performance of agriculture. But, equally importantly, the loss of forests affects basic nutrients and water, further affecting agriculture.

Finally, the Intergovernmental Panel on Climate Change (IPCC) predicts that the adverse effects of climate change on agriculture will be especially marked in Africa. Climate change may already have begun to contribute to increased water scarcity, increased frequency of severe weather shocks (including droughts), and increased coastal flooding.[23] These changes are likely to be already dampening agricultural yields and hence agricultural growth.[24] An analysis undertaken in 2010 projected that African staple crops will have 8-22% lower yields by 2050 due to climate change, all other things equal.[25]

More fundamental causes of poor agricultural performance

It is increasingly clear that public policy is often a more fundamental cause of poor agricultural performance in Africa than the proximate causes discussed above. Public policy in most African countries has hindered private investment in agriculture, agriculture marketing, marketing of farm inputs, and processing of outputs. In addition to the problems with fertilizer and infrastructure described above, poor policy has inhibited the use of improved seed, livestock services, chemical inputs, and farm mechanization as well. Further, government policy that hinders private investment, both local and foreign, reduces investment in marketing and processing of agricultural products.

The World Bank's Ease of Doing Business index, summarized in Annex Table A2 for Africa, shows that nearly all African countries make it difficult for private investors (which includes farmers) to do business.[26] The combination of poor economic policy, an excessively complex and often rent-seeking regulatory environment, inadequate courts and contract enforcement, inadequate protection of land rights, border controls on trade,[27] and frequent capital controls makes private investment in African agriculture and agro-industry risky and in many cases unprofitable.[28] Thus, private investment, both foreign and domestic, is curtailed. The lack of investment in fertilizer companies, agricultural

22. Glatzel, K. & the Montpellier Panel. (2014) No ordinary matter: Conserving, restoring, and enhancing Africa's soils. *Agriculture for Impact*.
23. Intergovernmental Panel on Climate Change. (2014a). *Climate Change 2014, Synthesis Report, Contributions of Working Groups I II, and II to the Fifth Assessment Report of the IPCC*. Geneva: IPCC.
24. FAO's *The State of Food and Agriculture: Climate Change, Agriculture and Food Security* (2016b) found that the impacts of climate change on African agriculture are already alarming.
25. Schlendker, W and Lobell, D.B. (2010). Robust negative impacts of climate change on African agriculture. *Environmental Resources 5*(1).
26. World Bank. (2017). Doing Business rankings. Washington: World Bank. Retrieved at http://www.doingbusiness.org/.
27. The share of intra-African trade remains low at 12% of total African trade, compared to interregional trade in other parts of the world (UNECA. (2010). *Assessing Regional integration in Africa IV: Enhancing Intra-African Trade*. Addis Ababa: UNECA.).
28. These factors are all reflected in the ease of doing business indicators.

A second and closely related issue has been a tendency by most African governments over the past 50 years to control some farm output and farm input prices, and to tax or otherwise inhibit agricultural trade.

Figure 5: Total forest area in Africa

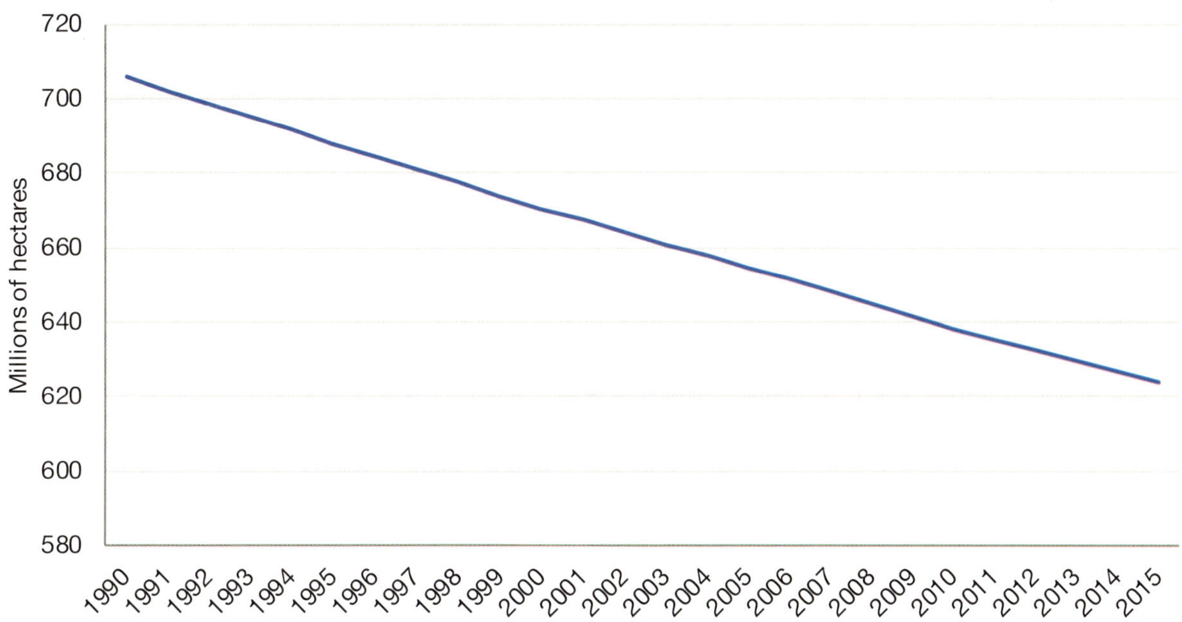

Source: FAO (2016a)

processing enterprises, private irrigation schemes, and transport companies, among others, is not surprising in this situation.

A second and closely related issue has been a tendency by most African governments over the past 50 years to control some farm output and farm input prices, and to tax or otherwise inhibit agricultural trade.[29] Controls similar to those discussed for fertilizer, with similar motivation, have been imposed on the price of food and export crops. Price controls on farm products at farmgate are often intended to reduce food prices for consumers, but they also reduce the incentive for farmers to produce the crops controlled. Price controls often require that governments operate crop marketing enterprises to purchase the crop from farmers to assure that the artificially low price at farmgate can be maintained. In some cases, crop movement controls were also imposed to suppress parallel or black markets that would pay more. Similarly, export crops were often marketed through parastatal enterprises, permitting governments to set low prices for export crops to farmers and to retain much of the revenue paid by foreign importers. This arrangement was common throughout much of Africa for cotton, cocoa, coffee, rubber, and tea. Again, these policies have been found to discourage production of these crops and technical innovation by farmers. Restrictions on trade in food crops between African countries has had the same effect as trade restrictions on fertilizer: African countries with surpluses of some food crops often found it difficult to sell into neighboring deficit countries in part due to trade restrictions. Of course, transport constraints and "dumping" by industrial countries also affected this trade.

These types of price and trade policies were nearly universal in Africa from the 1970s to the 1990s and are still more prevalent in Africa (and in the Middle East and

29. An important summary of this issue was published by the World Bank in World Bank (2008); pp. 10-13, p. 39, pp. 98-102.

Analysis shows huge gaps in agricultural technical and vocational training and, indeed, in rural education overall.

Central Asia) than in other developing countries,[30] although there has been a slow process of reversal of these types of policies over time.[31]

A third fundamental constraint involves the serious weakness of many local administrations and public institutions in rural areas. Local governments in rural areas are nearly always hindered by the lack of human capacities needed for planning and execution as well as by limited transparency and accountability. Agricultural development requires broad rural development including investment in and maintenance of rural roads, potable water, irrigation water, schools, health systems, land management,[32] contract dispute resolution, and more generally the rule of law. These key components of development are often done more poorly in rural areas than in urban areas. One reason is the lack of financial resources in rural compared with urban areas. Per capita GDP in Sub-Saharan Africa's urban areas was 5.5 times that of rural areas in 2010 (the last year for which data are available). In comparison, in India, urban areas had per capita incomes 2.7 times that in rural areas; the ratio was 2.1 in Mexico and 2.7 in Vietnam.[33] Thus, the fiscal base for local revenue in Sub-Saharan Africa rural areas is comparatively very weak, and it is not surprising that local services are badly managed and, in many cases, unavailable.

Analysis shows huge gaps in agricultural technical and vocational training and, indeed, in rural education overall.[34] Depending on the country, either weak local administrations or poor central government management and investment in rural areas are to blame.

The large number of donors working on African agriculture has contributed to weak policy and poor outcomes. Ahlers et al. (2014) found that in 2009, there were 225 bilateral donors operating in Africa, 242 multilateral donors, and 40 UN agencies.[35] Most had agricultural programs. These programs often come with advice and sometimes with conditions that must be met by governments to unlock the aid. Advice and conditions are often contradictory, differing from one donor to the next. For example, many donors support agriculture subsidies, but some are against. Many operate with public institutions only, others advocate limiting or eliminating public involvement in favor of the private sector. Others support agricultural services (research, extension, livestock) managed by their own nationals rather than locals. Many donors set up agricultural extension services following models developed elsewhere. It is common that in the same African country there will be European-style agricultural extension systems (several styles to choose from) uneasily co-existing in the same country with American- and NGO-style agricultural extension services. It should not, therefore, be surprising that there is often no national agricultural extension system in these countries but rather a hodge-podge of donor-supported services. The same situation holds for agro-processing, livestock services, and farm input distribution. Donors have thus been enablers of the confusion and lack of direction in government agricultural policy and investment.[36]

---

30. The Brookings Institution produced a report entitled *Ending Rural Hunger* (Brookings Institution 2015) that found that "the countries with the weakest [agricultural] policy environment are primarily, but not exclusively in Sub-Saharan Africa, the Middle East, and Central Asia," p. 25. It highlights the types of policy described here as "bad policy."

31. (Brookings Institution 2015). This was also the conclusion of World Bank (2008), p. 21, p. 30, p. 98. The World Bank's report stated that average effective taxation of agriculture in Sub-Saharan Africa declined from 28% in 1980-1984 to 10% in 2000-2004 (p. 98). This was still significantly higher than the effective taxation in other developing countries (pp. 98-101).

32. Only 10% of Africa's rural land is registered, the remaining 90% is undocumented and managed informally. Woman have serious constraints in many African countries as inheritance rights are not provided to widows or daughters, despite about 60% of African farmers being women See AfDB (2016).

33. Data from IFPRI cited in Ahlers et al. (2014), p. 273.

34. The Omidyar Network found that 70-80% of African youth lack an education beyond the primary level. IFAD shows that on average about 60% of those under 35 in rural areas have incomplete primary school, and many struggle with basic literacy and numeracy (Ahlers et al. 2014, p. 189).

35. Ahlers et al. (2014). Binswanger and McCalla also documented this problem in *The Changing Context and Prospects for Agriculture and Rural Development in Africa* (Binswanger-Mkhize, H. & McCalla, A. 2008).

36. The Brookings Institution's report, *Ending Rural Hunger* (2015) ranks the quality and quantity of bilateral aid donors (p.37). The rankings are generally low, reflecting poor quality agricultural aid. Denmark, Luxembourg, Iceland, Ireland, and Norway received the top scores. Slovak Republic, Czech Republic, Korea, Greece, Italy, Portugal, Slovenia, Poland, the United States and the European Commission received the worst rankings.

African governments must create the enabling environment for private investment in agriculture, agricultural input supply, agricultural marketing, and agricultural processing.

Trade and subsidy policy in OECD countries and much of the industrial world has been found by OECD and IFPRI to inhibit African agriculture. The OECD/DAC estimates that OECD member countries provide about $250 billion p.a. (though varying from year to year) on domestic farm subsidies.[37] Subsidized products are imported by Africa often in competition with its own production. African exports of farm products that compete with North American and European farm products are constrained. Tariffs on agriculture in the European Union and the US are currently 13.2% and 5.3% respectively, as compared with 4.2% and 3.1% for non-agricultural goods. Fewer OECD trade barriers and lower OECD agricultural production subsidies would be good for African agriculture.

Action agenda

The most important action to be taken to stimulate African agriculture involves a change in the role of the state. African governments must create the enabling environment for private investment in agriculture, agricultural input supply, agricultural marketing, and agricultural processing.

The actions suggested in the World Bank's Ease of Doing Business are a good place to start in improving the enabling environment for private investment in agriculture. These include better economic policy (removing agricultural price controls and product movement controls), eliminating government monopolies on agricultural marketing and processing, reducing barriers to private investment in these areas (both domestic and foreign), strengthening the court system and enforcement of contracts, improving land tenure laws to provide protection for land owners, and facilitating a land market, among others.[38]

No African country does particularly well on the World Bank Ease of Doing Business index, but there is considerable range in the severity of the problem. The least bad, listed from the best downwards are Mauritius, Rwanda, Botswana, South Africa, Tunisia, Morocco, Zambia, Namibia, Swaziland, Kenya, Ghana, Lesotho, Uganda, Cape Verde, and Egypt. Of these, all except Swaziland, Kenya, Lesotho, Cape Verde, Mauritius, and Egypt had significantly higher rates of increase in crop yields than the average for Africa (see Annex Table A2).

Government and donor resources for agriculture will not be sufficient to cover investment needs. The Rome-based UN agricultural agencies have estimated that agricultural investment requirements are about $53 billion p.a.;[39] the AfDB estimated the requirement at $120 billion p.a.[40] These estimates provide a range of investment requirements. Private investment, including foreign private investment, will be needed to respond to this need, whether the high or the low figure is taken. This magnitude of investment resources will not be forthcoming in the current poor investment climates in most countries in Africa. In the past, governments have responded to the lack of private investment in processing and farm input supply by creating public enterprises for processing, marketing, and supplying inputs. The number of failures of such enterprises over the past 50 years is staggering, representing billions of dollars of wasted investment. Governments should create the policies necessary to attract private investment into these activities, which will require a dramatic change in government policy in every African country, though more in some than in others.

The large financing gap that exists for private sector agriculture and agro-business needs to be filled. The World Bank's International Finance Corporation estimates that 84% of small and medium enterprises in Africa (which includes non-agricultural sectors) have limited or no access to finance. Smallholder farmers also have limited access to finance.[41] Given public sector financing

37. This figure is quoted in Brookings Institution (2015).
38. A good summary of the changes needed in this regard is provided in IFAD (2016). AfDB has also promoted this argument, AfDB (2016), Technical annexes, pp. 15-17. See also Thorpe, J. & Maestre, M. (2015). *Brokering Development: Enabling Factors for Public-Private Partnerships in Agricultural Value Chains*. Rome: IFAD and the Institute of Development Studies.

39. FAO, IFAD, WFP (2015). p. 11 (Table 4).
40. AfDB (2016), Technical Annexes, p. iii.
41. AfDB (2016), p. 14.

African governments should focus their direct investment interventions on infrastructure development, mediating land use, providing a social safety net and education in rural areas, improving tax policy affecting agriculture, promoting regional integration, and improving access to world markets by reducing trade barriers.

restraints, making more financing available will require the development of private financial intermediation, including banking services in rural areas. The most important action that governments can take to make this happen is not to create the banking services themselves but, again, to create the enabling policy environment for investment by private and cooperative banks.

There is, however, an important role for governments beyond creating a good policy environment and institutional environment for private investments. Government efforts are required to strengthen public institutions in rural areas, including their human capacity, their fiscal base, and their transparency. Where the local resource base is weak, the central government may also need to provide resources. Most certainly it will require creating rural technical and vocational training related to agriculture, improving rural education and health facilities more broadly, and improving rural infrastructure (rural roads, potable water, rural energy, and rural information and communications technology).

African governments should, therefore, focus their direct investment interventions on infrastructure development, mediating land use, providing a social safety net and education in rural areas, improving tax policy affecting agriculture, promoting regional integration, and improving access to world markets by reducing trade barriers. Reducing trade barriers between African countries would also help African agriculture.

There are other areas of intervention that will best be achieved through private-government-farmer-donor partnerships. These are quite difficult to manage. Most important in this regard is agricultural technical change, which needs to be more aggressively pursued than it is currently, because it is directly related to expanding agricultural productivity. In the past, technical change was thought to be best stimulated by governments and donors through public agricultural research, extension (farmer training), livestock services, and public irrigation projects. Much of the literature on African agricultural development focuses on the kinds of technologies that need to be introduced; these include introduction of quality seed, better weed management, reducing post-harvest losses, introduction of disease-resistant varieties of all crops, better soil nutrition management and irrigation water management, introduction of pest-resistant varieties, adoption of productivity-increasing methods such as zero tillage, sustainable feeding practices for livestock, and investment in bio-technology. Many of these improved practices have been introduced through donor-financed projects and by governments and have not taken hold at sufficient scale, if at all. Another approach to technological change is required, outside of the traditional donor-managed or government-managed service.

An alternative to government-managed technical services is privately managed services. The private sector often provides such services for crop and livestock production that serves a private sector interest. Is this the way to stimulate technical change? The problem with private sector-managed agricultural services and technology is that they are invariably targeted to export crops or profitable cash crops, typically produced by larger and more sophisticated farmers. Small farmers, who are the bulk of Africa's farm population, are frequently ignored. A newer and probably better approach is to avoid leaving technology services and irrigation exclusively to either government or the private sector. Rather, the best approach is through programs involving public-private partnerships with farmer participation and with donor participation, where there are willing donors. Projects at large scale involving the public sector, private sector, and farmer groups are difficult to organize, which is why they have been so infrequently done. But these now appear to have great promise, and one donor, IFAD, has had some surprising success with this approach.[42] This does not mean that private sector technical intervention should be discouraged, as it has been in much of Africa. The improvement of the investment climate should encourage such investment. But this

42. See Thorpe & Maestre (2015).

Donors will need to be more willing to be led and coordinated by governments, perhaps with the help of a few donor coordinators.

is unlikely to be enough, hence the premium on expanding public-private-farmer-donor partnerships.

Public sector-managed irrigation projects are found to be high cost in Africa, and thus there is very little new investment in irrigation. Donors now avoid irrigation investment in Africa due to high costs and poor public sector management. But private investors undertake small scale irrigation when it is profitable to do so. Government partnerships with the private and cooperative sectors to invest in and manage irrigation is the way to go. The combination of government, donor, private sector, and farmer financing and management can lead to expanded and better managed irrigation schemes.

A corollary to encouraging private investment and public-private partnerships is for governments in Africa to be more supportive of the development of independent farmers' organizations, cooperatives, and other types of farmer institutions. It is through these types of institutions that farmers can form true partnerships with governments, the private sector, and donors. Without such institutions, most farmers in Africa are too small to participate effectively in broad actions in agricultural development affecting their livelihood.

Donors will need to be more willing to be led and coordinated by governments, perhaps with the help of a few donor coordinators, as the African Development Bank has recently observed.[43] The Center for Global Development and the Brookings Institution have also published material pointing out this problem.[44] Having fewer donors would also make sense. This could perhaps be achieved by consolidating some of the many separate bilateral agencies handling agriculture in each donor country and by consolidating some of the multilateral agencies and UN agencies into fewer larger and more efficient agencies providing agricultural aid. Donors should also avoid the type of projects they have supported in the past to help governments create public enterprises to market, process, and supply inputs for agriculture. Rather, they should promote privately and cooperatively owned enterprises to provide these services, or public-private partnerships. Private and cooperative enterprises have a much better track record than do government enterprises not only in Africa but also everywhere in the world.

Climate change impacts need to be dealt with more aggressively than previously thought, beginning now.[45] Preparation for such action to date has not been sufficient. Changes in water availability, temperature, and severe weather need now to be factored into agricultural research, extension, and project planning.[46] The principal needed actions will involve measures in each African country to help farmers adapt to climate change, most often by adapting agricultural practices to temperature changes and changes in water availability. Where these changes are substantial, it may mean abandoning crops that require, for example, lower temperatures and more water in favor of crops that tolerate higher temperatures and less water. It will require agricultural research and extension to find and promote technologies that help farmers adapt their cropping practices to cope with these changes and, where possible, to profit from them. Again, this is likely to be most effectively accomplished through public-private-farmer (and donor) partnerships given the poor government track record and the narrow interest of the private sector.

OECD countries should agree, through the OECD Secretariat, to estimate the costs to African agriculture of OECD country trade and subsidy policy, and either make policy adjustments to mitigate impacts or provide compensation to African countries for negative impacts.

The above constitutes an expanded action agenda for African governments, donors, and OECD countries, which, if undertaken, could achieve the objectives of obtaining faster growth in agriculture, greatly reducing rural poverty,

43. AfDB (2016).
44. See the Brookings Institution (2015).

45. Schlenker and Lobell predict that in the absence of adaptation measures, climate change will lead to decreases in yields of 8 to 22% for Africa's top rain-fed staple crops. See Schlenker & Lobell (2010).
46. FAO (2016b) is an excellent summary of the issues of climate change and agriculture, with a comprehensive action agenda.

> *Combining the good practice of agricultural leaders into country policy and strategy in lagging African countries would be an excellent beginning for accelerated agricultural development in Africa.*

and contributing more to improved nutrition. What is the prognosis for such dramatic change?

There has been little change in the posture of African governments, donors, or OECD countries with respect to agriculture for years. The prognosis at this point for aid is not good, as economic and fiscal constraints are bedeviling most industrial countries and political resistance to aid by industrial country populations is increasing. The one exception to this trend is with respect to climate change where several climate funds have been created (for example, by the World Bank and IFAD) to help developing countries adapt to the effects of climate change.

A few African countries are doing better on some of these action points, though none at the level required. Rwanda has greatly eased constraints on doing business, and private investment has entered its export sector (especially tea). Rwanda has also dramatically improved its nutrition situation. Uganda has improved its ease of doing business, as has Ghana, and private investors have responded. Particularly notable is the vegetable oil sector in Uganda, which is an excellent example of the public-private-farmer-donor partnership extolled in this chapter. Côte d'Ivoire has begun to improve its economic policy and regulatory environment with respect to agriculture, and looks to be rejuvenating its cocoa sector. Nigeria, Zambia, and Ethiopia have taken some small steps with respect to ease of doing business, and Ethiopia's agricultural sector has responded surprisingly well. Ethiopia's floriculture sector is flourishing. Kenya has developed its financial sector in a public-private-donor partnership, which has facilitated capital flows to Kenya's commercial agriculture and to agro-business. Part of Kenya's success with its horticulture sector is in response to its improved climate for private investment in export agriculture and its improved rural finance situation. Burkina Faso has reformed its cotton sector, which appears to be healthy. Tanzania has become more inviting of private domestic and foreign investment.

Each of these countries has achieved higher growth of agriculture in recent years. Each has shown that foreign and domestic investors are willing to invest in agriculture and agro-industry where government policy creates an enabling environment. Each has shown that the private sector is willing to work with reliable governments and donors. These countries provide partial models for what might be done by the many lagging countries that have done nothing in these domains. Combining the good practice of these agricultural leaders into country policy and strategy in lagging African countries would be an excellent beginning for accelerated agricultural development in Africa.

Annex 1

Table A1: Land productivity, labor productivity, output growth (%), and TFP growth*

	Land productivity (gross production per hectare of agricultural land, constant 2004-2006 US dollars)				Labor productivity (agricultural gross production per economic active person in agriculture, constant 2004-2006 US dollars)				Output growth (%)			TFP growth (%)		
Country/ region	1990	2000	2005	2011	1990	2000	2005	2011	1991-2000	2001-2005	2006-2011	1991-2000	2001-2005	2006-2011
SSA	81	109	128	140	620	680	742	767	3.1	2.9	2.9	1.8	1.3	1.4
Angola	15	24	39	68	258	315	367	473	4.8	6.3	7.9	3.0	4.1	4.7
Benin	395	511	532	630	820	1175	1239	1300	6.1	3.5	1.7	3.3	5.2	0.4
Botswana	8	8	9	12	1055	728	783	913	-0.6	2.3	4.8	-5.2	2.5	4.6
Burkina Faso	110	147	205	190	294	338	363	344	4.4	4.3	1.5	0.2	1.5	-1.6
Burundi	487	396	428	500	412	348	337	230	-0.9	2.8	-3.9	-0.5	-1.2	-6.4
Cameroon	238	325	423	577	700	847	939	1171	3.2	3.8	3.9	1.7	2.6	4.0
Central African Rep.	108	152	158	193	521	643	679	760	3.5	1.7	3.1	2.1	1.3	2.7
Chad	17	23	30	28	456	509	505	515	3.6	3.1	2.3	-0.1	0.7	-0.1
Congo, Dem. Rep.	172	150	147	163	474	320	286	268	-1.8	-0.5	1.8	-2.0	0.3	1.3
	20	26	32	40	462	546	615	734	2.9	3.4	3.5	0.9	4.2	4.2
Côte d'Ivoire	209	289	273	306	1422	1823	1935	2240	3.5	1.1	2.5	1.2	3.6	2.4
Ethiopia	82	144	190	244	248	230	247	288	2.6	5.0	5.1	-1.4	2.6	3.2
Gabon	39	48	48	57	991	1179	1235	1615	1.7	0.3	4.5	1.6	-2.8	2.8
Ghana	160	294	352	430	696	907	977	1065	5.7	4.3	4.0	2.5	0.7	2.8
Guinea	73	111	127	147	435	447	491	530	3.7	3.7	2.6	-0.4	2.1	-0.3
Guinea-Bissau	105	130	150	198	437	534	571	620	3.5	2.9	3.5	0.8	0.0	2.2
Kenya	148	165	217	258	505	426	455	485	1.5	4.0	2.3	-0.5	2.2	1.5
Liberia	103	153	160	154	501	530	532	471	3.3	1.3	1.4	2.4	0.2	-1.8
Madagascar	69	65	76	89	624	505	472	477	0.5	2.2	3.7	-0.1	1.3	1.9
Malawi	244	410	324	562	302	450	466	557	5.6	3.1	4.9	4.7	1.9	1.5
Mali	46	47	65	88	759	838	879	1037	3.0	3.7	4.9	1.2	3.5	1.4
Mauritania	9	10	11	12	762	689	675	670	1.7	2.3	2.6	1.0	-0.5	0.3
Mozambique	24	34	40	65	202	246	247	236	5.3	2.2	1.7	3.0	0.9	0.1
Namibia	10	10	12	10	1747	1531	1694	1557	0.1	2.8	-1.2	-1.9	-3.7	0.2
Niger	34	46	56	71	483	584	644	872	5.2	5.9	8.0	1.9	2.4	6.4
Nigeria	235	390	458	471	1368	2249	2642	2943	4.9	4.0	1.9	3.6	2.0	1.9
Rwanda	590	742	830	1223	403	367	397	436	0.7	4.6	4.9	0.1	0.0	1.2
Senegal	101	139	141	129	403	367	335	369	1.5	0.0	1.5	-1.2	-1.5	-1.8
Sierra Leone	153	118	170	234	395	364	443	525	-1.2	8.7	4.4	1.3	5.3	2.4
Somalia	33	33	37	42	738	720	702	708	0.7	1.3	2.0	1.9	-1.6	1.5
South Africa	96	111	118	135	5594	6928	8057	10614	1.3	1.9	2.8	4.3	4.1	3.4
Sudan	31	55	69	0	829	1115	1211	1141	5.0	3.0	0.6	3.9	-1.3	-0.8
Tanzania	116	129	175	222	361	337	397	445	1.8	5.8	4.8	-0.6	2.8	2.1
Togo	151	176	214	247	518	616	603	620	3.8	1.1	2.5	2.5	-1.3	0.6

Source: IFPRI (2014)

Table A1 (cont.): Land productivity, labor productivity, output growth (%), and TFP growth*

Uganda	322	395	418	440	566	595	583	524	2.9	1.9	1.2	0.0	-0.1	0.0
Zambia	36	39	49	73	345	328	369	423	1.4	4.5	4.1	1.3	3.0	2.0
Zimbabwe	121	138	91	101	533	577	510	502	2.2	-3.4	1.0	1.0	3.4	1.4
Algeria	74	94	131	177	1599	1464	1681	1949	2.7	5.4	3.5	2.6	5.4	-1.1
Egypt	4178	5220	5623	6222	1565	2661	2932	3372	4.8	3.3	1.6	2.2	0.8	1.0
Libya	53	66	70	78	6253	10221	11947	15886	2.9	0.0	0.0	5.1	0.0	0.8
Morocco	167	170	224	315	1564	1697	2100	2777	1.2	4.2	3.1	-0.6	3.3	3.4
Tunisia	282	303	353	355	3617	3861	4266	4583	2.2	3.2	2.3	0.4	2.4	1.1
Comparators														
China	447	718	850	1067	717	1073	1249	1823	5.3	2.9	3.7	3.1	3.1	3.1
India	720	922	1034	1370	616	695	714	861	2.6	2.2	4.7	0.8	1.5	3.7
Vietnam	1588	2132	2387	2823	470	729	838	980	5.9	4.8	3.8	0.5	1.8	3.4
Peru	156	279	321	427	1274	1714	1898	2397	5.0	4.2	4.8	3.5	2.9	4.4
Mexico	219	279	319	351	2663	3444	3919	4546	2.9	2.5	1.0	3.2	3.5	1.2

Source: IFPRI (2014)

* TFP is the ratio of total output (crop and livestock products) to total production inputs (land, labor, capital and materials). The output values are the FAO-constructed gross agricultural outputs, measured in constant 2004-2006 US dollars and smoothed using the Hodrick-Prescott filter. Each output value is a composite of 190 crop and livestock commodities aggregated using a constant set of global average prices from 2004-2006. Inputs include agricultural land, measured by the sum, in hectares, of cropland and permanent pasture; labor, measured by the number of animals in cattle equivalents; machinery, measured by the total amount of horsepower available from four-wheel tractors, pedestrian-operated tractors, and combine-threshers in use; and fertilizer, measured by tons of fertilizer nutrients used." (IFPRI 2014).

Table A2: Ease of Doing Business Ranking compared to growth in food production and change in prevalence of malnutrition

Country	Ease of doing business rank, with low number best**	Average annual growth in cereal crop yields (tons per hectare) 2000-2011***	Percent change in prevalence of undernourishment, 2000-2014****
Top third in Ease of Doing Business rankings in Africa (2006-2011)			
Mauritius	26	-7.2	-2.1
South Africa	33	3.5	0.0 x
Botswana	46	10.4	-11.5
Namibia	49	2.6	11.9
Tunisia	71	5.2	0.0 x
Kenya	82	0.9	-11.1
Ghana	86	1.8	-12.5
Zambia	91	4.5	4.9
Seychelles	97	n/a	n/a
Uganda	103	2.8	-2.9
Ethiopia	104	4.6	-25.9
Swaziland	104	-2.4	5.1
Nigeria	114	1.2	-2.2
Lesotho	115	-0.7	-1.8
Rwanda	115	8.6	-29.0
Second third in Ease of Doing Business rankings in Africa (2006-2011)			
Tanzania	121	-0.4	-6.7
Morocco	121	14.4	-1.5
Egypt	123	0.0	0.0*
Malawi	125	2.0	-7.9
Algeria	126	4.6	-3.7
Guinea-Bissau	128	2.8	-7.7
Gambia	130	-3.6	-8.8
Mozambique	138	1.7	-16.7
Cape Verde	139	-12.7	-8.3
Madagascar	143	3.2	-1.8

Table A2 (cont.): Ease of Doing Business Ranking compared to growth in food production and change in prevalence of malnutrition

Sudan	143	1.0	n/a
Gabon	147	0.4	0.0*
Zimbabwe	147	-3.9	-10.3
Sierra Leone	152	4.1	-15.7
Togo	155	1.3	-17.8
Côte d'Ivoire	156	0.0	-1.6
Bottom third in Ease of Doing Business rankings in Africa (2006-2011)			
Burkina Faso	156	1.3	-5.9
Mali	157	-0.1	-8.9
Cameroon	158	-0.4	-22.4
Liberia	158	-0.6	-4.6
Senegal	158	0.9	-19.4
Benin	158	2.7	-16.4
Mauritania	159	4.4	-5.9
Guinea	164	-0.1	-10.8
Angola	164	1.8	-36.9
Equatorial Guinea	164	n/a	n/a
Eritrea	166	4.0	n/a
Niger	167	2.5	-13.3
Burundi	168	0.6	n/a
Chad	170	3.5	-5.7
Congo, Rep.	172	0.5	-5.6
Congo, Dem. Rep. of	175	-0.2	n/a
Comparators			
Peru	53	2.1	-14.1
China	88	1.7	-6.9
Vietnam	88	2.5	-17.1

Source: World Bank (2016d)
**Adapted from the World Bank Doing Business, Measuring Regulatory Quality and Efficiency; for years 2006 to 2011. See World Bank Group: www.doing business.org/rankings
***FAO Statistical Yearbook, Africa Food and Agriculture, 2014, Accra, Ghana; FAO Statistical Yearbook, 2014 Asia and Pacific For China and Vietnam; and FAO Statistical Yearbook 2014 for Latin America and the Caribbean for Peru.
**** FAO Statistical pocketbook, A large decline is positive. The countries with an x already had a low 5 prevalence of under-nourishment in the year 2000. Countries with a + show an increase in the prevalence of undernourishment.

Chapter 6

The Impact of Commodity Terms of Trade in Africa: Curse, Blessing, or Manageable Reality?

Claudio Loser and Ieva Vilkelyte

Introduction

Africa, like Latin America and the oil-producing areas of the Middle East, developed its trade links with the rest of the world on the basis of commodity exports. Over time some countries like Brazil, China, India, Mexico and South Africa have developed more advanced economies, more advanced technology, and more complex industrial exports. Nonetheless commodities remain at the center of their exports. In 2014, commodities represented about 76 percent of African exports, up from 71 percent in 1995 as prices and output went up sharply, but down from a peak of 82 percent in 2011.[1] These numbers for 2014 and 1995 for Latin America and the Caribbean were respectively 51 and 54 percent, and for the Middle East, 69 and 75 percent.

The increase in commodity prices, well over that of these regions' average import prices (even though these also include commodities), resulted in a marked improvement in terms of trade (price of exports relative to price of imports). Terms of trade increased by more than 90 percent from 2000 to 2012 for Africa, 37 percent for Latin America and the Caribbean, and about 75 percent in the Middle East. Since then, terms of trade for commodity exporters have declined, even after a moderate recovery since mid-2016, although relative prices remain higher than at the turn of the century. The impact of these enormous changes in relative prices has been a transfer of resources greater than any in the last thirty years. The rise of China and India, as well as the Newly Industrialized Countries of Asia (NICs) and other Asian countries, had resulted in a boom in demand for commodities, even as supplies were growing worldwide. Accordingly, African prosperity appeared to consolidate.

The major issue that the commodity-exporting countries face today is that most evidence suggests that this commodity-driven prosperity has ended, or at a minimum, has been interrupted for a long time, changing the perceived paradigm of the last decade. The key questions are how are the African economies being affected and reacting to this, and what can be done, if anything, to alleviate the process of adjustment. The answers are far from straightforward. The current reversal of prices is having a major adverse impact on income, and thus on output, through the multiplier effects of a decline in export income. Specifically, the growth of per capita income in Africa is well below that of the world and of advanced countries. In 2016 per capita income in Africa declined for the first time in some twenty years.

Output had been rising in both the export sector and the general economy. However, as major emerging markets like China, India, Brazil and Mexico mature demographically and economically, they face significant structural or macroeconomic impediments. The increase in demand observed in the last decades cannot be sustained and exporters will need to adapt to these new circumstances. The past may repeat itself in periods of growth and abundance followed by times of crisis and reform. The last 150 or more years bear witness to this pattern. The quantitative assessment of the consequences of a slowdown and possible responses to it should be among the tools of policy makers. That is the aim of this paper.

Terms of trade and output measurement

Globalization, the opening of trade opportunities, and reduced import restrictions of recent decades have resulted in a major increase in the importance of trade transactions in total GDP. Export and import prices have therefore become increasingly important in determining nations' real incomes, making the effects of their changes an integral part of macroeconomic developments. Over longer periods of time, terms of trade may revert, as has been the experience over the last thirty years, directly affecting available real income (GDI), even if real GDP has not changed. From the beginning of the century until 2011-12, in many emerging economies, income grew at a faster rate than GDP because of improved terms of trade. In these economies, foreign trade had a large role, and

1. UNCTAD (2017).

Terms of trade for commodity-exporting regions and countries have shown a marked secular cyclicality over the long term.

export and import prices were important determinants of prosperity. In more recent years, the decline in commodity prices has had a direct adverse impact on the relationship between GDP and GDI, with declines in the rate of growth of GDP and absolute declines in GDI.

GDI measures the purchasing power of the total incomes generated by domestic production when real variables, including terms of trade are taken into consideration. (See Annex 2 for further discussion.) When terms of trade change, the movements of GDP and real GDI may diverge. GDP is calculated in volume terms in order to measure the real change from one period to another. Changes in the terms of trade between a specific economy and the rest of the world mean that GDP is no longer identical to domestic final expenditure. Changes in import and export prices have an impact on real income. The effect of changes in terms of trade on GDI is generally taken into account by calculating what is known as the trading gains and losses from terms of trade changes.

There are other possible definitions but the effect of terms of trade gains and losses can generally be calculated as follows: GDP in volume or real terms, plus the trading gain or loss resulting from changes in the terms of trade equals real GDI. The difference between real GDP and real GDI can be decomposed into two key terms: the change in the terms of trade weighted by the average share of trade in GDP, and the change in the price of tradables (relative to the rest of the economy) weighted by the average share of the trade balance in GDP.[2] In practical terms, most emerging economies do not explicitly calculate trading gains and losses; thus, an adjustment provides an effective tool to capture these movements.

2. Reinsdorf, M. (2009). *Terms of Trade Effects: Theory and Measurement*. Washington: Bureau of Economic Analysis, Dept. of Commerce, provides this definition.

Developments in terms of trade, exports, and imports

Terms of trade for commodity-exporting regions and countries have shown a marked secular cyclicality over the long term. During the last century, terms of trade increased after World War I, collapsed during the Great Depression, and then tended to increase at the time World War II. Subsequently, commodity prices tended to fluctuate with the world business cycle, although they showed a sharp declining tendency until the 1970s, when, at least for energy exporters, terms of trade rose sharply. Even this increase was later reversed, due to the sharp slowdown associated with the anti-inflationary measures of the early 1980s.

The experience of Africa since independence has been one of cyclical reversals in the terms of trade. In the first years of this century, commodity prices started an almost continuous increase, except for the great recession of 2008-09, helped by economic growth in a number of emerging economies, and particularly in the newly industrialized countries (NICs), China, India, Brazil and Russia. However, conditions have changed in the last five years, and there has been a general weakening (Figure 1), particularly for fuel and metals. This experience is shared by other developing regions, particularly Latin America and the Middle East, although the effect on advanced commodity producers like Australia, New Zealand and Canada is also remarkable. Furthermore, as described in more detail in a later section, the prospects for both the next few years and the medium term look gloomy for commodity exporters, although currently unforeseen circumstances could change this outlook for individual goods.

Different series may show different paths because of differences in composition, measurement base, and other intervening factors, particularly in earlier years, where UNCTAD statistics show a smoother path of price changes than the International Monetary Fund (IMF) figures used in this study. Nonetheless, it is clear that prices moved rapidly up through 2011-12. They have fallen since to the levels

The volatility in terms of trade for the emerging economies has been much more marked than for the advanced economies.

Figure 1: Commodity prices deflated by advanced economy export prices (2002=100)

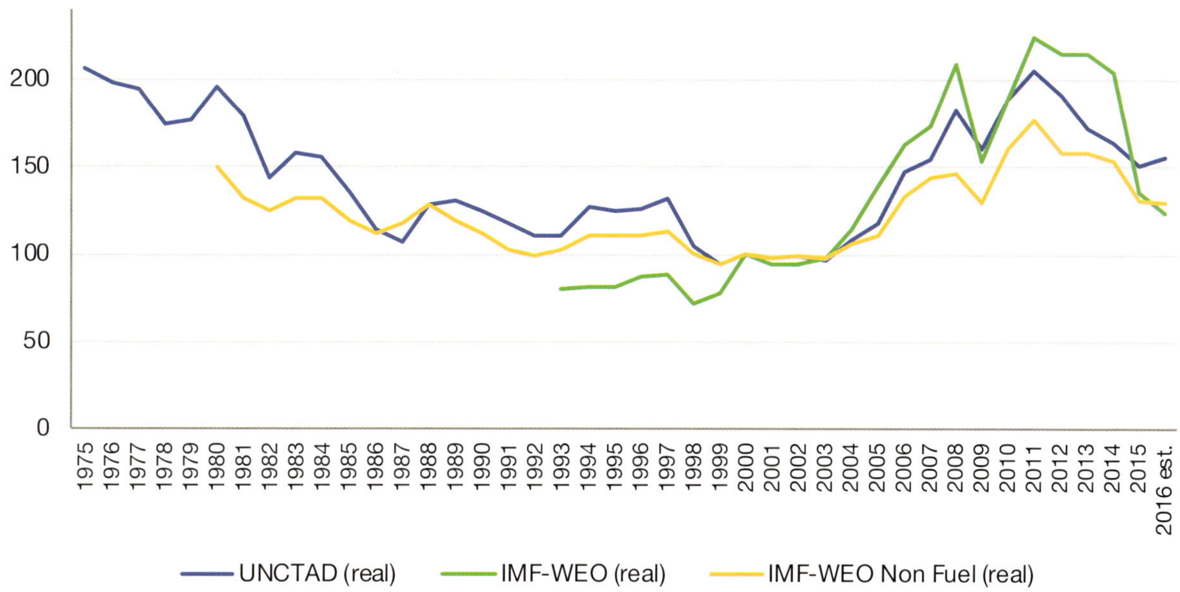

Source: IMF (2017); UNCTAD (2017)

observed in the early 2000s, although they remain higher than in the previous 20 years.[3]

The volatility in terms of trade for the emerging economies has been much more marked than for the advanced economies, as seen in Figure 2. The movements in terms of trade were also much more limited in Developing Asia. Furthermore, there is significant disparity within Africa, depending on the concentration of exports. Table 1 presents the average annual rate of change in terms of trade and the standard deviation for each region and for specific country groups in Africa. The Middle East shows the highest average annual change over the period in absolute terms both for goods and for goods and services, but it has the greatest volatility, as measured by the standard deviation. Africa follows, with smaller average rates of increase, but the rate of change and volatility are much higher for North Africa (which is also included in the Middle East and North Africa numbers) and for the exporters with high concentration of commodities. Countries whose exports are diversified or only moderately concentrated have tended to show changes and volatility in line with what is observed in Latin America. Developing Asia, the destination of exports from these regions, by obvious contrast shows an inverse trend in terms of trade, with some recovery in recent years, while the advanced economies show very limited changes and relatively low volatility (Figure 3).

The changes in commodity prices and in terms of trade have been highly correlated.[4] For all regions terms of trade have tended to move less markedly than the comprehensive real commodity index, in large part because commodities are imported as well as exported. However, at a broad regional level, terms of trade for Africa and the Middle East have the closest correlation with commodity

3. All series are deflated by the export price index for advanced economies, as published by the IMF. Alternative deflators, like the US CPI, would not produce significantly different results, except for the impact of world-wide slowdowns as observed in the early 1980s, early 2000s and 2009.

4. This is confirmed in Section 4, on the basis of regressions of terms of trade explained by commodity prices.

At a broad regional level, terms of trade for Africa and the Middle East have the closest correlation with commodity prices because of the high concentration of exports in a limited number of commodities.

Figure 2: Terms of trade for selected regions and subgroups (2000=100)

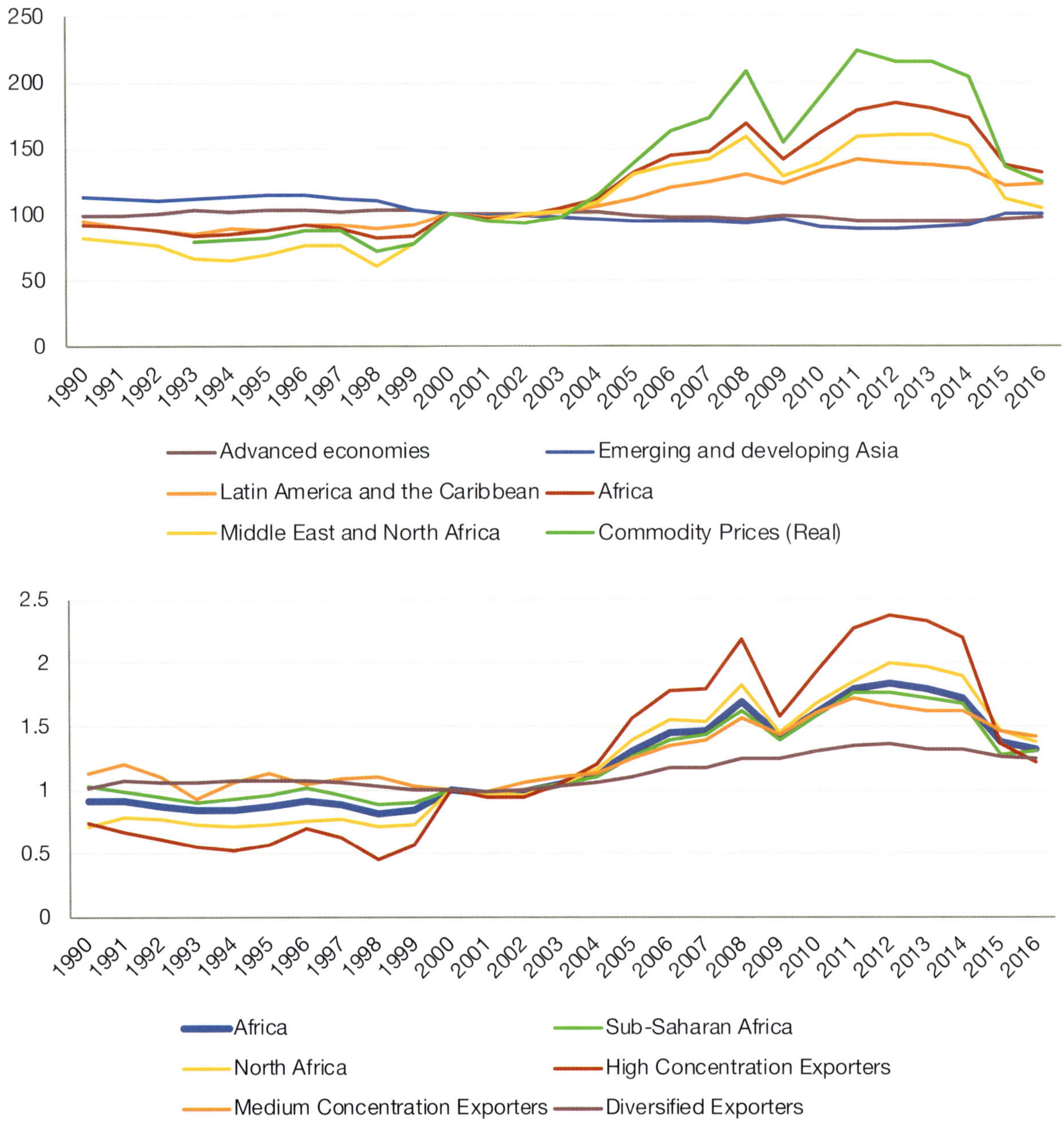

Source: IMF (2017); Centennial Group International (2017)

It is clear that terms of trade have had a strong secular cyclicality that suggests that the current downward trend in commodity prices and terms of trade cannot be expected to reverse soon.

Table 1: Terms of trade annual changes (in percent, average and standard deviation, 2000-2016)

Regions and groups	Average	Standard deviation
Advanced economies	-0.25	1.75
Emerging market and developing economies	1.16	3.54
Developing Asia	-0.12	3.14
Latin America and the Caribbean	1.87	4.95
Middle East and North Africa	2.62	13.12
Africa	2.04	11.04
Sub-Saharan Africa	1.61	10.91
North Africa	2.73	13.89
High concentration exporters	1.92	23.29
Intermediate concentration exporters	1.67	6.35
Diversified exporters	1.25	2.75

Source: IMF (2017); UNCTAD (2017); and Centennial Group International (2017)

prices because of the high concentration of exports in a limited number of commodities. This is particularly so for Africa because of the high level of exports of fuels in North Africa. In all cases, it is clear that terms of trade have had a strong secular cyclicality that suggests that the current downward trend in commodity prices and terms of trade cannot be expected to reverse soon (See a later section for a discussion of commodity price prospects). The impact of the observed decline should therefore be a major concern for policy makers.

Highly concentrated commodity exporters show a larger gain during episodes of price increases than less concentrated exporters. As the degree of concentration of exports decreases, so does the amplitude of movement in the terms of trade. In Africa, high-concentration exporters (15 countries) have considerably stronger terms of trade effects than countries in either the 20 countries in intermediate group or the 19 countries with diversified exports, which have the smallest changes, as seen in Figures 2 and 3.[5]

Terms of trade have had a significant effect on imports and exports. In general, exports have increased in real terms, helped by the increase in commodity prices. This effect is tempered by the real appreciation of national currencies that occurs at times of increases in terms of trade or export volumes, and the depreciation at times of declines.[6] Export volumes have tended to be linked to terms of trade effects. However, the pace of export growth in recent years has often fallen below that of GDP, as noted, reflecting the dampening effect of the real appreciation of the currencies. This has been evident in Africa, although not to the same extent as in Latin America.

In Africa, the ratio of the volume of exports to GDP has declined persistently since 2008, for a cumulative total of

5. As described in Annex 1, countries in Africa are divided into Geographical and Export Concentration subgroups. The Geographical subgroup distinguishes between countries in North Africa and Sub-Sahara. The Export Concentration has three categories: high concentration exporters, intermediate concentration exporters, and diversified exporters. This categorization is based on two criteria derived from UNCTAD indexing—the degree of concentration of exports by commodity, adjusted by the proportion of commodities in total exports

6. Real exchange rate movements are explained by many factors other than terms of trade, including changes in the amount and directions of capital flows, as well as domestic macroeconomic policies., The real exchange rate is also influenced by the degree of protection granted to domestic import substituting industries. Thus, it is not always easy to identify the pure effect of commodities.

In Africa, the ratio of the volume of exports to GDP has declined persistently since 2008, for a cumulative total of about 40 percent, after a sustained increase during the 1990s.

Figure 3: Changes in terms of trade for selected regions and subgroups (2000=100)

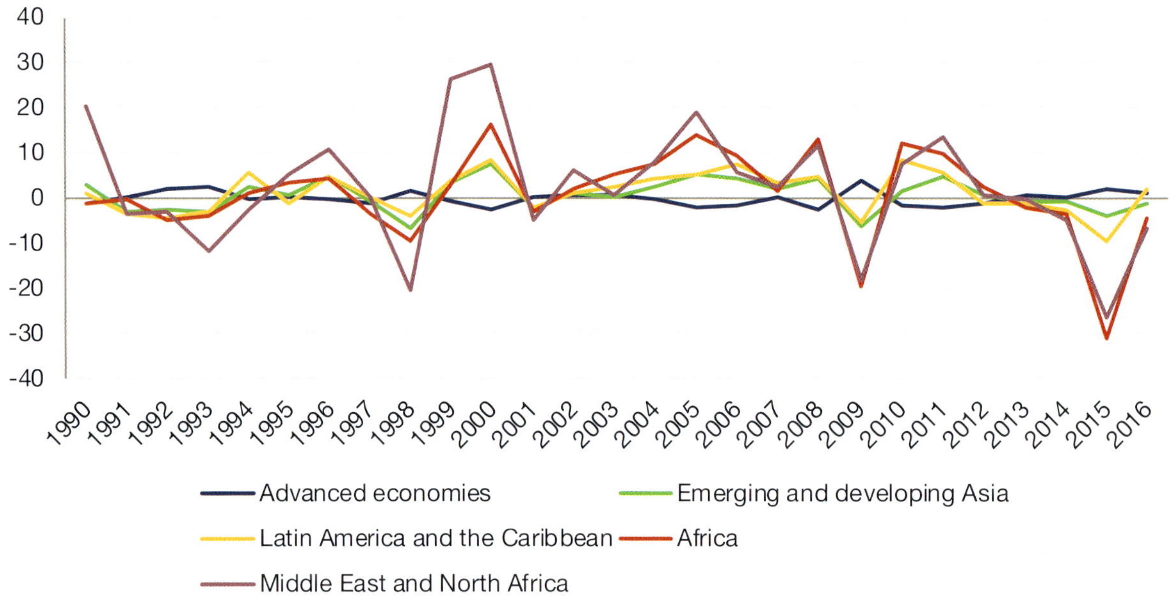

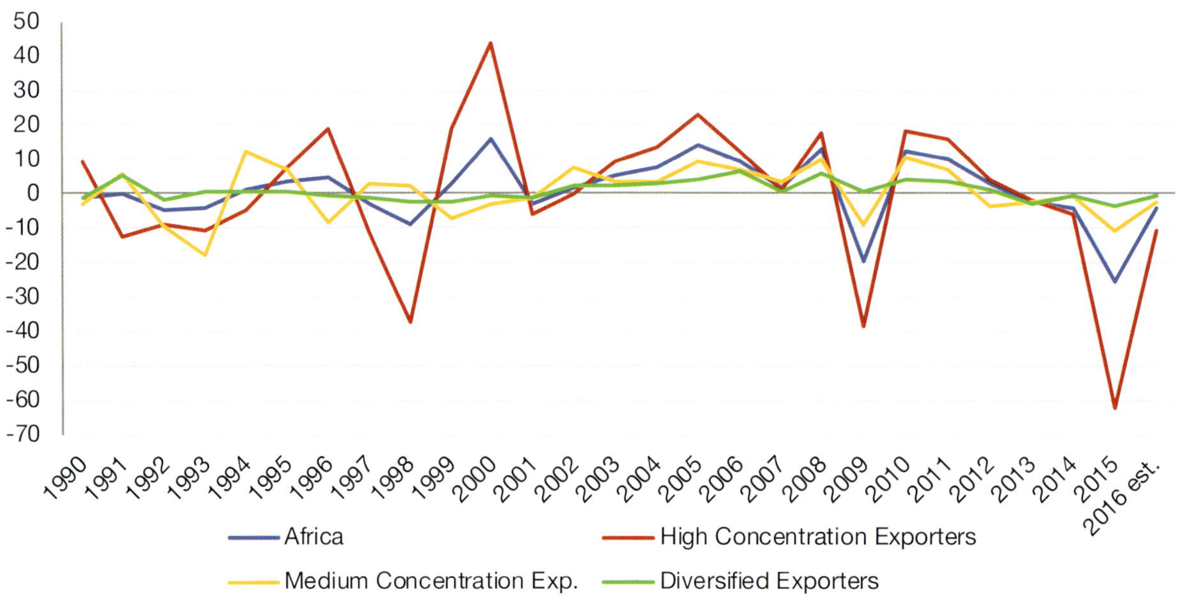

Source: IMF (2017); UNCTAD (2017); Centennial Group International (2017)

For the continent overall, there was a slight decline in investment and a sharp fall in savings, suggesting that the region had not adjusted to the decline in terms of trade nor, more generally, to the negative impact of the decline in commodity prices on public finances and the current account.

about 40 percent, after a sustained increase during the 1990s. The earlier change was most likely associated with a process of trade liberalization that was the common feature of emerging and developing countries during the 1990s.

The ratio of the volume exports to GDP has tended to move at a considerably different pace than that of the volume of imports. But when export volumes are adjusted to take into account the impact of terms of trade, specifically by adding the impact of terms of trade to the volume index to reflect the purchasing power of exports, the picture changes drastically. In fact, import volumes are more closely associated with the purchasing power than the volume of exports.

Figure 4 presents different aggregate variables for Africa with the simplifying assumption that all terms of trade effects reflect changes in the prices of exports. Import prices are estimated to change at the same pace as the domestic GDP deflator adjusted by real exchange rates and thus would not account for changes in relative prices.[7] Figure 5 looks at a different perspective, namely the ratio of the value of exports and imports to GDP. Exports are deflated by terms of trade, or more simply, are presented in real terms. In both cases, it is clear that exports in volume terms behave very differently than imports. However, when exports are corrected for their purchasing power (i.e. adjusted for terms of trade),[8] imports tend to follow export behavior more closely. In other words, as the export receipts of the countries in Africa have increased because of higher prices, there has been a concurrent change in the level of imports through 2011.

The increase in imports was associated with the sharp rise in the purchasing power of exports. However, starting in 2012 there was a significant gap, with both GDP and imports growing while exports decline. This reflected in a widening of the external current account deficit, which had been increasingly financed by debt flows and losses in reserves and with a concurrent decline in the pace of FDI to the region. In some cases, this may have reflected a continued high level of investment. But for the continent overall, there was a slight decline in investment and a sharp fall in savings, suggesting that the region had not adjusted to the decline in terms of trade nor, more generally, to the negative impact of the decline in commodity prices on public finances and the current account. Only in the very recent past, and as projected for the near future in the World Economic Outlook of the IMF (April 2017), has there been a change in trend toward adjustment, and a moderation in the rate of growth.

Regarding the behavior of exports, the decline in the ratio of exports to GDP in Africa in recent years does not signify stagnation of exportable output and of exports. On the contrary, export volumes have increased significantly, but that growth was outpaced by other sectors of the economy, reflecting in part the large increase in purchasing power derived from increased export prices. Investment and consumption, private and public alike, rose rapidly to accommodate the growing prosperity, observed in recent years as terms of trade skyrocketed. Real exports have moved with terms of trade (adjusted by real effective exchange rates) used as a proxy for domestic prices for exports. The growth in export volumes in the 1990s and early 2000s was also significant, at a time when terms of trade were generally stable, mostly attributable to a general opening of emerging economies to trade. Subsequently, the increase in output followed prices more clearly. Figure

7. In theory, the adjustment could be made on the basis of export prices and import prices separately and not on terms of trade. The results may not deviate much if that approach is taken. The estimates presented here follow the simpler approach. Furthermore, no adjustment is made to account for movements in real exchange rates as all variables would change in the same proportion. Real exchange rate estimates are obtained from Bruegel. (2016). Real effective exchange rates for 178 countries: a new database., which provides estimates since 1992, for most of the countries and certainly for the most important countries, in terms of their share of GDP.

8. The adjustment for terms of trade, as calculated in Figure 4, attributes all the change in commodity prices to exports. This allows to capture the full effect of changes in purchasing power of export prices on the estimated value of imports. A specific assignment of prices changes- for exports and imports- would provide somewhat different numbers, but the same correlation between imports volumes and adjusted export volumes presented here. In Figure 5, the adjustment is reversed, as the ratios of exports and imports are measured in value terms. Thus, the ratio of exports to GDP is corrected down (in case of improved terms of trade), to show the volume effect relative to GDP, and vice versa when terms of trade declines.

The key point is that terms of trade effects are not captured in the estimation of real GDP.

Figure 4: Exports, import, and the effect of terms of trade

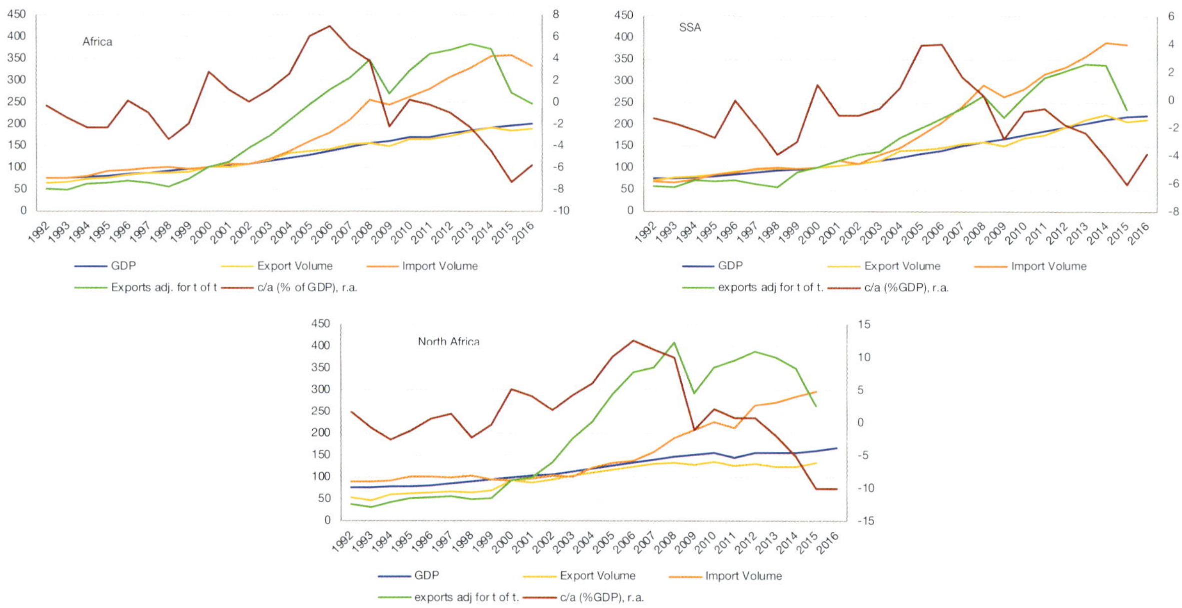

Source: IMF (2017), UNCTAD (2017), Centennial Group International (2017)

Figure 5: Ratios of exports, exports (net of terms of trade effect), and import values (in percent of GDP)

Source: IMF (2017); UNCTAD (2017); Centennial Group International (2017)

In recent years, per capita income has either declined or has increased negligibly, clearly showing the effect of lower prices.

6 shows the performance of exports (in volume terms) and terms of trade (adjusted for real effective exchange rates).[9] There is a clear correlation, although it is not perfect because of a complex investment process, including lags and long gestation periods.

Quantification of the effects of international price shocks

The impact of terms of trade on disposable income differs significantly from that on GDP. The key point is that terms of trade effects are not captured in the estimation of real GDP. Specifically, GDP in real terms underestimates the income or purchasing power available to the country because of an increase in export price, and vice versa.

Estimates of the cumulative change in terms of trade on GDI calculated for Africa and its subgroups (using the formulas presented in Annex 2) are presented in Table 2 with comparisons to a trend rate of growth (based on estimations explained in the next section). These trend values reflect the long-term growth potential without the impact of terms of trade. In the case of Africa, the direct effect of terms of trade changes on GDI (real income) has been 1.3 percent of GDP a year over the period 2000-12. But in the subsequent 4 years it was a negative 1.2 percent. In the case of the highly concentrated exporters, the corresponding values were 3.9 percent and -2.3 percent; in the case of the intermediate concentration exporters, 0.9 percent and -0.5 percent, and in the case of diversified exporters, with smaller changes in terms of trade, the values are 0.5 percent and -0.4 percent respectively. In recent years, per

9. The adjustment in terms of trade for movements in real effective exchange rates seeks to capture the true price effect of movements in export and import prices on domestic incentives. An improvement in terms of trade is frequently accompanied by a strengthening of the domestic currency with respect to others, beyond inflation differentials. In those circumstances, the relative price of export goods relative to the whole economy does not increase as much as the pure terms of trade effect would suggest, while that of imports would decline. The reverse would be the case if terms of trade decline, and the currency depreciates. On that basis, an adjusted terms of trade index provides a better indicator to measure existing incentives than the pure international price effect.

Figure 6: GDP, export volumes, and terms of trade adjusted by real exchange rates (2000=100)

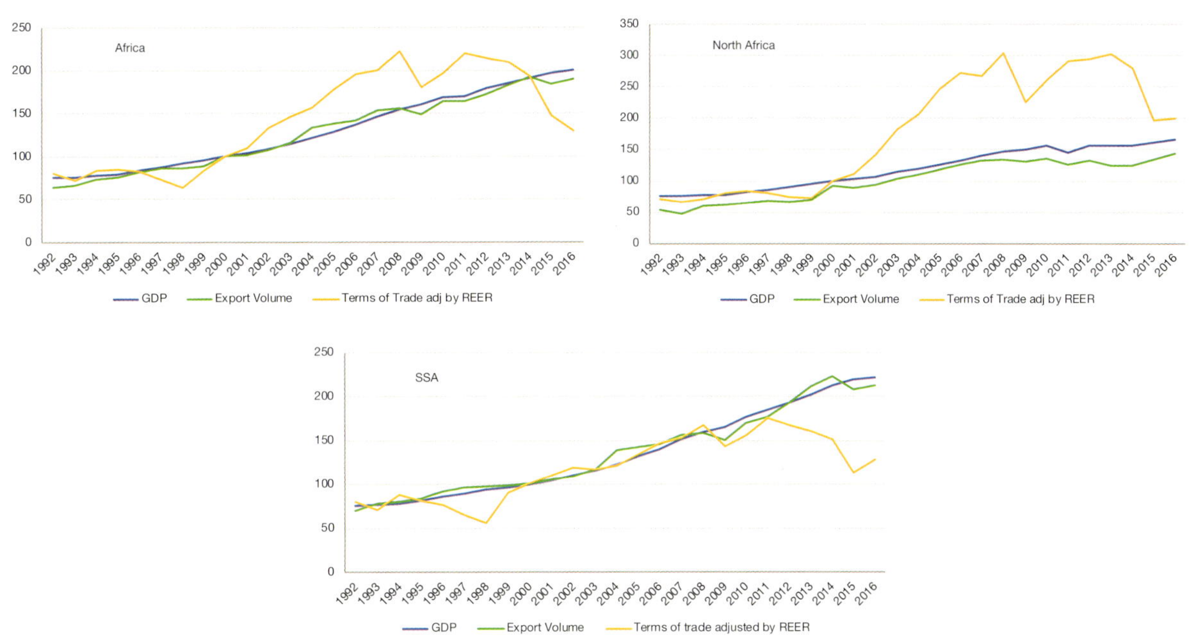

Source: IMF (2017); UNCTAD (2017); Centennial Group International (2017)

Actual losses have been smaller than estimated losses, very likely on account of unsustainable macro and borrowing policies, which have to date obscured the real situation of the region.

Table 2: Selected groups—Average annual rate of growth, 2000-2015

		Africa		Highly concentrated exporters		Intermediate concentrated exporters		Diversified exporters	
	Period	2001-12	2013-16	2001-12	2013-16	2001-12	2013-16	2001-12	2013-16
1	**Change in terms of trade**	0.056	-0.077	0.086	-0.138	0.045	-0.038	0.026	-0.020
2	**GDI**	0.063	0.019	0.101	0.000	0.060	0.061	0.045	0.024
3	**Trend growth rate**	0.036	0.036	0.052	0.052	0.035	0.035	0.037	0.037
4	**GDI-trend (Total terms of trade effect)**	0.027	-0.017	0.049	-0.052	0.025	0.026	0.008	-0.013
5	**GDP**	0.050	0.028	0.062	0.023	0.051	0.056	0.039	0.028
6	**GDP-trend**	0.014	-0.008	0.010	-0.029	0.016	0.021	0.002	-0.009
7	**Direct terms of trade effect (GDI-GDP)**	0.013	-0.010	0.039	-0.023	0.009	0.005	0.005	-0.004
8	**Terms of trade effect on GDP (estimated)**	0.013	-0.019	0.007	-0.011	0.010	-0.008	0.003	-0.003
9	**Total terms of trade effect (estimated)**	0.026	-0.028	0.046	-0.034	0.019	-0.004	0.009	-0.006
10	**Unexplained terms of trade**	0.000	0.011	0.003	-0.018	0.006	0.030	-0.001	-0.007
11	**GDI PC**	0.037	0.007	0.075	-0.020	0.025	0.036	0.023	0.003

Source: IMF (2017); UNCTAD (2017); and Centennial Group International (2017)

capita income has either declined or has increased negligibly, clearly showing the effect of lower prices.

For recent years, when the full effect of terms of trade is taken into consideration, including changes in GDP (with respect to trend explained by terms of trade, as detailed in a later section), the losses are higher. The full cumulative decline in income relative to trend in the period 2013-2016 was 7.4 percent of GDP for Africa, with a loss 21 percent for the highly concentrated exporters, and 3.5 percent loss for the diversified exporters. There was a 10 percent increase for the intermediate concentrated exporters, which can be explained by increasing borrowing. The cumulative effect of these gains and losses is very significant. However, actual losses have been smaller than estimated losses, very likely on account of unsustainable macro and borrowing policies, which have to date obscured the real situation of the region. These conditions are likely to change, and the actual losses will catch up, even if terms of trade do not deteriorate further.

The impact of commodity prices on GDP and export volumes

The previous section has covered the effect of prices on GDI, and also suggested total changes including those in GDP. In order to have a more accurate estimate of the latter, it is essential to analyze the impact of the external

The explanatory power of these described variables on African and African subgroups' GDP is extremely high, with an R2 on the order of 0.98 to 1.00, and coefficients for the different variables significant at the 95 percent level of confidence.

price shocks on real output, be it in exportables, other traded or non-traded goods in the economy. This is commonly described as the multiplier effect of exports. Here, the assessment is better done using a simple econometric model. It should be borne in mind that the coefficients show correlation and likely, but not necessarily, causality, and thus should be viewed with some caution.

The results for Africa and specified regions and subgroups are presented in Table 3. A set of regressions shows the impact of different variables on GDP growth for Africa and for specified subgroups. The regressions include as independent variables the terms of trade, and as additional variables either world GDP or a trend variable. Because world GDP growth and terms of trade behavior are highly correlated, the use of world GDP presents some technical problems that distort the results. As an alternative, a trend variable is used estimating an underlying annual constant rate of growth. This trend should be seen as a simplifying proxy for the underlying growth in labor and capital and in TFP. It would have been preferable to use these factors specifically. The explanatory power of these described variables on African and African subgroups'

Table 3: Summary of regressions for terms of trade: Key coefficients and statistics (1990-2015)

	Terms of trade	World GDP	Trend	Export values (deflated by US prices)	Specific variable	R-squared
Africa						
GDP	.13	1.08				1
GDP	0.24**		3.6** [1]			1
Real imports				.58**	0.66** [2]	0.99
Volume of exports	1.84**	0.05**				0.93
Terms of trade					0.51** [3]	0.99
Terms of trade		1.02**				0.92
Commodity prices		1.27**				0.9
Sub Saharan Africa						
GDP	0.05	1.25				1
GDP	0.3		4.0[1]			0.99
North Africa						0.99
GDP	0.13	0.84				0.99
GDP	0.21		3.3[1]			0.99
High concentration exporters						
GDP	-0.22	2.13				0.99
GDP	0.08		5.2[1]			0.99
Intermediate concentrated exporters						
GDP	0.34	0.8				0.99
GDP	0.22		3.5[1]			0.99
Diversified exporters						
GDP	0.15	0.94				0.99
GDP	0.13		3.7[1]			0.99

1. Annual rate of change in GDP; 2. Africa GDP; 3. Commodity prices (real)
Source: IMF (2017); Centennial Group International (2017); and estimates

The analysis also indicates a strong correlation between terms of trade and export volumes, suggesting that exportable output is price elastic.

GDP is extremely high, with an R2 on the order of 0.98 to 1.00, and coefficients for the different variables significant at the 95 percent level of confidence.

A second type of equation shows for Africa[10] the correlation between import volumes and export volumes adjusted for terms of trade. The results suggest that a considerable portion of the increased purchasing power from improved terms of trade is spent abroad. In that sense, if and when a correction in prices occurs, the impact on domestic activity will be somewhat reduced, even though the impact on expenditure will move in line with the loss in terms of trade.

The analysis also indicates a strong correlation between terms of trade and export volumes, suggesting that exportable output is price elastic. More research would be needed in this regard, in order to distinguish the short term and longer term investment-related elasticities.

10. Equivalent regressions have been run for the two sub-regional and the three export-concentration groups, with equivalent results.

In summary, the econometric results show a high degree of significance for terms of trade and the trend variable in explaining GDP behavior. They confirm the experience in the main commodity-exporting group about the multiplier effect of changes in prices and also indicate significant elasticities of output to changes in prices. These results hold for all the groups under analysis.

These results are technically strong. Nonetheless, Table 2 above shows significant deviations between the actual outcome for economic growth and the estimated result based on these regressions. Specifically, while there is a strong correlation between the actual results and the estimates for the period 2001-12, there are discrepancies for the period 2013-15 as shown on lines 4, 9 and 10 of Table 2. The equations overestimate the loss in GDP by 2 percent a year for Africa, and 3.3 percent for the intermediate concentrated exporters; and they underestimate the high concentration and diversified exporters by 0.9 and 0.5 percent respectively. To a large extent, these deviations are

Figure 7: External current account (percent of GDP)

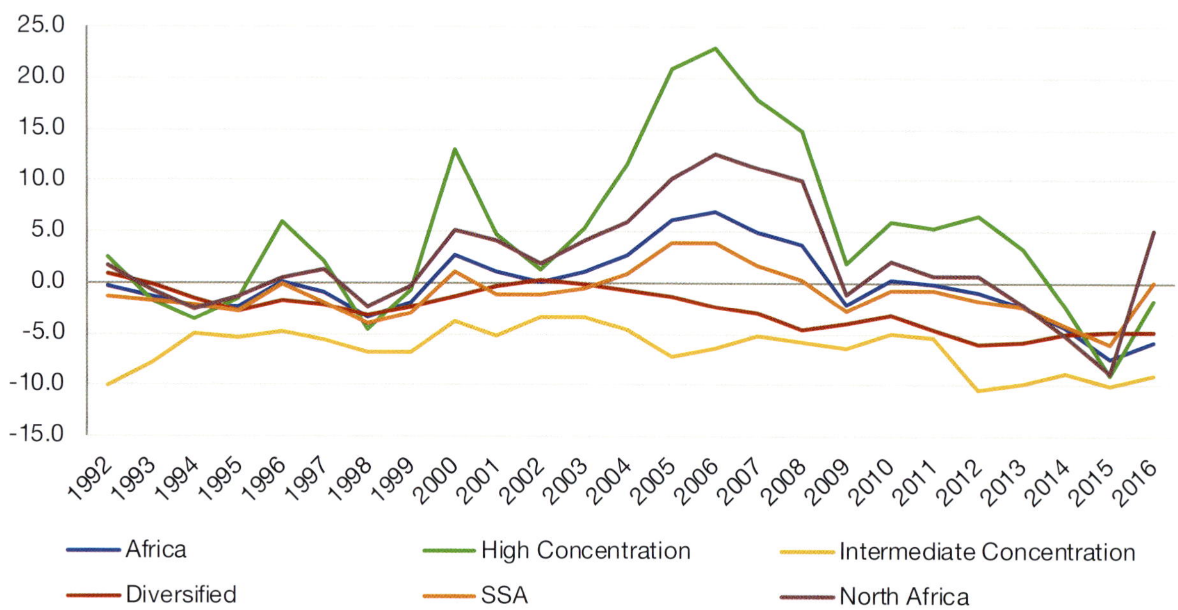

Source: IMF (2017)

It is clear that fluctuations in prices have an immediate impact on available income, and thus on expenditure and on output.

linked to the sharp increase in the external current account deficit and concurrent losses of reserves and heavy borrowing by the region in the last years (see Figure 7) where all subgroups show a clear and sharp deterioration in the external accounts, a trend that was only reversed in 2016, and is estimated to continue in 2017. As shown in Figure 8, the associated appreciation of the currency, initially linked to improved prices, and then expansionary policies, also was reversed in 2016, when the average real effective exchange rate declined (depreciated) by an estimated 14 percent (Figure 8). These changes suggest an increasing awareness of the unsustainability of previous policies.

This situation requires urgent corrective actions regarding both the exchange rate and the fiscal positions, which are extremely sensitive to terms of trade.

Macroeconomic implications of the terms of trade effect

It is clear that fluctuations in prices have an immediate impact on available income, and thus on expenditure and on output. Figure 9 provides an illustration of these magnitudes. It shows for Africa the rates of growth of GDP, GDI (that is, GDP corrected by the effect of terms of trade), and GDP trend, as described previously. Equivalent results are obtained for subcategories. It shows, again, the significant gap between output and income over time as a function of changes in terms of trade as well as the effect of lower prices. If no changes in commodity prices had occurred between 2000 and 2015, according to the above estimates, GDP and GDI would have been lower than actually observed by 15 and 23 percent, respectively, even after the recent declines in commodity prices. Other countries, GDP would have been lower by 19 percent, and GDI would have been lower by 41 percent. In the case of the intermediate concentration exporter countries, the values would

Figure 8: Real effect exchange rates (2000=100; increase entails appreciation)

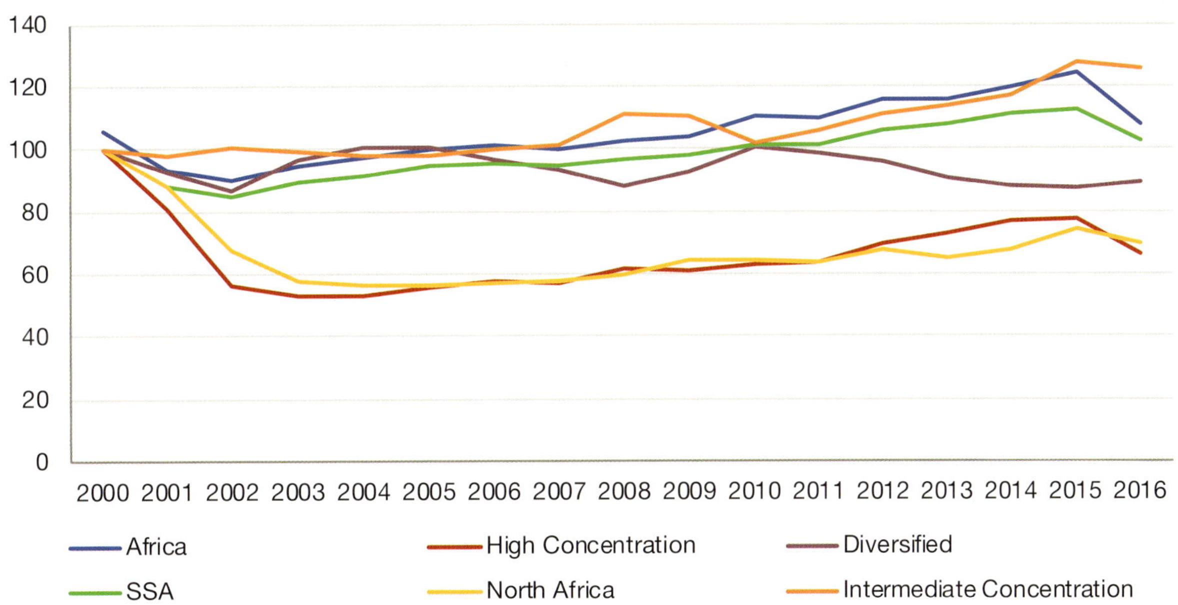

Source: Bruegel (2016); IMF (2017); Centennial estimates

In the case of the intermediate concentration exporter countries, the values would have been lower by 11 and 16 percent, respectively; and in the case of the diversified exporters, 5 and 9 percent respectively, a significant shortfall from observed values as of 2011.

Figure 9: Africa, GDP, GDI, and trend GDP per capita (annual growth rate)

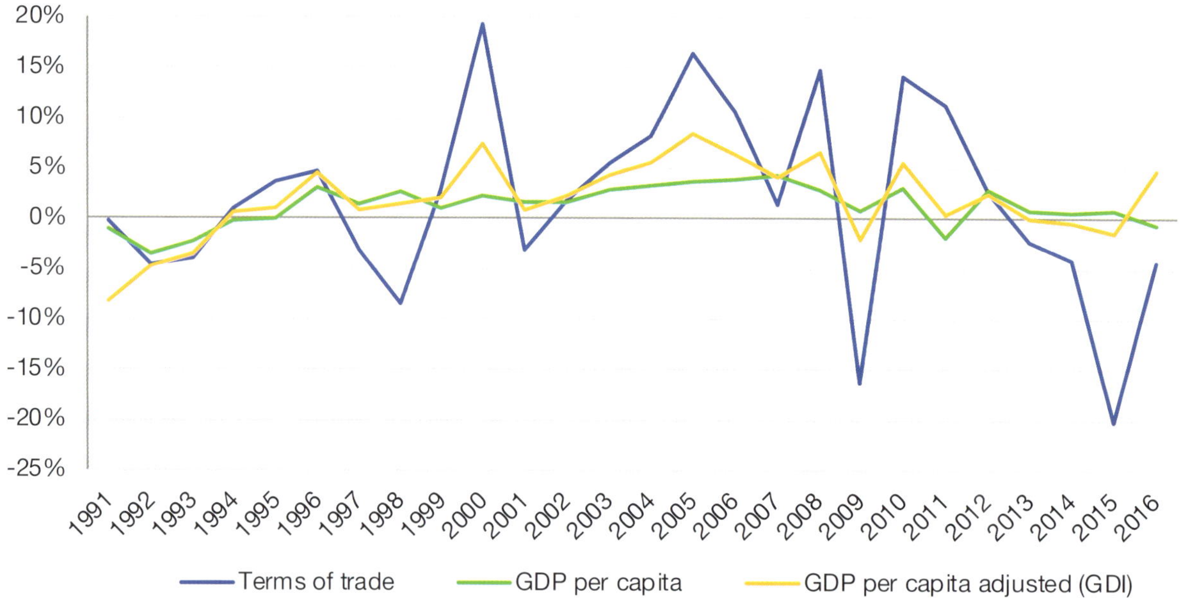

Source: IMF (2017); UNCTAD (2017); Centennial Group International (2017)

have been lower by 11 and 16 percent, respectively; and in the case of the diversified exporters, 5 and 9 percent respectively, a significant shortfall from observed values as of 2011. Equivalent declines would have been observed on a per capita basis.

The above estimates allow quantification of the impact of a "terms of trade event" on the economy. The results provide broad orders of magnitude for African subgroups but not for specific countries; still, they quantify the possible impact of external shocks rather well. Table 4 presents a summary of the key findings. It shows the percentage change in disposable income for the two main components: (1) the pure effect of terms of trade on income (which will be in addition to measured GDP, as developed

Table 4: Percentage change in selected variables associated with 1 percent change in terms of trade (elasticity)

Region/Subgroup	Total impact on GDI	Multiplier effect on GDP	Pure terms of trade effect on GDI*	Volume of exports
Africa	0.46	0.24	0.22	1.83
Sub-Saharan Africa	0.49	0.3	0.19	1.77
North Africa	0.38	0.21	0.17	1.93
High concentration	0.48	0.08	0.4	1.24
Intermediate concentration	0.48	0.22	0.26	1.41
Diversified	0.32	0.13	0.19	1.98

Source: Centennial Group International (2017)

Unless reforms take place, GDP growth rates would fall to the trend levels. Growth rates would fall further during periods of terms of trade decline because of the multiplier effect of export prices.

in section 4); and (2) the effect of the increased export receipts on real GDP (that is, the multiplier effect on real output, as described in the relevant section). The sum of the two effects will be the full effect of the price change on disposable income and would have to be added to (or subtracted from, as the case may be) the trend growth. The table also includes the effect of terms of trade on the volume of exports.

These results suggest that the impact on prices of a decline in world or regional activity or, as an alternative, an increase in world supply of commodities, would have a significant effect on the domestic economy. In the specific case of Africa, if terms of trade in the future were to stabilize at the current level, GDP growth rates would tend to fall to the trend growth rate of 3.6 percent, as the multiplier effect would disappear and the purchasing power of exports would stabilize. A further decline in terms of trade of 5 percent for Africa would entail an initial decline in GDI, resulting in a decline in output growth relative to the trend rate of growth and a effectively decline in the rate of change in per capita GDP to zero. A further decline of this nature, while steep, is not unusual and should be considered plausible as prices are about one third or more higher than in 2000 and are certainly within the realm of the long-term cycle of commodity prices. The effect tends to be similar for all regions and subgroups except for the diversified exporters, where the effect of a 1 percent change in terms of trade is in the order of 0.3 percent for GDP. Any argument that countries should not be concerned because GDP is growing beyond the terms of trade effect disregards the effect of export prices on domestic output.

The impact of the terms of trade on the growth rates for GDP and GDI is illustrated in Figure 10, which shows their average growth rates for the period 2000-15, an estimate for 2016, and a scenario for the period 2017-25.[11] For the period through 2016, the graph presents the average rates of growth for 2000-12 and for 2013-15 against the actual level of terms of trade. The numbers for 2016 shows a significant correction, reflected in a significant depreciation of the African currencies, associated with a reduction in borrowing but a slight deterioration in terms of trade of 6 percent for that year. Terms of trade are assumed constant for the period 2017-20, and declines are assumed for the period from 2021 onwards. If terms of trade where to remain constant in the near future, GDP and GDI growth rates would recover from the last few years but would fall substantially from experience since the turn of the century, even as terms of trade remain at current levels. Unless reforms take place, GDP growth rates would fall to the trend levels. Growth rates would fall further during periods of terms of trade decline because of the multiplier effect of export prices. For GDP to continue on the historical growth path, terms of trade would have to continue to increase on a long-term basis. Under the more realistic assumption of plateauing terms of trade, after a moderate decline to levels above those of 2000, GDP would be 10 percent lower in ten years than what would have been expected if the (unrealistically high) historical rate of growth of the period 2000-12 had prevailed after 2012. Available income, as measured by GDI, would be lower by 15 percent.

At this point, a word of warning is needed. The numbers presented here are estimates; they seem to fall within reasonable ranges on the basis of econometric tests. However, the actual values will fall within a range around the projected values. Thus, the estimates should be viewed with caution. Nonetheless, even if the projected GDI/GDP losses were to be one third or one half lower, they would remain considerable and would need to be taken into serious consideration in order to formulate a reasonable macro policy for the medium term.

The current levels of commodity price are likely to continue in the medium and long term, as discussed in the next section, while the high level of borrowing observed in recent years cannot be sustained. An assessment ignoring such likely developments would constitute a serious mistake by

11. As of the date of the review of this chapter, (May 2017), no final numbers were available for terms of trade of the regions and countries under consideration. Estimates have been included for some of the broader categories, but they should be seen as preliminary.

The complacency engendered by relatively high GDP growth rates is misplaced, given the very rapid rate of population growth in Africa in absolute terms, and as compared to most other regions of the world.

Figure 10: Historical and prospective terms of trade levels and rates of growth of GDP and GDI

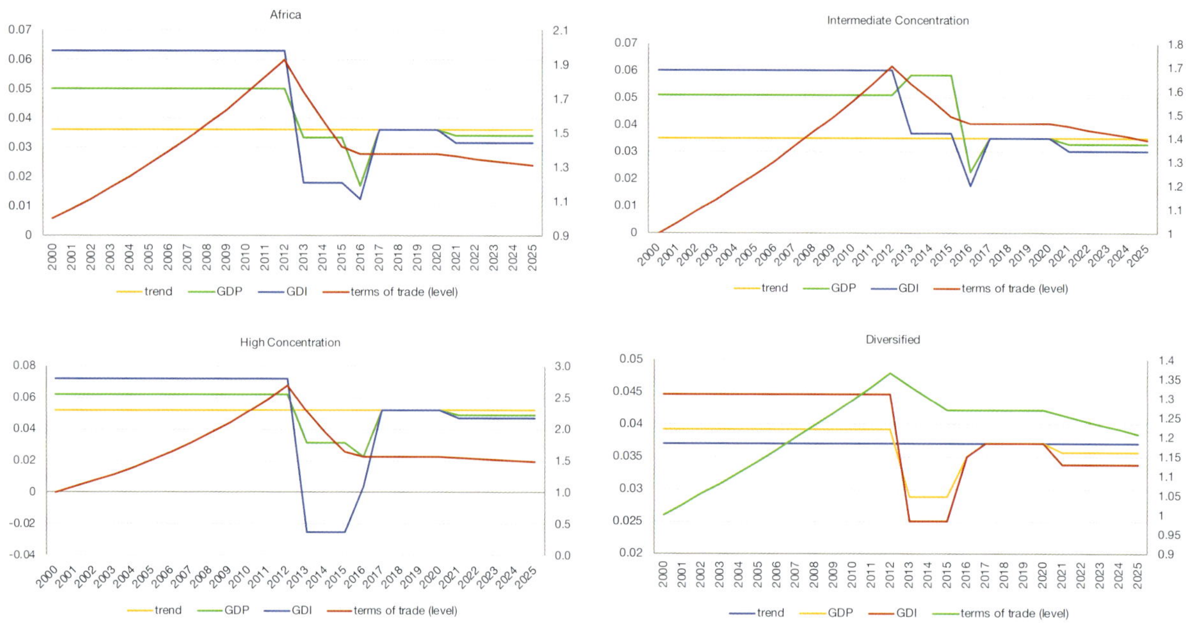

Source: Centennial Group International (2017)

emerging and developed countries alike, and needs to be corrected through appropriate economic policy. The consequences of a complacent dependence of governments on revenues from particular commodities (be they fuels, minerals, or agricultural goods) has had extremely negative effects throughout the history of commodity exporters.

Policy requirements in the new world of low commodity prices[12]

Economic growth in Africa has slowed significantly in recent years with average GDP growth declining from 5 percent a year during the period 2000-2012 to 2.6 percent during 2013-16. The decline was sharper among the more highly concentrated export countries. Furthermore, the measured decline underestimates the true magnitude of the slowdown as GDI (or domestic disposable income), which had been growing at a rate of 6.3 percent, decelerated to a rate of 1.8 percent in the period 2013-15, and very likely less in 2016, entailing an actual decline in per capita disposable income, with limited increases subsequently.

Of equal importance, per capita GDP growth has been consistently below that for the world at least since 2010. Moreover, it has been below that of the advanced countries for the last three years, as has been the case for Latin America and the Middle East.[13] The complacency engendered by relatively high GDP growth rates is misplaced, given the very rapid rate of population growth in Africa in

12. Many of these issues have been discussed in Ahlers et al. (2014). In particular, this section follows the principles presented in Chapter 9, Maintaining Macroeconomic Stability and Increasing Resiliency by Basu and Fajgenbaum, and Chapter 12, Harnessing Natural Resources for Diversification by Bond and Fajgenbaum. Also, see, Fajgenbaum, J. (2012) Macroeconomic Management—Implementing Responsible Fiscal and Monetary Policies, In *A New Vision for Mexico 2042: Achieving Prosperity for All.* New Delhi: Sage.

13. The Middle East is here defined as Middle East and North Africa, as generally presented by the World Bank and the IMF. To that extent there is some overlap in that series and that of Africa.

Even as the reality of low commodity prices is already sinking in, it is imperative for the African countries, both highly concentrated exporters and more diversified economies, to focus on macroeconomic sustainability.

absolute terms, and as compared to most other regions of the world.

The terms of trade effect ad a particularly strong impact for highly concentrated exporters, and more so in the case of oil producers, like, Angola, Gabon, Equatorial Guinea, Libya and Nigeria. Other countries have been hit by the Ebola epidemic (Guinea, Liberia and Sierra Leone) and several southern and eastern African countries, including Ethiopia, Malawi, and Zimbabwe, are suffering from a severe drought.

Some countries, mainly those with more diversified exports, may be doing better. Their terms of trade have tended to weaken by less or even to have benefited in net terms because of low oil prices. Some institutions, like the IMF, consider that the slowdown is temporary and focus on increased investment as a good indication of these prospects (IMF 2016). However, the analysis presented here suggests that any recovery will be slow in coming. Investment as a proportion of GDP has been declining, even as the external current account deficit has risen to levels not seen since at least the early 1980s. This rise has taken place at a time when the fiscal positions have tended to weaken.

Under these conditions, based on the current circumstances and prospects, the general policy approach has to be modified. In recent years, countries throughout Africa reacted differently but in general followed an unsustainable path, that only in 2016 started to be reversed, as noted above. The slowdown in activity became more marked last year, and per-capita income fell, while reserves fell and financing dried up. The previous average overvaluation of the currencies was reversed markedly, but a more drastic and sustainable effort is required for many of the countries in Africa.

Many policy-makers believed they were choosing between continued growth on the basis of their ongoing policies, or painful adjustment, usually imposed from outside. However, adjustment is inevitable. The real choice is between orderly and internationally supported correction and disorderly and disruptive crisis if polices are not corrected. Even as the reality of low commodity prices is already sinking in, it is imperative for the African countries, both highly concentrated exporters and more diversified economies, to focus on macroeconomic sustainability. It is important to promote physical investment and human capital formation.

The scenarios for growth in the next years presented here suggest some recovery after 2016, as prices stabilize or increase somewhat, and incipient adjustment efforts in some of the major countries. However, it is essential to correct the fiscal, monetary and exchange rate policies in addition to the necessary structural reforms mentioned elsewhere in this study, for the recovery to take place.

For many policy makers, the apparent policy options are continued growth of per capita GDP or painful adjustment. However, the true choice is orderly and internationally supported correction or disorderly and disruptive crisis, if current policies continue as they are for most of the countries in the region. It is difficult to design a single macroeconomic policy framework for all African countries given the diversity of circumstances. Nevertheless, it is generally recognized that for economic activity to expand equitably and on a sustainable basis, macroeconomic policies need to ensure stability and predictability. Broadly, this means sound fiscal and monetary policies, consistent with debt and balance of payments sustainability. Ideally, these policies would be supported by a flexible exchange rate regime, which would allow for an independent monetary policy and would provide countries with a critical policy instrument to help absorb external shocks. Furthermore, long-term trends suggest that many of these policies would need to be corrected even if terms of trade were not to change (see Box 1).

Policies need to be formulated to incorporate the effect of possible changes in terms of trade, particularly for resource rich countries. A commodity stabilization fund equivalent to the Copper Stabilization Fund of Chile together with structural fiscal targets, namely a budget

Fiscal policies will need to adjust as the economies continue to grow, if an indebtedness problem is to be avoided.

Box 1: Assessment of long-term fiscal and current account sustainability

The prospects for emerging economies are well represented by the Centennial/Emerging Markets Forum model[1], but this type of model tends to assume that the macroeconomic conditions will adapt to the underlying growth conditions. In practice, this may not be a straightforward result, and corrections may be required in macroeconomic policies. Corrections may also be required in the case terms of trade, as discussed here. For this purpose, it is possible to review the sustainability of the external outcome and of fiscal policies, broadly based on the debt sustainability methodology developed by the World Bank and the IMF.[2] The methodology addresses the consistency of policies and the ability of the economy to cope over the medium- to long-term for the attainment of higher growth. Specifically, it is possible to assess, in aggregate and stylized terms, the impact of the path of economic growth on (1) the external current account and, as a consequence, the level of indebtedness of the economy; and (2) the fiscal outcome and the corresponding increase in public sector debt.

This methodology suggests that without changes in the pattern of the fiscal and external variables, the economic growth path, represented by the trend variable, is characterized by a continued increase in per capita income based on investment and TFP. However, it does not necessarily entail a sustainable position over time., as both the external current account and the fiscal position may deteriorate, as is the case in most regions and subgroups (Figure B1).

The projections reflect the high dependence of exports and revenues on foreign income and changes in terms of trade for Africa. Econometric analysis suggests high elasticities of exports to world GDP and to terms of trade, and in the case of imports, high dependence to domestic GDP.[3] Under the assumption that terms of trade remain stable during the period under consideration, the external current account shows a progressive weakening in the current account surplus ratio to GDP over time for Africa. Furthermore, a decline in terms of trade has a significant impact on the current accounts of all regions and subgroups.

Regressions for government revenue and expenditure show a high correlation with domestic GDP and terms of trade. The model suggests that the fiscal outcome deteriorates for Africa overall and for most sub-regions over time as the economies grow, without changes in terms of trade. This result suggests that fiscal policies will need to adjust as the economies continue to grow, if an indebtedness problem is to be avoided. The results are worse when it is assumed that the terms of trade deteriorate. Below are charts showing for Africa the effect of changes in terms of trade of 20 percent in both directions over the next ten years on the basis of a central growth scenario, which does not fully reflect recent term of trade changes. Thus, it should be assumed that the prospective path of adjustment of both the external and the current account should be closer to the line showing a decline of 20 percent in terms of trade. The crossover point for the current account should be construed as a self-solving solution when commodity prices decline, as imports are highly sensitive to terms of trade declines, thus resulting in a more direct adjustment of the current account. This trajectory is of course influenced by possible borrowing, which will delay the adjustment to imports and therefore to the current account. In general, all subgroups (while not shown here) record similar behavior as for the continent.

In order to deal with these problems, the macroeconomic strategy will require specific policies to correct the fiscal and balance of payments positions as needed. For example, it will be important to increase the non-export related revenues in order to reduce dependence on commodities. Expenditure would have to be slowed down, while allowing for increased infrastructure spending and social expenditure. It may be argued that increasing external deficits in Africa may be offset by "naturally increasing" surpluses in other areas. That would entail large increases in inter-regional indebtedness or FDI, two assumptions that cannot be accepted in simple terms. In practice, these scenarios suggest that any solution to the problems of many emerging economies would need to be multi-pronged. Structural policies will help, but there is an overwhelming need

1. Kohli (2016). This section follows chapter 12 of that book.
2. See www.imf.org/external/pubs/ft/dsa/mac.htm for a discussion of the methodology currently being utilized by the IMF and World Bank.
3. The econometric results are not presented here to preserve conciseness but can be provided by the authors on request. Exports of goods and services (in real terms) are regressed against terms of trade and world GDP, while imports are regressed against domestic income and terms of trade. The current account is projected as the difference between exports and imports. Revenue and expenditure projections are regressed against domestic GDP and terms of trade.

A structural fiscal rule would smooth public spending patterns over time and reduce the pro-cyclicality of public expenditures observed at present as governments adjust expenditure to correct for declines in revenue associated with export price reversals.

Box 1: Assessment of long-term fiscal and current account sustainability (cont.)

to pursue adequate macroeconomic policies, particularly in response to changes in terms of trade, including through more depreciated currencies than is the case at present.

Figure B1: Africa's external current account and fiscal balance (percent of GDP)

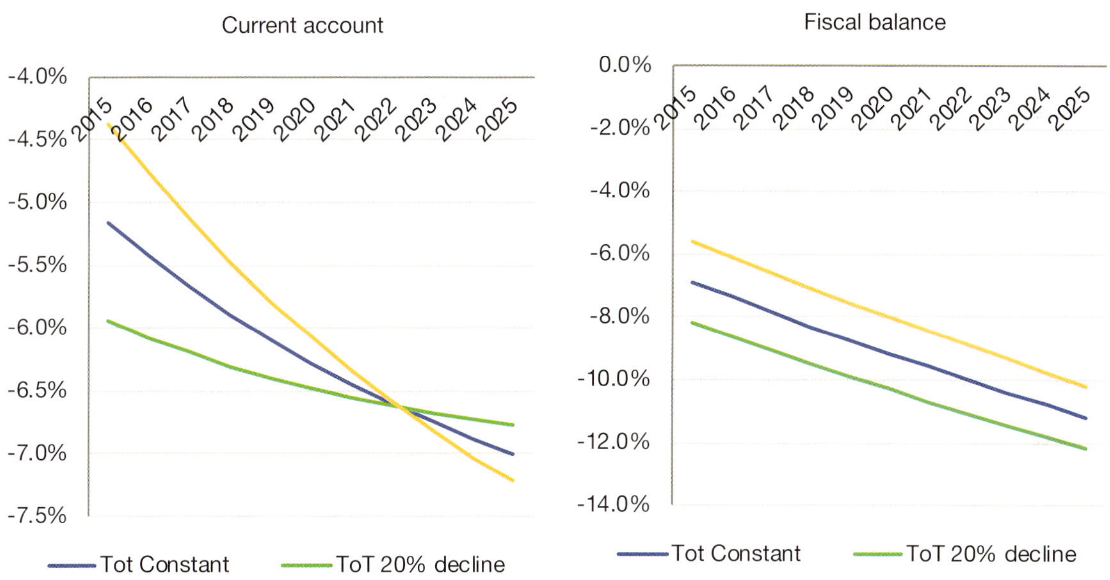

Source: Centennial Group International (2017)

based on long term trends and not only on current developments, would be optimal for these purposes. This initiative requires a predictable path for exports and a readiness by authorities to offset the deviations from this trend through fiscal policy, or a promotion of private stabilization schemes when production and trade are in the private sector.

The adoption of structural fiscal targets, as in Chile, would consolidate spending patterns by allowing better expenditure planning. A structural fiscal rule would smooth public spending patterns over time and reduce the pro-cyclicality of public expenditures observed at present as governments adjust expenditure to correct for declines in revenue associated with export price reversals. A structural fiscal rule reduces the impact of cyclical revenue fluctuations on expenditures as it allows for larger deficits and higher expenditures when the output gap is negative, and vice versa. It helps, in particular, to shield social spending and to protect the more vulnerable in times of crisis. Unfortunately, and contrary to the general experience in Africa today, this approach can only be started credibly during times of prosperity, i.e. high and/or increasing terms of trade. Thus, at this point, it is of the essence to make the necessary corrections to avoid an inordinate amount of public indebtedness at times of crisis. Some use of foreign financing is called for. The details of these policy

A balance has to be found between the welfare of future generations and the immediate needs to reduce poverty and invest in physical and human capital, which may well have a high social rate of return.

recommendations go beyond the scope of this chapter, but abundant material is available (Fajgenbaum 2012).

Efficient use of resource rents has an intergenerational dimension. Resource-rich countries need to make the trade-off between extracting the resource now and leaving it in the ground for future generations. Moreover, for a variety of reasons (including uncertain price developments), they may consider it advisable to extract now, especially when demand is expected to fall in the future, setting aside some of the proceeds in the form of financial assets for future use. The exhaustible nature of natural resources calls for intertemporal decisions about how much resource earnings to consume and invest and how much to save. A balance has to be found between the welfare of future generations and the immediate needs to reduce poverty and invest in physical and human capital, which may well have a high social rate of return. This tradeoff is especially acute for African countries where such expenditure is crucially needed. Spending resources beyond the economy's absorptive capacity will lead to the distortions typically associated with Dutch disease. Thus, for a lasting impact on development, part of the resource earnings needs to be saved, which has important implications for short- and long-term macroeconomic policies.

The prospects for commodities in the medium term[14]

This paper focuses mainly on the impact of commodity price fluctuations on Africa, both in the recent past and in the future. Previous sections have dealt with the behavior of prices, terms of trade, as well as income and GDP, particularly since the beginning the 21st century. While future developments are always subject to considerable uncertainty, it is crucial to provide an assessment of the future, to set the context in which African policy makers can establish adequate strategies. There are a number of respectable sources for this purpose. The recent writings of the IMF (WEO, April 2017 and earlier issues) and the World Bank (Commodity Markets Outlook, April 2016, and previous issues) capture the general trends. This discussion is principally based on their recent findings.

Share of world GDP

Commodity prices declined through mid-2016, and then recovered by year-end to the levels prevailing in 2015. maintaining the generally downward trend observed since early 2011 when they reached their peak. Diminishing growth prospects for emerging market economies, especially China, combined with abundant supply are putting downward pressure on the prices of most commodities, although the relative importance of each force differs across commodities. Oil prices have declined the most, on account of strong supply magnified by risk-behavior in financial markets. Metal prices have fallen owing mainly to slower demand growth from China. Food prices and agricultural raw materials have also declined as the result of record high harvests, although prices of selected food items have rebounded from unfavorable weather triggered by the waning El Niño.

The IMF's Primary Commodities Price Index declined by 56 percent from April 2011 to March 2016, and then recovered by 19 percent by the end of the year, for a total decline of 45 percent from April 2011 through end 2016. Oil prices decreased further, by 68 percent from April 2011 to March 2016, although there was a 29 percent recovery in recent months. Nonetheless, oil prices by end 2016, where 55 percent lower than in April 2011.

The weakness in oil prices is most recently explained by strong supply from members of the Organization of the Petroleum Exporting Countries (OPEC) and risk avoidance behavior in financial markets, with investors moving away from what they perceive to be riskier assets, including commodities and stocks. Even with the significant recovery, the fall in oil prices suggest that market expectations are for relatively low long term prices as is the case for natural gas and coal.

14. An expanded discussion is presented in Annex 3.

The consequences of stranded assets would be dramatic for coal and oil exporting countries that rely heavily on fossil fuel exports, as they would face heavy losses.

Metal prices declined by 44 percent in the last five years, after some correction in recent times, and are at about the same level as in 2009. Prices have been gradually declining because of a slowdown in investment in China, which uses roughly half of global metals. Metal prices may increase in 2017. However, futures prices point to continued low values, with rising uncertainty related to possibly weaker demand (especially from China) and stronger supply.

Prices of agricultural commodities leveled off since August 2015, and are down 32 percent from April 2011, with declines in most food items except sugar and a few oilseeds. El Niño has taken a toll on Asia and East Africa. International prices do not fully reflect the adverse weather shock, however, because of high prior inventory levels.

According to the World Bank, commodity prices in real terms are unlikely to recover from the levels observed in 2015-16. Fuel prices may increase but would remain below previous levels; this may be an overoptimistic assessment, as discussed below.

Longer term trends

The post-2000 commodity price increases, in part a reflection of demand growing faster than supply and of concerns about the security of supply, set in motion a boom in commodities exploration, investment and production, especially in mining and hydrocarbons. Less is known about the scale of investment that flowed into agriculture, but private sector investment in farmland in Africa increased significantly. With oil and metals price declines of 50-70 percent between 2011 and early 2016, many resource development projects have been delayed or put on hold. The result has been adverse consequences for commodity-exporting emerging market and developing economies facing shocks in the global economy.

After the United Nations' 2015 Climate Change Conference in Paris most countries around the globe have now firmly committed to reducing greenhouse gas emissions. At the heart of that implementation is the so-called energy transition, which consists of moving away from using fossil fuels (petroleum products, natural gas and coal) and toward clean energies to power the global economy. The technological forces unleashed by the anticipated public and private response to climate change may lead to a relatively swift transition, notwithstanding the potential delay implied by the current "low-for-long" fuel price environment. If such a scenario were to materialize, a number of emerging fuel exporters may see their mineral reserves and their concurrent investment assets become stranded or obsolete. The consequences of stranded assets would be dramatic for coal and oil exporting countries that rely heavily on fossil fuel exports, as they would face heavy losses.

The prolonged fall in metal prices is consistent with a typical commodity boom-and-bust cycle. High prices have led to downward adjustments on the demand side. Those adjustments have contributed to a gradual decline in metal prices since 2011. The lower investment will eventually reduce capacity, and lower production should eventually lead to a rebound in metal prices. The more prolonged the slump in metal prices, the sharper the likely eventual reversal. However, for the medium term, price prospects remain at best weak.

Over the next several years, the agricultural sector will adjust to lower prices for most farm commodities. For crops, production response to lower prices will lead to reduced planted acreage. In the livestock sector, lower feed costs will provide economic incentives for expansion. Following those near-term adjustments, long run developments for global agriculture reflect steady world economic growth and possibly continued global demand for biofuel feedstocks. Those factors combine to support longer run increases in demand. Most agricultural prices have fallen from recent high levels and are projected to fall further during the next few years, although they will recover somewhat in the long run, as presented in Table 5. Still, the prospects for increases in real prices are fairly low, at least during the next decade.

It is imperative for the African countries, be they highly concentrated exporters or more diversified economies, to focus on their macroeconomic sustainability.

Concluding remarks

The impact of terms of trade can be staggering - a decline of total disposable income and per capita income growth of half a percentage point for each one percentage point decline in terms of trade. The impact is divided equally between the pure decline in income because of lower prices, and the multiplier effect on real GDP because of its impact on demand. It is true that part of the impact will be defused because imports may decline as a consequence, with a smaller effect on the external current account than the reduction in export receipts. This may help in reducing the financing needs of individual countries. However, it clearly entails a reduction in disposable income and a below-par behavior of per capita income, with significant social, economic and political implications. The central issue as discussed here is related to the repeated occurrence of these events and countries' ability to withstand these shocks.

The evidence presented here is that there are long-term secular cycles. After a decade of affluence that was seen as permanent, the trend has reversed, and prospects are that the secular decline observed in recent years, as a minimum will not be reversed and might well continue. Countries throughout the region have reacted differently but in general have made an unsustainable use of borrowed resources and of their reserves, which have fallen dramatically.

It is imperative for the African countries, be they highly concentrated exporters or more diversified economies, to focus on their macroeconomic sustainability. Certainly, it is important to promote investment, both physical and in human capital. But it is also crucial to adjust the economy so as to attain a sustainable path, particularly in today's adverse external circumstances. Given the fragility of the fiscal positions and the mounting debt, aggravated by a weakening trend even in circumstances of moderate growth, actions in this field are of the essence.

Stabilization mechanisms and wealth management funds will need to be brought in to help consolidate the fiscal situation. Furthermore, monetary policy will need to be highly disciplined to avoid an acceleration of inflation and a weakening of the balance of payments that can only make the situation worse. Even though on average the currencies of African countries have depreciated in real terms in 2016, the authorities need to implement various measures to strengthen competitiveness in support of the recent devaluation efforts. The main message of this report is that time is of the essence if a sharp and disorderly adjustment process is to be avoided.

Annex 1: Country classification by export concentration

Table A1: Country classification by export concentration

	Concentration Index (2010-2014 average)	Primary Commodities (to total exports, 2014)	Primary Commodities excluding fuels (percentage of exports, 2014)	Concentration + primary comm. Index	Exceptional Classification	Export classification
Angola	0.96	0.99	0.3%	1.94		Highly concentrated
Guinea-Bissau	0.94	0.99	96.6%	1.93		Highly concentrated
Chad	0.88	0.99	4.9%	1.87		Highly concentrated
Congo	0.80	0.96	11.7%	1.76		Highly concentrated
Libya	0.80	0.95	0.7%	1.75		Highly concentrated
Nigeria	0.78	0.98	4.4%	1.77		Highly concentrated
Botswana	0.75	0.11	10.5%	0.86	Gold exporter	Highly concentrated
Gabon	0.72	0.89	23.7%	1.61		Highly concentrated
Equatorial Guinea	0.72	0.96	1.4%	1.67		Highly concentrated
Somalia	0.66	0.94	94.1%	1.60		Highly concentrated
Zambia	0.65	0.80	78.9%	1.45		Highly concentrated
Algeria	0.53	0.98	0.7%	1.51	High Commodity Share	Highly concentrated
Seychelles	0.49	0.91	86.8%	1.40	High Commodity %	Highly concentrated
Mauritania	0.47	0.94	85.1%	1.41	High Commodity %	Highly concentrated
Dem. Rep. of the Congo	0.42	0.95	80.2%	1.37	High Commodity %	Highly concentrated
Sudan	0.61	0.73	9.7%	1.34		Intermediate
Mali	0.55	0.42	39.6%	0.98		Intermediate
Comoros	0.53	0.45	45.4%	0.98		Intermediate
Sao Tome and Principe	0.51	0.70	69.9%	1.20		Intermediate
Burkina Faso	0.50	0.48	40.8%	0.98		Intermediate
Guinea	0.48	0.82	43.4%	1.30		Intermediate
Malawi	0.48	0.84	83.6%	1.32		Intermediate
Burundi	0.46	0.69	68.8%	1.15		Intermediate
Cabo Verde	0.43	0.77	69.4%	1.21		Intermediate
Rwanda	0.43	0.88	78.1%	1.32		Intermediate
Liberia	0.43	0.65	64.7%	1.08		Intermediate
Ghana	0.43	0.77	42.3%	1.19		Intermediate
Eritrea						Intermediate
Cameroon	0.42	0.90	89.7%	1.32		Intermediate
Niger	0.39	0.92	37.6%	1.31		Intermediate
Sierra Leone	0.39	0.72	34.8%	1.11	High Commodity %	Intermediate
Ethiopia	0.36	0.79	79.2%	1.15	High Commodity %	Intermediate

Table A1 (cont.): Country classification by export concentration

Côte d'Ivoire	0.35	0.88	78.7%	1.23	High Commodity %	Intermediate
Mozambique	0.34	0.78	58.0%	1.13	High Commodity %	Intermediate
Central African Republic	0.34	0.77	50.0%	1.11		Low
Lesotho	0.35	0.73	71.8%	1.08		Low
Gambia	0.33	0.06	6.3%	0.39		Low
Benin	0.31	0.73	72.6%	1.04		Low
Zimbabwe	0.29	0.74	59.6%	1.03		Low
Djibouti	0.27	0.72	60.8%	0.99		Low
Swaziland	0.25	0.56	46.8%	0.81		Low
Mauritius	0.24	0.44	43.0%	0.69		Low
Senegal	0.24	0.33	33.3%	0.57		Low
Madagascar	0.24	0.62	42.3%	0.86		Low
Namibia	0.23	0.66	63.6%	0.89		Low
Kenya	0.22	0.49	46.7%	0.71		Low
Togo	0.21	0.63	55.7%	0.84		Low
United Republic of Tanzania	0.20	0.50	34.2%	0.70		Low
Uganda	0.20	0.68	66.3%	0.88		Low
Egypt	0.19	0.66	65.1%	0.85		Low
Morocco	0.16	0.51	22.6%	0.67		Low
Tunisia	0.16	0.34	28.9%	0.50		Low
South Africa	0.15	0.24	12.4%	0.39		Low

	Main criterion: Concentration	Subsidiary criterion: High commodity percent & sum of share of commodities and concentration
Highly concentrated	.65 to higher	.90 and 1.35
Intermediate	.35 to .64	.75 and 1.10
Low	below .34	Lower

Source: UNCTAD (2017); Centennial Group International (2017)

Annex 2: Measurement of trading gains and losses

Gross domestic income measures the purchasing power of the total incomes generated by domestic production. It is a concept that exists only when real variables, including economic growth, are taken into consideration. When terms of trade change, there may be a significant divergence between the movements of GDP and real GDI. The difference between the change in GDP and disposable income, GDI, is generally described as the "trading gain" (or loss). The scope for trading gains and losses is substantial as a) imports and exports become increasingly large relative to GDP and b) the difference in the commodity composition of imports and exports grows.[1]

Domestic product, GDP, is calculated in volume terms in order to measure the real change that occurs from one period to another independent of price. Similarly, aggregates of income, GDI, are not broken down into quantity and price components. The effect of changes in the terms of trade for a specific economy and the rest of the world must be taken into account when moving from domestic product in volume terms to national income in real terms. GDP is no longer identical to domestic final expenditure as there is an impact on real income of changes in import and export prices. Incorporating the change in terms of trade into GDP is generally done by calculating the "trading gains and losses."

Trading gains or losses, T, is measured by the following expression:

$$T = \frac{X - M}{P} - \left\{\frac{X}{P_x} - \frac{M}{P_m}\right\} \qquad (1)$$

Where

- X = exports at current values
- M = imports at current values
- P_x = the price index for exports
- P_m = the price index for imports
- P = a price index based on some selected numeraire.

P_x, P_m, and P are all equal 1 in the base year. The term in brackets measures the trade balance calculated at the export and import prices of the reference year; the first term measures the actual current trade balance deflated by the numeraire price index. It is possible for these terms to have different signs.

As noted by the National Accounts Manual, there is an important choice to be made in the measurement of trading gains or losses: the selection of the price index P with which to deflate the current trade balance.[2] The literature on this topic is large but inconclusive, but there is general agreement that the choice of deflator, P, can sometimes make a substantial difference to the results. That the measurement of real GDI can be sensitive to the choice of P has prevented a consensus from being reached on this issue. The National Accounts Manual notes that trading gains or losses should be treated as an integral part of the System of National Accounts. The choice of appropriate deflator for the trade balance should depend on the particular circumstances of a country, and practical solutions are required, even with no consensus. No matter how defined, the formula to be used would be: GDP in volume or real terms plus the trading gain or loss resulting from changes in the terms of trade equals real GDI.

In discussing this issue, Reinsdorf (2009) at the US Department of Commerce, describes the best adjustment as follows: The difference between real GDI and real GDP can be decomposed into two key terms: the change in the terms of trade weighted by the average share of trade in GDP, and the change in the price of tradables (relative to the rest of the economy) weighted by the average share of the trade balance in GDP.[3]

1. This discussion draws heavily on European Commission, IMF, OECD, UN, and). *System of National Accounts 2008*; and Reinsdorf (2009), as well as material of the Australian Statistical office.

2. As described in European Commission et al. (2009): "If the prices of a country's exports rise faster (or fall more slowly) than the prices of its imports (that is, if its terms of trade improve) fewer exports are needed to pay for a given volume of imports... Thus, an improvement in the terms of trade makes it possible for an increased volume of goods and services to be purchased by residents out of the incomes generated by a given level of domestic production."

3. Estimates based on US national accounts data for 1974 to 2007 show significant terms of trade effects in many years. Trading gains subtract at least 0.21 percentage points from real GDI a quarter of the time, and that they add at least 0.18 percentage points a quarter of the time. Occasionally,

On that basis, the present discussion uses a simple formula, as follows:

$$dy^*/y^* = d(er^*(p_x{}^*x - p_m{}^*m))/dy^* \quad (2)$$

where dy/y is the difference between GDI and GDP, on the basis of changes in the terms of trade, and real exchange rates is er. In this presentation, the volume changes of x (exports) and m (imports) respectively are incorporated as part of GDP.

After manipulation, the operating formula for an annual change is

$$dy^*/y_0{}^* = (x_1/y_0)[(dp_x/p_x)-(dp_m/p_m)] + (ca_1/y_0)^*(drer/rer) \quad (2")$$

where rer is the real exchange rate denominated in local currency (appreciation entails a decline, and vice versa), and ca is the current account balance The relevant formula on a multi-year basis, i.e. based on the cumulative effect of terms of trade changes over time, for a three period horizon would be

$$dy_3{}^*/y_0{}^* = (1+(dy^*/y^*)_1)^*(1+(dy^*/y^*)_2)^*(1+(dy^*/y^*)_3)-1 \quad (3)$$

or in more general terms

$$dy_t{}^*/y_0{}^* = (\Pi_{1\ to\ t}(1+(dy_i{}^*/y_{i-1}{}^*))-1 \quad (4)$$

The result is the cumulative change of GDI relative to GDP, with regard to a base year. In this way the measurement captures the effect of the terms of trade over a period of time extending beyond a year. If a change occurs for one year only, the impact will be for that year alone. If the change extends for several years, the formula accounts for this effect over time.

---

however, the shocks are much larger. The petroleum price shocks that occurred at the end of 1973 and in 1980 subtracted more than a full percentage point from real GDI, and the one in the first half of 2008 in combination with rising prices of other imports subtracted almost 2 percentage points from the annualized growth rate of real GDI (Reinsdorf 2009).

Annex 3: The prospects for commodities in the medium term

Prospects in the next two years[1]

Commodity prices have recovered somewhat since mid-2016 reversing in part the downward trend observed since early 2011, when they reached their peak. Diminishing growth prospects for emerging market economies, especially China, combined with abundant supply put downward pressure on the prices of most commodities, although the relative importance of each force differs across commodities. Food prices and agricultural raw materials also declined as the result of record high harvest, although prices of selected food items have rebounded from unfavorable weather triggered by the waning El Niño (IMF 2016 and 2017)

The IMF's Primary Commodities Price Index increased by 15.5 percent from August 2016, the reference period for the October 2016 WEO, to March 2017. While energy and metals rallied, by 21.1 percent and 24 percent, respectively, food prices increased more modestly, by 5 percent. Oil prices e continued to increase, by 21 percent, following the agreement by OPEC members to cut oil production. Natural gas prices increased in Europe on account of supply tightening and higher oil prices. Coal prices rallied, by 21.0 percent, following government-led reductions in coal production in China and outages in Australia that affected production and shipment.

The recent reversal in oil prices has been explained by a strong supply response to low prices in the US, and the recent efforts by members of the Organization of the Petroleum Exporting Countries (OPEC) and others to curtail production and more willingness to take risks on the part of investors as conditions tightened. Even with the significant recovery in the recent past, oil prices have not reacted significantly to geopolitical tensions in the Middle East, suggesting that market expectations are for low long term prices. Moreover, the availability of medium level-cost energy in North America easily puts a limit to the likely increase. Natural gas and coal prices have also increased some, as the former is linked to oil prices, including through oil-indexed contract prices, but with a lag, and coal prices have been affected by curtailments of production in China.

Oil supply has been quite resilient in spite of low prices, mostly on account of strong OPEC and Russian production, as well as the Islamic Republic of Iran's return to world oil markets. However, the slowdown in shale oil production in the United States suggests that the relative resilience of shale oil production, due to the dramatic operational efficiency gains that have prevailed during the past year, is coming to an end. Oil futures contracts suggest average annual prices of $50 a barrel or more in 2017. There remains substantial uncertainty around the baseline assumptions for oil prices. Relatively high inventory levels and a rapid response from U.S. shale producers should limit the scope for a sharp price adjustment in the near future.

Metal prices declined by half in the five years ended in mid-2016, but rose by 23.6 percent since August 2016 and are at about the same level as in 2009. Prices had been gradually declining because of a slowdown and a shift away from commodity intensive investment in China, which uses roughly half of global metals. Iron ore was one of the best performing metals in 2016, almost doubling in. On the demand side, metal consumption in China, which accounts for half of global demand, rebounded in 2016 in response to the authorities' policies in support of credit growth. The Chinese authorities have also cut production of outdated factories. On the supply side, the declining investment in, and closure of, high-cost and high-polluting mining operations have driven price increases in iron ore, nickel, tin, zinc, and copper. However, overall excess capacity will probably put downward pressure on prices in many base metals.

Prices of agricultural commodities declined by 32 percent in the last five years, with declines in most food items. The agriculture index, which consists of food, beverages, and agricultural raw materials prices, has increased by 4.3

1. Based on IMF (2017); IMF. (2016). Primary Commodity Prices Database.; and World Bank. (2016c). *World Commodity Outlook, April 2016*. Washington: World Bank.

percent since August 2016. Although prices of palm oil, tea, and rubber have increased significantly, prices of rice and cocoa beans have decreased. Wheat prices reached an 11-year low in December 2016, but have since somewhat recovered. Overall, wheat prices have increased by 15.2 percent since August 2016. Maize prices have increased, although they remain near historical lows. The global stock-to-use ratios of wheat and maize remain significantly above the 10-year average, indicating that markets are well supplied. Soybean prices have remained broadly unchanged on account of continued strength in animal protein demand countering favorable supply conditions. Sugar and palm oil prices have increased because of a drought in India and Malaysia, likely caused by El Niño. El Niño has also taken a toll on East Africa. International prices do not fully reflect the adverse weather shock, however, because of high prior inventory levels. For example, Ethiopia suffered from its worst drought in 30 years. Unusually dry weather in North Africa is also likely to reduce harvests significantly, including for cereals. For the year 2016 prices rose by 7 percent.

Longer term trends

The post-2000 commodity price increases, in part a reflection of demand growing faster than supply and concerns about the security of supply, set in motion a boom in commodities exploration, investment, and production, especially in mining and hydrocarbons. Less is known about the scale of investment that flowed into agriculture, but private sector investment in farmland in Africa increased significantly. With oil and metals price declines of 50-70 percent between 2011 and early 2016, many resource development projects have been delayed or put on hold. Lead times—the time it takes from resource discovery to production—are a critical issue in many countries as these periods are associated with heightened macroeconomic vulnerabilities. This raises concerns about the ability of commodity-exporting emerging market and developing economies to withstand shocks in the global economy.

Discoveries

Several major discoveries transformed country prospects in Sub-Saharan Africa and Latin America and the Caribbean. Since 2000, 120 "giant" oil and gas fields (fields with recoverable reserves of more than 500 million barrels of oil equivalent) have been discovered world-wide, with estimated "proved plus probable" reserves of almost 250 billion barrels of oil. The fields are located in seven clusters, two of which are in Africa, mostly offshore in East and West Africa. In Tanzania alone (which accounts for almost 7 percent of these reserves) there have been 13 giant oil and gas discoveries. Other major discoveries are in Kenya, Madagascar, Mozambique and Uganda, as well as in six countries in West Africa and in the Gulf of Guinea. Another major frontier for giant oil and gas fields has emerged in the Bay of Bengal in South Asia.

Lead times from discovery to production

Bringing discoveries to actual production is a process that requires large upfront and sustained investment that varies across regions and time. Currently, there is high uncertainty about prices, as well as macroeconomic and policy environments.

- *Oil and gas*: Conventional discoveries can take 30 to 40 years to develop, but lead times for giant oil and gas discoveries can be shorter. For oil deposits, such as shale, the lead times are much shorter (2 to 3 years), a reflection of technological improvements and reduced entry barriers for small, agile firms. Monetizing discoveries in natural gas is harder than in oil because the former require investment in transport infrastructure (in addition to drilling) as well as long-term contractual arrangements with end-users (Hurdeman 2014).
- *Mining*: The time to develop resources ranges from a few years to decades, depending on the type of mineral, the size and grade of the deposit, financing conditions, country factors, availability of key inputs like electricity and commodity prices. For example, resource development takes an average of 10 years for gold but more than 15 years for base metals such as zinc, lead, copper and nickel. Given that resource development, production and revenue streams take place over decades, with substantial sunk costs along the way, longer term commodity price prospects are critical in deciding whether to develop a discovery into production. In 2016, the outlook for an era of low commodity prices has already set back many resource development projects. Ambitious improvements in business climates along with better and more predictable macroeconomic policies will be needed to offset these obstacles to resource development. Governments seeking to develop natural resources

may consider delaying new initiatives until the price outlook turns more favorable.

Table A2, prepared by the World Bank, shows that in general commodity prices in real terms are unlikely to recover from the levels observed in 2015-16. Fuel prices alone might increase but would remain well below previous levels. This may be an overoptimistic assessment, as discussed below.

Savings and investment

After the United Nations' 2015 Climate Change Conference in Paris most countries around the globe have now firmly committed to reducing their greenhouse gas

Table A2: Commodity price index forecasts (2010=100)

Commodity	2013	2014	2015	2016	2017	2018	2019	2020	2025
Nominal US dollars (2010=100)									
Energy	127.4	118.3	64.9	55.1	68.6	74.4	77.8	81.4	102.6
Non-energy commodities	101.7	97.0	82.4	79.7	81.4	83.2	85.0	86.8	97.3
Agriculture	106.3	102.7	89.3	89.2	90.5	91.9	93.3	94.7	103.0
Beverages	83.3	101.8	93.5	91.7	91.1	90.6	90.2	89.7	87.7
Food	115.6	107.4	90.9	92.4	93.8	95.2	96.7	98.2	106.8
Oils and meals	115.9	109.0	85.2	89.3	91.1	93.0	94.9	96.9	107.7
Grains	128.2	103.9	88.8	82.8	85.2	87.8	90.4	93.2	108.8
Other food	103.9	108.4	100.3	105.2	105.0	104.8	104.6	104.5	103.8
Raw materials	95.4	91.9	83.3	80.2	82.2	84.4	86.6	88.9	101.7
Timber	102.6	104.9	96.1	91.1	93.8	96.6	99.5	102.5	118.8
Other raw materials	87.6	77.7	69.3	68.2	69.5	70.9	72.4	73.9	82.9
Fertilizers	113.7	100.5	95.4	74.8	76.7	78.7	80.7	82.8	94.4
Metals and minerals[1]	90.8	84.8	66.9	60.8	63.3	65.9	68.4	71.0	86.0
Base metals[2]	90.3	89.0	73.6	66.4	70.1	73.0	75.8	78.7	95.6
Precious metals	115.1	101.1	90.6	97.4	95.4	93.5	91.7	89.9	81.6
Constant 2010 US dollars (2010=100), deflated by the MUV Index									
Energy	120.1	111.7	61.4	51.2	62.7	66.9	68.9	71.0	82.3
Non-energy commodities	95.9	91.6	78.0	74.1	74.4	74.8	75.2	75.6	78.1
Agriculture	100.2	97.0	84.5	82.9	82.7	82.6	82.6	82.6	82.6
Beverages	78.5	96.1	88.5	85.2	83.3	81.5	79.8	78.2	70.3
Food	109.0	101.4	86.0	85.9	85.7	85.6	85.6	85.6	85.7
Oils and meals	109.3	103.0	80.6	83.0	83.3	83.6	84.0	84.4	86.4
Grains	120.9	98.1	84.0	76.9	77.9	79.0	80.1	81.2	87.3
Other food	98.0	102.4	94.9	97.8	96.0	94.3	92.6	91.0	83.2
Raw materials	90.0	86.8	78.8	74.5	75.1	75.9	76.6	77.4	81.6
Timber	96.7	99.0	90.9	84.7	85.8	86.9	88.1	89.3	95.3
Other raw materials	82.6	73.4	65.6	63.4	63.5	63.8	64.1	64.4	66.5
Fertilizers	107.2	94.9	90.3	69.5	70.1	70.8	71.5	72.1	75.7
Metals and minerals[1]	85.6	80.1	63.4	56.5	57.9	59.3	60.6	61.9	69.0
Base metals[2]	85.2	84.1	69.7	61.6	64.0	65.7	67.1	68.6	76.7
Precious metals	108.5	95.5	85.8	90.5	87.2	84.1	81.2	78.3	65.4
Inflation indexes, 2010=100									
MUV index[3]	106.1	105.9	105.7	107.6	109.4	111.2	112.9	114.8	124.7
percent change per annum	-1.4	-0.2	-0.2	1.9	1.7	1.6	1.6	1.6	1.7
US GDP deflator	105.4	106.9	108.5	110.7	113	115.3	117.6	120	132.6
percent change per annum	1.5	1.3	1.6	2	2	2	2	2	2

1. Base metals plus iron ore; 2. Includes aluminum, copper, lead, nickel, tin, and zinc; 3. MUV is the unit value index of manufacture reports.
Source: World Bank (2016c)

emissions through the Intended Nationally Determined Contributions (INDCs). At the heart of that implementation is the so-called energy transition, which consists of moving away from using fossil fuels (petroleum products, natural gas and coal) and toward clean energies to power the global economy. While the energy transition is at an early stage, with important differences across countries, it is at a critical juncture. If the energy intensity of economic activity does not fall or if countries in the developing world do not adopt state-of-the-art technology for coal-powered plants to lower the carbon intensity of their electricity generation, global warming will worsen, and all will have to pay. One important lesson from earlier energy transitions is that these transitions take time to complete. However, the technological forces unleashed by the anticipated public and private response to climate change may lead to a relatively swifter transition this time, notwithstanding the potential delay implied by the current "low-for-long" fossil fuel price environment.

If such a scenario were to materialize, a number of emerging fuel exporters might find that their mineral reserves and their concurrent investment assets become stranded or, put differently, obsolete. The consequences of stranded assets would be dramatic for coal and oil companies and exporting countries that rely heavily on fossil fuel exports, as they would face heavy losses. Oil-exporting countries have attempted to diversify their economies away from oil, but this has proved challenging. Nevertheless, opportunities exist. Many high-income countries are reducing greenhouse gas emissions already and are committed to continue doing so. Consumption of fossil fuels by advanced economies can, therefore, be expected to continue to decrease. Though large economies account for the bulk of current emissions, emerging markets will continue to drive the growth of future emissions. In contrast to the falling emissions intensity of the advanced economies, emerging market and developing economies remain heavily reliant on coal, and their consumption of fossil fuels will continue to rise. However, as they become more dominant in the world economy, pressures for them to reduce demand for fossil fuels will increase. Already, China has adopted an ambitious plan to derive a significant fraction of its future energy needs from renewables. Shifting from coal to gas in electricity generation can help significantly in this regard. Still, while these trends are generally desirable and should continue to be promoted, fuel exporters will lose with considerable consequences for their future growth and welfare prospects.

Metals

Metal prices have been declining since 2011, and remain relatively low notwithstanding a recent recovery. The prolonged fall in metal prices is consistent with a typical commodity boom-and-bust cycle. Indeed, after a period of high metal prices during the 2000s, investment and, in turn, capacity in the sector have increased substantially. At the same time, high prices have led to downward adjustments on the demand side. Those adjustments have contributed to a gradual decline in metal prices since 2011, which has led to less investment in the sector due to the lower expected profits. The lower investment will eventually reduce capacity, and lower production should eventually lead to a rebound in metal prices. The more prolonged the slump in metal prices, the sharper the likely eventual reversal. However, for the medium term, price prospects remain at best weak.

From an economic point of view, iron ore is by far the most important base metal, with a $225 billion annual industry in terms of global sales. The top iron-ore-producing country is China, which accounts for about half of the world's production, followed by Australia and Brazil. Copper is the second-most important base metal by value—accounting for roughly a $130 billion industry annually. Chile is the largest producer, followed by China and Peru. Copper prices have been more transparent than those for iron ore because copper futures markets and London Metal Exchange settlements are used as benchmarks. The third most important base metal is aluminum (an annual $90 billion industry). Large producers of aluminum are located where electricity is cheap and abundant. The largest producer is China, followed by Russia, Canada and the United Arab Emirates. Aluminum prices are the most stable among those for metals because of the reliance on electricity in its production. The fourth most important base metal is nickel (accounting for a $40 billion market), which is used for alloys such as stainless steel. Nickel ore is mined in several countries, including the Philippines. Futures markets point to lower nickel prices, though the decline is projected to bottom out. On the demand side, the Chinese economy is projected to slow further. On the supply side, the drop in investment is unlikely to lead to a substantial price rebound in the near future. Low energy prices have in fact helped reduce mining and refining costs, including those for copper, steel and aluminum.

The secular expansion of the frontier of metal extraction to Latin America and Africa as a result of improvements in the investment climate is unlikely to revert to any great extent. Instead, those improvements should continue steadily. Thus, ample supply is likely to continue pushing metal prices down. The balance between weaker demand and a steady increase in supply suggests that, given the existing cost structure, metal markets are likely to experience a continued glut, leading to a "low-for-long" price scenario.

Agriculture

Over the next several years, the agricultural sector will adjust to lower prices for most farm commodities. For crops, production response to lower prices will result in reduced acreage planted. In the livestock sector, lower feed costs will provide economic incentives for expansion, although the timing of expansion for beef will be delayed by the building of beef cow inventories and biological lags. Following those near-term adjustments, long run developments for global agriculture reflect steady world economic growth and, possibly, continued global demand for biofuel feedstocks. Those factors combine to support longer run increases in consumption, trade and prices of agricultural products. Reflecting these market adjustments and price projections, export values will grow over the medium term. Developing countries are projected to have a growing role in the global economy and food demand. As incomes rise in developing countries and more consumers enter the middle class, diets tend to diversify, with increased consumption of meat, dairy products and processed foods (including vegetable oils).

World production of agricultural products is projected to increase more rapidly than world population, enabling a small increase in average world per capita use of most agricultural products. During this period, world trade in agricultural products is projected to maintain strong growth. Most agricultural prices have fallen from recent high levels and are projected to fall further during the next few years although they will recover somewhat in the long run. Still, the prospects for increases in real prices are fairly low, at least during the next decade and possibly beyond. World agricultural production is projected to continue rising in the coming decade as yield growth through technological enhancements and area expansion continue. The growth rate for world average crop yields has been slowing for nearly two decades and is projected to slow further in the next ten years. Reduced public funding for research and development over the last 25 years may have contributed to this slowdown. Increasing demand for higher quality food grain varieties can result in lower yields for specific countries. Water constraints in some countries are also impeding the expansion of irrigation. Where irrigation water is pumped from deep wells, the cost of pumping is projected to continue to increase due to falling water tables.

Chapter 7

Economic Diversification of African Economies

James Bond

Africa has not industrialized

With a few exceptions (Tunisia and Mauritius in particular), two decades of economic growth in Africa have not led to significant structural change of the economy. Compared to other developing regions of the world, Africa remains weak in terms of industrialization. By industrialization we mean more than just the "smokestack industries" comprising mining, manufacturing, utilities and construction. Modern industry comprises that part of an outward export-oriented economy based on manufacturing, as well as agro-industrial value chains and the tradable services sector (e.g. call centers, financial services). These all share the same firm-level characteristics and react to business environment parameters in similar ways.[1]

Africa's lack of industrialization is reflected in its trade patterns. From a trade perspective, Africa is the continent least integrated into the world economy. In 2015, the African continent (population: 1.186 billion people, or 16 percent of the world's population) represented around 2.9 percent of world trade (goods and services), less than France (population: 65 million people).[2] Intra-African trade is around 12.8 percent of the continent's GDP, compared to 68.6 percent in the EU or 53.4 percent in Asia.[3] African countries are thus not interconnected among themselves via trade links, and for the most part most have stronger trading relationships with their former colonial masters in Europe or with China than with each other.

A further indicator of the low rate of industrialization can be seen in export patterns. Africa's exports currently focus to a large extent on natural resources and not on the modern definition of industrial goods and services. Commodities represented about 76 percent of African exports, a proportion that had peaked in 2011 at 82 percent, as prices and output went up sharply over the last decade. With a few exceptions, Africa does not for the most part export processed or semi-processed natural resources either. Although processing of natural resources (bauxite into aluminum, oil into petroleum products, iron ore into pig-iron, etc.) does not create much value added, it does enable the development of associated industries around such installations ("clusters") and provides on-the-job training and skills enhancement for workers. Africa does not benefit from this.

Africa's recent economic growth has thus for the most part resulted from the combination of the effect of rising worldwide commodity prices over the past two decades (due China's export-led growth), which has since moderated, and from the move of low-skilled labor in many African countries from extremely low productivity subsistence agriculture in rural areas, into low- or moderate productivity services for domestic consumers. Such domestic services are generally delivered through the informal economy in urban areas and do not deliver skills enhancement, employment security or access to the modern economy, notably access to the financial sector or to healthcare[4]. Africa's economic growth has not led to the creation of "good jobs" and has not appreciably brought down poverty, largely because Africa has not yet embarked on an export-led growth pattern involving industrialization.[5]

Africa's pattern of growth without structural change goes against a widely-observed trend of industrialization around the world – the move of labor from low value-added agriculture into export-oriented industrial sectors – which has long been the model for development, most recently in Asia. In almost all developing countries the share of manufacturing in GDP increases as per capita income increases. However, in almost all African countries, the share of manufacturing is below what the per capita GDP would lead one to expect (Table 1). For two decades, African labor has moved out of subsistence agriculture into more productive

1. Definition taken from: Newman, C. et al. (2016). *Made in Africa – Learning to Compete in Industry*. Washington: Brookings Institute.
2. UNCTAD (2017)
3. WTO. (2013), quoted in ICA. (2015). *Infrastructure Financing Trends in Africa – 2015*. Abidjan: Infrastructure Consortium for Africa.
4. Such activities do not for the most part pay taxes either.
5. Some countries of course "buck" this trend: notably Mauritius, Morocco, South Africa and Tunisia. But the above summary is broadly in line with the vast majority of African countries.

Diversification into export sectors, including intra-Africa exports, will create jobs and reduce poverty, as well as lay the foundations of a long-term growth platform less dependent on natural resources and less vulnerable to terms of trade shocks.

Table 1: Africa's manufacturing deficit, 2014

Share of GDP (%)	Agriculture	Manufacturing	Construction	Mining and utilities	Services
Middle-income developing economies	16.8	16.5	7.1	8.7	50.9
Africa low income	30.3	8.3	7.8	10.2	43.4
Africa middle income	5.4	8.5	6.8	26.1	53.3

Source: UNCTAD (2017)

employment but not into industry, and not into sectors that export.

This means that while African countries do differ from one another in terms of economic structure – for example, in resource-rich countries the primary sector dominates -- they are almost all characterized by an underdeveloped manufacturing sector and a large unsophisticated service sector providing mostly low value-added services for the domestic economy only. (Tunisia and Mauritius are striking counter-examples of this, as shall be demonstrated throughout this paper.) The overwhelming majority of young African workers are engaged in informal self-employment or in micro-enterprises, in jobs that do not provide them with high wages, good working conditions and skills enhancement. Industrial sectors on the other hand, deliver employment that provides secure income and enhances skills, and is the best route to sustained poverty reduction because of its distributive effect in the economy.

Africa is the fastest growing continent, and the one where the rural-urban migration is most pronounced. African economies need urgently therefore to diversify their economies in order to create jobs to absorb the cohorts of young people leaving the land. Diversification into export sectors, including intra-Africa exports, will create jobs and reduce poverty, as well as lay the foundations of a long-term growth platform less dependent on natural resources and less vulnerable to terms of trade shocks.

Industrialization as part of Africa's development history

At the eve on independence few African countries had strong industrial sectors. Exceptions were Egypt, to a lesser extent, Algeria and South Africa. Other countries found themselves with trade patterns almost exclusively focused on exports of raw materials and agricultural produce, and imports of manufactured goods. There was a sense among the emerging leaders of the soon-to-be independent countries that they needed to transform the economies by reducing dependence on imports of manufactures and creating an indigenous manufacturing sector at home. Since independence, Africa has undergone three broad phases of industrialization policy to try to diversify the economy.

First phase: State-led industrialization (1960-1985)

Central role of the state

At independence, many countries undertook a strategy of state-led industrialization and import substitution. The leaders of the newly independent countries had for the most part similar views on the importance played by industrialization in the development process and shared the desire to move away from subsistence agriculture to a modern industrial state. The central element of this strategy was the development of large-scale manufacturing industries, in most cases owned and managed by the state. Such industries are capital intensive and require quite specific skills which were often not available in the

Mauritius became independent only in 1968, by which time the weaknesses of state-led industrial policies implemented in other African countries were becoming apparent. The government therefore sought local and foreign private investment into sectors geared toward exports.

domestic labor market. This industrial policy, the economic orthodoxy of the day, was designed around substituting for existing imports of manufactures in the domestic market rather than providing exports to international markets. Governments thus instituted protective measures on the local market such as import tariffs, non-tariff barriers (e.g. quantitative restrictions), and currency controls, as a way of achieving economic independence.

The state thus became the central actor in the industrialization strategy, both by ownership and operation of assets through newly created state-owned enterprises (SOEs), and by protective policies put in place around the new industries. It should be noted that in adopting these policies, the new African leaders were emulating the prevailing conventional wisdom concerning industrialization and economic development followed in Europe and elsewhere, where there had been a significant move toward a more central role for the state during and following post-World War II reconstruction.

Country examples

Examples of such state-led development were Ghana, where the state under President Nkrumah invested heavily in infrastructure and manufacturing, including producer goods (electrical and machinery industries). Other countries such as Tanzania, Uganda and Nigeria followed similar patterns. Apartheid South Africa also followed this path to some extent despite its already strong private sector, with the creation of strategic industries, including for example the manufacture of petroleum products from the country's abundant coal resources through a state-owned entity SASOL. Except for South Africa, these economic policies generally received both support and financing from the international donor community.

Some countries did not follow this model to the same degree. Examples are Kenya and Côte d'Ivoire, where the state had a smaller role and the private sector was allowed to flourish outside so-called strategic industries. Both built strong domestic private sectors based on exports of agricultural commodities: for Kenya, tea and later, cut flowers and vegetables; for Côte d'Ivoire, cacao and coffee by small-scale farmers. These sectors have remained strong today and still form the backbone of the economy of these two countries.

On the other hand, other countries followed an even stiffer centralized economy approach. Examples are Madagascar after the revolution of 1972 and institution of the Ratsiraka government of 1975, which nationalized most of the economy and instituted a North Korea-type centralized economy; Ethiopia, which after the 1974 Dergue revolution nationalized most privately owned manufacturing enterprises; and Mozambique, which after the Frelimo takeover from the Portuguese in 1975 nationalized many enterprises (which had until then been Portuguese-owned) and instituted import controls. In all three cases, long-lasting damage to the economic fabric ensued and per capita GDP plummeted. This was associated with increases in poverty and child malnutrition, and reduced live expectancy.

Success stories

Finally, a small number of countries did not follow this model at all. Mauritius became independent only in 1968, by which time the weaknesses of state-led industrial policies implemented in other African countries were becoming apparent. The government therefore sought local and foreign private investment into sectors geared toward exports. An export processing zone (EPZ) was created which offered duty-free entry of inputs and free repatriation of capital, and the government provided essential infrastructure and plant locations to increase competitiveness. It targeted first the sugar industry (Mauritius has the right climate for cultivating sugar cane), benefiting from the EU sugar protection and African, Caribbean and Pacific Group of States (ACP) import preferences; then, as these advantages began to decline, it moved into textiles and tourism; and finally, into IT and back-office financial services. This strategy has been very effective and has conferred on Mauritius the highest 50-year growth rate of any of the

By the 1970s, it was becoming clear across the world that excessive protection of domestic markets and the central role of the state in the economy imposed important costs on the economy in terms of reduced welfare and economic growth.

countries in Africa, pulling the country into the realm of upper middle income countries.

For its part, Tunisia instituted a dual economy that combined import substitution and export promotion, with an offshore sector dominated by private investors (often foreign) geared toward exports, and an onshore sector shielded from competition and regulated by the state. The offshore sector focused on the nearby European markets (notably France) while the onshore sector consisted of many small factories producing simple consumer goods for the local market. Heavy industry and the infrastructure sectors (transport, electricity, water, telecoms) were state owned. The two sectors diverged significantly in terms of labor productivity, with much higher productivity in the offshore sector.

Although in hindsight, these policies of state-led industrialization and protection from import competition were unlikely to succeed, it should be noted that in many cases newly independent African countries initially experienced a boom. Between 1965 and 1970 manufacturing output grew by more than 7 percent per year, and in some countries, by close to 10 percent per year (Tanzania, Uganda). However, this state-led industrialization policy was not financially sustainable in the long term and by 1975, economic growth in Africa had fallen back and production capacity became underutilized. By the end of the period (1985) manufacturing growth slumped and in some countries turned negative (Ghana, Nigeria and Tanzania). In some cases, the manufacturing sector was producing goods with negative value-added, i.e. the cost of intermediate inputs (and thus the domestic sales price) exceeded the border price for the same product. Countries were faced with foreign exchange shortages and loss of fiscal and monetary control. Only Tunisia and Mauritius, with their outward private sector orientation, were able to sustain the pace of industrial growth.

Second phase: Structural adjustment (1985 – 2000)

By the 1970s, it was becoming clear across the world that excessive protection of domestic markets and the central role of the state in the economy imposed important costs on the economy in terms of reduced welfare and economic growth. Moreover, Africa's prevailing industrialization policy, which was very capital intensive, could no longer be financed. Over the following decade, a set of economic policies known as "structural adjustment" were elaborated by the IMF, the World Bank and the donor community[6]. The specific policies proposed depended on country circumstances, but they included in particular:

- Trade liberalization
- Introduction of a competitive exchange rate
- Privatization of state owned enterprises
- Greater fiscal discipline, with public expenditures focused on human capital and essential infrastructure
- Promotion of foreign direct investment
- Deregulation

Very quickly these policies spread to Africa. By 1979, Senegal turned to the donor community for a stabilization and structural adjustment program, followed by Ghana in 1983. By 1988 eighteen countries had initiated macro-economic stabilization and structural adjustment programs with the IMF and World Bank and a further fourteen obtained support from the donor community for sector-specific adjustment programs. Over the course of the period (1985-2000) over thirty African countries adopted externally financed adjustment programs focusing on exchange rate and trade policy reforms, and others undertook internal adjustment without external support. State-led industrialization based on import protection was essentially at an end.

Privatization of state owned enterprises became a key part of the adjustment program. Privatization had a dual objective: first, to reduce pressures on the budget and create fiscal space for the government to invest in

6. This set of policies has since been termed the "Washington Consensus."

By 2000, almost all African countries had instituted a set of more open economic policies that included trade liberalization and exchange rate reform.

human capital and essential infrastructure; and second, to improve economic efficiency in the production process by introducing skills, techniques and financing from the private sector. In cases where there was no private investor interest, state owned enterprises were shut down.

Structural adjustment dramatically improved economic management in the countries concerned, with major improvements in fiscal deficits and freeing up of currencies. Trade was liberalized and the balance sheets of most governments were slimmed down to more manageable proportions through privatization. Quantitative restrictions were replaced by tariffs and budgetary processes became much more transparent and rational. However, structural adjustment, despite the name, did not lead to significant structural change. Most countries experienced a short burst of economic growth, but increased competitive pressures from abroad, the absence of appropriate skills and the scarcity of debt financing soon impacted the former state owned enterprises (now often privatized) which in some cases were operating at around 10 percent of capacity, and industrial output plummeted further. By the late 1990s many state-owned enterprises in Ghana, Nigeria and Tanzania were shut down awaiting privatization or liquidation. Mauritius and Tunisia, with their existing competitive manufacturing sectors, avoided this trend, and Kenya, Uganda and Tanzania were less effected (in part because of the strong private sectors of the former two countries).

An unfortunate negative outcome of the structural adjustment process was the reduction in funding going to public education, healthcare and infrastructure, the consequence of imposing stricter fiscal management. This has had the long-term effect of reducing investment in human capital and in infrastructure over the period and beyond, which has resulted in a weak skills base – particularly among cohorts who normally would normally be at their most productive in today's economy – and inadequate infrastructure. Two decades of lack of maintenance have degraded road systems, allowed rail networks to fall into disrepair and led to widespread shortages of electricity. Poor skills and infrastructure add to the cost structure of Africa's firms and reduce their competitiveness on international markets.

In hindsight, structural adjustment – by which we mean putting in place a set of rational economic policies – was unavoidable, but certainly not enough to achieve structural change in the economy.

Current phase: Investment climate reform (2000-Present)

By 2000, almost all African countries had instituted a set of more open economic policies that included trade liberalization and exchange rate reform. Fiscal deficits were beginning to improve and continent-wide, inflation had come down. Africa started to see positive per capita economic growth. But other than in a small number of countries the continent had not seen the development of an indigenous private sector-led industrial sector, and exports have remained focused on natural resources.

In an effort to attract foreign investors for the creation of manufacturing and service sector firms, countries began to take a closer look at their investment climate[7]. A number of very specific micro-economic policies were set in place to streamline business practices and regulation. Most African countries have instituted such investment climate reforms over the past decade and a half. In Kenya, for example, an investment climate program is in place to improve electric power supply, liberalize and streamline regulations of private firms, and introduce fiscal reforms. Ethiopia's Industrial Development Strategy, which dates from 2003, seeks to provide macroeconomic stability, improve access to finance, provide improved infrastructure and upgrade the country's skills base. In Senegal, the government instituted its Accelerated Growth Strategy in 2005 with similar policies; Mozambique followed suit in 2007 and Uganda in 2008. Even Mauritius and Tunisia

7. Defined as macro stability and openness; good governance and strong institutions; skills base; and quality and cost of infrastructure services.

Taking a leaf out of the book of successful East Asian economies, as well as from the experience of successful African industrializers like Mauritius, the need for a more interventionist industrial policy in Africa is becoming apparent.

implemented investment climate reforms to further improve their business environments.

Investment climate reform is still underway across Africa, and it is difficult at this stage to provide a definitive view of its efficacy. For sure, there have been improvements in the business environment across the continent, and economic growth has been sustained. However, it does not seem to have dramatically changed the structure of African economies, nor provide for the development of industrial sectors such as manufactures and tradable services. Most of the reform measures have been incremental, enabling countries to improve by one or two positions on the Doing Business table at most. African investment climates are for the most part so unattractive that to really influence potential investors, policy-makers cannot simply streamline the current system. The entire regulatory framework needs to be redesigned from the ground up.

Unlike other regions of the world like East Asia, there has therefore not been a major push of foreign investors into creating stand-alone industries nor integration into global value chains on the continent. Moreover, growth in African manufacturing output has remained below overall GDP growth over the past decade, indicating that if anything, Africa continues to undergo de-industrialization.

After half a century Africa is back where it started. In terms of industrial development, African countries have broadly ended up in 2016 where they found themselves at independence. But economic circumstances on the continent and across the globe have changed. Notable differences in African economies compared to half century ago are, first, much improved macroeconomic management; second, business regulations that are significantly more rational and business friendly (although more could be done on this front); and third, African infrastructure finds itself in a severely deteriorated condition due to lack of maintenance and replacement. Moreover, skills of African workers remain woefully below what an industrial sector would require, a result both of underperforming education systems and the lack of incentives for workers to acquire useful skills.

Increasingly, the view is emerging that the current trend in industrial policy in African countries – improvement of the business climate to improve the attractiveness of the country for private investors – is not enough for industrialization. The orthodox economic laissez-faire policies implemented over the past two decades have not delivered on significant private investment in manufacturing nor development of the industrial sectors and linkages to global value chains. Taking a leaf out of the book of successful East Asian economies, as well as from the experience of successful African industrializers like Mauritius, the need for a more interventionist industrial policy in Africa is becoming apparent. But the question remains, what should this interventionist policy look like?

Reasons for lack of industrialization in Africa

There are several specific reasons for Africa's unusual pattern of growth over the last two decades, which have prevented the development of strongly outward-focused industrial sectors. Some of these obstacles have been or are being addressed in ongoing investment climate reforms, while others have not received the attention they deserve.

- **Country size**. Africa has a large number of small countries – this results in high fixed costs for the administration, difficulty for firms and sectors in achieving economies of scale, little development of clusters.
- **Infrastructure**. Africa has a low overall infrastructure endowment and the quality of its infrastructure services is poor. This increases costs, particularly for its many landlocked countries.
- **Regional integration** is weak and focused more on political union than on improving competitiveness of African firms. Regional markets are inexistent or in an embryonic stage.
- **Business environment**. Despite significant reforms, regulatory and business frameworks still

Countries with small populations have difficulty in achieving economies of scale because their small internal markets do not provide significant opportunities for local providers of goods and services.

remain unattractive, and African governments penalize their firms.

- **Weak skills base**. Despite very significant progress in terms of school attendance, Africa remains the continent with the greatest number of low skilled or unskilled workers. Often, national education systems do not provide the right kind of skills development either.
- **Resource-rich countries**. These remain a special challenge because of the difficulty in managing fiscal flows and the terms of trade shocks that result from price swings.

Large number of small countries

Africa encompasses 54 countries, of which 48 are south of the Sahara and 15 are landlocked. The most populous country, Nigeria, has 180 million people and the second most populous, Egypt, 90 million. This compares to Brazil with 200 million people and Indonesia with 250 million, but generally, countries in Africa are far less populous. As a continent Africa has a lower population than India or China. Average country population in Africa is 21 million, less than or on a par with each of the world's five largest cities (Tokyo, Delhi, Mexico City, Mumbai, Sao Paulo). On average, Africa's countries are small, and no other region has such an agglomeration of small countries; and most African cities are small, too. No other continent has so many landlocked countries either. Smallness introduces three obstacles for development.

High fixed costs of running the national administration and essential government functions.

Small countries have specific economic challenges relating to the overhead cost of being an independent state. Irrespective of size, countries have certain central government functions that need to be performed (fiscal policy and management; legislative functions; central banking and monetary policy; etc.). In smaller countries, the tax base to finance such functions, and the skills pool to call upon to implement them, are more limited. In smaller countries, the quality of economic policy and administration can therefore suffer.

Lack of economies of scale

Countries with small populations have difficulty in achieving economies of scale because their small internal markets do not provide significant opportunities for local providers of goods and services. The only way to overcome these obstacles is to reach larger markets; and this requires having an economic policy that is strongly outward looking, with a major focus on exports, and to make a very significant effort toward regional integration and to integrating into global value chains. It is notable that the two African success stories have undertaken this path:

- **Mauritius** adopted from the start a strong focus on first sugar exports, benefiting from EU market access provided to ACP countries under the 1975 Lomé Agreement, as well as from the EU Common Agricultural Policy which pitched European sugar prices significantly above international market prices, offsetting Mauritius's geographic disadvantage compared to EU producers. As this opportunity began to decline with Europe's removal of its price controls, the government actively promoted the development of a textile industry within an export processing zone (EPZ) located on the island. Mauritius's textiles exports benefited specifically from the 2000 US African Growth and Opportunity Act (AGOA), particularly once clauses relating to origin of inputs were liberalized. At the same time the government actively promoted investment in the incipient tourism sector, including support through the creation of specialized training schools for tourism professionals and a modern international airport. More recently, as Mauritian labor has moved up the skills and pay curve and become less competitive in textiles the government has promoted the development of an

Most African countries have not been proactive in creating an aggressively outward-facing economy the way Mauritius and Tunisia have.

Box 1: Mauritius—How a small African country overcame its natural obstacles

Since independence in 1968, Mauritius has developed from a low-income, agriculturally based economy to a middle-income diversified economy with growing industrial, financial, and tourist sectors. For most of the period, annual growth has been in the order of 5 percent to 6 percent. It has also achieved an equitable income distribution with low inequality (Gini coefficient of 38.9). This has been reflected in increased life expectancy, lowered infant mortality, and a much-improved infrastructure.

Mauritius's development strategy has been articulated along four axes:

Heterodox liberalization and diversification policies: Mauritius has followed a pragmatic development strategy in which liberalization process was sequenced and tailored to its competitive advantages and weaknesses. The export-orientated approach has encouraged liberalization supported by strong state involvement as a facilitator (of the enabling environment for the private sector); as operator (to encourage competition); and as regulator (to protect the economy as well as vulnerable groups and sectors from shocks). Strategies were evidence-based and adapted according to results, and the country has consistency and stability, regardless of which political party is in power.

Concerted of nation building: Since independence Mauritius has focused on creating the foundations for sustained growth through nation building. Partnerships across ethnic groups allowed economic redistribution to be negotiated and the resulting better balance of economic and political power allowed strong and independent institutions. The political system encouraged a consultative approach to policy formation that allowed strategies for growth to be continued regardless of changes in the parties in power.

Strong and inclusive institutions: Strong institutions are critical in ensuring the country's competitiveness, economic resilience and stability. They have supported development strategies and ensured that export earnings are reinvested in strategic and productive sectors. In the financial sector, they have built a regulated and well-capitalized banking and financial system.

High levels of equitable public investment: Mauritius has a strong human capital foundation developed through consistent and equitable investment in human development, and among the most effective infrastructure services on the continent. This enabled Mauritius to exploit advantages, learn from expertise brought in through FDI and maintain competitiveness in a fast-evolving international market. Education and health services are free and have been expanded in recent years, in order to create further employment opportunities and ensuring inclusive growth.

Source: Overseas Development Institute

IT and a financial sector service industry, which is experiencing significant growth (Box 1).

- **Tunisia**, after an unfruitful period of state-led development until the early 1970s, adopted a policy focused more on export promotion combined with some import substitution (infitâh). The offshore sector focused on attracting foreign firms to invest in the country and on exports of manufactures to Europe. Tunisian manufacturing grew at 15 percent per year during the 1970s and close to 100,000 jobs were created in manufacturing. By the late 1980s manufacturing growth had slowed and the government started negotiations on a free trade agreement (FTA) with the European Union, concluded in 1998. This was supported by the government's proactive industrial modernization plan, including skills enhancement, with financial support from the EU. Exports to the EU grew at more than 10 percent per year. More recently, the political turmoil that followed the ouster of President Ben Ali and associated security issues have put a severe damper on growth in manufacturing and on exports.

Adequacy of infrastructure helps determine one country's success and another's failure in diversifying production, expanding trade, coping with population growth, reducing poverty, or improving environmental conditions.

Generally, however, most African countries have not been proactive in creating an aggressively outward-facing economy the way Mauritius and Tunisia have. It is informative to see that in both cases the governments followed heterodox private sector-friendly economic policies, with active promotion of specific sectors determined to be of greatest potential and benefiting from trade agreements with the EU and the US.

Lack of aggregation economies and difficulties in developing industrial clusters

Across the world, firms tend to agglomerate in clusters drawn by the markets they serve, by the products and services they produce, and by the skills they require. In France, the United Kingdom and the US, 75 percent to 95 percent of industry is clustered or concentrated relative to the overall economy. In Tunisia, more than half the large scale industrial firms are located in just two geographical areas.[8]

Africa has examples of such clusters:

- Morocco: Tangier (automobiles and automotive parts)
- Morocco: Casablanca/Fez (decoration, furniture, leather processing)
- Ghana: Suame Magazine (the largest artisan engineering cluster in sub-Saharan Africa – metal working: casting, lathe operators, foundries)
- Tanzania: Arusha cluster (furniture),
- Nigeria: Nnewe cluster (auto parts)
- South Africa: Durban auto cluster (auto assembly and auto parts)
- Egypt: Domiatt cluster (furniture)
- Uganda: Lake Victoria cluster (fish processing)
- Kenya: Nairobi cut flower cluster (horticultural products)

However, compared to emerging Asia, notably China, Africa has relatively few clusters and compared to their peers in other regions most have a relatively low level of sophistication in terms of access to financing, research and development, skills enhancement through specialized education institutions, and market intelligence. Also, they do not benefit from the same degree of government support. Indeed, the Nigeria Nnewe cluster for auto parts, one of the more successful examples in Sub-Saharan Africa, developed through a collaborative effort between Nigerian importers of equipment from Taiwan and their suppliers, who provided on the job training. The Nigerian Federal and State governments provided little tangible support. The Nnewi cluster overcame lack of infrastructure and absence of government support by providing its own electric power and water, and setting up its own business organizations such as the Nnewi Chamber of Commerce Industry, Mines and Agriculture.

Low infrastructure endowment and poor quality infrastructure services

Infrastructure endowment

Adequacy of infrastructure helps determine one country's success and another's failure in diversifying production, expanding trade, coping with population growth, reducing poverty, or improving environmental conditions. Good infrastructure, through the services it provides to the economy, raises productivity and lowers production costs, but it must expand fast enough to accommodate growth. The kind of infrastructure put in place also determines whether growth does all that it can to reduce poverty.[9] Rural roads, for example, linking rural and urban markets, or rural water supply, will do more for inclusive growth than other infrastructure services targeting higher income populations.

Africa does not have good infrastructure and is not well connected.[10] Overall, the African continent is by all measures the least endowed region of the developing world

8. Newman et al. (2016); World Bank. (2009b). *World Development Report 2009*. Washington: World Bank

9. World Bank (2009b).

10. There are various global indices of connectivity: see of instance McKinsey Global Institute's Global Connectivity Index.

Three constraints—poor initial conditions, low infrastructure endowment, and ineffective regional integration—taken together, have kept African economies relatively fragmented and high cost.

in terms of infrastructure, even compared to low-middle income countries in other regions. Moreover, performance of infrastructure in Africa is generally poor: high cost, erratic, and undependable. Transport costs are the highest in the world, twice level of other developing countries and significantly limit Africa's ability to trade regionally and globally[11]. Other infrastructure essential to competitive economies such as electricity networks, and fixed line telephone and broadband connectivity, are also relatively underdeveloped. Africa has by far the lowest percentage of the population with access to electricity (44 percent for the total population, of which only 26 percent in rural areas) and the lowest per capita electricity consumption for those who have access – average residential electricity consumption per capita is equivalent to around half the level of China or one-fifth of Europe.

Africa's combination of low infrastructure endowment and poor quality infrastructure services relative to other developing regions means that the continent has significant cost hurdles to be able to compete internationally in the exports of goods and services.

Unfinished regional integration

Since independence, African countries have supported regional integration through the creation of a large number of overlapping initiatives and organizations (Figure 1, expanded upon in Chapter 10). These have however focused more successfully on political coordination than on creating regional markets or production corridors. In particular, integration has lagged as concerns regional infrastructure, mobility of skills and trade in services, and "behind the border" non-tariff barriers.

Figure 1 shows country groupings for the different regional integration initiatives across the African continent

Three constraints—poor initial conditions, low infrastructure endowment, and ineffective regional integration—taken together, have kept African economies relatively fragmented and high cost. They have hindered firms' ability to operate in lean, just-in-time production mode needed to effectively participate in global value chains.

Unattractive regulatory frameworks, a key part of the business environment

The business environment may be defined as the nexus of policies, institutions, physical infrastructure, human resources, and geographic features that influence the efficiency with which different firms and industries operate. At firm level, it directly influences costs of production; at the industry level, it often relates to market structure and competition. Its impact is felt more heavily in traded sectors that are not particularly intensive in natural resources (that is, manufacturing, high-value services) than in primary production and extractive resource sectors. Even efficient firms able to transform inputs into outputs with high efficiency and low "factory-floor" costs can be driven out of business by a poor business environment.[12]

The business environment is made up of several different components. Several of the components (infrastructure, geographic features, human capital) are considered elsewhere in this paper. The regulatory framework is however a key feature of the business environment that warrants particular examination, because unlike certain other features (e.g. geography, or regional integration) it is almost entirely at the discretion of the government where the firm is located. There is, therefore, far more freedom to undertake systemic change to improve competitiveness than with the other components.

It is thus surprising that African countries figure almost universally at the bottom of the league tables concerning the attractiveness of their regulatory frameworks. The attractiveness of regulatory frameworks is generally

11. Aspen Institute. (24-25 March 2005). Trade Facilitation to Promote Intra-African Trade, Committee on Regional Cooperation and Integration. UNECA: Addis Ababa.

12. Eifert, B., Gelb, A., & Ramachandran, V. (2005). Business Environment and Comparative Advantage in Africa: Evidence from the Investment Climate Data. *Center for Global Development: Working Paper 56.*

In 2017, the average rank of African countries on the Doing Business indicators (from 1 as the best to 190 as the worst) was 142, i.e. the African continent as a whole was less competitive than Tajikistan or Lao PDR.

Figure 1: Africa's regional integration initiatives

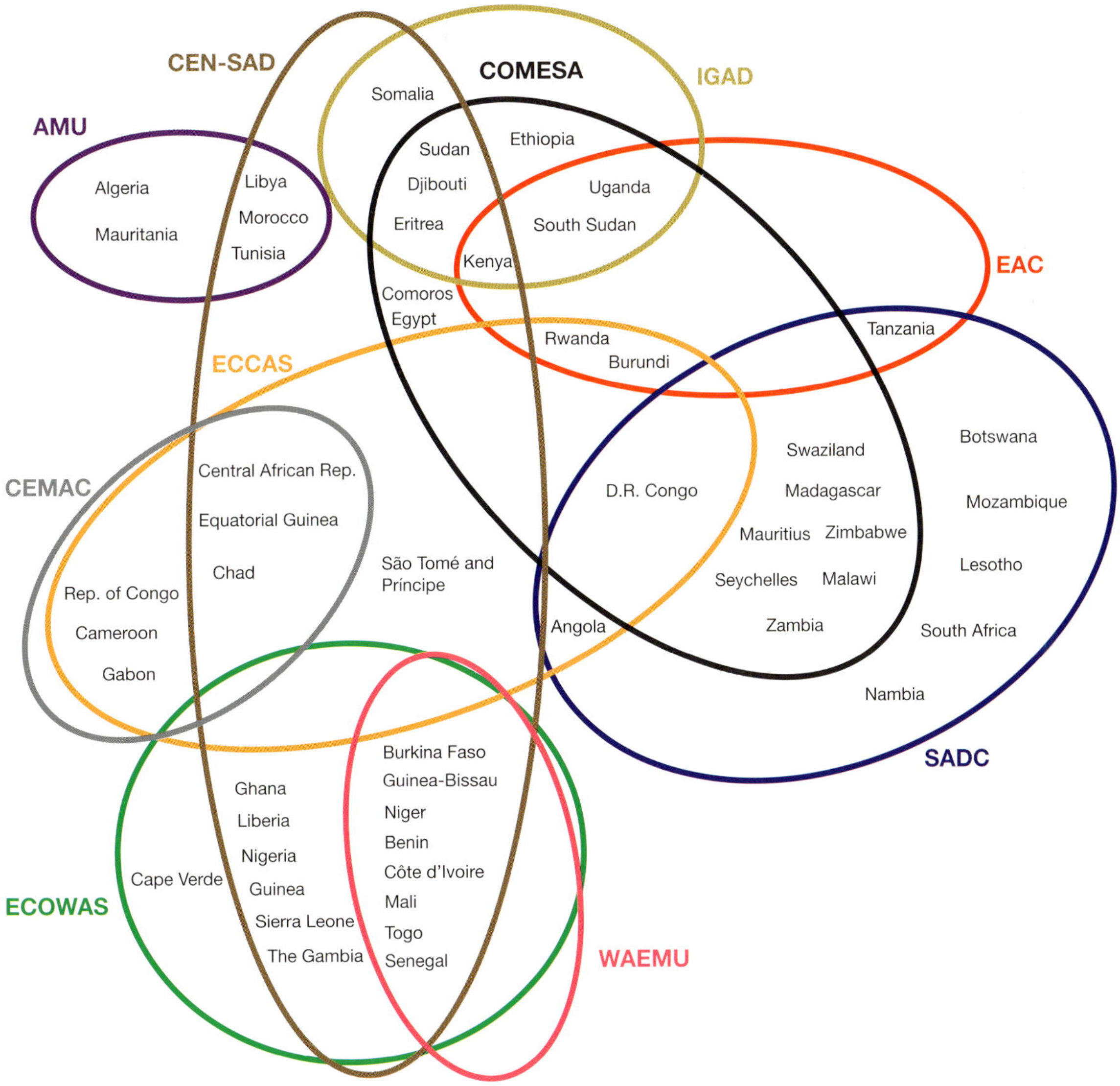

Source: Author

measured through the World Bank/IFC Doing Business surveys. Doing Business measures select business regulations in 189 countries and ranks countries on nine dimensions: starting a business; dealing with construction permits; registering property; getting credit; protecting investors; paying taxes; trading across borders; enforcing contracts; and closing a business. The Doing Business approach has been criticized as excessively mechanistic, and the system itself is open to gaming by countries to manage their outcomes in order to improve their rankings. However, flawed as it is, this indicator is the best

A review of the Doing Business report shows that firms in African countries are burdened with inefficient, time-consuming and costly regulations that increase overall cost and reduce their international competitiveness.

and most widely disseminated measure of the regulatory framework.[13]

In 2017, the average rank of African countries on the Doing Business indicators (from 1 as the best to 190 as the worst) was 142, i.e. the African continent as a whole was less competitive than Tajikistan or Lao PDR. However, the most competitive country in Africa in terms of Doing Business was Mauritius, at 49th place, ahead of Italy (50th) or Israel (52nd) (Table 2).

Broadly speaking, a review of the Doing Business report shows that firms in African countries are burdened with inefficient, time-consuming and costly regulations that increase overall cost and reduce their international competitiveness. For example:

- Outdated cadaster systems make registering real estate very difficult in many African countries, and these assets therefore cannot be used by firms as collateral when borrowing from banks.
- In cases where banks do take land as collateral, they often cannot obtain recourse before the courts in cases of non-payment of loans. This lessens or kills their appetite for further collateral-based lending.
- The financial sectors of many African countries do not provide term lending at reasonable interest rates for firms (maximum tenors rarely exceed 8 years, and generally less). Domestic debt securities – where they exist – are almost uniquely used by the governments to raise their own short term financing and there is little appetite in the markets for corporate issuances.[14]
- In countries as diverse as South Africa and Niger, labor legislation in the formal labor market has been modeled on that of European countries, although labor productivity is far below the levels of these countries. These labor protections drive up the marginal cost of labor beyond its marginal productivity, so workers cannot enter the formal labor market and are driven into the informal market where they cannot obtain good jobs.

Among the specific constraints outlined in this section, action on improving the regulatory environment would be a "low-hanging fruit" that would warrant close attention by African policy makers. Incremental change will not be enough; countries must re-engineer their regulatory environment toward supporting firms in a competitive environment.

13. Newman et al. (2016).

14. Morocco and South Africa are notable exceptions to this observation.

Table 2: Doing Business in Africa

Region/Category	Average Rank/Ranking
Africa	142
Sub-Saharan Africa	143
North Africa	130
East Asia & Pacific	94
Latin America & Caribbean	109
OECD High Income	26
Best in Africa	49 (Mauritius)
Worst in Africa = worst in the world	190 (Somalia)

Source: World Bank (2017)

The African continent has to make a significant effort to confer useful skills on the more than 60 percent of youth who do not attend high school, and the 7 out of 10 rural youth who do not attend school at all.

Weak skills base

Companies operating in African countries repeatedly cite insufficiently skilled labor as a bottleneck to growth[15]. By improving the knowledge and skills of workers through technical and vocational education and training, local economies can build a skilled workforce to increase their competitiveness in the production of goods and services.[16]

Significant strides have been made in recent decades in Africa in primary and secondary school enrollment:

- Africa has experienced an impressive increase in the number of students enrolled in primary school. Between 1990 and 2012, the number of children enrolled in primary schools more than doubled, from 62 million to 149 million children. In sub-Saharan Africa, 15 countries have abolished school fees since 2000, enabling more children to attend primary school. However, despite tremendous gains in primary school enrollment, no African country has achieved universal primary education.[17] Globally, of the 58 million children of primary school age were out of school worldwide in 2012, 38 million children were in Africa. About half of all out-of-school African children will never step foot in a school in their lifetime.
- Sub-Saharan Africa achieved the greatest gains in secondary education participation compared to all other regions of the world between 1999 and 2012. Worldwide, there were 552 million youth enrolled in secondary schools in 2012. Some 49 million secondary students resided in Africa. After graduating from primary school, many students find it difficult or impossible to attend secondary schools close to home. Across Africa, secondary schools can accommodate only 36 percent of qualifying secondary students. Young people living in rural communities are more likely to have limited access to secondary education compared to youth in urban areas, and even out of 10 rural youth have never attended school. They are to all intents and purposes unemployable in the modern economy.
- Beyond primary and secondary education, tertiary education (universities) and technical and vocational education and training (TVET—technical colleges) help to strengthen the local workforce, which creates an attractive economic environment for investors. African universities are often perceived as less attractive than universities in Europe or the US, and technical and vocational education and training has not been a top priority for many African countries, particularly during and after the structural adjustment policy phase. In 2012, technical and vocational programs accounted for only 6 percent of total secondary enrollment in the region, a decline from 7 percent in 1999. TVET programs markedly declined in the 1980s due to budgetary shortfalls in the education sector of many African countries and have never fully recovered. On average, only about 2 to 6 percent of educational budgets are devoted to technical and vocation skills development.

It is very difficult competing in the international economy without the right skills. The African continent has to make a significant effort to confer useful skills on the more than 60 percent of youth who do not attend high school, and the 7 out of 10 rural youth who do not attend school at all. As concerns the focus of this paper, firm-level and sector-level specialized training (e.g. in textiles, garment confection, etc.), tailored to the specific needs of emerging industry, holds the most promise to improve firm competitiveness in the short term, taking a lesson from the successes of countries like Mauritius and Tunisia. But more broadly African decision makers have to continue their focus on education, particularly as concerns skills for the modern economy.

15. World Bank. (2016a). Africa Enterprise Surveys. Washington: World Bank.
16. Africa-America Institute. (2015). *The State of Education in Africa 2015.*
17. For a country to achieve universal primary education, all children must have completed a full course of primary schooling.

Extractive industries are highly capital-intensive and neither create many jobs nor contribute significantly to development of skills and human capital.

The challenge for resource-rich countries

Africa's exports are mostly comprised of natural resources. Experience shows that mining and oil and gas make little direct contribution to the local economy other than generating fiscal revenues. Extractive industries are highly capital-intensive and neither create many jobs nor contribute significantly to development of skills and human capital. This is as true in Africa as it is in other parts of the world. Mining and oil and gas operations have few forward or backward linkages to the rest of the economy, and have often been managed as virtual enclaves without much impact on the economies of host countries other than payment of taxes and royalties.[18]

As can be seen from Table 3, Africa is essentially an exporter of natural resources. Resource-rich countries have particular challenges to develop sectors not associated with their natural wealth. Resource rents lead to Dutch disease and loss of competitiveness, and in some cases to widespread corruption, the hollowing out of local traditions and institutions and creating a culture of rent seeking and extraction, sometimes to armed conflict and war.

Dutch disease is the negative impact on an economy of an event that gives rise to a sharp inflow of foreign currency, such as exports of large amounts of natural resources. The currency inflows that result lead to currency appreciation, which makes the country's other products less price competitive on export markets. It also leads to higher levels of cheap imports and can lead to deindustrialization as industries apart from resource exploitation are moved to cheaper locations.[19]

Africa developed its trade links with the rest of the world based on its commodity exports. As of 2014, commodities represented about 76.5 percent of African exports, a proportion that had peaked in 2012 at 84 percent, up from 73.5 percent in 1995, as prices and output of commodities went up sharply. The increase in commodity prices, well in excess of these regions' average import prices (even though these also include commodities), resulted in a marked improvement in terms of trade, which increased by more than 90 percent from 2000 to 2012. Since then, commodity exporters' terms of trade declined, even after a very moderate recovery in mid-2016, although relative prices remain higher than at the turn of the century.[20]

Africa's major exporters of natural resources such as Algeria, Angola, Nigeria (oil); Guinea (bauxite and iron ore); Zambia (copper); and DRC and Zimbabwe (diamonds); have all undergone deindustrialization as their natural resource sectors have crowded out other emerging industrial sectors. The decade-long commodities boom that ended in 2015 accelerated this trend. In addition to the challenges that other African countries face (small size; low infrastructure endowment; weak regional integration; unattractive regulatory and business frameworks; and weak skills base), Africa's resource-rich countries have also

18. Ahlers et al. (2014)

19. First described in the Dutch economic crisis of the 1960s and 1970s following the discovery of North Sea natural gas.

20. See Chapter 6, "The Impact of Commodity Terms of Trade in Africa: Curse, Blessing, or Manageable Reality?"

Table 3: Share of Africa's exports, natural resources (2015)

Export category	Trade value (billions of dollars)	Percent of total exports
Primary commodities, precious stones and non-monetary gold	296.757	76.5
Labor-intensive and re-source-intensive manufactures	20.978	5.4
Combined	317.735	81.9

Source: UNCTAD (2017)

Africa must design and implement its own economic diversification program, based on its own specific features and geography.

to manage the fiscal flows resulting from their exports to offset their deleterious effects.

Possible policy directions for Africa's economic diversification

Given the dominance of East Asian economies (e.g. China, Thailand, Viet Nam, Indonesia) in global manufacturing and the emergence of new players geographically close to these players (Lao PDR, Cambodia, Philippines), it is unlikely that African countries can emulate East Asian industrial policy without adapting it to the continent's specific conditions. Also, economic circumstances have changed since these countries first elaborated their policies: trade and investment patterns have shifted from the historic north-south pattern to include increasing south-south flows (i.e. flows of investment and debt from developing countries such as China, Brazil or India, to other developing countries). This trend reflects increasing domestic savings in middle-income developing countries as their economies have matured, as well as a reduction in the appetite of industrialized countries for emerging market investments following the 2008 financial crisis. Economic circumstances are different, and Africa must design and implement its own economic diversification program, based on its own specific features and geography. This section outlines four specific policy directions that Africa might consider.

Creating regional markets and production centers: regional integration

Africa, made up as it is by many small countries, would benefit from more effective regional integration in two manners: first, by creating larger markets for the continent's producers, allowing them to lower their production costs; and second, by achieving aggregation economies, develop industrial production centers on a regional rather than national basis.

Creating regional markets

Africa's experience with regional integration: The integration model followed by the African continent, with leadership from the African Union (formerly the OAU) and support from the United Nations Economic Commission for Africa (UNECA), was to promote the creation of geographic integration blocs or Regional Economic Communities (REC). The goal of the RECs was to advance in a sequential, linear progression from free trade areas (FTA), to customs unions and to a single market, finally converging toward a continent-wide economic and monetary union.[21]

If such a development plan had been successful, one would expect regional markets for goods, services, capital and labor to develop within (and perhaps between) the different RECs. For example, if regional integration had gone according to plan one would expect that consumer products produced in Benin would access the large consumer markets in and around Lagos in Nigeria, and that the Ivorian telecommunications company Citelcom could be able to operate freely in Mali. These countries all belong to ECOWAS. Similarly, we would expect that an accountant or nurse trained in Uganda would be accredited to work in Kenya or Uganda, and a Kenyan bank would be able to provide a line of credit directly to a company in Tanzania, as these countries all belong to the East African Community, part of COMESA. This is far from the case and in practical terms, regional development has been very disappointing. There are reasons for this.

- First, there are too many regional integration initiatives. There are multiple conflicting regional arrangements with significant overlapping

21. Early RECs were: ECOWAS (for West Africa), ECCAS (for Central Africa), COMESA (for South and Eastern Africa), and AMU (for North Africa). In addition, other overlapping regional integration arrangements were set in place. For instance, in West and Central Africa WAEMU and CEMAC became active alongside ECOWAS, while EAC, partly overlapping membership with COMESA, was revived. Also, IGAD (Intergovernmental Authority on Development) organizes countries of the Horn of Africa, Nile Valley and the Great Lakes into a REC, while the inter-governmental Indian Ocean Commission (IOC) of 1984 regroups the five island communities of Mauritius, Seychelles, Comoros, Madagascar and Réunion.

Perhaps the comprehensive, sequential and top-down approach to regional integration undertaken by the continent needs to be reconsidered.

membership, in addition to bilateral trade arrangements. Countries pursue different objectives and hold differing views about relinquishing sovereign rights and regulatory authority.

- Second, groupings are too big and don't make economic sense. Excepting a handful of larger, diverse economies (like Tunisia, Morocco, South Africa, and Mauritius) countries in Africa have relatively similar economic and cost structures, requiring compensation for losers from regional economic integration. The larger the number of members, and the more similar they are to each other the economic structure, the harder it is to reach consensus on decisions and take effective action.
- Third, the private sector has been left out in designing integration policies. To date, private sector actors have not been required to play an active role in the design and implementation of the regional economic integration agendas, thus depriving the process of strong domestic champions. (However, it should be noted that the government and the private sector will have divergent views about competition; the latter will recommend policies that limit competition while policy makers should seek policies that widen markets and increase competitive pressures on firms.)

Developing regional centers of production

The Asian experience: Asian models of creating regional sectors of production such as clusters relied on the state playing a supportive and active role. This is also the experience of the two most successful industrial developers, Tunisia and Mauritius. States implemented policies that provided macro-financial stability, and maintained competitiveness of economies and of the exchange rate. Public policy in Asia delivered high quality, efficiently managed physical infrastructure (electricity, road, rail, port, airports, and communications networks) and maintained a reliable, predictable policy and investment environment that allowed for significant domestic and foreign investment in manufacturing and industry.

Where comprehensive changes were not possible, countries often created enclaves (special economic zones (SEZs), EPZs, etc.) with special fiscal and labor regimes, with high quality infrastructure investment and management that reduced cost and time to trade, and with appropriate legal investor protections. Again, this was the experience of Tunisia and Mauritius.

Asian countries also invested in human capital, with the development over time of a skilled, technically qualified labor force. The corporate sector in Asian economies acted as a partner to the active state and substantially benefited from the above features. In turn, the private sector acted as an important lobby for continued openness, competitiveness and deepening of regional economic integration. In addition, states often pursued selective, targeted industrial policies – providing investment incentives, credit facilities, import restrictions and public promotion and support of exports – in partnership with their private corporate sector.

Lessons for Africa: This Asian approach contrasts with the African experience. While macroeconomic management has markedly improved in Africa over the last two decades, African infrastructure is lacking both in absolute number of assets and in the quality of infrastructure services. Africa lags the rest of the world also in terms of skills development, the private sector has had little or no say in regional development initiatives, and African firms are weighed down with excessive business regulation and red tape.

Perhaps the comprehensive, sequential and top-down approach to regional integration undertaken by the continent needs to be reconsidered. What is required instead is an entirely new focus driven by and with the private sector, based on an economically and geographically coherent spatial entity. One approach could be to focus on **development corridors** centered around a regional port and associated transport infrastructure. The corridor would

To achieve economic diversification, focused integration efforts will need to be made to better integrate markets (generally situated around one or several large urban agglomerations as anchor), along transport corridors with access to ocean-going ports.

increase accessibility of hinterlands and provide them with access to urban markets. It would need to be associated with borderless regulatory environments to allow free flow of capital and labor, and with industry-specific regional skills enhancement initiatives such as vocational training (TVET) and industry schools. This approach is outlined in the section below.

Focused integration

To achieve economic diversification, focused integration efforts will need to be made to better integrate markets (generally situated around one or several large urban agglomerations as anchor), along transport corridors with access to ocean-going ports. These focused packages need to include the following elements:

- First, **variable geometry** in which a subset of like-minded countries around certain natural access corridors or with similar sector focus take specific actions to accelerate integration. Other countries operating at different speed could join at a later time.
- Second, involve **private sector** actors to generate demand for greater integration – for example, involving councils made up jointly of private and public sector players. But the focus on competition needs to be maintained.
- Third, **focus on few key integrated development corridors** and sectors or sub-sectors (Table 4). Critical infrastructure investments (ports, roads, rail, electric power) need to be provided, to the extent possible through private participation.
- Fourth, **trade policies** and **regulations** need to be reformed or eliminated to substantially reduce time and cost of importing and exporting through these corridors. Regulatory impediments such as registration, credit, and contract enforcement need to be addressed, and state distorting investment, such as privileges accorded to state-owned enterprises, need to be eliminated. This is not the

Table 4: Existing integrated development corridors

Corridor	Countries/Cities	Location of Industrial Hub	Port(s)
West African coastal	Lagos-Cotonou-Lomé-Accra/Tema-Takoradi	Lagos Takoradi	Lomé
West African Sahel	Cotonou-Niamey Lomé-Niamey Cotonou-Ouagadougou-Bamako Lomé-Ouagadougou-Bamako	Lomé Cotonou	Lomé Cotonou
Dakar Sahel	Dakar-Bamako	Dakar	Dakar
Abidjan Sahel	Abidjan/Vridi-Ougadougou Abidjan/Vridi-Bamako	Abidjan	Vridi
Douala Corridor	Douala-Yaoundé Douala-CAR-Chad	Douala	Douala
Central Corridor	Mombasa (Dar es Salaam)–Nairobi-Rwanda–Burundi–Uganda	Mombasa Nairobi	Mombasa
Trans Caprivi	Walvis Bay-Zambia-DRC Walvis Bay-Botswana-South Africa	Walvis Bay	Walvis Bay
North-South Corridor	Durban – Zimbabwe – Zambia – Mozambique	Durban	Durban
Maputo-South Africa	Mozambique-South Africa	Maputo Gauteng	Maputo

Source: Author

Whereas traditionally, an export good was produced more or less in its entirety in one country and exported to another, increasingly we are seeing the vertical disintegration of the manufacturing production process on a geographic basis.

case of simply improving a country's standing by one or two positions in the Doing Business ranking table, but systems and processes need to be entirely re-engineered. Essentially, an intermediate input imported into the Vridi port in Côte d'Ivoire for further processing in Mali must be able to move in a frictionless way to the factory, with little or no regulation between the two countries.

- Fifth, **illegal rent seeking behaviors** need to be eliminated, by perhaps the creation of public-private enclave entities with quasi-autonomous authority, removing the discretionary powers of mid-level civil servants. (An example would be the Dubai International Financial Center.) Elimination of inter-country regulation, and the reduced discretionary powers accorded to civil servants that result, would significantly help in this regard.
- Finally, **strengthen sub-regional institutions** by establishing high-level monitoring and dispute resolution mechanisms, and establishing a transitional compensation mechanism for less well-endowed and landlocked countries.

Trade in tasks: Value chains and tradable services

Over the last quarter century, worldwide changes in the nature of international trade have "complexified" the production process. Whereas traditionally, an export good was produced more or less in its entirety in one country and exported to another, increasingly we are seeing the vertical disintegration of the manufacturing production process on a geographic basis, so that different stages of production are carried out in different countries depending on their specific advantages and wage characteristics. For example, Mauritius might export garments made from cloth woven in India, with yarn spun in China, using raw cotton grown in Burkina Faso. We are also seeing a far greater degree of "embedded services" (design, after-sales service etc.) in the exported good. These two phenomena are introducing "trade in tasks"[22], which manifests itself in two manners: through **value chains**, and through **tradable services**. These two are similar to the extent that both have been enabled by the dramatic decline in the cost of international communications, transport and logistics over the past quarter century.

Value chains

A value chain[23] is a set of activities that a firm operating in a specific industry performs in order to deliver a valuable service for the market. Some of these activities can usefully be carried out in different locations. The very significant decline in costs now enable some of these tasks to be carried out in different countries. Worldwide, imported intermediates today represent nearly half total intermediate inputs,[24] for the most part carried out by multinational corporations operating in several sites. Value chain investors are very footloose, which both a blessing because they can be attracted quite easily by creating attractive business conditions, but a curse because when international competitive rankings change they relocate their centers of production to new localities.

Some African countries are beginning to achieve success in value chain development. Morocco has over the past decade developed a thriving automobile assembly business and auto part manufacturing industry in and around Tangier, with investment by the French auto companies Renault, PSA and others. Tunisia has had value chains operated by foreign firms (mostly European) in textile production and electrical/mechanical equipment manufacturing. South Africa has for many years had an auto assembly value chain centered around Port Elizabeth, with exports of finished autos to other countries on the continent. However, compared to other regions of the

22. See Newman et al. (2016).
23. The concept of value chain comes from business management and was first described by Michael Porter in Competitive Advantage: Creating and Sustaining Superior Performance (1985).
24. UNIDO. (2016). Statistical databases.

Developing a trade in services sector is less capital intensive than a more conventional manufacturing sector, but it requires the combination of world-class cost-effective fixed broadband Internet connectivity, and the right skills base.

world the African continent does not participate significantly in global value chains.

For instance, Kenya is one of the most developed countries on the continent and has a small manufacturing sector which is the most sophisticated in East Africa. It has a good but rather small port (Mombasa) and transport infrastructure between the port and the industrial areas around the capital is improving. However, despite a relatively diverse base of manufacturing companies, its main industries remain the transformation of agricultural raw materials (particularly of coffee and tea), still the principal industrial activity. Meat and fruit canning, milling, and sugar refining are also important, and there is some marginal activity in electronics and vehicle assembly, publishing, and soda ash processing. Kenya manufactures goods (e.g. ceramics, shoes, beer and soft drinks, soap, furniture, and leather goods) for its own market, but does not participate in any meaningful way in international value chains.

Policy prescriptions: Development of value chains seems to require two essential prior conditions: trade agreements to major markets (historically, the US or European Union); and a proactive heterodox government policy of actively attracting foreign investors. African decision makers should consider such measures in the elaboration of their industrial policies.

Tradable services

Tradable services are a subset of services that modern information and communications technologies allow to be carried out at a distance. Examples of tradable services are: call centers; computer and information technology services; back-office operations for financial firms; remote diagnostics of computer networks and engineering plants (refineries, power plants); tourism; and a range of services linked to design and fashion. Services represent worldwide a significantly larger share of GDP than manufactures, and over the last decade global trade in services has risen faster than merchandise trade, rising at 5.4 percent versus 4.3 percent, respectively. Exports of services by developing countries have nearly doubled in the past decade, growing at 11 percent per year.[25]

Regional trade in services: There are many sectors where there is a clear case for opening markets to tradable services between and among neighboring countries across the continent. Professional services (accounting, legal, banking, insurance), communications (fixed, mobile, broadband), and transport services (road, air, rail, maritime) are critical determinants of manufacturing productivity and competitiveness. Important intermediary professions for trade such as brokers, trade and customs agents tend to be protected by nationality requirements, and are therefore fragmented and costly. Countries along the integrated development corridor must agree on mutual accreditation of key skills. For example, there is no reason that an accountant registered in Benin cannot exercise her profession in Togo, Niger or Burkina Faso as these countries' accounting systems and education systems are practically identical, and all belong to ECOWAS.

International trade in services: While regional trade in services through increased economic integration has potential to diversify African economies, international trade in services would provide a much larger opportunity for African countries. The African continent lies on almost the same time zone as Europe and shares two of its most important languages (English and French). Investments needed for international trade in services are significantly less than those needed for manufacturing – for the most part, dependable, cheap fixed broadband Internet connections are sufficient. Africa has the potential to become the provider of services such as call centers and remote diagnostics for many European countries.

Policy prescriptions: Developing a trade in services sector is less capital intensive than a more conventional manufacturing sector, but it requires the combination of world-class cost-effective fixed broadband Internet connectivity, and the right skills base. In those countries where Internet connectivity is not up to par, African policy makers

25. World Bank (2016d)

African policy makers should integrate considerations of industrial clusters into their development plans, particularly urban planning, and promote skills-enhancement through industry-focused vocational training programs developed in partnership with the private sector.

need to focus on dramatically improving the quality and cost-effectiveness of service. This will in some cases require removing statutory monopolies on provision of Internet services, and requiring open access to fiber-optic cables for Internet service providers. Also, policy makers need to consider TVET institutions in conjunction with the private sector, to ensure that the labor force has the requisite skills.

Developing industrial clusters

Firms tend to agglomerate in clusters drawn by the markets they serve, by the products and services they produce, and by the skills they require. Africa has examples of such clusters, but they are relatively less developed than in other parts of the world.

Africa's lower cluster development likely stems in part from the continent's lower degree of urbanization. A review of clusters in other parts of the world highlight the importance of cities for the development of clusters, and studies have shown that doubling the size of cities is associated with productivity gains.[26] Geographical agglomeration of firms in urban areas allows them to obtain access to skills, financing and markets, although some studies have underlined that such advantages can be achieved through industrial clustering, e.g., in EPZs rather than in urban centers.

Another reason behind Africa's lower development of clusters might be due to the continent's industrialization history. At a time when other developing regions were beginning to see cluster development oriented toward export industries (in the late 1980s and 1990s), Africa was dismantling its state-led industries and embarking on macroeconomic reform. There were few opportunities for firms, either domestic or international, to invest in manufacturing capacity. Subsequently the development of trade in tasks (value chains and trade in services) has not been as pronounced in Africa as in other regions, and for this reason the continent has not been able to develop strong clusters of industrial firms.

Policy prescriptions: African policy makers should integrate considerations of industrial clusters into their development plans, particularly urban planning, and promote skills-enhancement through industry-focused vocational training programs developed in partnership with the private sector.

Africa's economic transformation—An agenda for action

Africa's 54 countries display a wide diversity, from upper middle income economies (Mauritius) to extremely low income (Niger); from landlocked (Central African Republic) to well-placed for exports (Tunisia). It is unlikely that any one set of policy recommendations would fit the entire continent, hence the need to adapt economic diversification policies to country specifics. However, a complete set of measures would include both those that create the right environment and those that proactively promote development of new sources of economic growth.

Indeed, the central lesson from this review of economic diversification of African economies is that while stable macroeconomic policies and streamlined business regulations are essential, they may not of themselves be sufficient to enable African countries to diversify their economies through development of manufacturing sectors and trade in services. Policies implemented by African policy makers over the past two decades have for the most part focused on orthodox macro management and investment climate reform. These have created the platform for the next stage, the focus of the policy recommendation below.

The second key lesson from this review is that governments of the most successful countries (notably the two diversification stars Mauritius and Tunisia), in addition to ensuring macroeconomic stability and streamlined regulations, implemented heterodox private sector-friendly economic policies. In particular, the governments undertook proactive steps to attract investors, both through

26. Newman et al. (2016)

Economic diversification is not a stable economic state, but requires constant policy adjustment by policymakers for countries to remain globally competitive.

direct outreach and by working with the private sector to tailor education and infrastructure to their needs. This approach needs to be flexible and to be adapted through time, to adjust to conditions as they change (e.g. Mauritius moving from sugar to textiles).

Creating the right environment. Getting the economic environment right to enable diversification will involve policies that are for the most part widely understood among African policymakers:

- Ensure a coherent and predictable macroeconomic management
- Streamline business regulations and red-tape for businesses
- Invest in infrastructure and improving its operation and maintenance
- Develop a skilled labor force through continued focus on basic education, coupled with vocational training programs designed in collaboration with the private sector
- Pursue targeted regional integration to enlarge regional markets

Proactive action on diversification. In addition to the above, policymakers must:

- Invest in regional infrastructure to allow the creation of industrial centers along transport corridors
- Promote investment by international operators of value chains, including proactive outreach to potential investors
- Promote the development of a tradable services sector by proactive outreach to potential investors

The third and final lesson from the above review is that economic diversification is not a stable economic state, but requires constant policy adjustment by policymakers for countries to remain globally competitive. Policymakers must have their "ear to the ground" to understand international business trends and to be able to adjust policies accordingly. Unless African governments become more business-friendly they will not be able to attract the new private sector players who will help them diversify out of basic agriculture and low-value services.

Annex 1

Table A1: Country typology and diversification priorities

Country Type	Characteristics	Countries	Key challenges
Industrialized	Have penetrated international markets with goods and services in a significant way	Botswana, Gabon, Mauritius, Namibia, South Africa, Tunisia	Maintain global competitive position through productivity gains, notably continued skills enhancement (TVET) Seek to diversify sectors
Emerging coastal	Emerging Africa with access to the coast	Benin, Cameroon, Cape Verde, Côte d'Ivoire, Djibouti, Egypt, Gambia, Ghana, Guinea, Kenya, Mauritania, Morocco, Mozambique, São Tomé and Príncipe, Senegal, Tanzania	Expand existing export sectors Promote investment by foreign investors in value chains Develop skills (basic education and TVET) Strengthen infrastructure Promote regional markets
Emerging landlocked	Landlocked emerging Africa	Burkina Faso, Ethiopia, Lesotho, Malawi, Swaziland, Uganda, Zambia	Reduce connectivity and other infrastructure costs (transport and Internet) Develop skills (basic education and TVET) Develop trade in services Promote regional integration along transport corridors
Resource-rich	Significant portion of their export revenues, and budgetary re-sources, stem from the export of natural re-sources	Algeria, Angola, Rep. of Congo, Equatorial Guinea, Nigeria	Implement strong fiscal management to avoid Dutch disease Seek to diversify the economy into areas related to natural resource (cluster development)
Fragile	In, or coming out of, a period of major civil or military unrest and the economy has not re-turned to normal	Burundi, Central African Republic, Chad, Comoros, D.R. Congo, Eritrea, Guinea-Bissau, Liberia, Libya, Madagascar, Mali, Niger, Rwanda, Sierra Leone, Somalia, South Sudan, Togo, Zimbabwe	Rebuild the economic and institutional fabric Ensure sound macro-economic management Reduce business regulations Strong focus on basic education (primary and secondary) Rebuild infrastructure

Source: Author

Africa's Infrastructure Deficit: Closing the Gap

Chapter 8

James Bond

Africa's infrastructure—An overview

Africa's infrastructure lags behind the rest of the developing world

Infrastructure endowment

As a continent, Africa is the lowest income region in the world and is characterized by a large number of small low-income countries (54 in total). Of the 30 World Bank-classified low income countries in the world, 25 are in SSA. This presents a challenge for infrastructure development. Overall, the African continent is by all measures the least endowed region of the developing world in terms of infrastructure endowment, even compared to low-middle-income countries in other regions (Figure 1).

Quality of infrastructure services

Countries in Africa are far from homogeneous, and their infrastructure problems and solutions vary across the continent. Infrastructure stocks are closely correlated with income,[1] and in this regard Africa's low infrastructure endowment reflects above all its low GDP per capita income levels. However, infrastructure performance across countries – that is, the delivery of services related to physical infrastructure stocks (transport services, communication services, delivery of quality electricity and water services) – is generally not strongly related to income levels. Some countries with low infrastructure endowments deliver relatively good infrastructure services, whereas other countries with greater amounts of physical infrastructure may deliver far poorer infrastructure services. The quality of infrastructure services delivered depends on intangible elements (the "service content" of infrastructure) which

1. Indeed, cross-country and time series analyses demonstrate that per capita GDP and infrastructure stocks rise in almost lock step across the world: an increase of one percent in per capita GDP is met by an increase of one percent in infrastructure stocks. It is not clear, however, what the causality mechanism is (World Bank. (1994). *World Development Report 1994: Infrastructure and Development.* Washington: World Bank.)

Figure 1: Africa's infrastructure endowment (Middle-income countries = 100)

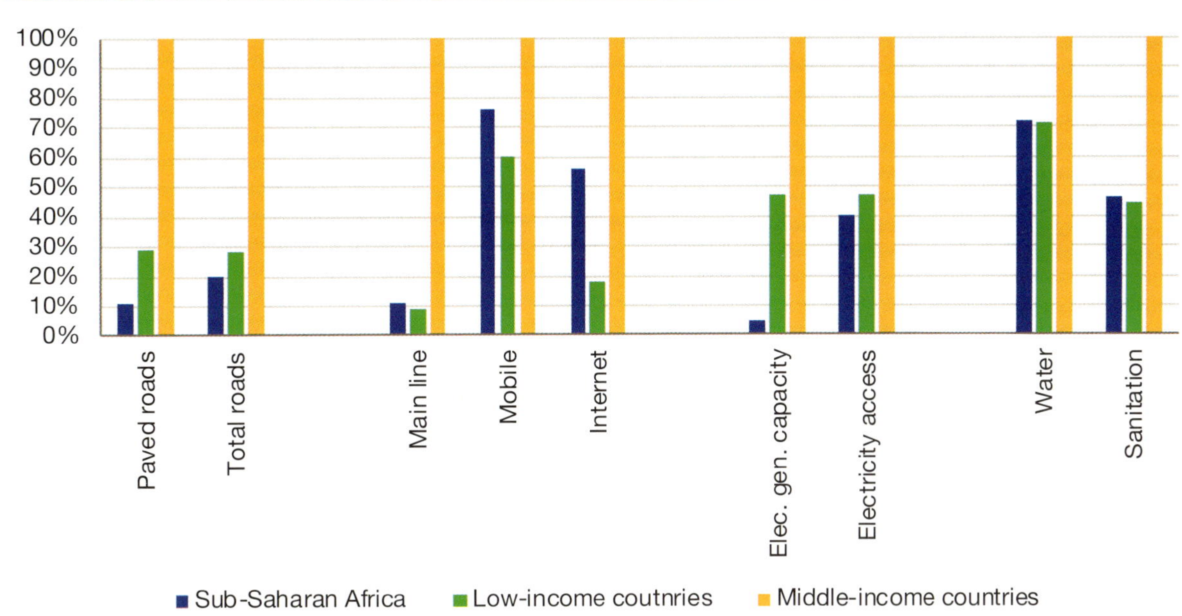

Source: Gwillian et al. (2008); World Bank (2016d)

Africa does not perform well on either the endowment of physical infrastructure or on the quality of infrastructure services delivered.

relate to levels of skills and human capacity, the efficiency of public administration, and the service focus of the business environment. For example, the ease of obtaining an electric power connection can vary significantly from one country to the next irrespective of the density of electric power networks and, in countries with more extensive electricity networks, it is not necessarily easier to obtain a connection. The cost of transporting merchandise on a road network is not simply a function of the road density of the country; informal roadblocks will significantly degrade the quality of transport services by increasing cost and time for the transporter.

Africa does not perform well on either the endowment of physical infrastructure or on the quality of infrastructure services delivered. Performance of infrastructure in Africa is generally poor: costly, erratic, and undependable.

Implications for infrastructure financing

As indicated above, Africa has both low infrastructure endowments and inefficient supply of services related to this infrastructure stock. The implication of this dual weakness is that it will not be enough simply to increase financing flowing to infrastructure investments in Africa. Simply increasing finance for infrastructure would address the problem of low physical stock but not improve its efficiency in delivery of services. Systemic changes to the way infrastructure services are delivered, a greater focus on maintenance of existing capital stocks, and an enhanced attention to managerial capacity for the operation of these stocks will also be needed to ensure that Africa's infrastructure is operated efficiently and maintained effectively. Better operation and maintenance will ensure that capital stocks, whatever the level, deliver quality infrastructure services to the continent's citizens.

Infrastructure's role in development

Adequacy of infrastructure helps determine one country's success and another's failure in diversifying production, expanding trade, coping with population growth, reducing poverty, or improving environmental conditions. Good infrastructure raises productivity and lowers production costs, but it has to expand fast enough to accommodate growth. The kind of infrastructure put in place also determines whether growth does all that it can to reduce poverty.[2] Rural roads, for example, linking rural and urban markets, or rural water supply will do more for inclusive growth than other infrastructure services targeting higher income populations.

Africa's combination of low infrastructure endowment and poor quality infrastructure services relative to other developing regions means that the continent has additional development hurdles to overcome. These development hurdles include:

- Products and services tradable on international markets have higher costs than those exported by other regions (Box 1). This reduces the international competitiveness of African exporters and limits sectors that African firms can compete in.
- Domestic markets, e.g. for agricultural produce, are less developed. Local suppliers are not always able to meet demand, e.g. because electric power is not readily available. Products are more expensive for consumers.[3]
- Infrastructure contributes to inclusive growth. The absence of infrastructure means that the fruits of growth are not widely shared throughout the country. For example, the absence of transport linkages between rural and urban markets reduces opportunities for the evolution of agriculture from subsistence to market-based.
- Regional integration requires both a coordinated set of rules across the region, and physical interconnections such as road, rail, and electricity transmission lines between and within countries. It

2. World Bank (1994)
3. In past decades, localized famines in countries like Ethiopia and Malawi persisted despite local food surpluses elsewhere. This was due to the inadequacy of transport infrastructure able to channel the surpluses to famine areas.

A sometimes overlooked but critically important factor in the development of infrastructure services is the importance of technology choice within infrastructure sectors.

Box 1: Importing and exporting are costly in Africa

To import a 20-foot container in Sub-Saharan Africa:

- Average cost: $2,793
- Average time: 38 days

To import a 20-foot container in Singapore:

- Average cost: $440
- Average time: 4 days

For the 16 landlocked countries in Africa, the cost of trading is 50 times higher and the volumes of trade are 60% lower than in African coastal countries.

Source: ICA (2015)

is not enough simply to create regional institutions and coordinate tariffs and regulations at a regional level. Countries need to be connected by road, rail, electricity, and communications networks. These are absent or weak in much of the continent. Africa's low infrastructure endowment means that these physical interlinkages are tenuous at best.

Technology choice

A sometimes overlooked but critically important factor in the development of infrastructure services is the importance of technology choice within infrastructure sectors. For example, mobile telephony has better corresponded to the communication needs of Africa's population than fixed line communication. The introduction of mobile phones – a then-new communications technology – two decades ago allowed a very significant increase in voice and texting communication compared to what would have been the case with landlines. Similarly, in the electric power sector, new renewable technologies such as solar electricity allow for a new paradigm of electric power delivery (mini-grids or solar home systems) rather than traditional grid delivery through an incumbent monopoly utility, which has not been a success on the continent. In urban transport, hybrid systems involving mini-buses, linking to large buses or rail, are making inroads into traditional transport service delivery models. In some cases, however, earlier technology choices constrain later choices. Also, it seems that the African continent has had more success with decentralized approaches and multiple operators (e.g. mobile) than with centralized approaches.

Overall, astute adoption of new technologies permits very significant possibilities for poorly endowed countries because of the ability to leapfrog the older technologies prevalent in more developed countries. Again, mobile phones are a striking example of this phenomenon. Decision-makers should be sensitive to the technological choices of infrastructure-related decisions.

Electric power

Electricity consumption and access

Africa generally, and Sub-Saharan Africa in particular, is starved for electricity. The region's power sector is significantly underdeveloped, whether gauged by energy access, installed capacity, or overall consumption. African countries struggle to sustain GDP growth in part because of the lack of electricity.[4] Measured in terms of gross electricity generated[5], Africa represents 3.2% of total world generation, slightly more than Germany (2.7%) and two-thirds the level of Japan (4.3%) (Figure 2).

On-grid power generation capacity in Africa was 167 GW in 2015, of which close to one-third was located in

4. Castellano, A., Kendall, A., Nikomarov, M., and Swemmer, T. (2015). *Powering Africa*. McKinsey.
5. i.e before transmission and distribution losses.

The paradox is that Africa is rich in energy resources, and huge renewable resources (solar, wind, hydroelectric, and geothermal in the Rift Valley) remain untapped.

South Africa. One-third of this capacity is powered by coal (mainly South Africa and Botswana) while one-fifth is hydroelectricity. Modern renewables account for less than 2% of the total, but they have also grown significantly in recent years. Insufficient, unreliable, or inaccessible grid supply has resulted in widespread private ownership of small oil-fueled generators and increasing focus on developing mini- and off-grid power systems based on renewables (Table 1).

The paradox is that Africa is rich in energy resources, and huge renewable resources (solar, wind, hydroelectric, and geothermal in the Rift Valley) remain untapped. Sub-Saharan Africa started late with renewable energy although these sources are particularly appropriate for mini- and off-grid systems and more relevant for low-density populations such as those in Sub-Saharan Africa's rural areas. In North Africa, the situation concerning renewables is different. In February 2016, Morocco commissioned the world's largest concentrated solar power plant, the Noor 1 Complex, near the city of Ouarzazate, with a capacity of 160 MW. This plant will produce enough energy to power over one million homes by 2018 and reduce carbon emissions by an estimated 760,000 tons per year.[6] The plant was built and is being managed by a consortium led by Saudi Arabia's ACWA Power, which will sell the electricity produced for $0.19/kWh. The project is co-financed by the World Bank and the European Investment Bank. Noor 1 is expected to be followed by two subsequent phases with a total final capacity of 2000 MW.

Infrastructure services delivered by the electricity sector cannot be measured by total gross generation alone, which is an indicator of overall electricity consumption. Access to electricity is also an important indicator (or indeed more so) of the quality of the service delivered. In the case of electricity access, North Africa is for the most part on a par with the rest of the world, with electrification

6. Climate Investment Funds (CIF).

Figure 2: Electricity generating capacity in Africa

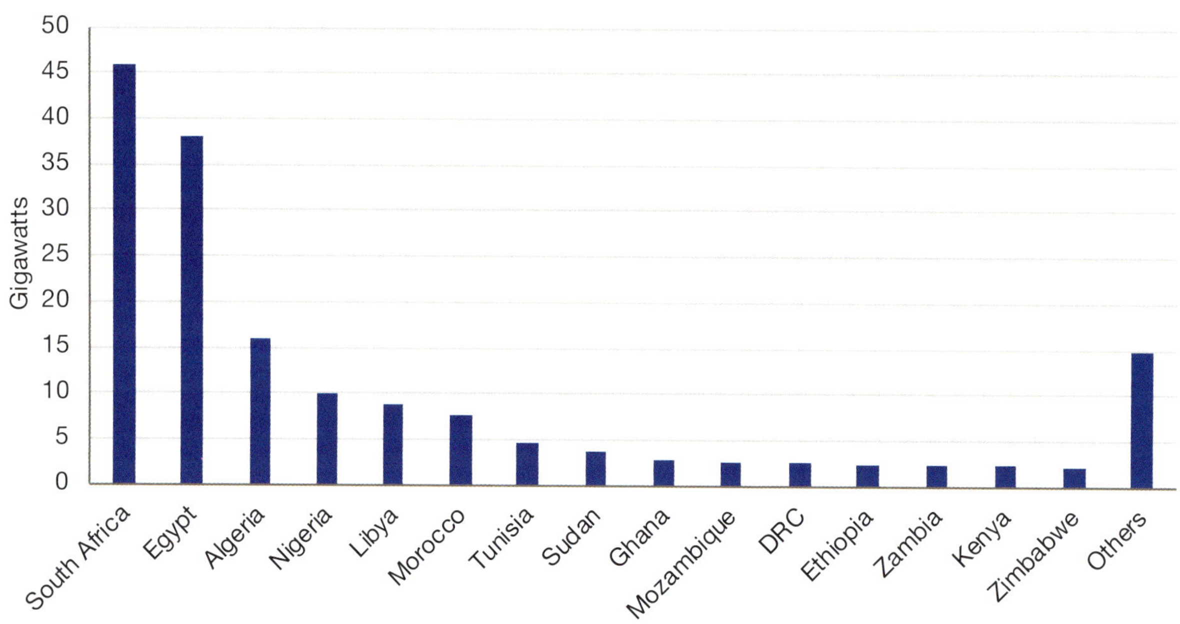

Source: ICA (2015)

In many, if not most, Sub-Saharan African countries the generation segment of the sector is theoretically open to private investment in the form of Independent Power Producers (IPPs), but they must sell to the incumbent public sector operator, which is for the most part insolvent.

Table 1: Access to electricity and power consumption

Region	Access to electricity (% of population)	Access to electricity, rural (% of rural population)	Access to electricity, urban (% of urban population)	Electric power consumption (kWh per capita)
Sub-Saharan Africa	35	15	72	496
Africa	44	26	70	846
Best, Africa	Algeria, Egypt, Libya, Mauritius, Morocco, Seychelles, Tunisia, Gabon (100)	Algeria, Egypt, Libya, Mauritius, Morocco, Tunisia, Gabon (100)	Algeria, Egypt, Libya, Mauritius, Morocco, Seychelles, Tunisia, Gabon (100)	South Africa (4407)
Comparators	79	68	97.4	844
Best, Comparator	Kyrgyz Republic, Moldova, Uzbekistan (100)	Kyrgyz Republic, Moldova, Uzbekistan (100)	Kyrgyz Republic, Moldova, Uzbekistan, Vietnam (100)	Uzbekistan (1611)
East Asia and Pacific (developing)	96	93	98	2720
Latin America and Carib. (developing)	96	86	99	1849
South Asia	78	69	97	640
Low and middle income countries	81	69	95	1666

Source: World Bank (2016d)

rates of more than 99%. Sub-Saharan Africa however is significantly underserved compared to other regions. More than 630 million people in Sub-Saharan Africa are without access to electricity; two out of three Sub-Saharan Africans have no access to electricity at all. In urban areas in Sub-Saharan Africa, electrification reaches 63% compared to a worldwide average of 95%. In rural areas, electrification is only of the order of 19% compared to a worldwide average of 71%. For those who do have electricity access in Sub-Saharan Africa, average residential electricity consumption per capita is equivalent to around half the average level of China or one-fifth of Europe, and nearly 730 million rely on the traditional use of solid biomass for cooking. Sub-Saharan Africa is literally a "continent in the dark" (Table 2).

The reasons for Sub-Saharan Africa's electric power scarcity are multiple. Africa has almost universally chosen a public-sector model for the delivery of electricity. Côte d'Ivoire is a notable exception, with a privately owned and managed enterprise, Compagnie Ivoirienne de l'Électricité, operating under a concession system. The results of the Ivorian system have been very good, but there are questions about how easy it would be to replicate the example in other Sub-Saharan countries.[7] In many, if not most, Sub-Saharan African countries the generation segment of the sector is theoretically open to private investment in the form of Independent Power Producers (IPPs), but they must sell to the incumbent public sector operator, which is for the most part insolvent. Poor creditworthiness of power utilities and their inability to pay for electricity delivered by the IPPs have severely constrained the amount of private financing available.

In essence, the centralized utility model of public sector ownership and operation has not been good at mobilizing

7. An attempt to replicate the model in Guinea was unsuccessful, for example.

The consequences of low electricity access rates in rural areas constrain the possibilities for inclusive growth.

Table 2: Electricity access, regional aggregates (2013)

Region	Population without electricity (millions)	Electrification rate (%)	Urban electrification rate (%)	Rural electrification rate (%)
Developing countries	1200	78%	92%	67%
Africa	635	43%	68%	26%
North Africa	1	99%	100%	99%
Sub-Saharan Africa	634	32%	59%	17%
Developing Asia	526	86%	96%	78%
China	1	100%	100%	100%
India	237	81%	96%	74%
Latin America	22	95%	98%	85%
Middle East	17	92%	98%	79%
Transition economies and OECD	1	100%	100%	100%
World	1201	83%	95%	70%

Source: IEA (2015)

financing for electricity investments (generation, transmission, and distribution) nor has it been good at operating installed assets. Sub-Saharan Africa's power utilities also have not pursued the most appropriate technologies and have in many cases preferred large investments in conventional equipment over more distributed investments in renewable technologies. Perhaps most importantly, these utilities have been unable to assure adequate maintenance of existing assets, which have often fallen into disrepair and are operating at a fraction of their installed capacity.

Sector issues

Low electricity access: The consequences of low electricity access rates in rural areas constrain the possibilities for inclusive growth. Lack of electricity reduces the ability for transformation and cold storage of agricultural products, and hence constrains incomes in rural areas; it eliminates the supply of clean lighting and thus reduces the productive period to daylight hours only, with negative consequences for cottage industries and after-hours learning. Nearly 730 million rely on the traditional use of solid biomass (mainly fuelwood and charcoal) for cooking. Each year nearly 600,000 premature deaths in Africa can be attributed to household air pollution resulting from the traditional use of these solid fuels.

In urban areas, low electrification rates constrain the development of industries such as manufacturing and of a modern service sector. Many middle-income Africans, desperate for electricity, install high-cost diesel generators in the absence of supply from the formal system. Such generators are polluting and the cost of electricity produced is multiples of what electricity from a modern sector with appropriate technology would cost. Such added costs reduce competitiveness for African firms (Box 2).

Inefficient system operation: Systems in Sub-Saharan Africa are in many cases poorly run. (North African power utilities, on the other hand, have a significantly better track record at operation and maintenance.) The most egregious weakness concerns the commercial aspects of the operation, notably inadequate billing of electricity consumed and low rates of collection of outstanding bills. Non-technical losses – essentially, theft of electricity – can be very high, sometimes as much as one-third of total electricity generated. Poor billing and collection, as well

Distributed electricity generation and supply models based on renewables would in many cases be a useful addition to existing centralized systems, particularly to accelerate access in rural areas where population densities are low.

Box 2: Nigeria—A failed electric power system

Nigeria, with a population of 175 million, has installed generating capacity of an estimated 8,000 MW, of which only around 4,000 MW can function at any given time given poor operation and maintenance. At 125 kWh per capita, Nigeria's electricity consumption is one of the lowest in the world. (South Africa, with a population of about a quarter of Nigeria's, has 45,000 MW installed and functional, nine times superior.) The Nigerian middle class has installed an estimated further 10,000 MW of expensive, polluting diesel generators to make up for failings of government utility. Inefficiencies in Nigeria's power sector have traditionally been a major constraint to growth, costing the economy as much as $100 billion per year according to government estimates.

Nigeria ranks among the worst performers in the world when it comes to power, according to the World Bank's most recent *Doing Business* report. Nigeria is placed 180th out of 190 countries surveyed in terms of ease of getting electricity, behind South Africa (111th) and Kenya (106th).

The lack of a reliable supply of electricity is seen as a major impediment to growth in Nigeria's industrial sector, adding to the cost of doing business for many firms. The private sector's backup diesel-fueled generators run at a cost of $0.30-0.50 per KWh, compared to the average grid tariff of $0.13.

Supported by the development community, Nigeria has embarked on a very ambitious reform program to completely overhaul the system and bring in private capital and expertise. It is still not clear whether this reform can work, given its complexity. Notably, the reform does not address the underlying poor financial viability and lack of creditworthiness of local distribution companies

Source: ICA (2015)

as theft of electricity, reduces utility income with the result that power utilities are financially weak and often unable to finance maintenance and new investments.

Insufficient maintenance of installed assets, as indicated above, due in part to the fragile financial situation of most of Sub-Saharan Africa's power utilities, has allowed these systems to fall into disrepair. This reduces the life span of investments in the power sector and diminishes the economic return on assets.

Poor technology choice: Sub-Saharan Africa's utilities have traditionally invested in centralized systems using conventional energy sources (e.g. coal, petroleum products, and natural gas), associated with a transmission network for transport of electricity generated to centers of consumption. Distributed electricity generation and supply models based on renewables would in many cases be a useful addition to existing centralized systems, particularly to accelerate access in rural areas where population densities are low. Such decentralized investments represent a real opportunity for African countries, particularly as they could seek greater amounts of private financing.

Inadequate regional integration of national electricity systems: Power trading in Africa started in the 1950s in the form of bilateral agreements between Democratic Republic of the Congo and Zambia. Over the past two decades, electricity transmission systems have begun to be more integrated on the African continent with the creation of several regionally integrated systems. However, country systems are integrated only to a very limited extent.

The North African countries created an Association of Power Utilities, the Comité Maghrébin de l'Électricité (COMELEC) established in 1989. The Southern African Power Pool (SAPP) was created in 1995, covering South Africa and other Southern Africa Development Community (SADC) countries. It is now the most advanced power pool on the continent. SAPP introduced the short-term energy market (STEM) in April 2001. The West African Power Pool (WAPP) was established in 2001 to promote energy trade between member countries. Currently the power trade in

Transport infrastructure in Africa is significantly less developed than in other developing regions of the world.

WAPP is still under bilateral or multilateral agreements, and energy trade through WAPP has not yet started. The Central Africa Power Pool (CAPP) was launched in 2003 and the Eastern Africa Power Pool (EAPP), in 2005. The two power pools are still in the developmental stage, with more progress for the EAPP.

All four power pools in South, West, Central, and East Africa and COMELEC are recognized, specialized institutions in their respective RECs. Although all power pools are working to promote energy trade, the level of energy traded in 2009 ranges only between 0.2% (in CAPP) and 7.5% (in SAPP).

Inadequate financing for electricity, is due most notably to the inability of public sector power utilities to generate sufficient cashflow to finance existing investments and roll out new capacity. The combination of regulated tariffs that do not cover long run marginal costs and inadequate billing and collection means that financial returns are not adequate and utilities can afford to finance neither needed investments nor maintenance.

Transport

Roads, rail, airports, ports

Transport infrastructure in Africa is significantly less developed than in other developing regions of the world (Table 3). Transport costs are twice the level of other developing countries and in landlocked countries up to 4 times as high as developing countries. The high cost of transport services significantly reduces African competitiveness and exports, and constrains economic growth.

- Road density in Africa is 152 km/km^2, compared to 211 km/km^2 for low-income countries worldwide, and 757 km/km^2 for middle-income countries. Under one third of African roads are paved compared to over 60% for low- and middle-income countries. Road quality is lower and road transport costs higher than in other regions of the world. Also, non-physical constraints such as road blocks and trucking cartels significantly reduce the efficiency of transport of goods by road.
- Rail could be an alternative, but rail networks outside South Africa are underdeveloped, poorly maintained, and of incompatible gauges. According to the International Union of Railways, in 2014 Sub-Saharan African trains carried about 158 billion tonne-kilometres of freight, or roughly half of what Australia's railways carried. Of that, 84% was in South Africa, which has a modern network. Elsewhere, railways carry a fraction of the volumes of two or three decades ago, due to absence of maintenance and deterioration of networks. However, several new rail regional projects are under consideration or construction, notably in East Africa (Kenya-Uganda, and Djibouti-Ethiopia) and West Africa (Benin-Niger)[8]
- Air transport has grown strongly in Africa in recent years. The availability of air freight services, in particular, has helped boost exports. However, air transport in Africa is expensive, connections are patchy, and safety is a problem. Airports are often inadequate, and landing charges are high owing to the absence of support from concessions enjoyed in many parts of the world. Air traffic control requires major upgrades to improve the continent's baleful safety record. Policy challenges include strengthening regulatory oversight and achieving full liberalization of the air transport sector. In particular, cartelization of national systems and the absence of a regional open skies policy significantly increase the cost of air transport.[9]
- African ports are small compared to their peers worldwide. Only Durban in South Africa, and Damietta/Port Said in Egypt have annual capacities equivalent to other developing country ports

8. The Economist. (4 June 2016). *Railways in Africa: Puffed out*. The Economist.
9. African Development Bank

In Africa, not only is there a low overall endowment of transport infrastructure but the African transport sector also does not use its physical assets efficiently.

Table 3: Key transport statistics

Region	Air transport, freight (million ton-km)	Air transport, passengers carried (million)	Air transport, registered carrier departures worldwide (million)	Container port traffic (million TEU: 20 foot equivalent units)
Sub-Saharan Africa	2755	44.9	0.7	1.4
Best, Africa	South Africa (1062)	South Africa (16.6)	South Africa (0.2)	Egypt (8.8)
Best, Comparator	India (1739)	India (82.7)	India (0.7)	India (11.7)
Africa	3232	72.3	1.0	28.0
East Asia and Pacific (developing)	24,458	641.3	5.3	240.9
Latin America and Carib. (developing)	3580	204.4	2.2	39.2
South Asia	37,192	99.1	0.9	20.9
Low and middle income countries	2688	1,157.2	10.7	342.0

Source: World Bank (2016d)

(4-5 million TEU/year). Only six of the continent's ports are able to accommodate Post and Super Panamax vessels (Durban, Damietta/Port Said, Port Elizabeth, Cape Town, Port Louis, and Tangiers). Many of the ports operate at below capacity due to low berth/docking facilities, weak terminal freight and handling management, and inadequate maintenance and dredging capacity. As a result, port services are costly and shipments are often delayed leading to physical and financial losses.

Issues in the transport sector

The quality of transport services is important in an economy. Transport services underpin all logistics operations, i.e. the detailed coordination of interactions involving many people, facilities, or supplies. Logistics underpin trade and the market economy. Inefficient logistics operations thus constitute a dead weight that reduces growth and overall welfare in the economy. The quality of transport services is a function of both the country's endowment in physical infrastructure and the efficiency with which it is used. In Africa, not only is there a low overall endowment of transport infrastructure but the African transport sector also does not use its physical assets efficiently. This is for several reasons, given below.

"Soft" infrastructure constraints: Not only is physical transport infrastructure less dense and its quality lower than infrastructure in other developing regions of the world, there are significant constraints in policy, regulations, procedures, norms, standards, and certification, which increase the cost and time of transport. Soft infrastructure has not received the same degree of attention as physical stocks from policy makers and development finance institutions although, in recent decades, countries have reduced high tariff levels and tariff complexity. Nevertheless, average tariff levels in Africa remain above those in other developing countries, and there are still many exemptions.

Non-tariff barriers also remain a significant issue and similarly have not received attention proportional to their importance. Non-tariff barriers include the number and complexity of procedures and administrative processes, different and incompatible technical regulations, norms, and product standards, and certification. These allow discretion on the part of officials and increase the time and

Development of transport infrastructure has in most cases been undertaken at national rather than regional levels.

cost of trading. By some estimates some 75% of delays on major transport corridors are due to the shortcomings in soft "behind the border" infrastructure, rather than the constraints due to physical infrastructure[10].

Lack of competition and cartelization of transport services: In many African countries (particularly Sub-Saharan Africa) there is an insufficient degree of competition among transporters. Trucker cartels exist, for example, in West Africa where the added cost hinders development of landlocked countries (Niger, Burkina Faso, Mali). Air transport is controlled by a small number of airlines leading to excessively high ticket prices, and air links between African countries are spotty. Maritime transport is in many cases cartelized as well. Such lack of competition is in certain cases reinforced by national legislation and regulations, e.g. the absence of region-wide open skies policies and requirements that foreign truckers unloading in ports return to their home base empty. A regional approach to transport regulation and competition has the potential of significantly reducing transport costs even with existing physical infrastructure.

National systems rather than regional systems: Development of transport infrastructure has in most cases been undertaken at national rather than regional levels. For example, countries compete for air transport, so that air hubs have not been able to develop (other than South Africa and Ethiopia). Inter-country competition in maritime transport has underpinned the development of a number of small ports dimensioned at the level of national rather than regional requirements, increasing overall port costs. Africa has several landlocked countries (16 in total) and the development of transport corridors into the interior would significantly improve competitiveness of the continent.

Rural roads provide inclusive growth and accelerate agricultural transformation

10. Harmon, L. M., Simataa B., and van der Merwe, A., (July 2009) Implementing Facilitation on Trade and Transport Corridors. Proceedings of the 28th South African Transport Conference (SATC), Pretoria, SA.

Finally, in addition to underpinning trade and competitiveness, transport infrastructure has an important role in supporting inclusive growth. Rural roads play an essential part in connecting rural communities to urban centers, to export points, and to each other. Interconnection of rural areas enables greater participation by poor rural communities in the fruits of growth and accelerates the transformation of agriculture from subsistence to market-based.

Information and communications technologies (ICT)

Fixed line, mobile, and internet connectivity

From a very low base two decades ago, Africa has undergone a revolution in communication technologies. Africa's incumbent fixed line telephone operators, operating for the most part under a utility model, had been unable to deploy fixed lines ("POTS": plain old telephone service) to a sufficient segment of the population. The introduction of new mobile technologies, and a new delivery model based on private investment and operation coupled with competition between operators rather than on incumbent state owned enterprises, completely overturned the situation. The number of subscribers in Africa has grown by 13 percent a year during the first half of this decade—more than twice the global average of six percent. Today, there are nearly as many mobile cellular subscriptions in Africa as the population (Table 4). The rapid growth in the first half of the decade was partly due to starting from a low base, with less than a quarter of the population having a mobile subscription in 2010.

The rapid penetration of mobile telephony in Africa, based on new and more appropriate technologies and private operators operating in a competitive environment, provides a useful model for other infrastructure sectors such as electric power.

Internet penetration via fixed broadband links has been notably less successful. With 13.9 Internet users per 100 people the continent lags other low- and middle-income

Africa's mixed performance with fixed broadband Internet connections, associated with the high cost of Internet usage for those with connections, represents a cost to economy and a missed opportunity.

Table 4: Key global telecom indicators for the world telecommunication service sector, 2014

Indicator	Global	Developed nations	Developing nations	Africa	Arab states	Asia and Pacific	CIS	Europe	The Americas
Mobile cellular subscriptions (millions)	6915	1515	5400	629	410	3604	397	780	1059
Per 100 people	95	121	90	69	110	89	141	125	108
Fixed telephone lines (millions)	1147	511	636	12	33	512	70	245	256
Per 100 people	16	41	11	1	9	13	25	39	26
Active mobile broadband sub-scriptions (millions)	2315	1050	1265	172	92	920	138	399	577
Per 100 people	32	84	21	19	25	23	49	64	59
Mobile broadband growth (2013-2014)	N/A	11%	26%	43%	19%	21%	15%	12%	16%
Fixed broadband (millions)	711	345	366	3	12	313	40	173	163
Per 100 people	10	27	6	<1	3	8	14	28	17

Source: International Telecommunication Union (2014)

developing countries, which stand at 31.1 users (Table 5). Africa's best performer, Mauritius, has rates of Internet usage close to that of developing countries and this connectivity has underpinned the island's strong trade links and international competitiveness.

Mobile telephony: An African success story

Infrastructure services provided by connectivity, particularly mobile communications, have the potential to spur development of other sectors. The most important of these has been mobile banking (Box 3). However, other uses, such as providing market information (e.g. prices for cacao on international markets) or weather-related information, improve the functioning of the market as well.

Internet still lags

Africa's mixed performance with fixed broadband Internet connections, associated with the high cost of Internet usage for those with connections, represents a cost to economy and a missed opportunity. More Africans access the Internet through smartphones than via a fixed broadband connection. Because of poor Internet connectivity African countries find it more difficult to tap into highly attractive openings for trade in services such as call centers, provision of back-office financial services, tourism, although the continent has some clear-cut advantages for such developments (proficiency in English and French, and being on the same time zones as Europe). African firms are also less competitive than their peers because of inability to interconnect efficiently with customers and suppliers in a timely fashion.

Kenya's M-Pesa brought banking-by-phone to Africa. Since its introduction the service has grown into a bona fide payment network.

Table 5: Key ICT statistics

Region	Internet users (per 100 people)	Mobile cellular subscriptions (per 100 people)	Fixed broadband subscriptions (per 100 people)	Fixed telephone subscriptions (per 100 people)
Sub-Saharan Africa	19	71	<1	1
Africa	14	78	1	3
Best, Africa	Mauritius (57)	Gabon (171)	Mauritius (15)	Mauritius (30)
Comparators	23	96	3	8
Best, Comparators	Vietnam (48)	Vietnam (147)	Moldova (15)	Moldova (3)
East Asia and Pacific (developing)	42	101	12	14
Latin America and Caribbean (developing)	47	111	9	17
South Asia	17	75	1	2
Low and middle income countries	31	90	6	9

Source: World Bank (2016d)

Box 3: Mobile banking in Kenya—A real success story

Kenya's M-Pesa brought banking-by-phone to Africa. Since its introduction, the service has grown into a bona fide payment network. More than 60 million Africans use basic mobile phones to transfer money from one person to another, take out insurance policies and collect payment from government agencies. Africa's "mobile money" market exceeded $61 billion in 2012—greater than the amount of money sent via mobile in Europe and North America combined. In some months the value of Kenya's mobile money transactions equals or exceeds 60 percent of GDP (Source: GSM Association).

Launched in 2007 by carriers Safaricom and Vodacom, M-Pesa's success is based on its simplicity. Customers buy credit on their mobile phone accounts to pay bills or buy products. To transfer money to a person, merchant, or government agency, all they need is the creditor's related phone number. The debits are deducted directly from the mobile phone account, with no need to fuss over a bank account. Customers give debtors their mobile number to use in settling up; when a debt payment comes in, their mobile phone account is credited.

Mobile phones have spread faster than bank branches. Mobile money accounts outnumber bank accounts in Kenya, Tanzania, Uganda and Madagascar. Today, 150 mobile money services such as M-Pesa serve more than 81.8 million customers in Africa, the Middle East and Asia; 41 new mobile money operators launched in these emerging economies over the past year, the GSMA reported. Africa is the world's largest market: In Sub-Saharan Africa, more people have a mobile money account than are signed up for Facebook.

These systems have obvious appeal for people without bank accounts, or what the financial services industry calls the "unbanked." In Kenya, this represents more than 80 percent of the market. For many Kenyans, their first mobile phone contract served to introduce them to the world of debit and credit. With minimal banking regulations in the region, African mobile companies were able to add various retail banking services (insurance, microfinance, remittances) to the traditional pay-as-you-go contract.

Source: Bloomberg (2013)

While electricity, transport, and telecommunications infrastructure supports country competitiveness and trade, and also (perhaps to a lesser extent) inclusive growth, provision of safe water and sanitation is directly responsible for reducing poverty and supporting inclusive growth.

Water and sanitation

Installed water and sanitation capacity

While electricity, transport, and telecommunications infrastructure supports country competitiveness and trade, and also (perhaps to a lesser extent) inclusive growth, provision of safe water and sanitation is directly responsible for reducing poverty and supporting inclusive growth. Serious waterborne illnesses such as diarrhea are leading causes of infant mortality and malnutrition, with impacts that extend beyond health to the productive sectors of the economy through lost work days and school absenteeism. Meeting the Millennium Development Goal (MDG) for access to safe water would produce an economic benefit of US$3.1 billion (in 2000 dollars) in Africa, through time savings and health benefits.

Adequate sanitation (defined as any private or shared, but not public, facility that guarantees that waste is hygienically separated from human contact) also makes a key contribution to public health, particularly in densely populated areas. Adequate sanitation reduces the risk of a broad range of diseases—including respiratory ailments, malaria, and diarrhea—and reduces the prevalence of malnutrition. Access to this standard of sanitation produces direct health gains by preventing disease and delivering economic and social benefits. A reduction in diarrheal illness would produce a gain of 99 million days of school and 456 million days of work for the working population ages 15–59 in Africa.

The international adoption of the MDGs in 2000 created a framework for focusing poverty reduction efforts. MDG 7 calls for reducing by half the number of people without sustainable access to safe drinking water and improved sanitation. The world overall is on track to meet the MDG drinking water target, but Africa lags. The gap is most acute in Sub-Saharan Africa, where only 58 percent of the population enjoys access to safe drinking water, and the gap is widening as the increasingly urban population places a greater strain on existing service providers (Table 6). Of the 828 million people in the world whose water sources remain unimproved, 37 percent live in Sub-Saharan Africa.[11]

Key issues

Access to improved water and sanitation remains inadequate, particularly in rural areas: In rural areas, reliance on surface water remains prevalent, and boreholes are the principal improved source of water, accounting for a further 40 percent of the population. Access to piped water and standposts is very low. Indeed, in many countries, less than 1 percent of the rural population receives piped water. In urban areas, coverage of piped water fell markedly over the past decade owing to rapid population growth but is still the single largest source of urban water. Coverage of standposts saw a similar decline. Overall, about two-thirds of the urban populace depends on utility water. Utilities are the central actors responsible for water supply in urban areas.

For sanitation, traditional pit latrines are by far the most common facility in both urban and rural areas, but more than a third of the population—mostly in rural areas—still defecates in the open. Improved sanitation (septic tanks and improved latrines) reaches less than 20 percent of Africa's population, and less than 10 percent in rural areas. Coverage of improved latrines is no greater than that of septic tanks, despite the significant cost difference between them. Only 10 percent of the population uses a septic tank; coverage in rural areas is practically negligible. In urban areas, septic tanks are much more common than improved latrines, and less than 10 percent of the population practices open defecation.

High water tariffs: African water utilities operate in an environment of high costs. However, overall, Africa's experience in recovering operating costs is positive, with many utilities setting tariffs at levels high enough to recoup

11. Banerjee, S. and Morella, E. (2011). *Africa's Water and Sanitation Infrastructure—Access, Affordability, and Alternatives*. Washington: World Bank.

African tariffs are highest among the developing regions, but African utilities are still not able to adequately fund either capital expenditures or maintenance.

Table 6: Key water and sanitation access statistics

Region	Improved water source (% of pop. with access)	Improved water source, rural (% of rural pop. with access)	Improved water source, urban (% of urban pop. with access)	Improved sanitation facilities (% of pop. with access)	Improved sanitation facilities, rural (% of rural pop. with access)	Improved sanitation facilities, urban (% of urban pop. with access)
Sub-Saharan Africa	66	55	86	30	23	40
Africa	75	65	89	40	32	51
Best, Africa	Mauritius (100)	Mauritius (100)	Egypt, Tunisia, Niger (100)	Seychelles (98)	Seychelles (98)	Seychelles (98)
Comparators	87	81	95	71	64	84
Best, Comparators	Vietnam (96)	Vietnam (95)	Nicaragua (99)	Uzbekistan (100)	Uzbekistan (100)	Uzbekistan (100)
East Asia and Pacific (developing)	93	89	97	75	64	85
Latin America and Caribbean (developing)	94	83	97	81	62	86
South Asia	92	91	95	45	35	65
Low and middle income countries	89	83	95	61	47	76

Source: World Bank (2016d)

operations and maintenance costs. In fact, African tariffs are highest among the developing regions, but African utilities are still not able to adequately fund either capital expenditures or maintenance.

Water sector performance: Many African governments have reformed their water supply and sanitation (WSS) systems in the past two decades to provide better services for their citizens. Countries that have pursued institutional reforms have built more efficient and effective sector institutions and achieved faster expansion of higher quality services. The potential dividend of such efforts is large, because addressing utility inefficiencies alone could make a substantial contribution to closing the sector funding gap in many countries. Utilities that have decentralized their WSS services or adopted private sector management have done a better job of eliminating inefficiencies and other hidden costs than those that have not. Unbundling of services can also be beneficial, but unbundling is rare in Africa and exclusively concentrated in middle income countries, whose superior performance can be explained for many other reasons. The reform agenda has had two major thrusts: increasing private participation and improving governance from within. Private sector participation has helped to improve utility performance, with Senegal being particularly noteworthy (Box 4).

Low-cost infrastructure services are key for export competitiveness by reducing transport costs and providing connectivity between suppliers and their markets, and allows for greater economic diversification.

Box 4: Senegal's successful experience with private sector participation

Water supply and sanitation in Senegal is characterized by a relatively high level of access compared to the average of Sub-Saharan Africa. Water supply and sanitation has been provided under a public-private partnership that has been operating in Senegal since 1996, with Senegalaise des Eaux (SDE), a subsidiary of Saur International, as the private partner. SDE does not own the water system but manages it on a 10-year lease contract with the Senegalese government under an affermage contract. Between 1996 and 2014, water sales doubled to 131 million cubic meters per year, and the number of household connections increased by 165% to more than 638,000.

The Senegal experience under the affermage is characterized by significant expansion of access and a large increase in operational efficiency that mainly originated from a reduction of nonrevenue water (NRW).

Expansion of access was mainly related to a massive subsidized connection program sponsored by donors and, in part, to the cash-flow surplus generated by the private operators. The social connection program, implemented with donor support, provided about 129,000 connections (75 percent of all new connections installed) benefiting poor households living in targeted neighborhoods.

Improved efficiency was related to contract innovations geared toward increasing the operator's incentives to perform efficiently. The affermage contract included targets for reduction of NRW and improved bill collection, backed by financial penalties for noncompliance.

Another innovation in Senegal's public-private partnership was the responsibility of the private operator to finance part of the network's rehabilitation using cash flow. This approach provided the operator with more flexibility to identify and reduce water losses, lessening its dependency on the public asset-holding company.

The impact of these innovations on efficiency has been remarkable, making Senegal's affermage a prominent example of private participation in Africa. Today, Senegal can report a level of NRW comparable to the best water utilities in Western Europe. These results also confirm that operational efficiency is perhaps the area in which a private operator can make the most positive and consistent impact.

Source: Adapted from Banerjee and Morella (2011)

Future infrastructure requirements and financing needs

Drivers of physical infrastructure needs

Infrastructure underpins development of the domestic economy and contributes toward inclusive growth. It is also the enabler of regional integration. Low-cost infrastructure services are key for export competitiveness by reducing transport costs and providing connectivity between suppliers and their markets, and allows for greater economic diversification.

While countries in Africa are far from homogeneous, Africa's low infrastructure endowment is above all a reflection of its low GDP per capita income levels. Therefore, estimating future needs of physical infrastructure will depend to a large extent on expected growth in GDP and population over the period. But irrespective of growth assumptions, financing needs for new physical infrastructure and maintenance of existing stocks are likely to be very significant.

Financing needs for infrastructure in Africa

Current infrastructure financing

In 2015, total funding for infrastructure in Africa reached $83.5 billion, an increase of $8.9 billion (11.9%) over 2014. Of this total, African national governments themselves provided the highest share: $28.4 billion (34.1%), through their own, mainly fiscal, resources; multilateral and bilateral partners provided $25.5 billion (30.6%), most of

Public sector budgets remain both dominant and the primary source of funding for infrastructure in Africa as in other regions of the world.

which was on concessional or near concessional terms; government-to-government lending, almost entirely from China, represented $22.0 billion (26.4%); and the private sector provided $7.4 billion (8.9%) (Figure 3). Private sector financing nearly doubled from 2014 to 2015, with the increase focused almost entirely on renewable energy investments in Morocco and South Africa, including the successful bidding round in the country's REIPPP program.

African infrastructure commitments in 2015 were focused mainly in electric power and transport, with roughly similar amounts ($34.7 billion) committed in each of these two sectors. Together, these sectors make up more than four-fifths of total infrastructure commitments in Africa. Historically, electric power has on average attracted more financing than transport, due to an extreme outlier situation in 2010 when very major financial commitments were made for North African energy projects and for the Eskom Investment Support Project in South Africa.

In geographic terms, Southern Africa (including South Africa) has been and remains the most important destination for infrastructure investments in Africa, attracting $27.6 billion in 2015 (33.1% of the total). This region saw a significant increase in commitments in 2015 compared to 2014, due to an increase in commitments to South Africa from $4.9 billion to $11.7 billion under the REIPPP program, as noted above.

Financing for infrastructure in Sub-Saharan Africa has tripled since 2004. Over this period, financing from international financial institutions (IFIs) increased (especially from the World Bank and African Development Bank, and China emerged as a major bilateral source. The most striking feature of this surge is the changing share of financing offered by traditional and non-traditional partners and private sector sources.

The funding increase since 2004 has benefitted a wide range of Sub-Saharan African countries. In absolute terms, the top recipients of external financing have been South Africa, Nigeria, Ghana, Kenya, and Ethiopia.[12] The electricity sector has had the fastest growth across all external financing sources. Excluding telecom, private finance for other sectors, especially energy, is highly concentrated in a few countries. Official Chinese investments are now expanding beyond the country's earlier focus on financing for resource-rich economies only and is reaching sectors in which it has particular technical expertise—such as hydropower—and those that are amenable to private sector participation—such as transport (especially road and rail).

As indicated above, public sector budgets remain both dominant and the primary source of funding for infrastructure in Africa as in other regions of the world. Public sector budgets are critical, as they establish the strategic framework within which support through external financing is coordinated. However, any future increase in financing for infrastructure will need to call to a greater extent on private financing, both as active investors and as providers of long-term capital (notably debt) from financial markets and the banking sector, as the fiscal situations both in African countries and among traditional development partners preclude the necessary increases in public funding.

Future infrastructure financing needs

Worldwide infrastructure spending has been estimated at some $2.5 trillion a year, or 2.8% of Gross World Product.[13] In Africa, infrastructure spending represents about 3.5% of the continent's GDP.

It is not easy to estimate future infrastructure financing needs in Africa, or indeed in any region of the world. Development practitioners advocate a benchmark of 5-6% of GDP for infrastructure financing to sustain growth.[14] Currently, across Sub-Saharan Africa there is a wide variation of the share of GDP devoted to infrastructure financing, with some countries (e.g. Lesotho, Cape Verde, Angola) investing over 8%, while Nigeria invests less than 3% and South Sudan less than 1%. The results do not appear

12. Gutman, J., Sy, A., and Chattopahyay, S. (2009). *Financing African Infrastructure – Can the World Deliver?* Washington: World Bank.
13. McKinsey Global Institute. (2016 June). Bridging global infrastructure gaps.
14. World Bank.

Any future increase in financing for infrastructure will need to call to a greater extent on private financing...as the fiscal situations both in African countries and among traditional development partners preclude the necessary increases in public funding.

Figure 3: Infrastructure financing by sector, region, and source

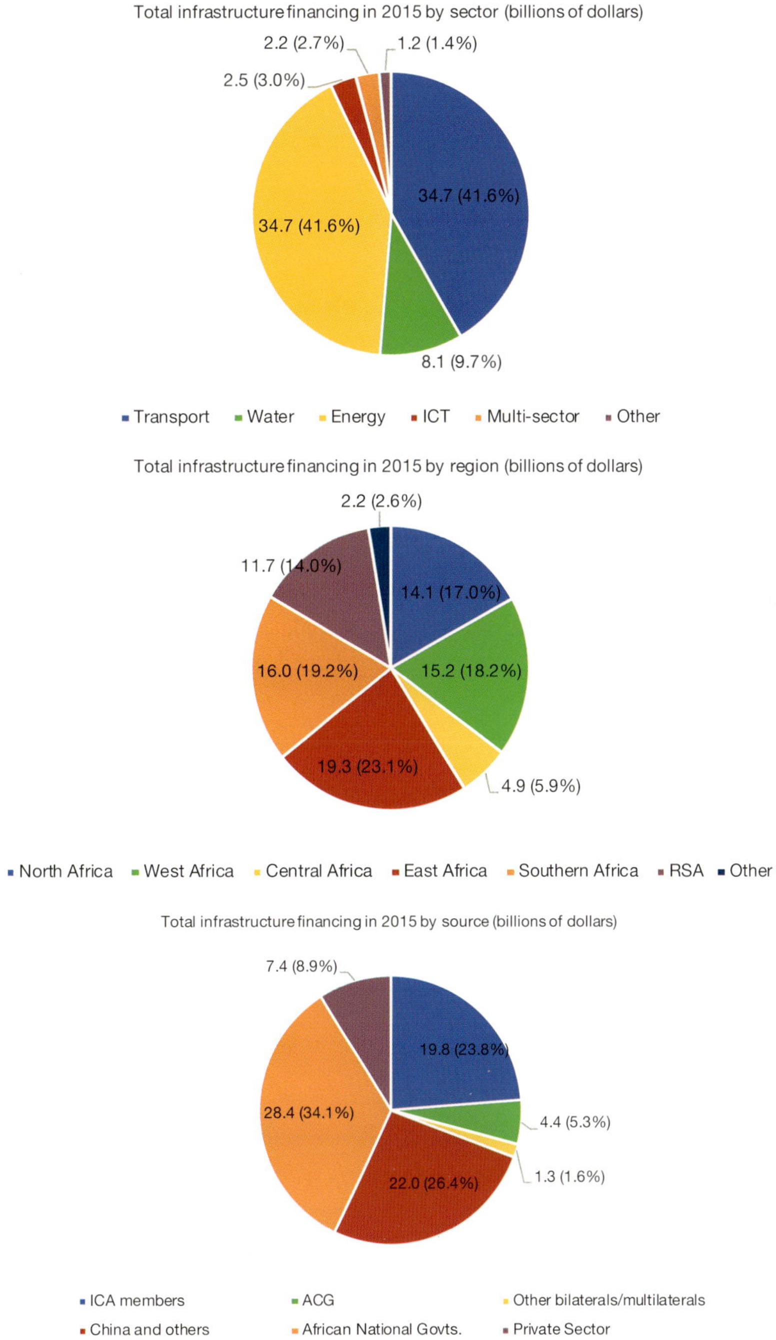

Source: ICA (2015)

Note: ICA members include G8 countries, the World Bank Group, African Development Bank Group, the European Commission, the European Investment Bank and Development Bank of South Africa.

For Africa, applying a 5% to 6% benchmark across the continent for future needs would lead to infrastructure spending requirements of around $120 billion to $140 billion per year in the short-term (2015 US$), compared to current infrastructure spending of $83.5 billion.

to reflect any direct relationship of budgetary allocation with either infrastructure capacity or needs.[15] For Africa, applying a 5% to 6% benchmark across the continent for future needs would lead to infrastructure spending requirements of around $120 billion to $140 billion per year in the short-term (2015 US$), compared to current infrastructure spending of $83.5 billion.[16][17]

Sources of finance for future infrastructure investments

Potential sources of finance for future infrastructure spending include:

- *Government money*
    - **From domestic resources**: government fiscal resources through the budgetary process
    - **From external resources**: cross-border IFI loans and guarantees, cross-border sovereign and sub-sovereign loans, governments issuing sovereign-guaranteed offshore bonds
- *Private money*
    - **Private sector investors**: conventional equity and debt investments including through public-private partnerships (PPPs)
    - **Institutional investors**: tapping domestic and international financial markets through infrastructure bonds and other securities purchased by insurance companies, pension funds, and the like

As noted previously, the African continent relies heavily on government sources of finance to fund its infrastructure spending. Taken together, governments' own fiscal resources plus offshore public money from DFIs and other governments represent 91.1% of total financing. Private sources in their different forms represented 8.9% of the total in 2015 (a near doubling compared to 2014) and rarely exceeds 5% in a typical year. This private money is largely from private sector investors, both direct and through PPPs, rather than from institutional investors via securities markets. Institutional investors, both domestic and international, contribute a small fraction of the total, although these sources of potential finance represent approximately $80 trillion worldwide.[18] Increasing Africa's annual infrastructure investments by $40 billion to $60 billion per year will require tapping into funds held by institutional investors, thus mobilizing domestic and international savings currently held in insurance companies, pensions, sovereign wealth funds, and private equity funds and endowments.

Obstacles to attracting financing from the private sector

Even in developed markets, there is the belief that the private sector, particularly institutional investors, could be better harnessed to support investment in new infrastructure. In the developing world, this problem is exacerbated, although larger middle income developing countries have started to see a trend toward greater involvement of institutional investors in their infrastructure sectors for larger projects. In Africa, by contrast, these investors are almost invisible in the infrastructure space. The question can be asked why this is so.

Private investors require a return on their investment. It is important to note that this source of potential funding is therefore not appropriate for all infrastructure subsectors but must be reserved for those subsectors able to generate revenues through user fees (energy, telecoms, ports and airports, toll roads, and toll bridges). Three major

15. Gutman, Sy, and Chattopahyay (2015) and other recent World Bank data.

16. In 2009, the World Bank issued a comprehensive report on African Infrastructure that estimated that $93 billion per year is needed to meet the infrastructure needs of Sub-Saharan Africa alone.

17. Infrastructure economists estimate magnitudes of investment needs based on countries' existing physical infrastructure stocks and the elasticity of stocks' growth with respect to national income. For most countries, elasticities are close to 1 for most infrastructure sectors. Therefore, as a first approximation, physical infrastructure stocks increase more or less in line with GDP growth.

18. Worldwide assets under management are estimated at $120 trillion, of which $80 trillion by institutional investors and $40 trillion by banks (McKinsey Global Institute 2016).

African governments and regional securities markets can do more to streamline and harmonize financial sector and business regulations to attract more investment, in general, and from institutional investors, in particular.

obstacles need to be addressed to allow private investors to participate in financing African infrastructure:

1. *Circumscribing investor risk*
   - **Private sector-friendly business environment**: African governments do not always encourage dynamic private sector engagement in their countries. Financial sector regulation and cross-border investment rules on the African continent also often limit investor appetite for infrastructure projects, and many overlapping and contradictory national regulations create barriers to investment.[19] African governments and regional securities markets can do more to streamline and harmonize financial sector and business regulations to attract more investment, in general, and from institutional investors, in particular.
   - **Streamline and standardize Africa's investment frameworks**: Different political, regulatory, and legal frameworks and policies lead to inconsistent regulatory decisions across the continent that balkanize markets and increase investor uncertainty. African governments at a regional level need to establish and enforce a body of laws and regulations that (i) provides for fair and equitable treatment, national treatment, and most-favored-nation treatment of foreign investment; and (ii) provides for resolution of disputes between business and government through binding offshore dispute-resolution mechanisms. Adoption by African countries of the OECD Declaration on International Investment and Multinational Enterprises could be an important first step. African countries need to think of development in terms of multi-country economic corridors and refashion their regulatory frameworks accordingly.
   - **Risk management and credit enhancement at the project level**: For institutional investors, infrastructure investment is an alternative to government securities: they generate higher yield, yet can be relatively low-risk. Risks can be circumscribed and financing costs brought down through credit enhancement mechanisms such as partial risk guarantees, mezzanine investment tranches which absorb first-loss, and political risk insurance. Multilateral development banks (MDBs), such as the World Bank, IFC, African Development Bank, and MIGA, all have these mechanisms in their toolboxes but do not deploy them sufficiently[20] to support Africa's infrastructure. Instead, these institutions seem to prefer deploying their own scarce resources in the form of sovereign loans and credits. These do not crowd in institutional lenders and simply add to governments' sovereign debt burden. Much can be done to strengthen the MDBs' game to crowd in the private sector better.
2. *Developing African infrastructure as an asset class*
   - **Regional exchanges**: In most cases, Africa's national exchanges will be too modest in scope to attract major international players on their own. The major regional securities exchanges need to be strengthened to serve multiple countries in the region and attract large institutional investors (e.g. JSE in South Africa, WAEMU securities exchange in Abidjan, Nairobi Stock Exchange, Bourse de Casablanca). Multilateral development

19. Basel III and Solvency II also create barriers to investment: they mandate high-risk capital allocations for infrastructure, which runs counter to the actual profiles of infrastructure investments that (once operational) are often low-risk.

20. With, perhaps, the exception of MIGA.

Unless pipelines of bankable projects are established and made public, involving the private sector will be difficult.

banks need to step up to play the role of market makers, for example, by financing project preparation to make greenfield infrastructure projects bankable and creating and securitizing pipelines of bundled brownfield assets for listing on the exchanges.

- **Standardization**: Institutional investors require standardized documentation, transparent and recognized credit ratings (the quality of investments must often be of investment grade and above), and consistency of security instruments. Financial terms and risk categories need to be consistent, risk-return reviews and credit ratings established, and market indexes developed. This needs to be done at the supranational level to ensure regional consistency.
- **Pooling in order to tap financial markets**: Many African infrastructure projects are simply too small on their own to attract institutional investors, and this is true also for some countries. Pooling of projects (including across countries), development of investment funds, and securitization will be needed.[21] In particular, experience with private sector financing of infrastructure in the developed world underlines the potential of refinancing brownfield assets through market mechanisms and recycling the freed-up resources into new greenfield projects. A widely recognized and respected market maker such as an MDB will be needed to undertake these tasks.

3. *Pipelines of bankable projects*

- **Project feasibility**: Identified infrastructure gaps have often not been fleshed out into project concepts; feasibility studies have not been undertaken; or the project has not been adequately structured financially to ensure bankability. The essential prior work needs to be financed and undertaken before private sector financing can be secured. Unless pipelines of bankable projects are established and made public, involving the private sector will be difficult.
- **User-fee reservation for debt service**: Where infrastructure subsectors have the potential to generate revenues, these revenues should be used to service the associated debt. In cases where such projects have been adequately prepared, potential revenues have often not been demarcated as user fees and reserved for this purpose. Instead, they are often absorbed through the tariff structure into an often-insolvent public utility, which, because of its precarious financial situation, is unable to service the debt. For the private sector to be able to invest in such cases, either the user fee must be paid into an escrow mechanism established for the purposes of servicing the debt or an external body must step in and guarantee the utility's payment obligations.
- **Brownfield assets will be simpler to finance than greenfield projects**: Even when projects have been well defined and user fees earmarked, the overall riskiness of the project increases the risk spread that investors will require. This can make the cost of financing prohibitively expensive for the investment. To create an infrastructure asset class with a manageable risk profile, a clear first step would be to refinance a pool

21. In this regard, a salutary first step has been taken by the African Development Bank with the creation of the Africa50 Infrastructure Fund to tap into the institutional investor segment.

Depending on the infrastructure sector concerned, African governments need to consider moving away from the existing SOE utility model, just as they did with the telecom sector following the introduction of mobile phones.

of existing revenue-generating infrastructure assets where construction risk is minimal and cashflows are already well known. Refinancing such brownfield assets would allow the initial investment capital to be freed up and recycled into new infrastructure investments.

To put in place the above prior conditions, action is needed at the supranational and regional level. There is a clear role for one or several MDBs to support the harmonization of regulatory and business environments at the sub-regional level: develop African infrastructure as an asset class; and create pipelines of bankable projects with manageable risk. This could, for example, be achieved through a dedicated African Infrastructure Facility with very clear mission and guidelines.

Key findings for infrastructure financing

Inadequate private financing: Africa does not call on significant private financing of infrastructure and current financing is mostly in the form of sovereign (fiscal revenue or government-guaranteed borrowings) or Official Development Assistance (ODA). In particular, Africa makes almost no call on assets managed by institutional investors although these represent a significant potential source of funding to finance the required increase in spending on the continent.

Private financing will not flow regularly for infrastructure until the different sectors are creditworthy, which in most cases involves moving away from the rigid SOE utility models to new institutional setups. This has been done successfully in a number of examples, most notably delegation of water and sanitation to a private enterprise in Senegal and a privately-run electric power system in Côte d'Ivoire. Still, this approach does not seem to attract much enthusiasm from the continent's decision makers. However, there is considerable scope to create African infrastructure as an asset class to attract institutional investors and bring fresh funding to the table.

Action agenda

As this paper indicates, Africa needs more infrastructure investment, and it needs better operation and maintenance of its infrastructure stocks to achieve better infrastructure services for its economies and its population from these stocks. These dual but compatible objectives suggest that African decision makers need to focus on three sets of actions.

New models for the delivery of infrastructure services

Depending on the infrastructure sector concerned, African governments need to consider moving away from the existing SOE utility model, just as they did with the telecom sector following the introduction of mobile phones. A model based on multiple privately owned and financed operators is in many cases not applicable (e.g. for road infrastructure), but where technology allows, this model should be considered. Specifically, the following might be considered:

- **Power**: This is the sector with the most potential for tapping new technologies, notably solar and other renewables, in a delivery model that involves privately owned and financed off-grid and mini-grid systems. However, governments must accept dismantling the de facto and de jure monopolies that currently favor the incumbent utility.
- **Transport**: The sector needs to move away from national systems and toward a regional (multi-national) planning and investment program. Notably, governments need to seek real physical integration by developing transport corridors with significant private sector investment (ports, rail, toll-roads) and with bonded transport and storage facilities, such as inland ports.
- **ICT**: Mobile telephony functions for the most part quite well, although better attention could be paid to interconnectivity of competing systems. The most urgent need is to strengthen fixed broadband Internet access by introducing open access

The most glaring area for progress in infrastructure financing is to increase flows of private finance, particularly institutional investors (pension funds and insurance companies).

to trunk-line fiber-optic cables and gateways, encouraging competition. Again, this needs a policy decision from governments to move away from current monopoly situations, in many cases run by the rump of the former fixed line telecoms operator (e.g. in Niger), and to encourage competition and open markets.

- **Water and sanitation**: This sector has had the greatest success in moving to privately run (and to some extent financed) operational models, notably concessions and affermages. Other countries need to consider such institutional setups.

Improved management of assets

New institutional setups, such as those outlined above, will begin to address the poor operation and maintenance records of African infrastructure operators. In the case of concessions and affermages, specific maintenance requirements can be included in relevant contractual documentation, with penalties in case of non-respect. In the case of privately owned assets (telecoms), investors have an economic incentive to operate and maintain their asset correctly.

Cost-reflective tariffs: In addition to new institutional setups, there needs to be a focus on principles to ensure that operation and maintenance are fully funded. Current tariff mechanisms often set prices for consumers below long-run marginal costs, with the result that the investor/operator is not financially viable and is therefore unable to cover its costs. Maintenance, as it can be deferred (unlike direct costs such as salaries), is generally the first cost item to be cut, which leads to deterioration of the physical asset.

Payment by government: Governments and government agencies have a poor track record for paying infrastructure tariffs (electricity and water, in particular) across the continent. This forgone revenue contributes to sector operators' financial hardship and inability to fully finance operation and maintenance. African governments need to consider approaches, such as hard budget constraints and fixed line-items in national budgets, to cover payment for these services. It should be noted that there have been interesting experiences for payment of tariffs by government agencies, e.g. through the use of pre-paid mobile telecoms cards, that could be further explored.

Innovative financing

Need for private financing: The most glaring area for progress in infrastructure financing is to increase flows of private finance, particularly institutional investors (pension funds and insurance companies). The measures outlined above (new delivery models and improved operations and maintenance), associated with cost-reflective tariffs and payment by government for the services it consumes, will go some way toward improving the financial viability of the sector and hence its creditworthiness and ability to attract private financing.

However, the priority for African governments must be to develop domestic financial markets and instruments to channel national savings to long term infrastructure projects. This will involve, in particular, development of domestic debt markets at the regional level, and the creation of African infrastructure as an asset class to attract institutional investors.

Annex 1: African infrastructure financing commitments, 2015

Table A1: Commitments by region and sector (billions of dollars)

	Transport	Water	Energy	ICT	Multi-sector	Other	Total
North Africa	5,141	2,109	5,144	269	838	632	14,132
West Africa	7,114	1,371	5,412	576	650	72	15,195
Central Africa	2,252	622	1,350	562	135	–	4,921
East Africa	11,779	1,960	5,350	177	26	–	19,293
Southern Africa	2,694	1,452	10,631	704	28	463	15,971
RSA	4,763	509	6,254	12	132	–	11,669
Other	943	94	526	220	409	–	2,191
Total commitments	34,686	8,117	34,668	2,519	2,216	1,167	83,372

*Source:*ICA (2015)

Table A2: Commitments by region and source (billions of dollars)

	ICA	ACG	RDBs	China and others	European non-ICA	National governments	Private sector	Total
North Africa	4093	1921	–	–	691	6199	1229	14132
West Africa	4014	1201	359	4449	14	3879	1280	15195
Central Africa	1308	498	55	482	68	2190	320	4921
East Africa	4702	467	5	7084	74	6915	45	19293
Southern Africa	1793	325	–	7727	8	5364	755	15971
RSA	1740	–	–	2238	23	3855	3813	11669
Other	2191	–	–	–	–	–	–	2191
Total commitments	19841	4412	418	21980	876	28402	7442	83372

*Source:*ICA (2015)

Table A3: Commitments by source and sector (billions of dollars)

	Transport	Water	Energy	ICT	Multi-sector	Other	Total
ICA members	6771	3184	8635	616	634	–	19841
ACG	2072	378	1555	17	392	–	4412
RDBs	174	48	95	76	26	–	418
China and others	9932	268	10748	1032	–	–	21980
Non-ICA Europeans	346	–	458	73	–	–	876
National governments	15278	4125	5962	705	1165	1167	28402
Private sector	114	114	7215	–	–	–	7442
Total commitments	34686	8117	34668	2519	2216	1167	83372

Source: ICA (2015)

Note: ICA members include G8 countries, the World Bank Group, the African Development Bank (African Development Bank) Group, the European Commission, the European Investment Bank and Development Bank of South Africa. ACG: Arab Coordination Group; RDB: Regional Development Bank (Central African States Development Bank, Development Bank of South Africa, ECOWAS Bank for Investment and Development, East Africa Development Bank, West African Development Bank).
Donor financing is assumbed to group ICA members, RDBs, and non-ICA Europeans.

Urbanization and Demographics: Planning Cities That Work

Chapter 9

Gregory K. Ingram

Introduction[1]

Africa, a large and heterogeneous continent, is experiencing high population growth and rapid urbanization. This paper reviews the interactions between Africa's total and urban population growth, highlights the key challenges posed by projected demographic changes, develops the implications that urban population growth has for the physical expansion of its cities, and relates such physical expansion to the investment in, and financing of, needed urban infrastructure. The paper also surveys the substantial challenges that climate change poses for urban growth in Africa and assesses how new technology associated with smart cities may help address Africa's looming urban growth and climate change issues. This analysis sometimes subdivides Africa into North Africa, comprising the five middle-income countries on its Mediterranean coast, and SSA, comprising the remaining 53 countries. Data are also examined from all of Africa's 58 countries and from a random sample of 25 African cities. The two regions are compared with seven other global regions to offer a global perspective, while data on individual countries and cities underpin more detailed analyses.

After placing Africa in the global context in terms of its current population, urbanization, and income; UN population projections from 2010 to 2050 are reviewed. Africa will have the largest regional increase in total and urban population—both absolutely and in percentage terms—over the forecast period. Africa's increase in total population is a key driver of its urban population increase. Its high rate of population growth makes it the only global region experiencing a declining dependency ratio,[2] which potentially can yield a demographic dividend spurring economic growth. At the same time, the population's share of young adults will remain very high, potentially threatening social stability if adequate economic growth is not realized. National and municipal policies likely will have little if any effect on these demographic trends in the short or medium run, due to the built-in demographic momentum.

Recent global trends in urbanization suggest that growing urban populations will expand urban areas greatly because urban population densities will continue to decrease, causing urbanized areas to grow at rates much higher than urban populations. Urban expansion will create tremendous needs for infrastructure investment. Installing a basic grid of arterial roads before urban development occurs is a high priority. Such a grid can guide urban development away from cultivated land, provide rights of way for transit and trunk utilities, improve urban productivity, and do so at less cost than the inevitable later efforts to retrofit infrastructure. Financing infrastructure will require new borrowing approaches and municipal finance reforms that enhance local revenue mobilization.

Climate change will have large impacts on Africa and its cities, causing increased stress on water systems throughout the continent and even speeding the movement of people from country to city in some areas. New infrastructure facilities need to take account of its effects. Smart city technology has the potential to improve the efficiency of existing infrastructure and make new infrastructure more productive. Africa's rapidly growing use of mobile phones and associated innovative applications are potential precursors of the benefits of new technology for cities.

Current population and income levels

Figure 1 provides a global context by displaying the 2010 populations for nine global regions (seven developing and two high income).[3] SSA ranks fourth in terms of 2010 population, and its urban population share is second lowest, just above that of South-Central Asia. North Africa is the smallest of the nine regions, and half its population is urbanized.

1. The author thanks H. Kohli, T. Ahlers, and B. Ormond for comments, and has drawn ideas from Ingram, G. (2016). Demographics and Urbanization, Ch. 3 in Kohli (2016).

2. Dependency ratio is discussed further below.

3. These nine regions are similar to those used by the United Nations, except that Japan has been grouped with Europe, and four high-income, land-rich countries (Australia, Canada, New Zealand, United States) have been grouped separately. See Annex 1 for country groupings.

SSA is projected to have the largest absolute (1.3 billion) and percentage (150 percent) increase in total population across regions, so that by 2050 its total population will be second only to South-Central Asia and well ahead of East Asia.

Figure 1: **Population and urban share, by region (2010)**

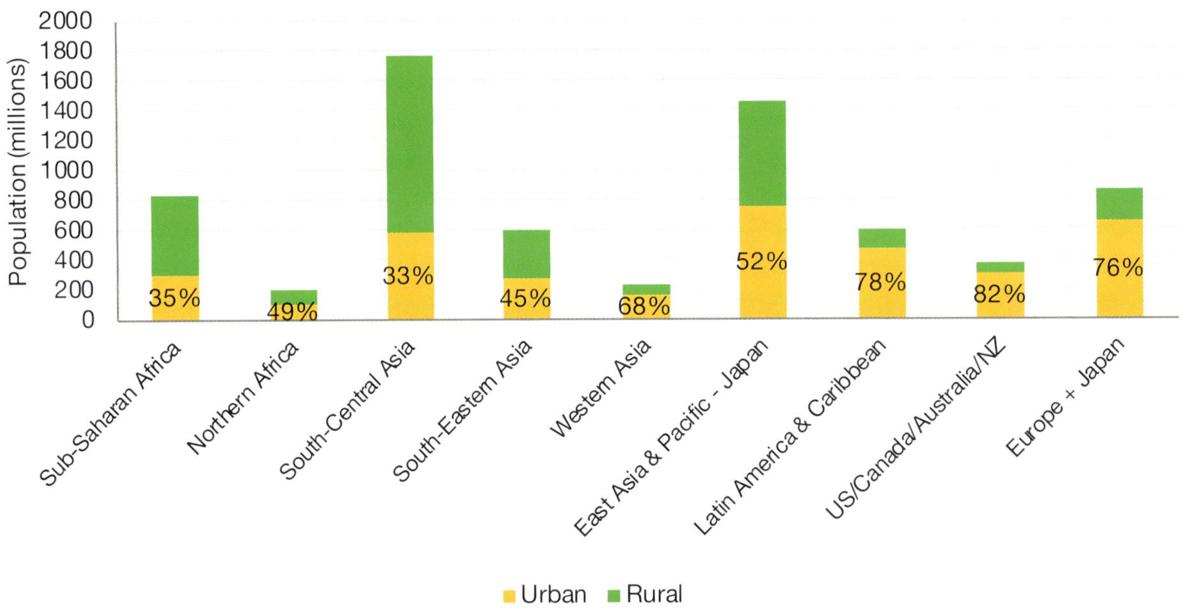

Source: United Nations (2014. 2015)

Figure 2 presents information on current country population and income for all countries in the seven developing regions. It displays the cumulated country populations by region with the countries ranked by per capita Gross National Income (GNI). Many of the 53 SSA countries are low income (GNI per capita less than United States$1,045 in 2014). The Sub-Saharan region contains 25 of the 30 countries ranked as low income by the World Bank, and these 25 countries currently hold about 40 percent of the region's population. The Latin America and Caribbean region also contains a large number of countries (43), but, unlike SSA, many of its small countries are middle or high income. It includes only one low income country, Haiti. South-Central Asia, dominated by India, is also a poor region, but it has only two low income countries, Afghanistan and Nepal, representing about 3 percent of that region's population. The East Asia and Pacific region has two low income countries, Cambodia and North Korea. North Africa is fairly homogeneous in terms of income, and all countries in that group are middle income. Referring back to Figure 1, the two regions with the lowest shares of urbanized population—South-Central Asia and SSA—are the poorest in Figure 2, reflecting urbanization's typical relation with income.

Projections of total populations to 2050

Planning for development requires projections of population growth; the projections used here are from the United Nations' most recent estimates for national (2015) and urban (2014) populations. Figure 3 shows 2010 total populations and projected regional populations for 2050. SSA is projected to have the largest absolute (1.3 billion) and percentage (150 percent) increase in total population across regions, so that by 2050 its total population will be second only to South-Central Asia and well ahead of East Asia. While the absolute population growth of North Africa is modest, it is tied for second in percentage terms with a projected 60 percent increase. The East Asia region,

Lower income countries have high annual projected population growth rates—most ranging from 2 to 3 percent—while middle income country rates center around one percent.

Figure 2: Developing regions: Cumulative country population by ascending GDP per capita

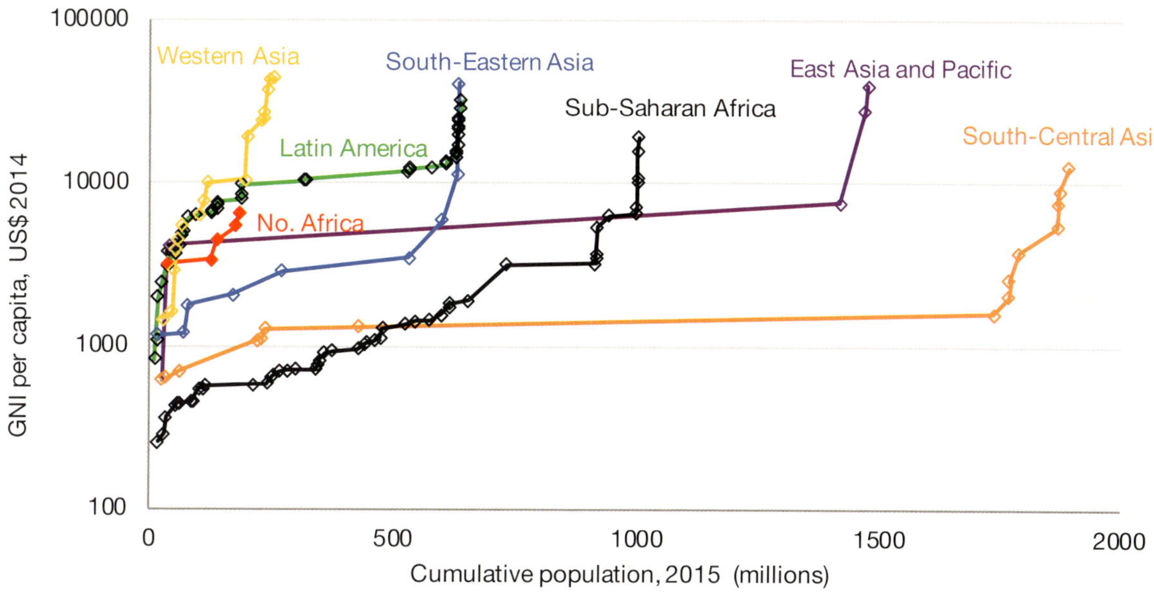

Source: World Ban k (2016d), United Nations (2015)
Note: Based on gross national income per capita in 2014. The World Bank income groups are: low income, $1,045 or less; lower middle income, $1,046-4,125; upper middle income, $4,126-12,735; and high income, $12,736 or more. Of the 30 low income countries, 25 are in SSA.

second largest in 2010, is projected to have essentially no overall population growth to 2050, while the population of Europe plus Japan declines because of the rapidly aging populations in both regions. The land-rich high income group (United States/Canada/Australia/New Zealand) is projected to experience moderate growth (up 27 percent) with international immigration making an important contribution.

Projected population growth varies inversely with current country GDP per capita at the aggregate level. Figure 4 shows this correlation using average per capita GDP and growth rates for the World Bank's four income groupings. Projected annual population growth falls steadily across the three lowest income groups, from 2.3 to 1.1 to 0.3 percent. There is virtually no difference in projected growth rates between upper middle and high income groupings. Figure 4 also shows the averages for the Sub-Saharan and Northern Africa regions. These two regional averages reflect the income group pattern but with above average population growth for their current income groups.

Figure 5 shows projected population growth and current GDP per capita at the country level for the Sub-Saharan and Northern Africa regions combined and reveals substantial variation around the underlying averages. Lower income countries have high annual projected population growth rates—most ranging from 2 to 3 percent—while middle income country rates center around one percent. The few outliers (high incomes and high growth rates) are labeled, and their situations are enlightening: Angola, Equatorial Guinea, and Gabon are oil exporters with high GDP per capita and very unequal income distributions. But in general, higher incomes are associated with lower population growth.

The good news for SSA is that its dependency ratio falls continuously over this period, potentially creating a demographic dividend that will enhance economic growth.

Figure 3: Population by region: 2010 & projected 2050

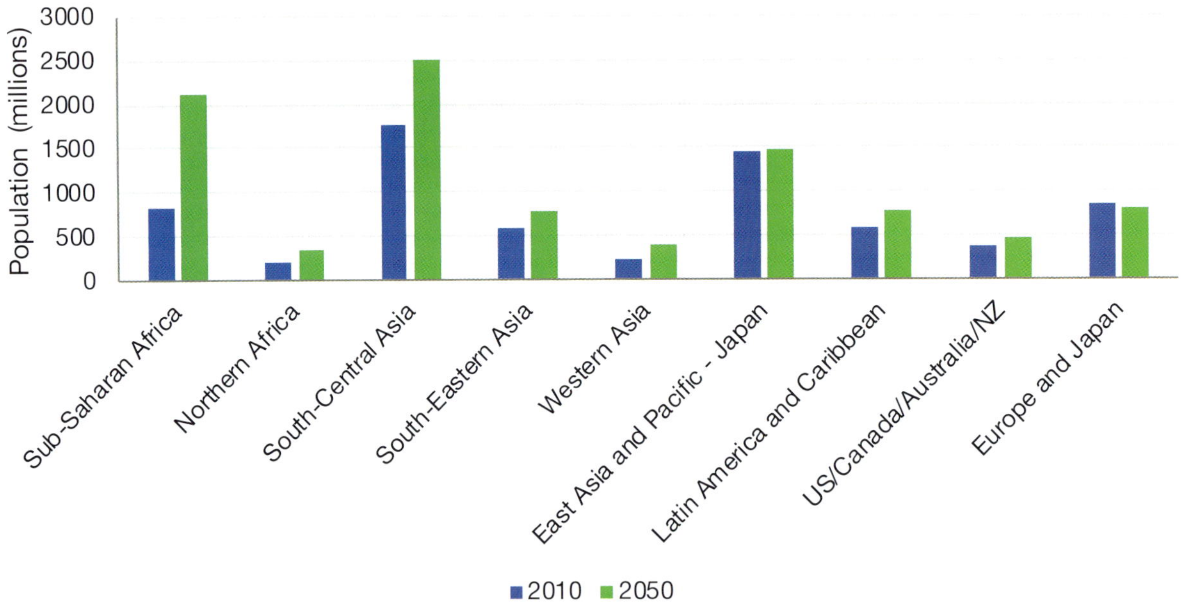

Source: United Nations (2015)

Figure 4: Projected population growth and current income

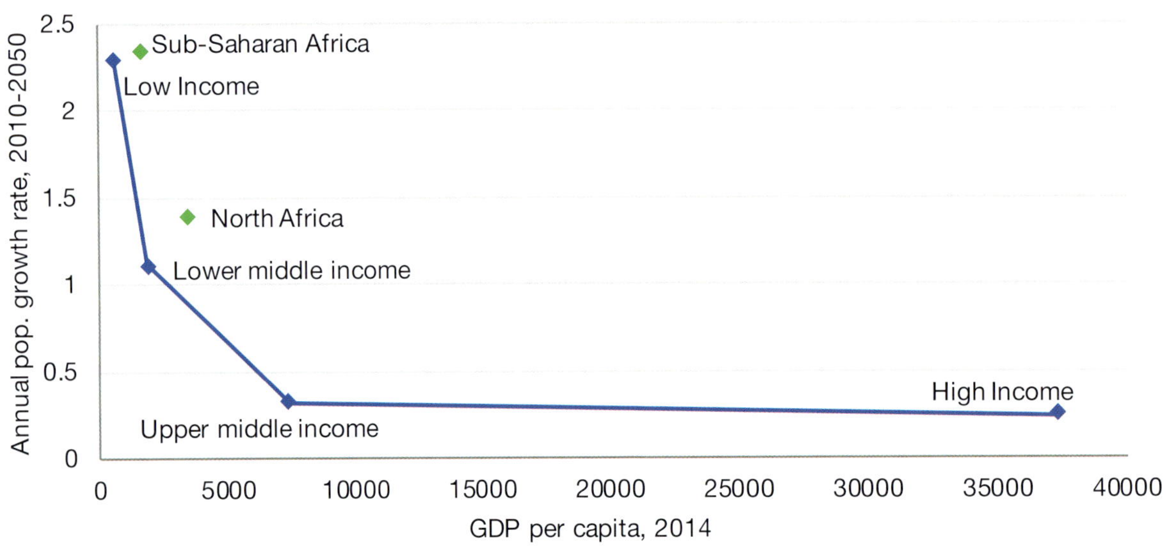

Source: United Nations (2015); World Bank (2016d)

Underlying the trend in SSA is the projected reduction in birth rates, reducing the share of the population 14 and younger well before the proportion 65 and older increases.

Figure 5: Projected country growth and current income

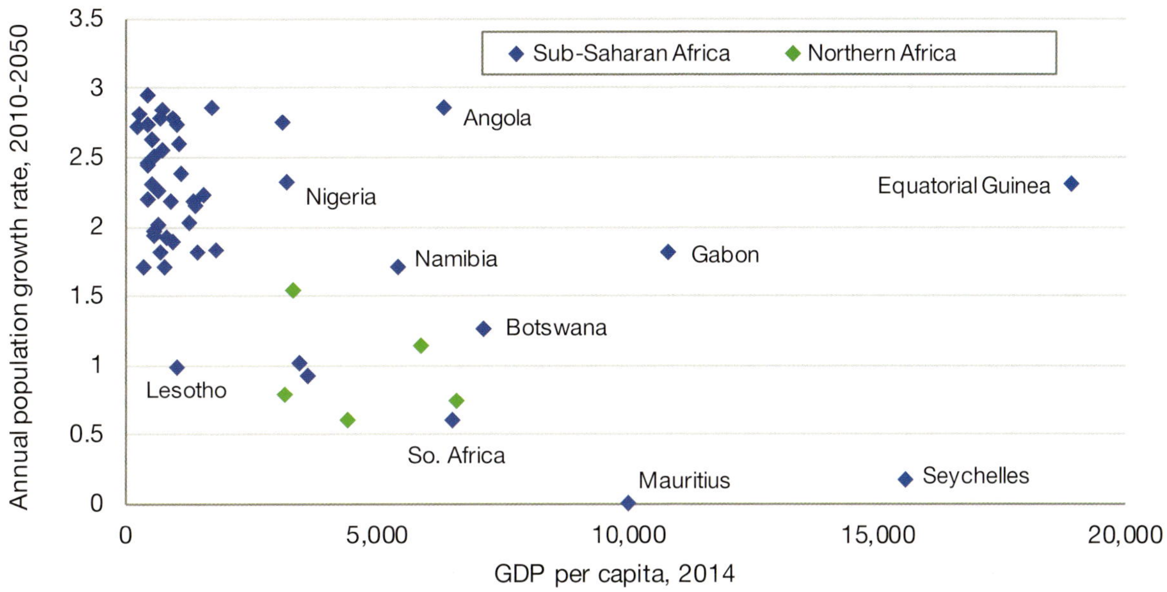

Source: United Nations (2015); World Bank (2016d)

Projected changes in demographic composition

The demographic composition of country populations will change in important ways from 2010 to 2050. The dependency ratio measures the ratio of "dependents" (those aged 0 through 14 plus those aged 65 and older) to the working age population (those aged 15 through 64) and so measures the economic burden that dependents place on an economy. High or rising dependency ratios are characterized as a headwind to economic growth; falling dependency ratios are characterized as a demographic dividend that facilitates economic growth. High dependency ratios can result from high birth rates (a growing share 14 and younger) or from increases in life expectancy and aging populations (a growing share 65 and older). Figure 6 shows projected dependency ratios from 2010 to 2050 by global region. The ratios increase continuously for Europe plus Japan and East Asia, and increase and then flatten for the United States/Canada/Australia/New Zealand—reflecting the aging populations of those regions. The good news for SSA is that its dependency ratio falls continuously over this period, potentially creating a demographic dividend that will enhance economic growth. North Africa shows a modest decline followed by an increase over this period with little net change. Underlying the trend in SSA is the projected reduction in s, reducing the share of the population 14 and younger well before the proportion 65 and older increases.

Figures 7 and 8 present data on the net change in dependency ratios from 2010 to 2050 by income group for the two Africa regions (Figure 7) and for each country in Sub-Saharan and North Africa combined (Figure 8). The patterns are similar to those in Figures 4 and 5 relating population growth to GDP per capita. The low income country group experiences a substantial demographic dividend; the lower middle income country group, a nearly neutral impact; and the upper middle and high income country groups experience substantial demographic headwinds

Starting in 2015, the projected percent of the population aged 15 through 29 in SSA is the highest across regions.

Figure 6: Dependency ratios by region

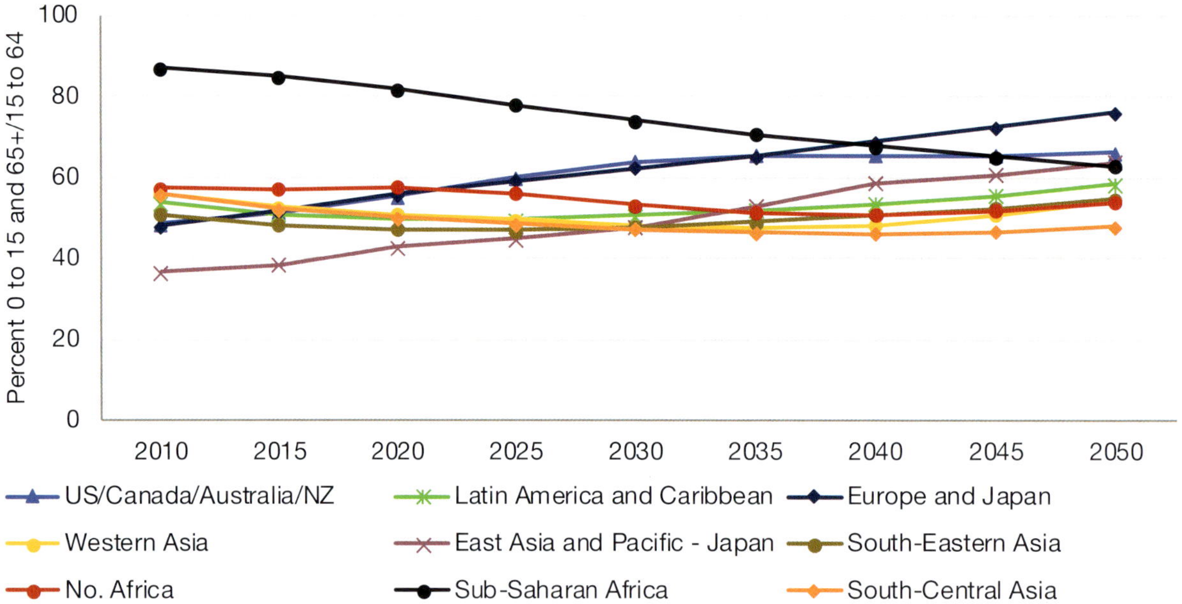

Source: United Nations (2015)

Figure 7: Projected change in dependency ratio and current income

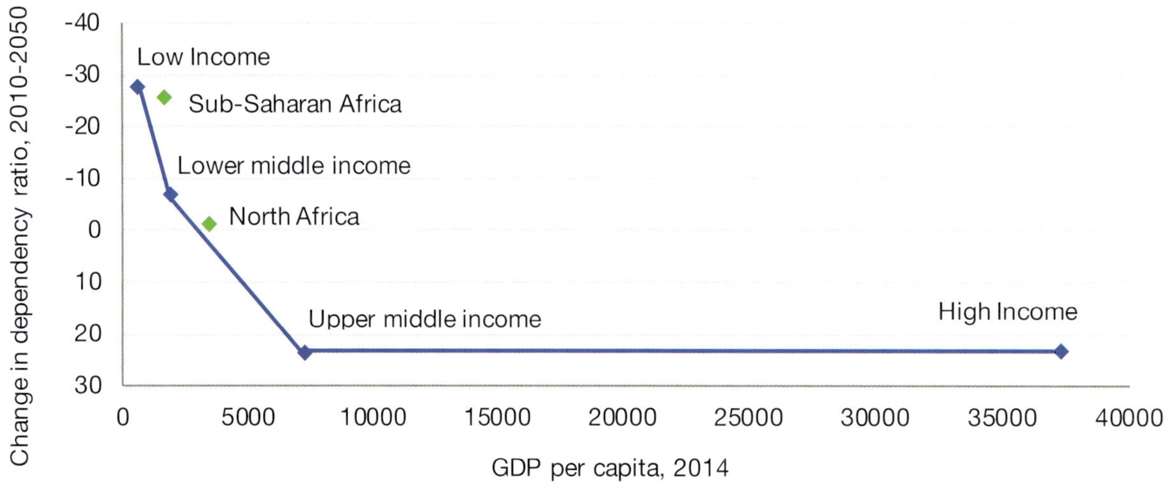

Source: United Nations (2015); World Bank (2016d)

While the demographic dividend that SSA will experience is positive, the high young adult population share could create problems if economic growth is low and unemployment is high.

Figure 8: Dependency ratio change, 2010-2050, and current income

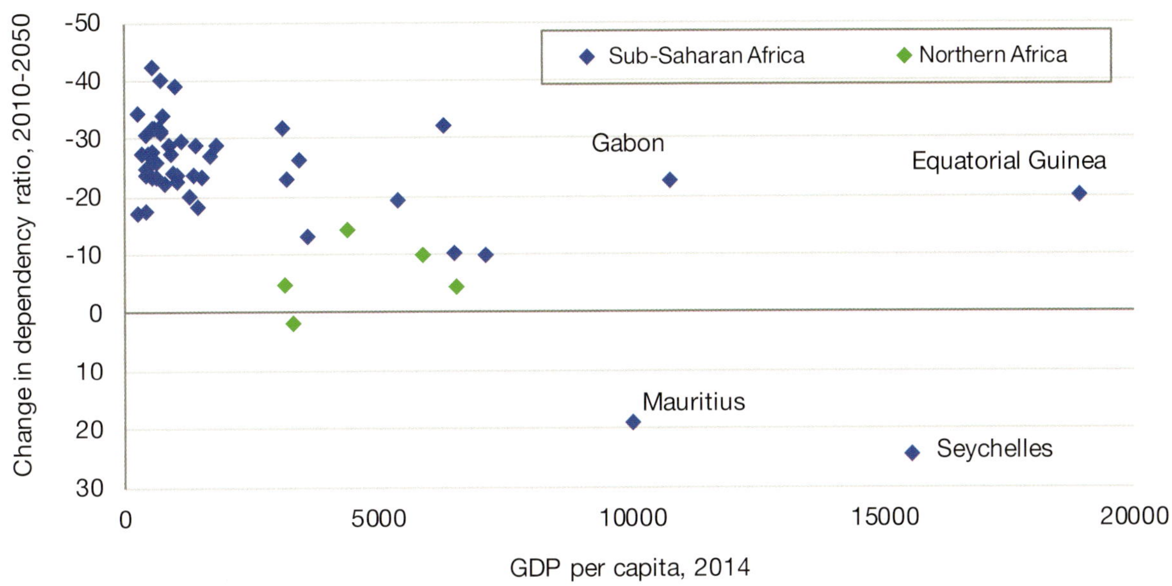

Source: United Nations (2015); World Bank (2016d)

from increased dependency ratios (Figure 7). The net changes shown in Figure 8 at the country level are varied, but they are clustered around the income group averages.

While a falling dependency ratio can produce a demographic dividend that aids growth, it can also create social challenges if economic growth is inadequate to provide jobs and incomes for the growing population. Unemployment is normally concentrated among younger workers, and young adults also have higher propensities to be restive and engage in illegal, antisocial, and risky behavior. The young adult share of the population can be measured directly as a "restiveness ratio;" Figure 9 shows the share of each region's population aged from 15 through 29, from 2010 to 2050. If growth is insufficient to keep unemployment rates down, civil unrest and domestic security issues are likely to be greater when this share is large.

The striking result is that, starting in 2015, the projected percent of the population aged 15 through 29 in SSA is the highest across regions. For North Africa, the young adult share is the highest in 2010, falls, and then rebounds to be the second highest from 2030 on. This demographic feature will be a challenge for the whole African continent and is the potential downside of SSA's demographic dividend. Meanwhile, the young adult share decreases for all other regions—most dramatically for East Asia, where the percentage is similar to that of Europe+Japan by 2025 and eventually falls below it by 2050. While the demographic dividend that SSA will experience is positive, the high young adult population share could create problems if economic growth is low and unemployment is high. It is unlikely that national or local policies will have much effect on Africa's overall population growth or the projected changes in the demographic composition of its population over this time period.

Projected increases in urban populations

The growth in total populations has significant economic impacts, but so does the growth of population in

SSA's urban population is projected to grow by close to 300 percent—nearly quadrupling from the level in 2010. North Africa's projected gain is 100 percent—a doubling of 2010 urban population.

Figure 9: Young adult population share by region, 2010-2050

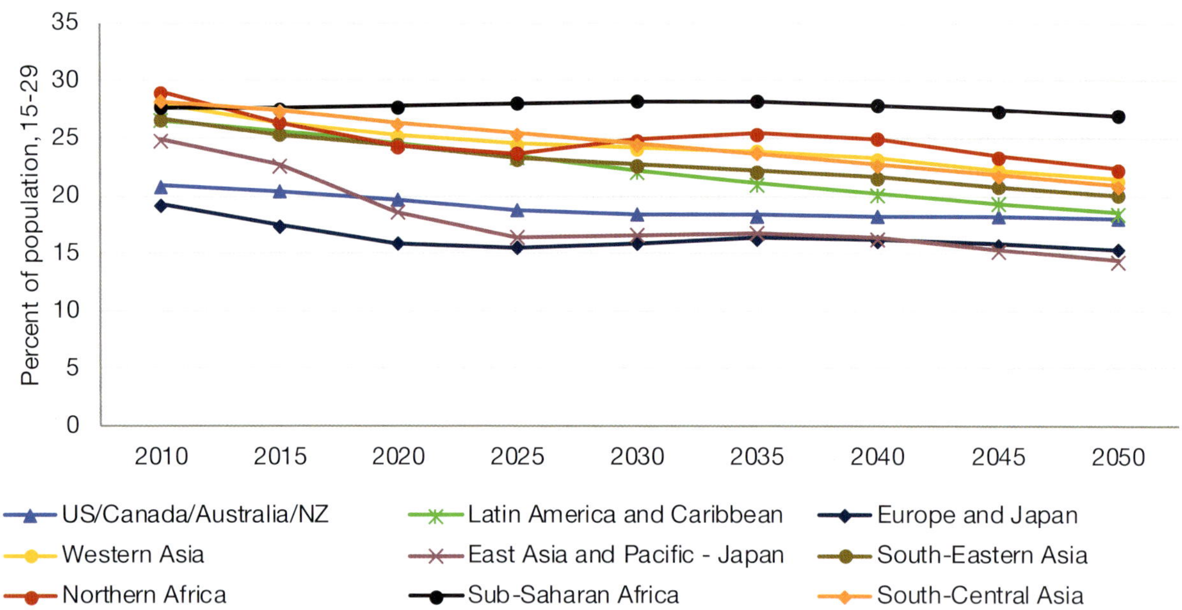

Source: United Nations (2015)

urban areas. Figure 10 shows the absolute change in total and urban population by region from 2010 to 2050. In most regions except SSA and North Africa, the urban population increases by more than the total population—implying that the rural population will decrease absolutely (and the most in East Asia). SSA is projected to experience the largest absolute increase in urban population across the regions.

The projected absolute increases in urban population are large, but even more remarkable are the percentage increases. Figure 11 shows that SSA's urban population is projected to grow by close to 300 percent—nearly quadrupling from the level in 2010. North Africa's projected gain is 100 percent—a doubling of 2010 urban population. The percentage increase projected for SSA's urban population is unprecedented.

Another perspective on urban population growth is the change in the share of total population over time that is urban. Shown in Figure 12 for each region, the pattern is one of smooth and steady progression for most regions. One exception is East Asia, whose urbanization is projected to accelerate and then slow over the next few decades. SSA and South Central Asia, the two poorest regions, have the lowest urban population shares throughout the period, and each reaches or exceeds 50 percent from 2040 to 2045. The declining difference in urban population shares over time illustrates a pattern of convergence across regions. Figure 12 makes it clear that the large increase in urban population projected for SSA is driven mainly by the large increase projected for its total population because its urban population share grows in a very regular manner—similar to that of most other regions.

Figure 12 also provides global evidence that increases in urban population shares tend to be larger for poorer and less urbanized regions. This pattern is also observed in Africa— Figure 13 relates each country's projected change in the percent of its urban population from 2010 to 2050 to its current income. Low income tends to be associated with higher increases in projected urbanization, consistent

The large increase in urban population projected for SSA is driven mainly by the large increase projected for its total population because its urban population share grows in a very regular manner—similar to that of most other regions.

Figure 10: Population change, urban and total, 2010 to 2050

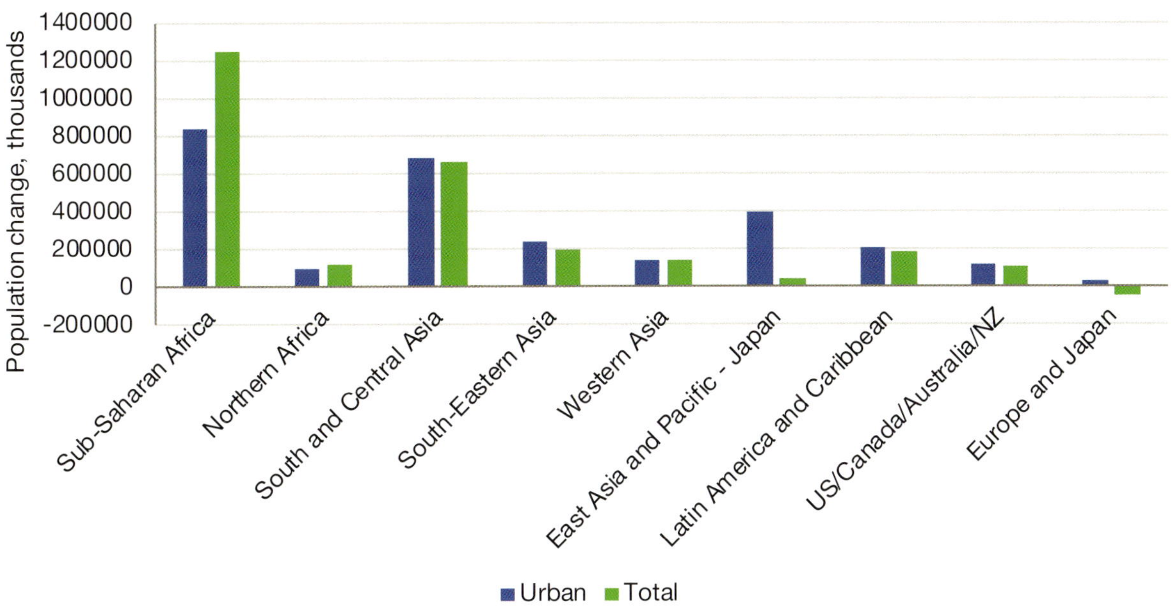

Source: United Nations (2014)

Figure 11: Percent change in population, urban and total, 2010 to 2050

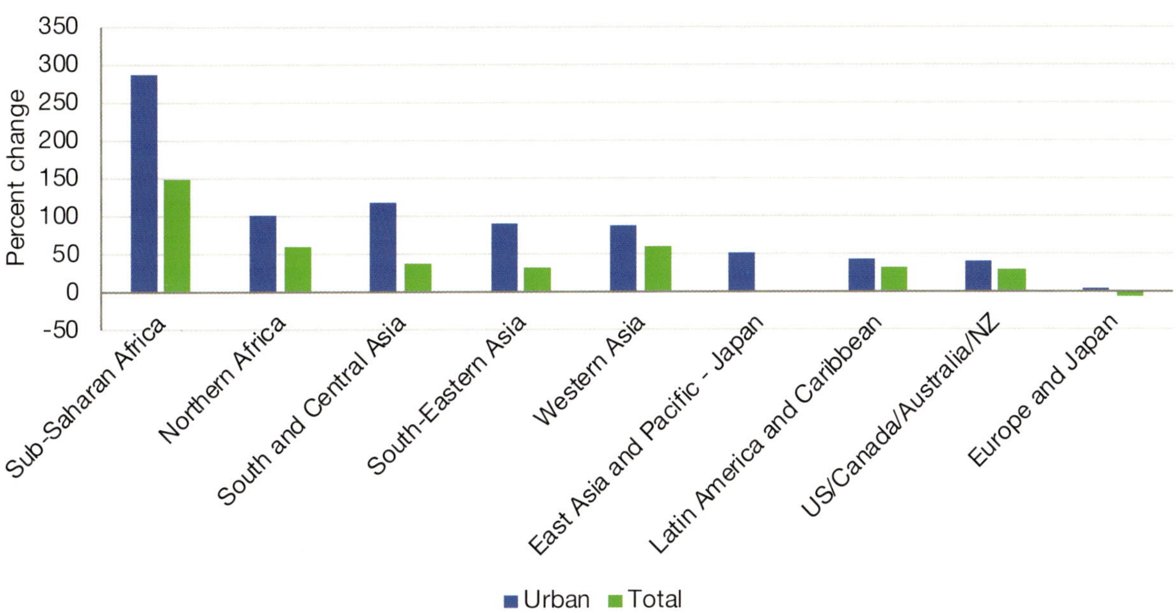

Source: United Nations (2014)

A growing concern among African urban scholars is the globally and historically unprecedented disconnect between increased urbanization and economic growth in many African countries

Figure 12: **Percent urban by region**

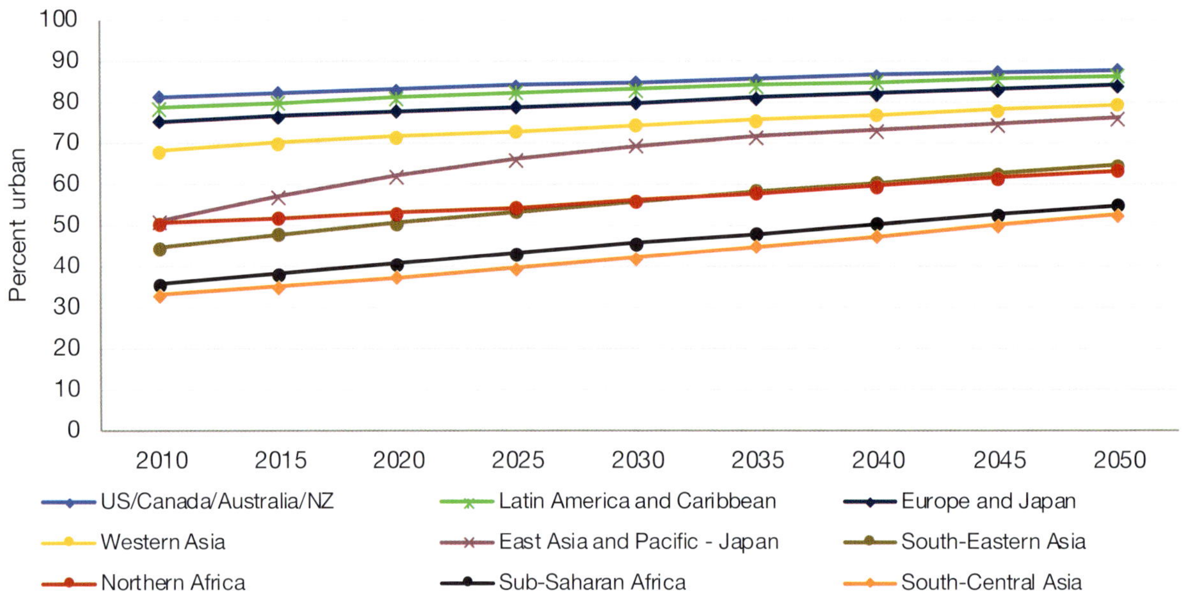

Source: United Nations (2014)

with an overall pattern of convergence. In recent decades, however, a growing concern among African urban scholars is the globally and historically unprecedented disconnect between increased urbanization and economic growth in many African countries (OECD 2016a; Gore 2015).[4] A continuation of this disconnect, combined with the high share of the population aged 15 through 29, is likely to produce social unrest.

Urban population densities

Improvements in the use of satellite imagery and data now allow the identification of urbanized land as distinct from forests, crop land, or other uses. Moreover, satellite data allows consistent definition of urbanized areas across countries and over time.[5] These estimates of urban areas combined with urban population data allow measurement of urban population density and its change over time for individual cities. Population density is an important parameter because it allows the transformation of forecasts of urban population growth into projections of the physical growth of urbanized areas. The expansion of urban areas is a key input for planning transport, utilities, and other infrastructure investments.

Shlomo Angel and his colleagues have recently compiled data on urbanized areas and urban densities at decadal intervals (approximately 1990, 2000, and 2014) for a random sample of 200 global cities drawn from the global total of 4,245 cities with 2010 populations over 100,000 (Angel, Blei & et al. 2016).[6] This random sample includes

4. OECD. (2016a). *African Economic Outlook 2016*. Paris: OECD.; Gore, C. (2015). Climate Change Adaptation and African Cities: Understanding the Impact of Government and Governance on Future Action. Ch. 11 in Johnson, C., Toly, N., & Schroeder, H. (eds.), *The Urban Climate ChallengeRethinking the Role of Cities in the Global Climate Regime*. Routledge: London and New York.

5. For a description of the analysis, see Angel, S. (2012). *Planet of Cities*. Cambridge, MA: Lincoln Institute of Land Policy.

6. Angel, S., Blei, A., Parent, J., Lamson-Hall, P. & Galarza Sánchez, N. with Civco, D., Qian Lei, R. & Thom, K. (2016). *Atlas of Urban Expansion, 2016 Edition, Vol. 1: Areas and Densities*. NYU Urban Expansion Program at New York University, UN-Habitat, and the Lincoln Institute of Land Policy.

The average annual rate of decline of population densities across all 25 African cities from 1990 to 2014 was 1.83 percent, a result that is close to the long term global average of two percent.

Figure 13: Increase in urban population share and current income

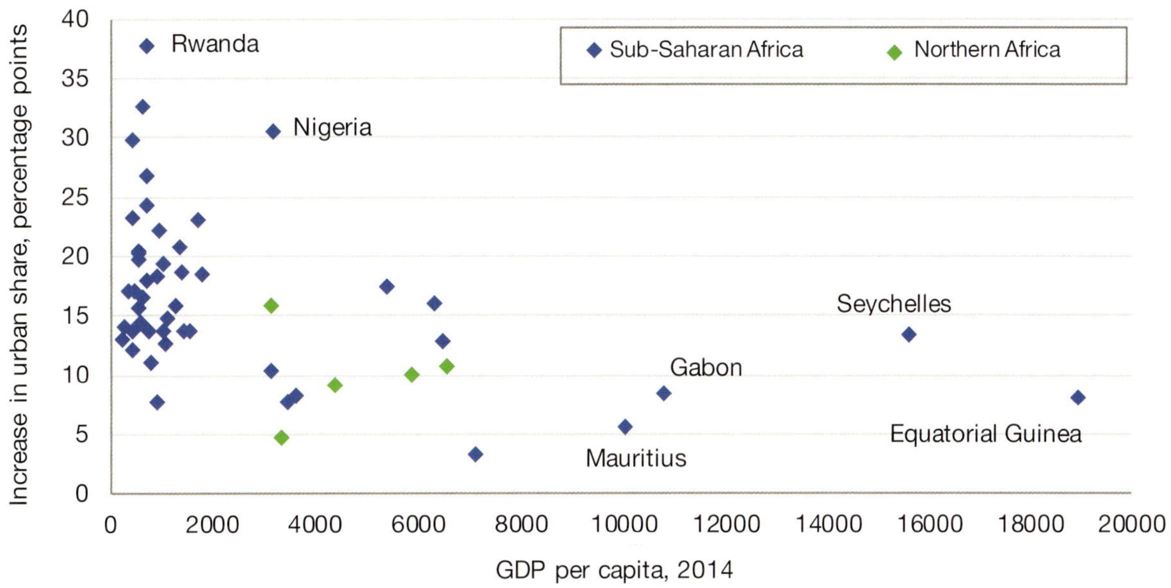

Source: United Nations (2015); World Bank (2016d)

25 cities from Africa.[7] Angel and his colleagues have examined changes in urban densities over two decades for this global sample of 200 cities and also over much longer periods of time for select U.S. and global cities (Angel 2012). They found that, over long periods of time, urban population densities have declined about two percent per year on average, with variation around this mean.

How does this compare with the experience of African cities? Population density and population size for the 25 African cities are shown in Figure 14, along with the sample averages. The population of all cities grew over this period, so for each city the 2014 density is the right-most point. Urban population densities decreased over the period for 19 of the 25 cities. The exceptions were Bamako, Ibadan, Johannesburg, Kampala, Lagos, and Oyo (interestingly, three of these are in Nigeria). Cities with high population densities experienced the largest decreases; in 2014, the sampled city densities ranged from 50 to 250 persons per hectare—down from 50 to 550 in 1990. The average annual rate of decline of population densities across all 25 African cities from 1990 to 2014 was 1.83 percent, a result that is close to the long term global average of two percent reported by Angel.

Projected increases in urbanized land area

One often overlooked aspect of urban population growth is the expansion of urbanized land area that accompanies increases in urban populations. Extensive analysis of both historical and satellite data, including the review of experience in 25 African cities above, indicates that urban population densities have declined by about two percent per year over the last century. A rough rule of thumb is that a doubling of urban population is associated with a tripling of urbanized land (Angel 2012). Figure 15 presents data on urban land cover by region in 2000; it shows that across regions urban land cover occupied less than one percent of the land area in all nine regions, with particularly

7. The 25 cities are listed in Annex 2.

With declining densities, by 2050 urban land areas in SSA and North Africa grow to 12 and 7.5 times their size, respectively, in 2000.

Figure 14: Population density, 1990, 2000, and 2014 for 25 African cities

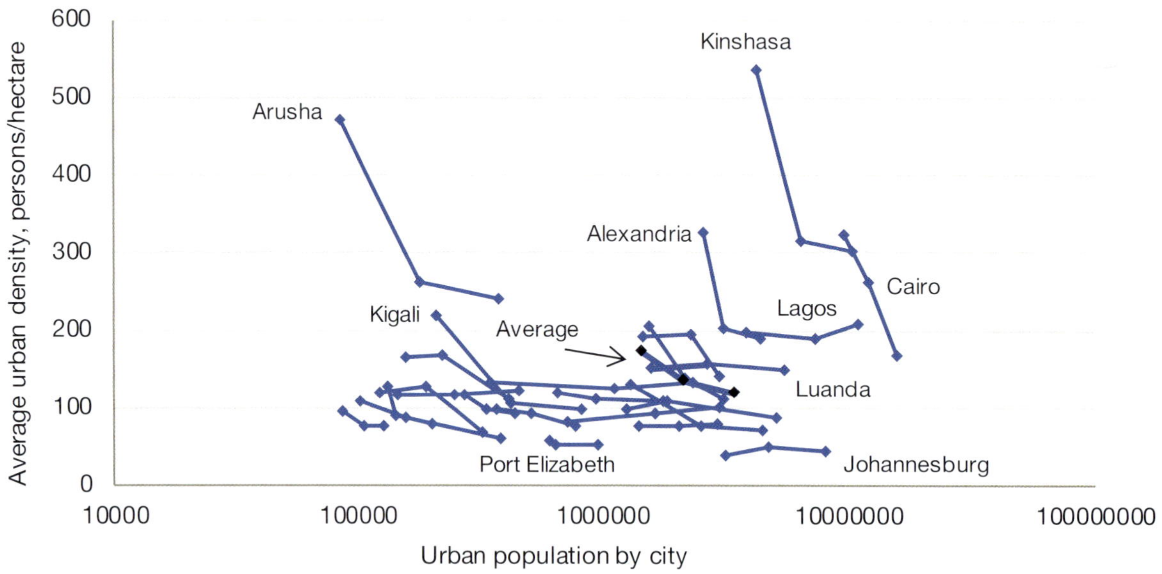

Source: Angel, Blei & et al. (2016)

Figure 15: Urban land cover share of total land area, 2000 and 2050

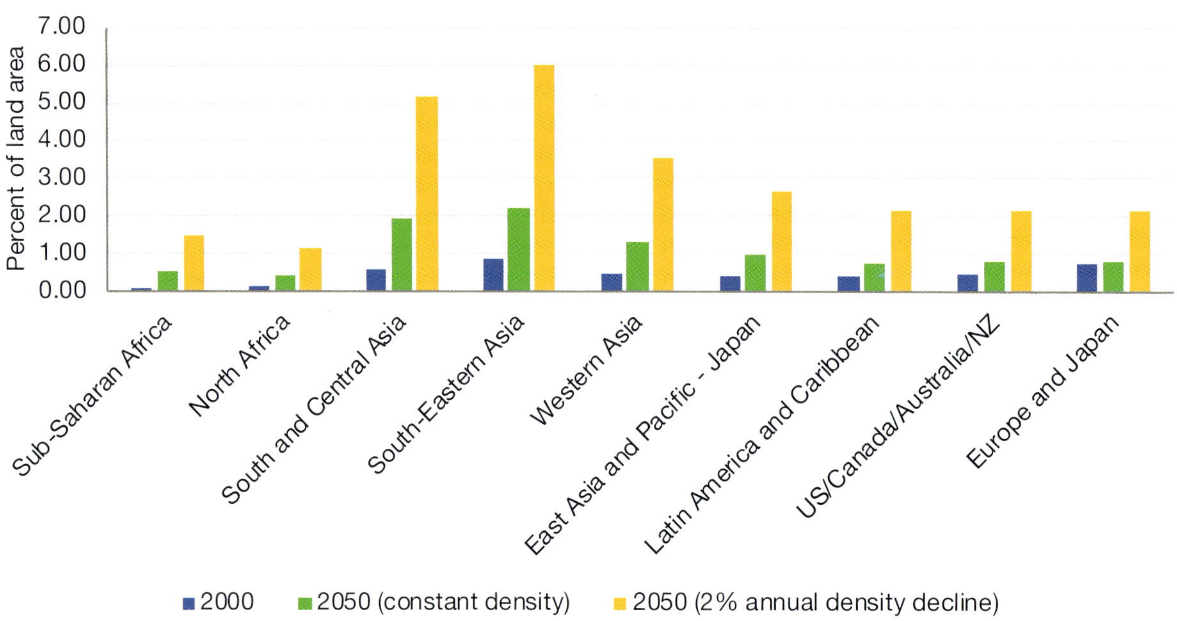

Source: Angel (2012), calculated from Table 10.2, p. 166 and Table 15

Guiding urban expansion to reduce the development of cultivated land is a clear priority, but how can it be accomplished? One way is to provide some key infrastructure facilities ahead of development located to help direct development away from cultivated land.

low shares for SSA and North Africa, 0.12 and 0.15 percent respectively. Figure 15 also presents two forecasts of the urbanized land area in 2050 based on the projected urban population increases in Figure 10. The first makes the very conservative assumption that average urban population densities in each region remain the same in 2050 as in 2000, and the second assumes that urban population densities will continue their historic trend of declining by 2 percent per year.

With constant urban population densities, urban land areas in SSA and North Africa will grow to 4.5 and 3 times their size, respectively, in 2000 (0.54 and 0.42 percent of total area). With declining densities, they grow to 12 and 7.5 times their size, respectively, in 2000 (1.48 and 1.13 percent of total area). While the absolute size of these expansions is less than those projected for other regions, the large percentage increases have important implications for the expansion of urban areas and associated infrastructure in Africa.

When urbanized areas expand, they often encroach on cultivated land. Satellite data allows the identification of cultivated land, so it is possible to develop rough estimates of the extent to which urban growth subsumes cultivated land. Figure 16 shows the regional share of cultivated land in 2000 that would be lost to urban expansion by 2050—with the simplifying assumption that urban areas will expand over land uniformly in all directions (like inflating a balloon) and the assumption that urban population densities continue to decline at historic rates of two percent per year. The share is particularly large for North Africa (over 9 percent) but also of concern for SSA (at 5 percent). To put these numbers in perspective, the Food and Agricultural Organization (FAO) has forecast that global cultivated land area will need to increase by 10 percent by 2050 to meet food requirements at that time (FAO, 2012). This FAO forecast does not take into account any loss of cultivated land to urban expansion, so undirected business-as-usual urban expansion is a potential threat to food security in Africa and elsewhere.

Guiding urban expansion to reduce the development of cultivated land is a clear priority, but how can it be accomplished? One way is to provide some key infrastructure facilities ahead of development located to help direct development away from cultivated land. Providing infrastructure ahead of development also costs about a third as much as retrofitting after development, so it is cost-effective. Moreover, some types of infrastructure—particularly arterial roads—are very difficult to build after development occurs because households and businesses would need to be displaced. Arterial roads also provide rights of way for trunk infrastructure, such as water and power, as well as routes for transit service. Implementation of this policy would need to be at the local or metropolitan level, not at the national level.

Recent analysis of satellite data provides information on the extent to which cities have been providing arterial road grids either historically or more recently. Angel and his colleagues have calculated for their global sample of 200 cities the percentage of urbanized area that has a system of arterial grids for two time periods: urbanized areas developed before 1990, and those developed from 1990 to 2014 (Angel, Lamson-Hall & et al. 2016).[8] These data are available for 24 of the 25 African cities in the global random sample of cities and are shown in Figure 17.

The share of built-up area with gridded arterial roads is very low, the share is typically higher for areas developed before 1990, and planned arterial road grids are the exception for urbanized areas developed post-1990. For example, 15 of the 24 cities in the sample have no arterial grids in their areas developed since 1990. The lack of arterial road grids makes transportation within cities difficult, impedes the efficient operation of urban labor markets by increasing the costs of commuting, and hinders the installation of other trunk infrastructure—thereby increasing the cost of water, electric power, and other networked utilities.

8. Angel, S., Lamson-Hall, P., Madrid, M., Blei, A., & Parent, J. with Galarza Sánchez, N. & Thom, K. (2016). *Atlas of Urban Expansion, 2016 Edition, Vol. 2, Blocks and Roads*. NYU Urban Expansion Program at New York University, UN-Habitat, and the Lincoln Institute of Land Policy.

The lack of arterial road grids makes transportation within cities difficult, impedes the efficient operation of urban labor markets by increasing the costs of commuting, and hinders the installation of other trunk infrastructure—thereby increasing the cost of water, electric power, and other networked utilities.

Figure 16: Percent of cultivated land lost with 2 percent annual urban density decline, 2000 to 2050

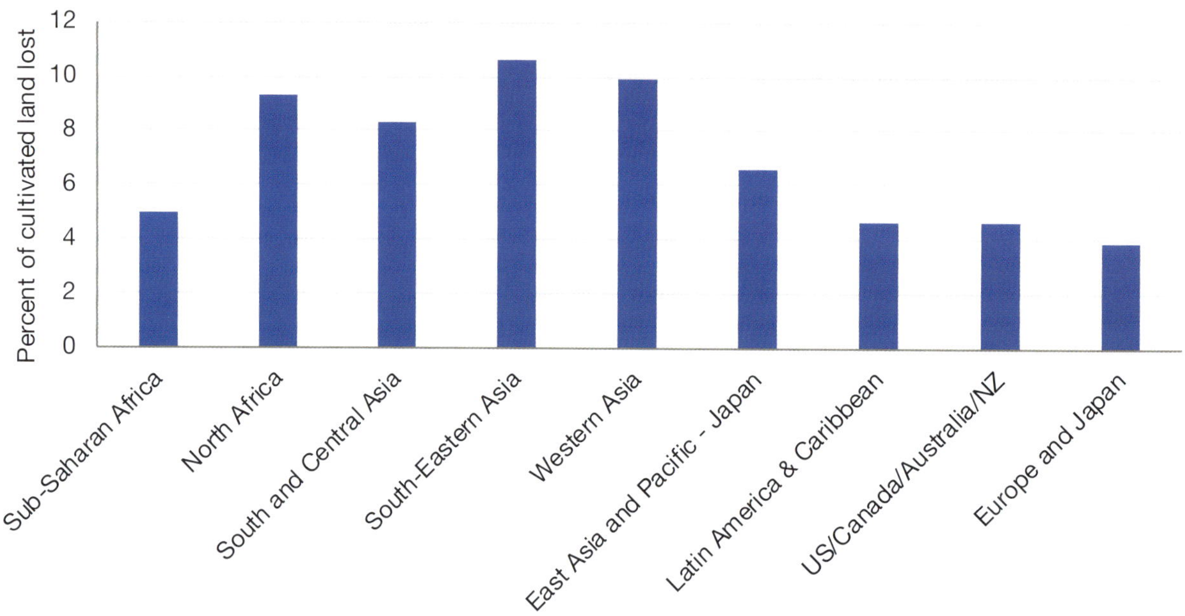

Source: Angel (2012), based on Figure 16.12, p. 281

Figure 17: Past and recent share of built up area with arterial grid

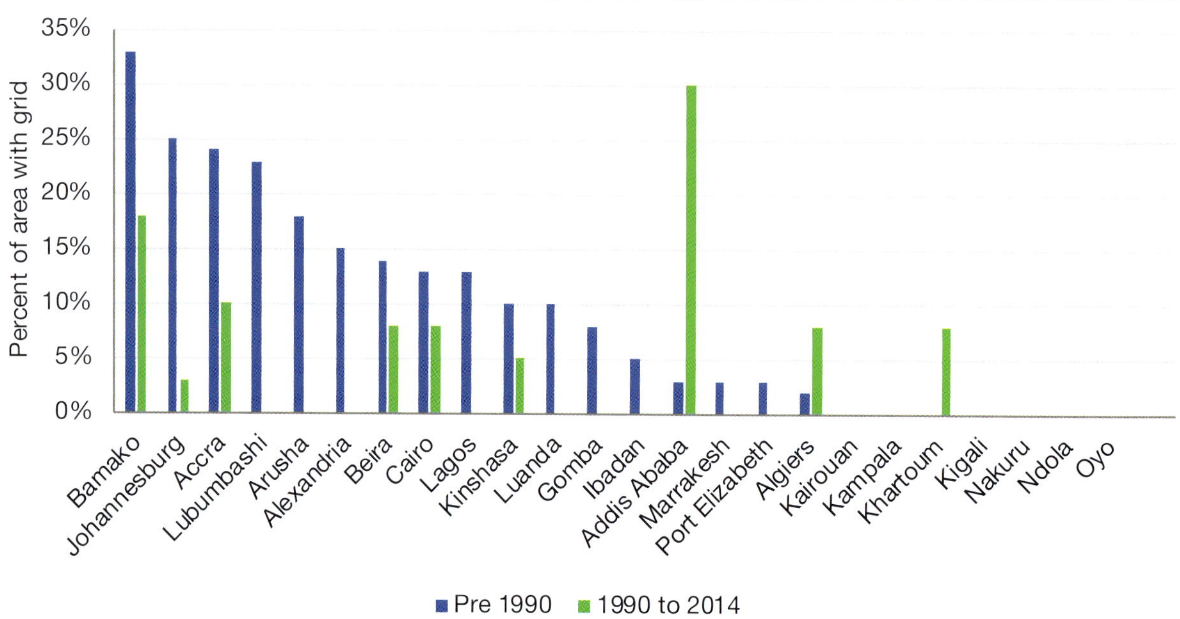

Source: Angel, Lamson-Hall & et al. (2016)

Getting ahead of development with designated rights of way and the installation of infrastructure before development raises questions about how low income households will pay for these facilities.

Remedying this situation for future urban development must be a priority in order to increase the productivity of African cities while directing urban development away from cultivated land.

Planning urban infrastructure

Thus far, the terms cities and urban areas have been used interchangeably. Except for those in South Africa, the reality is that large metropolitan areas are typically composed of many municipal jurisdictions—with a main central city municipality surrounded by smaller urban centers and suburbs with their own municipal status. Moreover, planning and land use decisions are often made at the municipal or city level with little metropolitan-wide coordination. Given the dramatic expansion of African urban areas that will accompany the growth of urban populations, capacity must be developed to implement metropolitan-wide planning to accommodate the expansion if rapidly growing urban areas are to avoid being overwhelmed by informal settlements. Such an initiative preparing in advance for urban growth is underway in four cities in Ethiopia (Lamson-Hall et al. 2015).[9]

Planning will involve: (a) identifying urban expansion areas that minimally subsume cultivated land, (b) reserving rights of way for an arterial grid of roads, and (c) coordinating infrastructure investments across transport, water and sanitation, electric power, and telecommunications. Integrating plans across these infrastructure sectors must be done at the metropolitan level to take advantage of economies of scale and incorporate related network effects. Installing metropolitan-wide governments to accomplish the needed coordination is likely to be a political non-starter in many countries, so metropolitan-wide commissions or councils of government will need to be given oversight of metropolitan-wide planning. Development activities that do not involve large-scale systems effects or inter-jurisdictional spillovers can continue to be handled at the city or municipal level.

Development regulations also influence how urban areas grow. In many countries, the least-cost dwelling that meets existing standards for formal housing (relating to lot size, building materials, and size) is unaffordable to low income households. As a result, low income households construct dwellings in informal settlements that are below minimum formal standards, often in areas that are poorly served by transport, ecologically fragile, or distant from existing infrastructure services. Over time, informal dwellings are improved through progressive construction, and services and regularization are eventually provided, often years after the community is developed and at high cost. Standards should be consistent with affordability and not provide an incentive for informal development.

Getting ahead of development with designated rights of way and the installation of infrastructure before development raises questions about how low income households will pay for these facilities. One approach is that households should pay for private goods and the community should pay for public goods. For example, the cost of arterial rights of way and trunk infrastructure should be paid for by all beneficiaries at the city or metropolitan level, and households would bear the cost of service provided at the lot level. Because low income households often have irregular incomes and often expand their dwellings by progressive construction—spreading out costs over time—a similar extended payment scheme could be used for infrastructure installation at the lot level.

Estimates of national infrastructure investment and maintenance expenses are presented in Chapter 8, but how much of national investment is needed for cities? Direct estimates of infrastructure and maintenance expense for individual cities are virtually nonexistent in part because little information is available about infrastructure stocks (e.g., length of paved roads) or infrastructure investment (e.g., annual expenditure on paved roads) at the city

9. Lamson-Hall, P., Degroot, D., Martin, R., Fafesse, T., Angel, S. (2015). *A New Plan for African Cities: The Ethiopia Urban Expansion Initiative.*

The share of national infrastructure investment and maintenance needed to support the growth of cities can be set proportional to cities' shares of national GDP.

or metropolitan level. However, indirect estimates of city level investment needs can be made.

Analysis indicates that a country's quantity of physical infrastructure stocks has little relation to its urbanization level but is strongly related to GDP (Ingram, Liu, & Brandt 2013).[10] The lack of a relation between urbanization and infrastructure seems surprising, but infrastructure costs per person vary inversely with population density (making infrastructure provision in cities less costly per capita), and much infrastructure located in rural areas (roads, power lines) serves urban residents. Accordingly, the share of national infrastructure investment and maintenance needed to support the growth of cities can be set proportional to cities' shares of national GDP. For example, if cities produce 60 percent of a country's GDP, a rough estimate of required funds for annual infrastructure investment and maintenance in that country's cities would be 60 percent of its estimated national infrastructure investment needs. Thus, if national infrastructure investment needs were 5 percent of such a country's national GDP, urban investment needs would be 3 percent of its national GDP.

Financing infrastructure investment and raising local revenue

When urban infrastructure is long-lived, it is equitable to spread its cost over time and to have future beneficiaries pay their fair share. This can be accomplished by partially funding it from longer term public or private debt or from international aid and other transfers. Several options exist for local borrowing. In some middle-income countries, municipal development funds have helped to develop both local government loan facilities and local urban government capacity to access loan financing, often with reliance on external aid (Kharas & Linn 2013).[11] Some middle-income countries, including South Africa, now have municipal bonds (Martell & Guess 2006), and some municipal bonds have been sold directly on international markets.[12]

Municipal bonds pose risks for both issuing governments and investors. Some risks of general obligation bonds can be lowered by issuing bonds in local currency, by utilizing third party guarantees or insurance, and by establishing a national fiscal responsibility framework specifying prudential conditions, such as maximum debt service ratios or the use of credit rating agencies. The risks associated with bonds used to finance privately operated projects can be reduced by (a) requiring that the project operator is legally separated from the local government, (b) assuring that tariffs will be adjusted to maintain a minimum debt service ratio, (c) including a clause to prohibit the government from building directly competing investments, and (d) including performance standards allowing the government to replace management or call in the credit if standards are not met (Ingram, Liu, & Brandt 2013).

Official development assistance (ODA) and lending from the International Bank for Reconstruction and Development (IBRD) and International Development Association (IDA) can be an important source of infrastructure investment funds in developing countries. ODA and World Bank (IBRD plus IDA) commitments for infrastructure in the past few years have each been in the range of $20 billion per year. Private investment in infrastructure has been a growing source of infrastructure finance over the past 25 years, and it has, for example, played a very important role in the remarkable expansion of mobile telephone service in Africa. Private participation in infrastructure (PPI) commitments have been four to six times larger than combined ODA and World Bank funding for infrastructure since 2006 and are now a major element of infrastructure finance, peaking at $195 billion in 2012. PPI and development assistance to infrastructure in 2012 together were about 40 percent

10. Ingram, G., Liu, Z., Brandt, K. (2013). Metropolitan Infrastructure and Capital Finance, in Bahl, R., Linn, J., & Wetzel, D. (eds.) *Financing Metropolitan Governments in Developing Countries*. Cambridge, MA: Lincoln Institute of Land Policy, 339–366.

11. Kharas, H. & Linn, J. (2013). External Assistance for Urban Finance Development: Needs, Strategies, and Implementation, in Bahl, R., Linn, J., & Wetzel, D. (eds.) *Financing Metropolitan Governments in Developing Countries*. Cambridge, MA: Lincoln Institute of Land Policy, 393–420.

12. Martell, C. & Guess, G.M. (2006). Development of Local Government Debt Financing Markets: Application of a Market-based Framework. *Public Budgeting and Finance 26*(1), Blackwell Synergy.

Taxing local citizens to fund local services gives them a real incentive to engage with and oversee local services.

Box 1: Lessons of experience for successful Private Participation in Infrastructure (PPI)

The considerable experience of municipal and metropolitan areas with PPI projects over the last 30 years has yielded a number of insights about the potential impediments encountered and good practices developed:

- PPI projects are more successful when carried out under a well-specified national program or policy, often using model concession documents, rather than in an opportunistic way.
- Municipal governments often lack the institutional capacity to negotiate PPI agreements and so benefit from assistance from multilateral development banks or from a national public-private partnership unit that helps to facilitate and manage infrastructure investments.
- Legal constraints, such as national prohibitions on the use of arbitration for contract disputes between the government and private firms, may need to be addressed.
- A lack of bankable projects and a generally poor business climate are frequent impediments in the lowest-income countries.
- Decentralization of revenue and investment responsibilities, which replaces a central national agency with many local agencies, can complicate PPI because local municipalities often lack the technical expertise to implement projects; a lack of coordination among neighboring municipalities may also lead to policy incoherence between municipalities, particularly for water supply and sanitation.

PPI has been concentrated in three sectors: telecom, energy, and transport. Two African countries, Nigeria and South Africa, were among the top ten recipients of PPI from 2001 through 2008.

Source: Ingram, Liu, & Brandt (2013)

of the total new infrastructure investment estimates for all developing countries (Ingram 2016), and are poised to play a key role in financing the infrastructure investment needs of rapidly growing cities in the coming decades. Past experience with PPI has provided some useful guidelines to promote success (see Box 1).

Public finance principles hold that each level of government should have enough budgetary autonomy to fulfill its expenditure responsibilities (Musgrave 1959), and metropolitan infrastructure investment will require local funds to cover investment directly or to repay debt.[13] Lack of local revenue sources is a major issue in African metropolitan areas and municipalities (and in most developing countries). In addition, local tax systems often perform poorly.

In many countries, central governments have had little enthusiasm for transferring taxing authority to local governments. In some cases, central governments may be able to raise revenues more efficiently (with lower collection costs) than local governments. However, political considerations can also be relevant. Local governments that are independent of central and provincial governments can become potential rival centers of political power, particularly when municipal and city officials are locally elected. By centralizing revenue collection and the funding of local governments through intergovernmental transfers, local governments become an extension of higher levels of government, and local accountability is reduced. However, taxing local citizens to fund local services gives them a real incentive to engage with and oversee local services.

User fees and benefit charges are attractive local sources of revenue that create appropriate incentives for both suppliers and users of services. User fees are most easily implemented in transport and public utilities having a fee-for-service regime, but the fees must be set

13. Musgrave, R. (1959). *The Theory of Public Finance*. New York: McGraw-Hill.

Forecasts of the effects of climate change for Africa raise many concerns for both rural and urban areas. Projected effects include increases in average temperatures across the continent, less rainfall in northern and southwestern areas, and increasingly stressed water systems everywhere.

at an appropriate level. Fees that are below costs promote overuse of services—a serious problem in electric power and water where subsidized rates undermine end-user efficiency by stimulating demand for services—and hence for more investment. In Africa, only one in ten water companies' tariffs cover full costs, though over half cover operating costs (Banerjee et al. 2010).[14] Low fees also create the need for subsidies. Recent estimates are that SSA governments spent $4.1 billion annually (0.7 percent of GDP) on power and water subsidies (Foster & Briceno-Garmendia 2010).[15] While subsidies are often defended on social welfare grounds, their beneficiaries are predominantly the non-poor who have access to regular services while the poor are left with higher-cost, non-regular suppliers. Applying user fees and setting them at levels that cover costs is a goal that metropolitan and municipal governments should move toward.

As a local revenue source, the property tax is inherently attractive because real estate benefits from local services and is immovable, making the tax difficult to evade. It is used in many African municipalities and has been adapted in various ways to local conditions (Franzsen and Youngman, 2009). However, local property tax systems often have low tax rates, low yields, and many exemptions. Because the property tax is an appropriate local tax and already exists in many metropolitan and municipal areas in Africa, its performance should be improved. Moreover, its scope can be extended to include value capture, which taxes some of the increased land value associated with new infrastructure investments. Technological improvements, such as mass appraisal (using statistical techniques) and computer based mapping (using satellite images), are reducing property tax's administrative costs (McCluskey & Franzsen 2013).[16] Some countries are experimenting with simpler area-based systems that levy the tax on land area, built area, or per parcel rather than on an estimated market value.

Addressing climate change

Forecasts of the effects of climate change for Africa raise many concerns for both rural and urban areas. Projected effects include increases in average temperatures across the continent, less rainfall in northern and southwestern areas, and increasingly stressed water systems everywhere. These changes are forecast to lead to more extreme meteorological events including heavy rainfall, intense heat events, and more severe arid intervals. Such changes are likely to have a negative impact on the extensive rainfed agriculture that supports a large proportion of the population and to reduce crop yields (Intergovernmental Panel on Climate Change 2014a).[17]

If agricultural livelihoods become more precarious, migration flows from rural to urban areas may grow, particularly to cities whose economies are based on activities other than agricultural services. Some analysts argue that climate change may already have increased the rate of urbanization in Africa (Henderson et al. 2016).[18] In urban areas, climate change may intensify the severity of threats to human health because climate change acts as a multiplier of existing health vulnerabilities. This multiplier effect manifests itself through inadequate access to safe water and improved sanitation, limited access to health care and education, and food insecurity (Intergovernmental Panel on Climate Change 2014b).[19]

Populations in urban areas residing on low lying coastal areas and river flood plains are likely to be increasingly vulnerable to displacement from flooding caused by strong

14. Banerjee, S., Foster, V., Ying, Y., Skilling, H., Wodon, Q. (2010). Cost Recovery, Equity, and Efficiency in Water Tariffs: Evidence from African Utilities, *Policy Research Working Paper* (5384). Washington: World Bank.
15. Foster, V. & Briceño-Garmendia, C. (eds.). (2010). *Africa's Infrastructure: A Time for Transformation*, Washington: World Bank.
16. McCluskey, W. & Franzsen, R. (2013). Property Taxes in Metropolitan Cities. Bahl, R., Linn, J., & Wetzel, D. (eds.) *Financing Metropolitan Governments in Developing Countries*. Cambridge, MA: Lincoln Institute of Land Policy, 159-181.
17. Intergovernmental Panel on Climate Change (2014a)
18. Henderson, J., Storeygard, A. & Deichmann, U. (2016). Has climate change driven urbanization in Africa?,
19. Intergovernmental Panel on Climate Change. (2014b). *Climate Change 2014: Impacts, Adaptation, and Vulnerability. (Report of Working Group II)*, Cambridge, UK and New York: Cambridge University Press, pp. 1199-1265.

If agricultural livelihoods become more precarious, migration flows from rural to urban areas may grow, particularly to cities whose economies are based on activities other than agricultural services.

Box 2: Lessons on adaptation drawn from African experience

Five common principles for adaptation and building adaptive capacity have been distilled from a review of Africa's experience to date. Improving adaptation will require:

- supporting autonomous adaptation through a policy that recognizes the multiple-stressor nature of vulnerable livelihoods;
- increasing attention to the cultural, ethical, and rights considerations of adaptation by increasing the participation of women, youth, and poor and vulnerable people in adaptation policy and implementation;
- combining "soft path" options and flexible and iterative learning approaches with technological and infrastructural approaches and blending scientific, local, and indigenous knowledge when developing adaptation strategies;
- focusing on building resilience and implementing low-regrets adaptation with development synergies, in the face of future climate and socioeconomic uncertainties; and
- building adaptive management and social and institutional learning into adaptation processes at all levels. (22.4) IPCC WGII.

The assessment of significant residual impacts in a 2°C world at the end of the 21st century suggests that, even under high levels of adaptation, there could be very high levels of risk for Africa.

Source: Intergovernmental Panel on Climate Change (2014a)

Figure 18: Floods per year in Africa

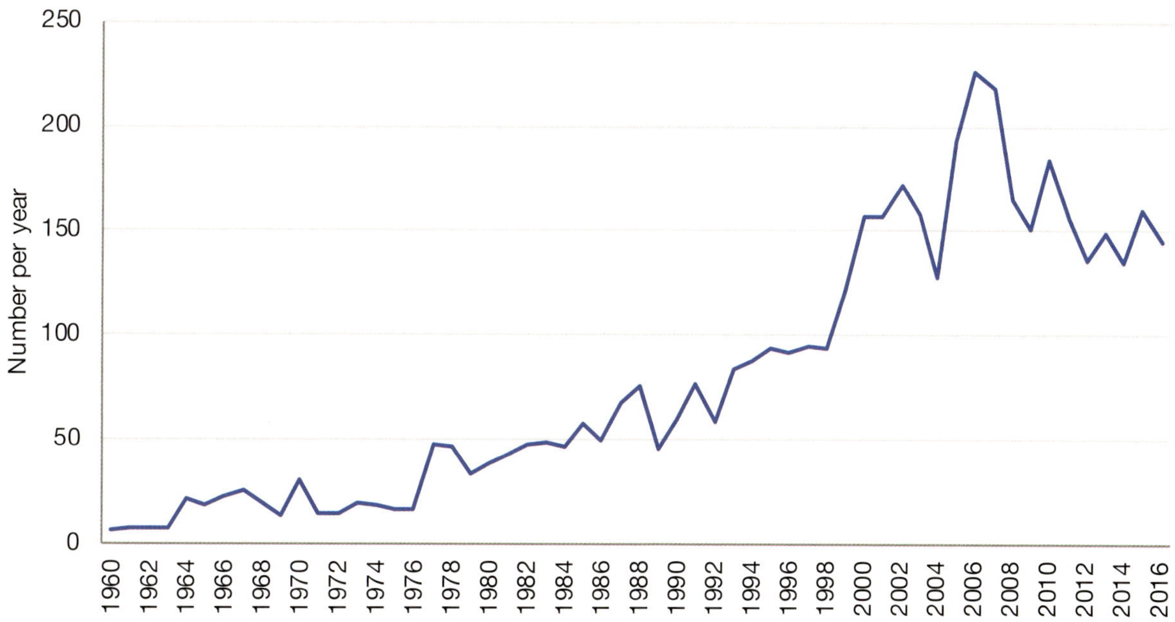

Source: EM-DAT (2016)

New technology as embodied in the concept of the smart city may have the potential to address many of the problems faced by African cities that are related to rapid population growth and the need to adapt to climate change.

storms and from sea level rise. Inadequate urban infrastructure combined with heavy rain events will particularly affect poor and vulnerable populations (Gore 2015). These projections of more severe weather events imply a continuation of trends since 1960 that show a dramatic increase in flood events in Africa (Figure 18). Populations in low lying coastal areas are vulnerable to sea level rise that could be as much as a meter by 2100. In Africa, about 12 percent of the urban population and 7 percent of the total population live in coastal areas less than ten meters above sea level. These percentages are similar to global shares: 13 percent of the world's urban population and 10 percent of its total population are similarly situated (McGranahan, Balk, & Anderson 2007).[20] These are very large populations in low-lying coastal areas that are likely to be affected by storm surges and sea level rise.

Africa is highly vulnerable to climate change and faces many challenges in adapting to this threat. Local government capacity is often weak both in raising its own financial resources and in governance. Regulatory capacity and planning are often weak, data are fragmentary, infrastructure (particularly waste management and drainage) are inadequate, and residential settlements often have been established in fragile or vulnerable areas, such as floodplains, wetlands, and coastal zones. While local governments have been addressing climate change issues, most adaptations remain autonomous and reactive to short-term problems, and local adaptive capacity is typically low. Increasing adaptive capacity to climate change is very important; experience-based suggestions are noted in Box 2.

Adapting to climate change and investing in infrastructure each place huge burdens on African economies, and the concomitant need to improve governance and government capacity is also daunting. African cities typically have better services than rural areas (e.g., water, sanitation, education, and health), and these contribute to producing urban life expectancies that are above national averages (Satterthwaite et al. 2009).[21] However, urban infrastructure is often poorly maintained and basic infrastructure services are not keeping up with urban growth, resulting in a decline in coverage relative to 1990 levels in many cities, especially for piped water (Banerjee et al. 2009).[22] Adapting existing infrastructure to climate change and adding facilities to reduce flood risks compounds the task. The challenge is to promote urban economic growth and to devote a sufficient share of that growth to investments in infrastructure and in metropolitan-area public goods so that infrastructure coverage can increase and events associated with climate change become less life-threatening and costly to urban residents.

New technologies and smart cities

New technology as embodied in the concept of the smart city may have the potential to address many of the problems faced by African cities that are related to rapid population growth and the need to adapt to climate change. The hope is that the relative lack of infrastructure and facilities will be an asset, allowing African cities to leapfrog directly to new technologies without being hampered by a legacy stock of aging and obsolete facilities. Underpinning this hope is Africa's experience with mobile telephone technology that has grown rapidly, allowing the telecommunications sector essentially to bypass investments in costlier fixed-line telephone service.

Smart city technology normally involves integrating information technology—especially digital technology—into the expansion, management, and operation of the city and its infrastructure. It involves collecting and using

20. McGranahan, G., Balk, D., Anderson, B. (2007) The rising tide: assessing the risks of climate change and human settlements in low elevation coastal zones. *Environment & Urbanization, International Institute for Environment and Development (IIED) 19*(1), pp. 17–37.

21. Satterthwaite, D., Huq, S., Reid, H., Pelling, P. & Romero Lankao, P. (2009). Adapting to climate change in urban areas: the possibilities and constraints in low- and middle-income nations. In icknell, J., Dodman, D., & Satterthwaite, D. (eds.).*Adapting Cities to Climate Change. Understanding and Addressing the Development Challenges*. Earthscan: Abingdon, UK and New York.

22. Banerjee, S., Diallo, A., Foster, V. & Wodon, Q. (2009). Trends in Household Coverage of Modern Infrastructure Services in Africa, *Policy Research Working Paper* (4880). Washington: World Bank.

Smart city technology normally involves integrating information technology—especially digital technology—into the expansion, management, and operation of the city and its infrastructure.

data to make infrastructure and urban systems more intelligent and efficient. The results are manifested in three ways. First, the integration improves the operating efficiency of existing systems so they produce more output per unit of input. This could be more vehicles per hour down a highway lane, less leakage or loss of water or power in distribution systems, higher completion rates of phone calls, lowered peak loads on power grids, or lower costs of toll collection or meter readings. Second, the integration may transform existing systems. For example, it could enable the generation of electric power to be distributed widely using solar panels rather than concentrated in large generating stations, or sanitary waste to be processed by composting rather than using water intensive methods. Third, the changes could be unexpected or difficult to predict. For example, the internet-of-things could automatize food shopping based on continually updated records of household inventories. These three types of results could improve efficiency and/or performance of urban systems by saving capital or operating costs in African cities.

Of course, this technology is not without its own risks and drawbacks. Most immediate is the loss of privacy that accompanies the collection of data about individuals, whether it is driving habits, records of purchases, or detailed data on telephone calls. In addition, the aggregation and use of digital data often is subject to scale economies and network effects, so that average data analysis costs fall as the quantity of data to be analyzed increases. These effects are likely to lead to the data being analyzed by one or a few large firms that would not be subject to the discipline of competitive markets, so prices could become high for these services. Finally, these systems might be subject to hacking or systemic failure. Actual experience with recent failures of computerized municipal traffic light systems or air traffic control systems indicate how disabling such breakdowns could be.

African cities do have other advantages, besides an absence of legacy facilities, that may facilitate the adoption of new urban technologies. The high rate of urban population growth and the looming problems of climate change create great pressure to improve service delivery, to promote economic diversification and growth, to seek solutions with lower capital costs, and to increase operational efficiency. In addition, the demographic composition

Box 3: Smart city innovations in Africa

Many projects in Africa embody smart city approaches; here is a sampling:

- **Data collection for social change**: The Ushahidi project, initially developed by Juliana Rotich and her team to map reports of violence in Kenya after the post-election violence in 2008, expanded across the world and is now one of the most-used platforms of its kind.
- **Mobility and traffic congestion**: Twende Twende (Swahili for "let's go") is a mobile phone service developed in IBM's research center in Nairobi that takes images captured by existing low-cost cameras and applies network-flow algorithms to estimate traffic flow. The solution does not require road construction but provides information that helps facilitate traffic flows.
- **Innovation anywhere**: The iHub project in Nairobi, Kenya, is an open community space—part vector for investors and venture capital funders, part incubator—providing a space where young entrepreneurs can receive mentorship, Internet connectivity, and the possibility of funding through connections with the international venture capital community.
- **Ethical energy**: The iShack Project, a social enterprise, provides a pay-for-use solar electricity service to people living in slums of the South African city of Stellenbosch.

Source: Ratti (2016)

Many African municipalities are engaged in smart city projects to improve the quality of life of their citizens, enhance the experience of businesses, and provide an environment that is conducive to economic development.

of the population, with many young adults, may facilitate the adoption of new and technologically intense solutions. The high penetration of mobile phones in African countries and the local development of innovations, such as mobile-based payments, provide the basis for optimism about the adoption of new technologies.

Although smart city approaches may seem to have modest relevance in less developed countries, many developing countries are surprisingly engaged with intelligent urban systems. Several countries have been constructing new green cities as platforms for smart technology. These efforts include Songdo in Korea, the Tianjin eco-city in China, Masdar in the United Arab Emirates, and Konza Techno City in Kenya. Many African municipalities are engaged in smart city projects to improve the quality of life of their citizens, enhance the experience of businesses, and provide an environment that is conducive to economic development (Walker 2016).[23] Some examples of the many projects that involve smart city technology and techniques are summarized in Box 3.

Although smart city approaches are likely still in their infancy, a review of experience that cities have had so far provides some insights. First, cities that have mainly responded to proposals from private vendors in an ad hoc fashion have not done as well as cities that have first developed a technology vision or plan that emphasizes productivity and connectivity. Second, allowing open access to data and broadband along with collaboration with citizens and technologists has fostered inclusiveness and support from citizens for new technologies. Demonstration projects focused on a neighborhood or specific problem have helped identify issues before applications are scaled up to the city or metropolitan level. New projects that seem not to involve smart technology should be vetted to ensure their future potential compatibility in order to avoid costly retrofitting later. Finally, establishing and using a public-private support and advisory group of knowledgeable persons can aid in educating citizens about the potential of smart city technology (Puentes & Tomer 2014).[24]

The decision to implement smart city approaches in a top-down or bottom-up fashion is related to the decision about open versus closed access to data and approaches. Top-down approaches typically employ a single large vendor who is responsible for data gathering (and installing associated sensors), data analysis, central control, and management. Such top-down single vendor approaches often use closed access proprietary systems with the vendor having control of the data and its analysis. The opposite approach is an open data operation—usually web-oriented—that enables individuals and firms to develop software solutions independently. Several smart phone applications have been developed in this fashion for transit agencies to provide customers with access to current transit system data on service schedules.

Many observers have a preference for bottom-up decentralized systems because such an approach produces more innovation and lowers smart technology costs. In fact, cities and metropolitan areas may use a top-down approach for some systems where engineering efficiency is paramount and a bottom-up approach where consumer service is more critical. Cities need to recognize the existence of the two alternative approaches and to consider their benefits and costs when choosing technologies because it may be costly to shift from one technological path to another.

Conclusion

SSA is the poorest global region (containing 25 of the 30 countries ranked as low income by the World Bank in 2014), and the region is projected to have the largest absolute (1.3 billion) and percentage (150 percent) increase in total population across nine global regions from 2010 to 2050. North Africa's population growth is the second

23. Walker, M. (2016). Smart Cities in Africa: Hype or Hope?.

24. Puentes, R. & Tomer, A. (2014). *Getting Smarter about Smart Cities.* Washington: Brookings Institution.

Urban expansion's potential conversion of cultivated land is particularly large for North Africa but also of concern for SSA.

largest in percentage terms with a projected increase of 60 percent.

A potential benefit for SSA from its strong population growth could come from its continuously falling dependency ratio, potentially creating a demographic dividend that will enhance economic growth. North Africa shows a modest decline followed by a modest increase in dependency over this period. However, demographic change can create social challenges if economic growth is inadequate to provide jobs and incomes for the growing population—particularly for young adults aged 15 through 29. SSA's projected percent of population aged 15 through 29 is consistently high (and the highest among global regions from 2015 on). For North Africa, this age group's share is the second highest from 2030 on. The demographic dividend that SSA will experience is good demographic news, but the high population share of young adults could create problems if economic growth is low and unemployment is high. This is an ongoing concern because recent increases in urbanization in many African countries have not been accompanied by the structural transformations in national or urban economies that have accompanied urbanization in other regions. While national and municipal policies can influence economic growth, they are unlikely to have much impact on demographic trends in the short and medium run.

SSA is projected to experience the largest absolute increase in urban population across the regions, but even more remarkable are the percentage increases: SSA's urban population is projected to quadruple and North Africa's to double. The large increase in urban population projected for SSA is driven mainly by its large projected total population increase; because its urban population share is projected to progress in a very regular manner.

Urban population growth will increase urbanized land areas. If urban population densities continue to decline following historic trends, urbanized land areas in SSA and North Africa will grow to be 12 and 7.5 times their size in 2000. Urban expansion's potential conversion of cultivated land is particularly large for North Africa but also of concern for SSA. Guiding urban expansion to minimize building on cultivated land is a clear priority, and this can be aided by installing a one kilometer grid of arterial roads prior to development. Investing in infrastructure ahead of urban expansion is also critical because retrofitting urban infrastructure in developed areas is three times as costly as installing urban infrastructure before development. Analysis of a random sample of African cities reveals that only small shares of their urbanized areas have road grids, and a majority of African cities do not have any arterial road grids in areas urbanized since 1990.

Given the dramatic expansion of African urban areas that will accompany the growth of urban populations, capacity must be developed to plan for such growth at the metropolitan-wide level, likely through a metropolitan commission; planning at the municipal level cannot take account of economies of scale and network effects that pervade urban infrastructure. The costs of infrastructure investment are difficult to calculate at the city level, but existing analysis suggests that the urban share of national infrastructure costs would be proportional to the urban share of national GDP. Because much infrastructure is long-lasting, spreading its cost over time by using debt financing is sensible. Several middle-income countries have begun to issue municipal bonds, and development assistance in the form of grants and loans can help fund infrastructure. Private participation in infrastructure has grown dramatically, and its annual total has recently been five times larger than infrastructure-related development assistance. It has played a key role in the expansion of mobile phone systems in Africa.

Setting the tariffs for infrastructure services appropriately is important both to cover the costs of supply and to promote end-user efficiency by preventing over consumption. Recent estimates are that SSA governments spent \$4.1 billion annually (0.7 percent of GDP) on power and water subsidies. Funding urban infrastructure will require larger expenditures at the municipal level, and in Africa

Within a supportive national framework, the success of cities and metropolitan areas will be determined to a great extent by policies pursued at the metropolitan and municipal level—including planning for urban expansion and provision of basic infrastructure services.

municipal governments have few sources of local revenue. This needs to change. The property tax is widely used but relatively ineffective in African cities. It is well suited as a revenue source to fund infrastructure, and recent technological advances, such as satellite imagery, can reduce collection costs.

Africa is highly vulnerable to climate change and faces many challenges in adapting to its threats. Key issues are overall increased stress on water systems, more numerous extreme meteorological events, and the threat of coastal flooding potentially affecting the 12 percent of Africa's urban residents who live in low-lying coastal areas. Inadequate urban infrastructure combined with heavy rain events will particularly affect poor and vulnerable populations.

Local governments have been addressing climate change issues, but most adaptations remain autonomous and reactive to short-term problems and local adaptive capacity is typically low. Increasing adaptive capacity to climate change is very important. The challenge is to promote urban economic growth and to devote a sufficient share of that growth to investments in infrastructure and in metropolitan-area public goods so that infrastructure coverage rates can increase and climate change events become less life-threatening and costly to urban residents.

New technology embodied in smart city approaches has real promise in Africa, and many local initiatives are underway. One model for smart city technology's appeal in Africa builds on African experience with mobile phones—where the new mobile technology leapfrogged over the old, and Africa essentially bypassed costly land-line systems. The hope is that Africa's lack of infrastructure and facilities will become an asset, as there would be little burden from legacy systems as new technologies emerge.

Experience to date indicates that cities that have a technology vision or plan for smart city technologies do better than cities that merely respond to vendor proposals. Choices need to be made between top-down and bottom-up technological approaches, and these choices are often related to decisions between systems that are open and closed in terms of access to data and its analysis. Smart city technology also poses challenges for personal privacy (data often can track individual behavior) and for the robustness of the systems (they must be reliable and resist hacking).

To handle successfully the forecast large increases in total and urban populations and the unprecedented expansion of urbanized areas over the next 40 years, African countries must pursue national policies that promote economic growth, health care, and education within a supportive macroeconomic and regulatory framework. Within a supportive national framework, the success of cities and metropolitan areas will be determined to a great extent by policies pursued at the metropolitan and municipal level—including planning for urban expansion and provision of basic infrastructure services. Sound national policies are necessary but not sufficient for success at the metropolitan level. Within a supportive national policy, metropolitan areas can underperform by pursuing poor policies. But with poor national policies, even excellent policies at the metropolitan level are unlikely to succeed. National governments and metropolitan areas need to work together to manage an effective transition to an urbanized African society.

Annex 1: Classification of countries into nine groups

This classification is a variation on the country groups used in *World Population Prospects: The 2012 Revision* produced by the UN Department of Economic and Social Affairs Population Division.

SSA

Angola
Benin
Botswana
Burkina Faso
Burundi
Cameroon
Cape Verde
Central African Republic
Chad
Comoros
Congo
Côte d'Ivoire
Democratic Republic of the Congo
Djibouti
Equatorial Guinea
Eritrea
Ethiopia
Gabon
Gambia
Ghana
Guinea
Guinea-Bissau
Kenya
Lesotho
Liberia
Madagascar
Malawi
Mali
Mauritania
Mauritius
Mayotte
Mozambique
Namibia
Niger
Nigeria
Réunion
Rwanda
Saint Helena
São Tomé and Príncipe
Senegal
Seychelles
Sierra Leone
Somalia
South Africa
South Sudan
Sudan
Swaziland
Togo
Uganda
United Republic of Tanzania
Western Sahara
Zambia
Zimbabwe

Northern Africa

Algeria
Egypt
Libyan Arab Jamahiriya
Morocco
Tunisia

East Asia and Pacific excluding Japan

East Asia

China
China, Hong Kong SAR
China, Macao SAR
Democratic People's Republic of Korea
Mongolia
Republic of Korea

Pacific

American Samoa
Cook Islands
Fiji
French Polynesia
Guam
Kiribati
Marshall Islands
Micronesia
Nauru
New Caledonia
Niue
Northern Mariana Islands
Palau
Papua New Guinea
Samoa
Solomon Islands
Tokelau
Tonga
Tuvalu
Vanuatu
Wallis and Futuna Islands

South-Central Asia

Kazakhstan
Kyrgyzstan
Tajikistan
Turkmenistan
Uzbekistan
Afghanistan
Bangladesh
Bhutan
India
Iran (Islamic Republic of)
Maldives
Nepal
Pakistan
Sri Lanka

South-Eastern Asia

Brunei Darussalam
Cambodia
Indonesia
Lao People's Democratic Republic
Malaysia
Myanmar
Philippines
Singapore
Thailand
Timor-Leste
Viet Nam

Western Asia

Armenia
Azerbaijan
Bahrain
Cyprus
Georgia
Iraq
Israel
Jordan
Kuwait
Lebanon
Oman
Qatar
Saudi Arabia
State of Palestine
Syrian Arab Republic
Turkey
United Arab Emirates
Yemen

Europe and Japan

Albania
Andorra
Austria
Belarus
Belgium
Bosnia and Herzegovina
Bulgaria
Channel Islands
Croatia
Czech Republic
Denmark
Estonia
Faeroe Islands
Finland
France
Germany
Gibraltar*
Greece
Holy See
Hungary
Iceland
Ireland
Ireland
Isle of Man
Italy
Japan
Latvia
Liechtenstein
Lithuania
Luxembourg
Malta
Monaco
Montenegro
Netherlands
Norway
Poland
Portugal
Republic of Macedonia
Republic of Moldova
Romania
Russian Federation
San Marino
Serbia
Slovakia
Slovenia
Spain
Sweden
Switzerland
Ukraine
United Kingdom

Latin America and Carribean

Anguilla
Antigua and Barbuda
Argentina
Aruba
Bahamas
Barbados
Belize
Bolivia
Brazil
British Virgin Islands
Caribbean Netherlands
Cayman Islands
Chile
Colombia
Costa Rica
Cuba
Curaçao
Dominica
Dominican Republic
Ecuador
El Salvador
Falkland Islands
French Guiana
Grenada
Guadeloupe
Guatemala
Guyana
Haiti
Honduras
Jamaica
Mexico
Nicaragua
Panama
Paraguay
Peru
Suriname
Uruguay
Venezuela

Land rich industrial countries

Australia	United States of America
Canada	
New Zealand	

Annex 2: Random sample of 25 African cities

Table A1: **Random sample of 25 African cities**

City	Country	2014 Population
Accra	Ghana	4,429,649
Addis Ababa	Ethiopia	3,009,130
Alexandria	Egypt	4,345,193
Algiers	Algeria	3,085,560
Arusha	Tanzania	377,169
Bamako	Mali	2,358,106
Beira	Mozambique	382,574
Cairo	Egypt	15,734,934
Gomba	Nigeria	416,874
Ibadan	Nigeria	2,954,967
Johannesburg	So. Africa	8,000,158
Kairouan	Tunisia	127,569
Kampala	Uganda	3,017,000
Khartoum	Sudan	5,061,792
Kigali	Rwanda	821,881
Kinshasa	D.R. Congo	10,226,182
Lagos	Nigeria	11,008,356
Luanda	Angola	5,555,024
Lubumbashi	D.R. Congo	1,746,414
Marrakesh	Morocco	770,422
Nakuru	Kenya	326,159
Ndola	Zambia	443,326
Oyo	Nigeria	452,476
Port Elizabeth	South Africa	952,746
Tebessa	Algeria	203,542

Regional Economic Integration in Africa

Chapter 10

Hasan Tuluy

Introduction

There is significant evidence that countries benefit from openness and participation in the global economy. Trade, whether in goods, services or finance, and increasingly through participation in global value chains—contributes to growth through access to deeper markets, enhanced competition and new technology, all driving productivity and efficiency. In the same manner, greater intra-regional trade and economic integration overcomes market fragmentation to achieve greater economies of scale, allowing for more efficient resource allocation from higher-cost to lower-cost producers, thereby increasing overall efficiency.[1] Larger, lower-cost markets tend to crowd in more foreign and domestic investment and thus bring knowledge and technology to the regional markets. This has been found to be true for both large and for smaller economies.[2]

From 1995-2004, global trade grew faster than global GDP as the world became increasingly integrated. Trade in constant prices (US$2005) grew by 5.7 percent compared to 3.7 percent growth of global GDP from 1995 to 2004. However, that growth has been more volatile, and slowed significantly in the last decade (2005-2015), bringing it more in line with GDP growth, at 4.0 percent compared to 3.8 percent for GDP (Figure 1).[3]

By way of comparison, Africa's[4] share in global trade over the period also grew, albeit more slowly, from 2.3 percent (1995) to 2.9% percent (2015) (Figure 2). Moreover, when extractive commodities[5] are excluded, the share

1. In addition to static, one-time gains from reallocation, there is considerable evidence of dynamic gains generated by greater competition, acquisition of technology and managerial know-how from operating in deeper competitive markets.

2. Kathuria, S. & Shahid, S. (2015). *Opening up markets to neighbors: Gains from smaller countries in South Asia*. Washington: World Bank.

3. Growth rates are given as constant annual growth rates.

4. This paper takes a view of the African continent covering both North Africa and Sub-Saharan countries.

5. Ores and metals, fuels, pearls, precious stones, and non-monetary gold.

Figure 1: Growth of global GDP and trade

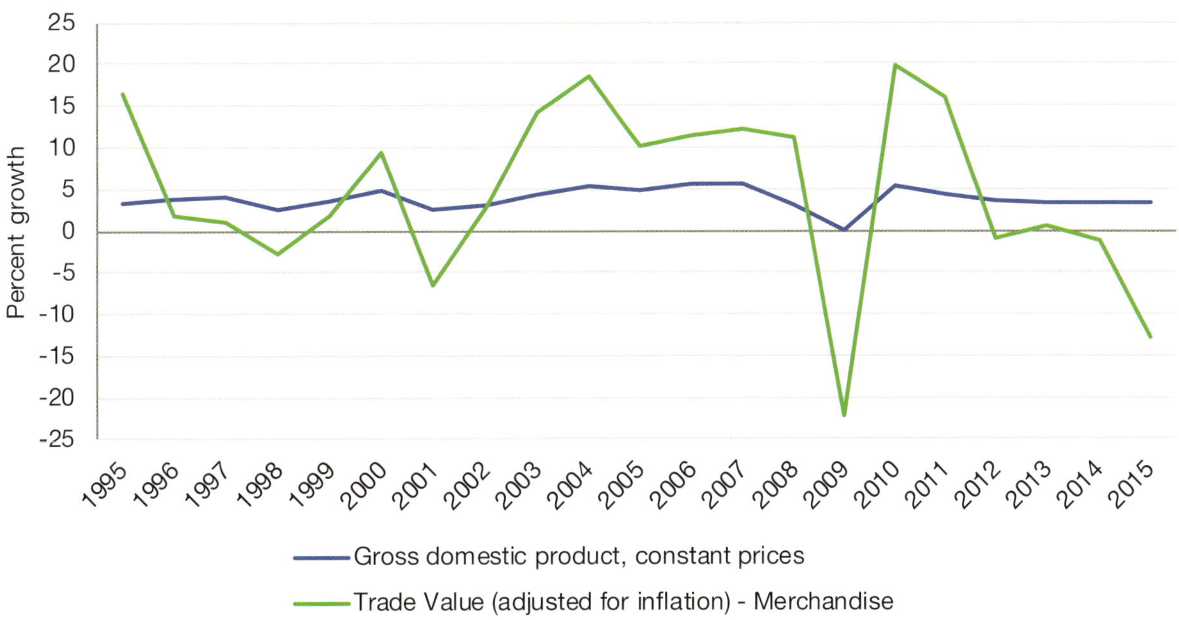

Source: IMF (2017); UNCTAD (2017)

Trade in finished manufacturing goods has tended to decline, as producers in open economies have increasingly linked into the global economy through trade in intermediate goods, services and components that form regional segments of global value chains (GVC).

has grown only marginally from 1.8 percent to around 2.2 percent. Typically, a few countries have tended to dominate the trade flows; the 10 largest countries represented 67 percent of Africa's total trade and 73 percent of the non-extractives trade in 2015.[6]

A second noteworthy feature is that global trade patterns have shifted over time: Trade in finished manufacturing goods has tended to decline, as producers in open economies have increasingly linked into the global economy through trade in intermediate goods, services and components that form regional segments of global value chains (GVC).[7] An important implication of this shift is the diminished importance of labor costs, but the growing importance of non-labor costs and of speed to market in competitiveness.[8] The continued shortening of GVC timelines points to the importance of efficient low-cost transport, communications and services.

The share of emerging economies[9] in global trade has also grown from 28.2 percent to 41.9 percent of total global trade in the past two decades. Even when extractive commodity trade is excluded, the share of emerging economies in global trade has grown from 27.1 percent to 42.1 percent over the period. Emerging economies increasingly participated in global trade through contributions to regional segments of global value chains; while systematic regional data are uneven, it is clear that most Eastern European countries, newly industrializing nations of Asia and some Latin American countries such as Mexico have deepened their participation by increasing their production into segments of larger value chains. In Africa on the other hand, only Mauritius, Morocco and South Africa have recently had a major presence in GVCs.

6. For all goods trade in 2015, top three accounted for 37.9 percent: South Africa 17.3 percent, Nigeria 12.7 percent, followed by Algeria 7.9 percent. (UNCTAD. (2017). UNCTADSTAT.)

7. OECD & World Bank. (2015). *Inclusive Global Value Chains*. Report prepared for submission to the G20 Trade Ministers Meeting, Istanbul.

8. See McKinsey Global Institute. (2016 March). Digital Globalization: The new era of global flows.

9. UNCTAD Developing Economies group of countries.

Figure 2: Africa's share in global trade (total & net of extractives)

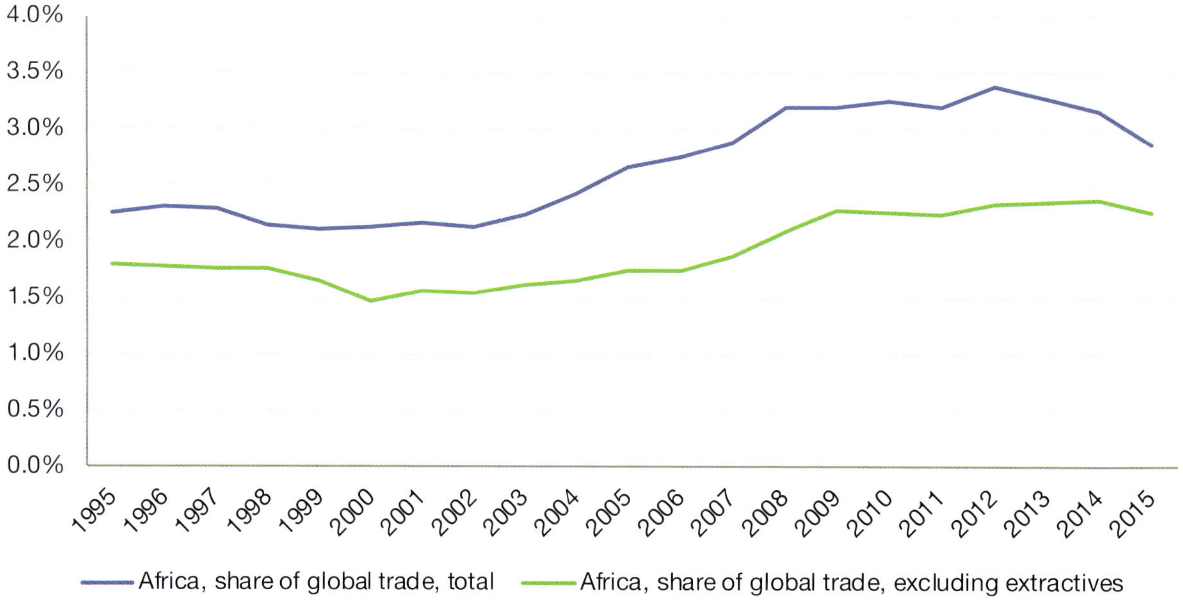

Source: UNCTAD (2017)

Unlike other regions that have open regional and global trade arrangements, Africa's trade flows have tended to be predominantly with the industrialized northern countries of Europe, North America and more recently China, often under preferential trade agreements, such as ACP and AGOA.

A third important feature of global trade over the past decades is the strengthening of regional trade and economic agreements to boost growth and create jobs. Integration through lower tariffs and reduced trade costs has allowed for scale economies and productivity gains around larger markets.

Unlike other regions that have open regional and global trade arrangements, Africa's trade flows have tended to be predominantly with the industrialized northern countries of Europe, North America and more recently China, often under preferential trade agreements, such as ACP and AGOA. In the period 2005-2015, intra-African trade was only around 11-15 percent of total trade flows compared to 45-60 percent in the European Union, 41-50 percent in the NAFTA area and 59-62 percent in Asia.[10] Further, when extractive commodity trade is excluded, intra-African trade has been largely flat, representing only 6-9 percent of trade flows.

The challenge for Africa—Constraint of initial conditions should favor economic integration

Many of the countries and economies of the African continent are small and fragmented, the enduring legacy of the continent's colonial past. Of the 53 countries for which data are available[11] 24 had GDP of less than $10 billion in 2016, and only 5 had GDP greater than $100 billion. Were Africa a single country it would have a GDP of $2,184 billion, about 2.9 percent of global GDP, and equivalent only to India[12]; 23 have population of less than 10 million, and only 6 have a population greater than 50 million; 16 (or nearly 30 percent) of the continent's countries are land-locked and 6 (11 percent) are island economies. While this represents a relatively large number of countries, in terms of GDP and population they account for only 11 percent and 26 percent (Figure 3).[13]

African countries also tend to be more rural – even with a growing trend toward urbanization – affecting density of infrastructure and services. On average, 40 percent of Africa is urban, ranging from 87 percent in Gabon to 12 percent in Burundi.

Furthermore, African economies on the whole have not been able to materially diversify their economic structures (Figure 4). Colonial production and trade patterns tended to favor production and export of raw, primary goods in exchange for imports of finished goods. Official trade patterns (and indeed the layout of infrastructure) favored South-North flows over intra-continental flows. While African economies began to transition away from rural activity in the past two decades, the move toward greater share of services has occurred without having built a substantial manufacturing base.[14] The continued heavy dependence on commodities has made African economies particularly subject to the risks of "Dutch disease" and to significant terms of trade shocks.[15]

Countries have sought to overcome the constraint of fragmentation, small size and land-locked settings by participating in the global economy and, often, by joining regional economic integration arrangements. In Africa, regional integration also holds the promise of increasing the size and depth of markets to achieve critical mass, to enable greater diversification of the economy, to expand business opportunities and create jobs, and to stimulate greater competition to spur productivity increases.

10. UNCTAD (2017)
11. Does not include Somalia, for which data are not available.
12. Of the total regional GDP of $2,262 billion, six countries: Nigeria, Egypt, South Africa, Algeria, Morocco, and Angola, represent two-thirds (66.9 percent) of the total.
13. Nevertheless, the large number of landlocked countries and island nations becomes an issue where regional arrangements require consensus decisions
14. See also Rodrik, D. (2015). Premature deindustrialization. *Kennedy School of Government, Harvard University Working Paper*. Also see Dutt, P. & Traça, D. (2009). ion and its impact on trade: Extortion or evasion?. *VoxEU*. Similarity in economic structure and low Trade Complementarity Index tend to constrain intra-African trade (see De Melo, J. and Tsikata, Y., (2014) Regional Integration in Africa: Challenges and prospects. *UN University-WIDER, Working Paper* (37)).
15. See Chapter 6, "The impact of commodity terms of trade in Africa: Curse, blessing or manageable reality?"

In Africa, regional integration also holds the promise of increasing the size and depth of markets to achieve critical mass, to enable greater diversification of the economy, to expand business opportunities and create jobs, and to stimulate greater competition to spur productivity increases.

Figure 3: Africa GDP and population quintile totals

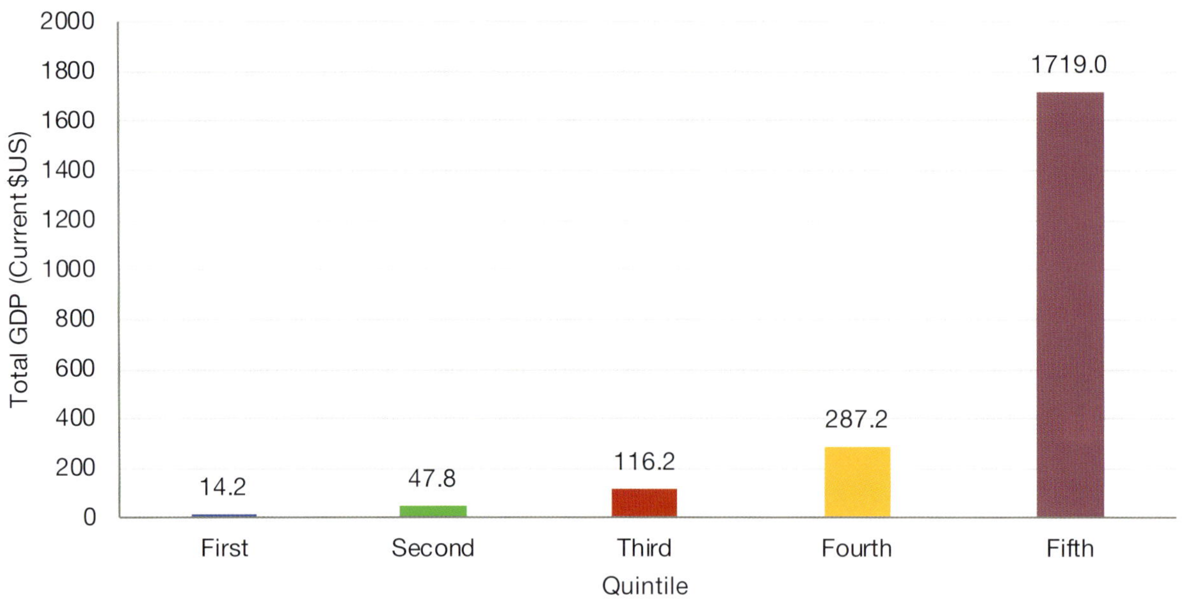

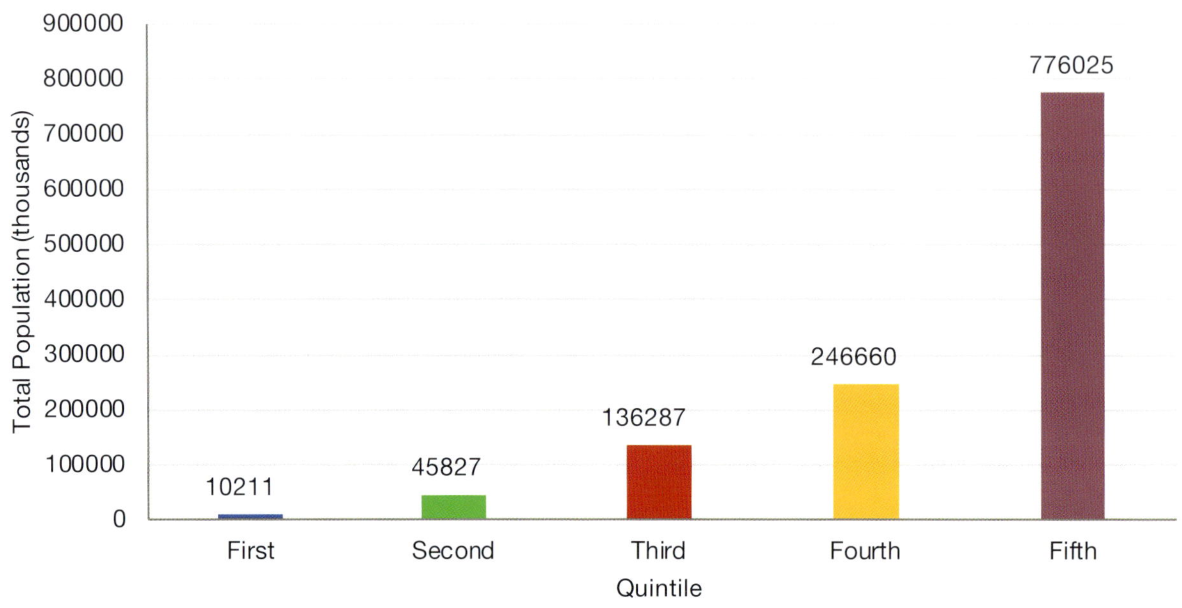

Source: IMF (2017) and UN Population Division (2015)

Regional integration has indeed been a founding principle of the African Union since its establishment in 1963 (OAU until 2001).

Figure 4: GDP sector composition, 1995-2015

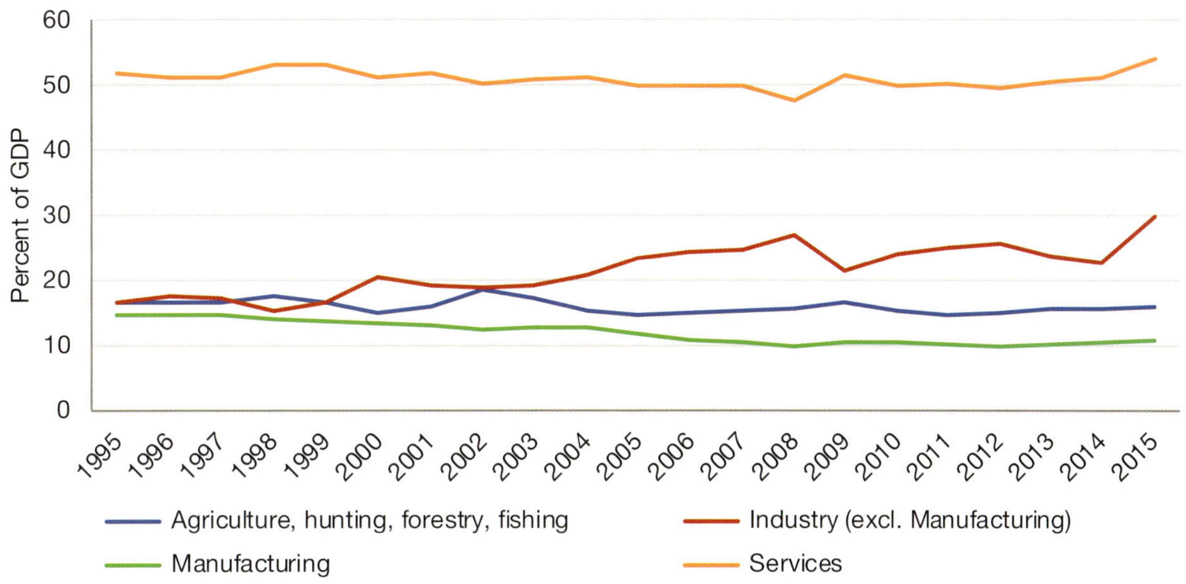

Note: Manufacturing is a sub-category of industry [UNCTADSTAT].
Source: UNCTAD (2017)

Regional integration is a founding principle of African Union

Regional integration has indeed been a founding principle of the African Union since its establishment in 1963 (OAU until 2001). It is a cornerstone of policies designed to overcome a legacy of fragmentation and conflict, to promote peace, security, stability and cooperation, and to spur economic and social development toward a political union of the continent. Not surprisingly, these efforts to integrate the African markets and economies toward a political union have been essentially driven by the political leadership.

In its early stages, when central planning was still favored, regional integration was seen as a means to enable import-substituting industrialization.[16] From the 1980s a more outward-oriented approach to regional integration received added push with the adoption of the Lagos Plan of Action (LPA) in 1980 followed by the Abuja Treaty in 1991. These undertakings called for "solidarity, self-reliance and endogenous development through industrialization" as a stepping-stone to the African economic community.[17] AU's political leadership received active operational support from UNECA. UNECA promoted organization of the continent into geographic building blocs, referred to as RECs. The goal of the RECs was to advance in a sequential progression from free trade areas (FTA), to customs unions and to a single market, finally converging toward a continent-wide economic and monetary union (the African Economic Community) by 2025. The eight UNECA promoted and supported RECs were[18]: ECOWAS (for West

16. Only a stylized summary of the evolution of African regional integration arrangements can be presented here. For a more thorough discussion see Fouroutan, F. (1992). Regional Integration in Sub-Saharan Africa: Past Experience and Future Prospects, in de Melo, J. & Panagariya, A. (eds.), New Dimensions in Regional Integration. Cambridge: Cambridge University Press.; Aryeetey & Oduro (1996) Regional Integration Efforts in Africa: An Overview in Regionalism and the Global Economy: The case of Africa, FONDAD, The Hague; Hartzenberg, T., *Regional Integration in Africa*, WTO, Economic Research and Statistics Division Staff Working paper ESRD-2011-14, October 2011; and De Melo & Tsikata (2014).

17. Hartzenberg, T., (2011).

18. It is important to note that the number and configuration of these ar-

It is worth recalling that over the centuries African traders have successfully and reliably operated complex trade routes in integrated cross-border markets.

Africa); ECCAS (for Central Africa); AMU (for North Africa); COMESA (for South and Eastern Africa); EAC (for East Africa); SADC (for Southern Africa); IGAD (for countries of the Horn of Africa, Nile Valley and the Great Lakes); and CEN-SAD (the community for Sahel-Saharan states).

In addition, states formed or revived other arrangements through parallel initiatives, resulting in frequent overlaps of countries in multiple regional integration arrangements. For instance, in West and Central Africa WAEMU and CEMAC became active alongside ECOWAS, while EAC, partly overlapping membership with COMESA, was revived. IOC formed in 1984 regroups the five island communities of Mauritius, Seychelles, Comoros, Madagascar and Reunion.

In 2001, African leaders established New Partnership for African Development (NEPAD) to further facilitate the design, funding and implementation of significant intra-country programs and investment projects in support of regional integration. In 2008, the 26 member states of COMESA, EAC and SADC, representing a population of about 620 million and total GDP of $1.3 trillion, committed to establish a grand Tripartite-FTA. Finally, heads of state at their meeting in Kigali in 2010 set an ambitious new goal to form a Continental Free Trade Agreement (CFTA) by 2017, and a Continental Customs Union (CCU) by 2019.

Successful examples of cooperation and collaboration

It is worth recalling that over the centuries African traders have successfully and reliably operated complex trade routes in integrated cross-border markets. Even today—in parallel to the officially and politically driven integration efforts, and in spite of multiple obstacles—a substantial amount of unofficial and unrecorded trade in agricultural commodities and in artisanal mining takes place across the continent. Examples include the substantial cross-border trade in grain, tubers, fruits and vegetables, an active livestock trade from the Sahel to coastal consumer markets (and even from Somalia, a quasi-failed state, to the Middle East), and much of artisanal mining output that is moved and marketed across multiple borders. Other examples of unofficial cross-border supply chains—the kola-nut trade in West Africa or the khat trade from the horn of Africa to Yemen—are remarkable in the sophisticated, time-sensitive distribution and payments chains across multiple borders and jurisdictions that these trade channels require. These integrated markets and dynamic trade circuits, with their sophisticated production, storage, handling, shipping and distribution, credit and payment systems, remain essentially informal and are often not captured in official trade statistics.

There have also been successful larger scale official cooperation and collaboration experiences in Africa around regional public goods where joint and coordinated action has yielded benefits to all participants. Regional cooperation in sectoral areas on such issues as communicable diseases (Onchocerciasis, Guinea worm, Ebola); natural resources management (river basin management); agricultural and livestock research; and the fight against terrorism have functioned relatively successfully because solutions are sub-regional in nature and benefits visibly accrue to all members of the region, irrespective of their size.

Similarly, groups of African countries have worked out joint negotiation positions to gain greater voice in matters ranging from ODA, trade and climate change. Further, some sub-regions such as WAEMU have pursued policy harmonization with regard to fiscal and monetary policy.[19]

Proponents of integration have rightly argued that the regional integration agenda would be significantly advanced with the achievement of intra-regional projects

rangements evolved over time. For instance, EAC was initially organized in 1967, became EAC II in 1999. In Southern and Eastern Africa, SACU - the Southern Africa Customs and Monetary Union - became SADCC 1975 and formed a Preferential Trade Area (PTA) in 1981; in 1992 after the end of Apartheid South Africa, SADCC transformed itself into SADC, and COMESA replaced the PTA in 1994. IGADD formed in 1986 (Intergovernmental authority on drought and development) became IGAD in 1996. The region also has a large number of functional groupings. See UNECA website for a more detailed historical treatment.

19. These examples of close economic and monetary integration and policy coordination are built on history and colonial administrative legacy of the CFAF countries.

In parallel to the more top-down process of RECs, a number of promising initiatives are underway that advance regional economic integration in a pragmatic way in the Horn of Africa, in East and South Africa.

and harmonization efforts that reduce costs and bind markets closer together. The creation of NEPAD (2001), the AU's Minimum Integration Program (MIP)[20] of May 2009, and other similar institutional arrangements reflect this desire. There have been a few notable examples of such intra-regional projects, particularly in East Africa, including the Mombasa-Nairobi-Addis Ababa Corridor and the Kenya-Uganda Railway Concession, as well as some capacity building projects, including the East Africa Centers of Excellence and the Africa Economic Research Consortium, though there are some questions as to their sustainability.

Recent developments in regional integration

In parallel to the more top-down process of RECs, a number of promising initiatives are underway that advance regional economic integration in a pragmatic way in the Horn of Africa, in East and South Africa. For instance, the recently completed Addis Ababa-Djibouti Railway, linking Addis Ababa with the Port of Doraleh in Djibouti,could substantially reduce cost and time of transit. Early estimates are a reduction of cargo transit time from 3 days by road to 12 hours by train. SAPP, which aims to develop a common power grid and common electricity market for SADC countries, has seen relative success with major connections established between nine SADC members, and others currently in development (e.g. Zambia-Tanzania, Mozambique-Malawi, etc.). Another major project is the West Africa Gas Pipeline (WAGP), the first regional natural gas transmission system in sub-Saharan Africa. The 678-km pipeline runs through four countries, from Lagos to Takoradi. While both projects have had setbacks and much progress remains, they still stand out as some of the better examples among Africa regional projects.

There have also been other useful examples on the soft infrastructure side, particularly where there is already a consistent administrative system between countries, such as WAEMU. For example, the Organisation for the Harmonization of Business Law in Africa (OHADA) has led to notable progress in harmonizing business laws and institutions among West and Central African states. As a result of OHADA and its harmonization, the time to start a business has decreased from 67 to 26 days, and cost has decreased from 250% of per capita income to 75%, in the last decade.[21]

Two features emerge from these initiatives. First, the larger sub-regional economies are playing the lead role with a few like-minded countries that share a common interest in pressing for changes: South Africa leading the SAPP and Nigeria leading the WAGP. Other examples are being developed currently across the continent: Kenya is leading the inter-governmental discussions with East African Community partners (Uganda, Burundi, Rwanda and Ethiopia) with a view to expanding the capacity of Mombasa port and replacing the Northern corridors multiple gauge railway with a standard gauge (SGR).[22] South Africa has invested substantially in the Maputo corridor, which is an important element of the country's bilateral trade with and foreign direct investment to Mozambique. The port-railway corridor has been a major channel for the trade of the sub-region as well with sub-regional exports to the global markets. A second important feature is the active role of the private sector is playing lobbying the governments for investments, changes in policies and regulations to lower costs and barriers to sub-regional trade. On the WAGP, Chevron and Royal Dutch Shell were two of the key partners in initiating the project and collectively own more than 50% of the pipeline. Kenya's private banking, telecoms, retail and wholesale traders, and air transport operators[23]

20. MIP is not an incremental planning or financing mechanism. Rather, it consists of those investment plans that RECs commit to implement on an accelerated basis.

21. Nosal, L., & Saltane, V. (2016 January). Harmonization strike a chord of success: Doing Business in OHADA economies. *IFC SmartLessons*.

22. Brenton, P. & Hoffman, B. (eds.). (2016). Political Economy of Regional Integration in Sub-Saharan Africa. Washington: World Bank, p. 12. There is some recent uncertainty on project design with possibility that Uganda may prefer upgrading the Southern corridor to Dar es Salaam. Ethiopia is also evaluating a possible Northern link with the SGR in addition or as an alternative to the rail line from Djibouti to Addis.

23. Safaricom, Kenya Commerce Bank and Equity Bank, Nakumatt, Tusky's, and Uchumi (retailers) and Kenya Airways are actively expanding their market presence in the sub-region (Brenton et al. 2016, p. 7).

Despite the promise of significant potential gains that regional economic integration holds for Africa, and the high-level declarations of commitment to further the regional integration agenda over multiple decades, Africa clearly has not made as much progress toward integration as it wished and as it could.

have expanded their operations into neighboring countries and are actively partnering with and lobbying authorities for *inter alia* improvement in efficiency in Mombasa Port, to eliminate road blocks, reduce red-tape and to ensure One-Stop Border Posts (OSBP)[24] are fully functioning.

However, by and large, regional, multi-country projects have not shown much success in the past. There have been a large number of programs and plans put forth, but with few tangible results to show to date. Finance has not necessarily been the binding constraint. The challenge has been that even multi-country projects that have demonstrable joint benefits are implemented locally by national administrations. For instance, even the WAGP, as well as the West Africa Power Pool, potentially important instruments designed to reduce costs along a more efficient energy mix, are not functioning to their projected capacity due to a combination of divergent national sector policies, distortions in domestic price, and continued concerns about sovereignty and source reliability.

Constraints to deeper economic integration

Despite the promise of significant potential gains that regional economic integration holds for Africa, and the high-level declarations of commitment to further the regional integration agenda over multiple decades, Africa clearly has not made as much progress toward integration as it wished and as it could. Three sets of constraints impede realization of potential gains from deeper[25] regional economic integration: (a) the density and quality of "hard" physical infrastructure; (b) the burdensome "soft" infrastructure; and (c) the complexity of historical regional integration arrangements.

Dearth of physical infrastructure[26]

Africa is not well connected.[27] The continent suffers from poor physical infrastructure in both density and quality, contributing to high cost structure of the economies and loss of competitiveness. According to the World Bank's Logistic Performance Index 2014, the vast majority of African countries rank toward the bottom on trade logistics, with only South Africa (3.43) ranking in the top quartile. African countries (including North African) account for a little more than half (23 out of 40) of the bottom quartile, with D.R. Congo (1.88) and Somalia (1.77) ranked last.[28]

Transport costs are the highest in the world—twice level of other developing countries—and significantly limit Africa's ability to trade regionally and globally.[29] Costs vary significantly by sub-region and depend on whether the country is landlocked or has port access: landlocked countries' transport costs are up to four times as high as those of developing countries.[30] Perkins and Robbins further estimate that the cost of transporting goods in East Africa is 30 percent higher than in South Asia, and up to 60-70 percent higher than in the USA, thereby reducing annual GDP growth by 1 percent.[31] Average road density is low. Among the RECs, road density ranges from 214 km/1000 km^2 in SADC to 105 km/1000 km^2 in the EAC.[32] This is compared to an average road density of 306 km/1000 km^2 in South Asia, 237 km/1000 km^2 for East Asia and Pacific, and 740 km/1000 km^2 for Latin America and the Caribbean. Paved all-weather road density is even lower, ranging from

24. JICA is supporting investments into the establishment of 80 operational OSBPs across Africa. The challenge is not only improving the hardware of such OSBPs but also in simplifying and harmonizing policy, procedure and functioning of such posts (NEPAD. (2016 May). *Move Africa: Launch of Initiative*).
25. "Depth" in regional integration generally refers to moving from a Free Trade Area to closer integration of markets (Customs Union, Common Market) and institutions (Political Union), and inclusion of behind-the-border issues such as services, investment and competition policy in the regional integration agenda (Hartzenberg 2011).

26. See Chapter 8, "Africa's Infrastructure Deficit: Closing the Gap."
27. There are various global indices of connectivity that generally track each other. In general, African economies tend to rank low on these indices. See of instance McKinsey Global Institute's Global Connectivity Index.
28. World Bank. (2014). *Logistic Performance Index 2014*. Washington: World Bank.
29. Aspen Institute (2005)
30. Christ, N. & Ferrantino, M. (2009). Land Transport for Exports: The Effect of Cost, Time and Uncertainty in Sub-Saharan Africa. *Office of Economics Working Paper, U.S. International Trade Commission* (2009-10-A).
31. Perkins, D. & Robbins, G. (2011 March). The Contribution to Local Enterprise Development of Infrastructure for Commodity Extraction Projects: Tanzania's Central Corridor and Mozambique's Zambezi Valley. *Making Most of Commodities Programme (MMCP) Discussion Paper*, (9).
32. See Yepes, T., Pierce, J., & Foster, V. (2008.) Making Sense of Africa's Infrastructure Endowment: A Benchmarking Approach. *World Bank Policy Research Working Paper* (4912).

The African continent has many small ports that serve shallow local markets and compete for regional trans-shipment trade, yet these facilities are unable to reach scale to be internationally competitive.

92 km/1000 km^2 in SADC to only 8 km/1000 km^2 in the EAC,[33] compared to an average paved road density of 14 9 km/1000 km^2 in South Asia and 419 km/1000 km^2 in Latin America and the Caribbean. Moreover, routine and periodic maintenance has been a challenge for most African roads; in 2008, while roughly half of the main road network in sub-Saharan Africa was rated in good condition and one-third in fair condition, the situation was dramatically worse in rural road networks (where 50 percent were rated in poor condition, with only 25 percent rated each in good and fair condition).[34] The adverse effect on cost and time of Africa's low density, poor road conditions and inadequate maintenance is further aggravated by the frequent lack of compliance of transport norms (load standards) that in turn further degrades the network.[35]

The African continent has many small ports that serve shallow local markets and compete for regional trans-shipment trade, yet these facilities are unable to reach scale to be internationally competitive. Only Durban (South Africa) and Damietta and Port Said (Egypt) have the annual capacity of around 4-5 million TEU (twenty-foot equivalent unit). These plus Port Elizabeth and Cape Town (South Africa), Port Louis in Mauritius, Tangiers in Morocco are the only ports able to accommodate Post and Super Panamax vessels today. A handful of others, notably Dakar (Senegal), Abidjan (Côte d'Ivoire), Mombasa (Kenya) and Djibouti have capacity of around 500-900,000 TEU per year. Many of the continent's ports operate at below capacity due to low berth/docking facilities, weak terminal freight and handling management, and inadequate maintenance and dredging capacity. As a result, port services are costly and shipments are often delayed leading to physical and financial losses. The Port of Durban, widely considered one of the more efficient ports in Africa, has turnaround time of more than two days (51 hours), compared to less than 24 hours for ports such as Shanghai and Klang (Malaysia) and less than 48 hours for ports such as Singapore and Rotterdam, all of which also have significant higher volumes than Durban.[36] The continent also is poorly served by inter-country rail networks.[37] Major inter-country rail corridors are limited in reach (coverage/extent) and service is considered generally unreliable due to lack of maintenance and new investment. The colonial legacy also left to the continent a fragmented network. For instance, in East Africa, the Northern corridor linking Uganda, Rwanda and Burundi to the coast, still carries three separate rail gauges.[38] Air travel and air freight is similarly underdeveloped, costly and generally lacking in capacity and connections. Notwithstanding recent improvements, few of the continent's airports have adequate connections and capacity to make regional passenger and freight traffic convenient. A simple connection between two major West African cities—Dakar and Lagos—lacks a single nonstop flight, requiring passengers to change planes in Lomé or stop to refuel Abidjan. Air cargo levels for all Africa were 1.73 million tons in 2013,[39] comparable to the air cargo traffic for just Los Angeles International Airport, which fails to rank in even the top 10 airports in the world for cargo traffic. The top performers, Hong Kong International Airport and Memphis International Airport (FedEx), each handle more than 4 million tons per year.[40] Other infrastructure essential to competitive economies—electricity and telephone and broadband connectivity—are also relatively underdeveloped in Africa. Electricity generation capacity across the continent is only 37 MW/million population, or 11 percent of comparable low-income countries, which have a generating capacity of 326 MW/million population. Further, only 11 percent of the population has access to electricity, which is

33. Yepes, Pierce, & Foster (2006)
34. Gwilliam et al. (2008)
35. In addition, transport services are fragmented by country, frequently organized in cartels with many small providers that have no incentives to consolidate and make efficiency gains.

36. Port Regulators of South Africa. (2016). *Port Benchmarking Report: SA Terminal 2015/2016*.
37. Note that many African countries also have limited local/domestic rail service and some have specialized (e.g. for ore) rail transport networks.
38. Aspen Institute (2005), p. 9
39. Boeing. (2015). *World Air Cargo Forecast 2014-2015*.
40. Airports Council International. (31 March 2014). *Preliminary World Airport Traffic and Rankings 2013*.

The constraints of low density and quality of physical infrastructure on global competiveness and regional integration are amplified by significant border and behind-the-border constraints in policy, regulations, procedures, norms, standards and certification, often collectively referred to as "soft" infrastructure.

highly concentrated in urban centers, as compared with 41 percent in comparable low-income countries. In addition, electric power is expensive and highly unreliable. African mobile telephone penetration increased dramatically, such that today mobile density is at 55 lines per 1,000 population, compared to 76 lines in low-income countries. Yet importantly, in Internet density Africa still lags significantly behind other regions.[41]

Major trade corridors are intermodal networks of ports, roads and railways that connect hubs of economic activity and move the bulk of trade within and between countries. Most effective corridors go beyond integrating intermodal infrastructure only, to also harmonizing and aligning the entire logistics chain along the corridor. Thus, well-functioning corridors contribute to competitiveness and integration through smooth, efficient, low cost, timely and reliable services. Africa has a number of potentially significant trade corridors that link the landlocked countries and the coast (including Durban and Maputo to Harare, Gaborone and Lusaka, Mombasa to Kampala and Kigali, Douala and Central Africa, Lagos, Cotonou, Abidjan and Dakar to the Sahelian states) and others that link a number of coastal countries (Douala to Abidjan, or Tangiers to Algiers).[42] Yet many of these corridors operate at below their potential, and remain much costlier than comparable data from competitor countries.[43] These high costs do not serve Africa well. They act as a real deterrent to global competitiveness and closer regional integration, yet present an opportunity to make significant gains, if reforms are brought to priority corridors.

41. AfDB. (2015). *African Competitiveness Report*. Abidjan: AfDB, p. xiv, notes that, "Only one-fifth of the region's population is using the Internet, compared with 30 percent in Southeast Asia, 40 percent in Latin America and the Caribbean, and 80 percent in…OECD economies."

42. See for instance, African Development Bank. (2011). *Programme for Infrastructure Development in Africa (PIDA)*. Abidjan. AfDB. PIDA is a joint initiative of the AU, NEPAD and ADB multi sector program covering transport, energy, water and ICT, and is dedicated to facilitating continental integration in Africa through improved regional infrastructure.

43. For instance, according to the World Bank's Doing Business 2015, the cost to import a container in Africa was as high as $9,285 (South Sudan) with an average for Sub-Saharan Africa of $2,930/container and an average for North Africa of $1,307 as compared to $1,100 for OECD high income countries and the lowest cost of $440 in Singapore.

Africa still faces significant "soft" infrastructure constraints

The constraints of low density and quality of physical infrastructure on global competitiveness and regional integration are amplified by significant border and behind-the-border constraints in policy, regulations, procedures, norms, standards and certification, often collectively referred to as "soft" infrastructure.

While governments and international agencies have devoted attention to upgrading physical infrastructure, "soft" infrastructure has not received the same degree of attention. Policy reforms have tended to emphasize the "at the border regimes," the formal thickness of the border. These include lowering relatively high tariff levels, reducing their complexity (number of bands) as well as minimizing recourse to exemptions regimes for allegedly "sensitive sectors."

African economies have been relatively less open to international trade. Africa's openness has been around 65 percent in past decade (2005-2014), compared to Asian Developing Economies (at 80 percent) and Europe (at 77 percent). Only Latin America at 43 percent (on account of Brazil) and rapidly opening Southern Asia at 48 percent (on account of India, Pakistan and Bangladesh) have had less open economies over the past decade.[44] Over this period Africa's tariff structures have been simplified and average tariffs have come down from 13.9 percent to 12.8 percent. While this represents good progress three observations are in order: (a) There are still wide tariff variations between African countries (from a simple average MFN tariff of 21.2 percent in Sudan to 1.0 percent in Mauritius);[45] (b) The average tariff levels still remain above those in other parts of the world (Figure 5); and (c) Exemptions lists remain long and broad.[46]

44. UNCTAD (2017)

45. Trade taxes remain a significant share of total revenue for many African countries representing 11 percent of Sub-Saharan countries' total revenue in 2010, compared to 4.8 percent in North Africa, 4.4 percent each in East Asia and Latin America (and 0.6 in Europe and 1.7 in North America) (World Bank 2016d).

46. For example, the ECOWAS Common External Tariff (CET) signed in

While governments and international agencies have devoted attention to upgrading physical infrastructure, "soft" infrastructure has not received the same degree of attention.

Figure 5: Simple average MFN applied tariffs and frequency of tariff rates

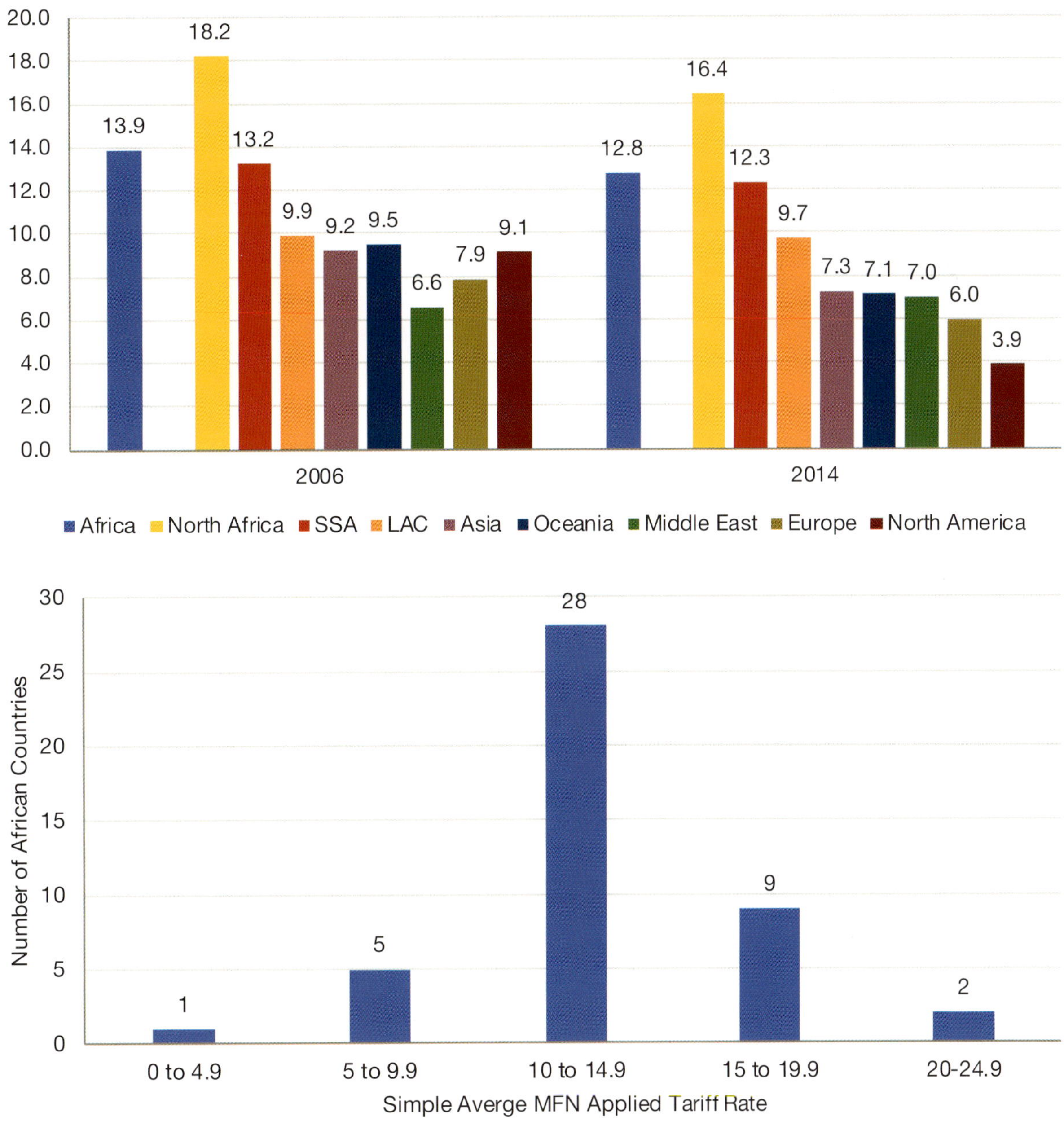

Source: WTO (2016)

In contrast to the attention formal trade regimes have received, other critical "soft" infrastructure barriers, non-tariff measures (NTMs), those measures that collectively represent the cost of getting to the border, have typically received much less attention.

In contrast to the attention formal trade regimes have received, other critical "soft" infrastructure barriers, non-tariff measures (NTMs), those measures that collectively represent the cost of getting to the border, have typically received much less attention. These include the number and complexity of procedural requirements, administrative processes, the recourse to different technical regulations, norms and product standards and certification.

As an example of the complexity and multiplicity of documentation, it takes 11 documents to export goods from Cameroon, DR Congo, and Malawi, whereas Mauritius, Morocco and Tunisia require only 4 documents to export. By comparison, the best in class, Ireland, requires only 2 documents.[47] It takes 17 documents to import goods into CAR, but only 5 to Djibouti and Mauritius. The global best in class Ireland requires only 2 documents to import.[48] Similarly, whereas 31 African countries use UNCTAD's Automated System for Customs Data (ASYCUDA), in principle laying the foundation for expedited transactions, it is notable that most major economies (e.g. Nigeria, South Africa, Egypt, etc.) do not use the system. Even minor differences between countries of such items create impediments and the need – or the opportunity – for low value compliance controls at borders,[49] which raise the elapsed time and cost of transactions. For instance, in the absence of regional/multi-country agreement on transport guarantee bonds, shippers are obliged to obtain guarantee bonds for each country traded goods are transited through at added cost and lost time.

While some of these NTMs legitimately protect national interests of health and safety, many needlessly introduce discretion and increase the time and cost to trade. Multiple checkpoints along highways add hours of delay and often lead to bribes exceeding the official highway toll charges.[50] By some estimates, as much as 75 percent of delays on major transport corridors are due to these types of soft "behind-the-border" shortcomings, rather than the constraints due to physical infrastructure.[51]

There is strong global evidence that service productivity is important for increasing manufacturing productivity. Yet today in Africa, services and intermediary professions so critical for trade tend to be protected (by nationality requirements) leaving the activity fragmented into many small and higher-cost domestic markets. Integrated, cross-border services markets present a missed opportunity to boost productivity for greater competitiveness – a must if Africa is to participate more actively in regional and global value chains. Lack of competition and low levels of integration results in higher costs of critical intermediary services (such as brokers and agents); professional services (such as legal and accounting, banking, insurance); communications (fixed, mobile and Internet); transport services (road, air, rail, maritime); and retail and wholesale commercial services.

In addition, the quality of the basic overall economic governance environment in Africa, from contract enforcement to the ease of starting up a new business, remains a major contributor (or hindrance) to the effectiveness of the "behind-the-border" environment. Investors, producers, shippers and traders require predictability of policy and its enforcement, and reliability in the supply and availability of tradable goods and services. In this regard, while overall performance has improved since 1995-2005, African countries' average Doing Business ranking in 2017 was 142, compared with 94 in East Asia and Pacific, 107 in Latin America and 26 in OECD high-income countries.[52]

January 2015 includes an "exceptions list" of about 300 products eligible for exemption from the new tariffs that includes 200 products from the former Nigerian Import Ban list. (De Melo, J. (26 August 2015). Regional integration arrangements in Africa: Is large membership the way forward?. *Brookings Africa in Focus Blog*.)

47. In 2015, the Sub-Saharan average for export documents is 8, Middle East and East Asia required 6, and OECD 4 documents to export (World Bank 2017).

48. In 2015, the Sub-Saharan average number of import documents is 9, while Middle East required 8 import documents, East Asia 7, and OECD 4 (World Bank 2017).

49. The multiplicity of regulatory and control agencies set up to manage quality and control fraud have come to serve in good part a non-tariff barrier.

50. The Economist. (16 April 2016). Obstacle Course: Africa's trade suffers from dismal infrastructure, lack of investment and corruption. *The Economist*. Checkpoints along the Burkina-RCI corridor had even acquired an acronym: PDG for Police-Douane-Gendarmerie, and bribes could run as much as 10% of product value.

51. Harmon, L. M., Simataa B., & van der Merwe, A. (2009)

52. The Doing Business approach has been criticized as excessively mech-

An important impediment to deepening regional economic integration in Africa is undoubtedly related to the complexity and multiplicity of regional integration arrangements.

For the 2017 rankings, 61% of African countries ranked in the bottom quartile, and none in the top quartile – best in class was Mauritius (49), just shy of the top quartile, and Rwanda (56) (Figure 6).[53]

Complexity of approach impedes greater progress toward regional integration

A third important impediment to deepening regional economic integration in Africa is undoubtedly related to the complexity and multiplicity of regional integration arrangements. African countries have historically approached regional integration in a formal, relatively rigid, sequential and linear manner: Countries would form regional economic communities (RECs), which would progress from free trade areas (FTA) with free flow of goods followed by free flow of services and labor and then the formation of customs unions, proceeding toward fiscal and monetary unions and culminating in a continental political union.

African leaders have periodically reconfirmed their strong political commitment to the goal of an integrated African economic community and to this linear approach. Their political commitment, however, has not yielded commensurate results in the face of significant practical implementation challenges. Intra-REC trade, on average has been only 8.2 percent of RECs total trade value. This drops to merely 6.7 percent when SADC—the best performer with intra-REC trade at 19.1 percent of total trade value—is removed. A similar story emerges with each REC's trade with the rest of Africa, which is, on average, only 7.9 percent, with SADC again as the best performer at 15.3 percent of total trade value. The vast majority of RECs' trade is with the rest of the world, on average, 83.9 percent of total trade value (Figure 7).

A first challenge is that the politically motivated, relatively rigid, sequential approach covering a wide range of sectors and issues may not be best suited to the African context today.

A second challenge is the multiplicity of regional arrangements with significant overlapping membership where members often pursue different economic objectives and may hold divergent views about relinquishing their sovereign rights. Smaller, landlocked countries, for instance—a large share of Africa's countries—tend to have a rather different perception of policy and implementation risk, of being overwhelmed by the larger countries in the regional grouping (Figure 8).

Third, except for a handful of larger, diverse economies (such as Kenya, Morocco, Mauritius, South Africa), African countries tend to have relatively similar economic and cost structures. The larger the number of members, the more divergent the size of membership, the more similar the economic structure, the harder it is to reach consensus on decisions and to take effective action in the absence of credible transition and compensation arrangements for losers from regional economic integration.

Fourth, with few exceptions to date, private sector actors have not been actively brought in to play an active role in the design and implementation of the regional economic integration agendas, thus depriving the process of strong domestic champions.

And finally, institutions tasked with advancing regional integration, whether at the regional or national level, have not always had the requisite institutional, financial and

anistic, and the system itself is open to gaming by countries to manage their outcomes in order to improve their rankings. However, flawed as it is, this indicator is the best and most widely disseminated measure of the regulatory framework. At the same time Doing Business tracks other similar measures of countries' competitiveness and receptivity to investment. For instance, according to latest WEF Global Competitiveness Index (2016-17) Africa ranked toward the bottom of GCI. Only 4 African country placed in the top 50 percent in rankings out of 138 countries: Mauritius (46), South Africa (47), Rwanda (52), and Botswana (64). Meanwhile, nearly three-quarters of the lowest quartile were countries of the continent. (World Economic Forum (WEF). (2017). *Global Competitiveness Report*.)

53. Note that the Doing Business 2017 Report breaks down cost and time to export and import into border compliance and documentary compliance. Among these, there is significant variation within the continent. For example, South Sudan ranks the worst for time to import in documentary compliance, at 360 hours, but for border compliance, it is closer to the middle of the list at 179 hours, far below the worst performer in that category, Dem. Rep. of the Congo at 588. If African countries could seek to emulated the best in each category and take took on their best practices, whether it be Swaziland's fast border compliance practices for exporters, at only 3 days, or Namibia's comparatively inexpensive documentary compliance at $63, there are several countries who can stand out as best practice for the various aspect of cross-border trade it would substantially contribute to reduced costs and time and increase the competitiveness of Africa's trade.

While these challenges make intra-regional trade and integration a particular challenge, with growing population, rising incomes, increasing demand for foodstuffs, manufactures, and quality services there is significant potential for deeper regional economic integration in trade and investment in regional value chains.

Figure 6: Cost and time to export and import

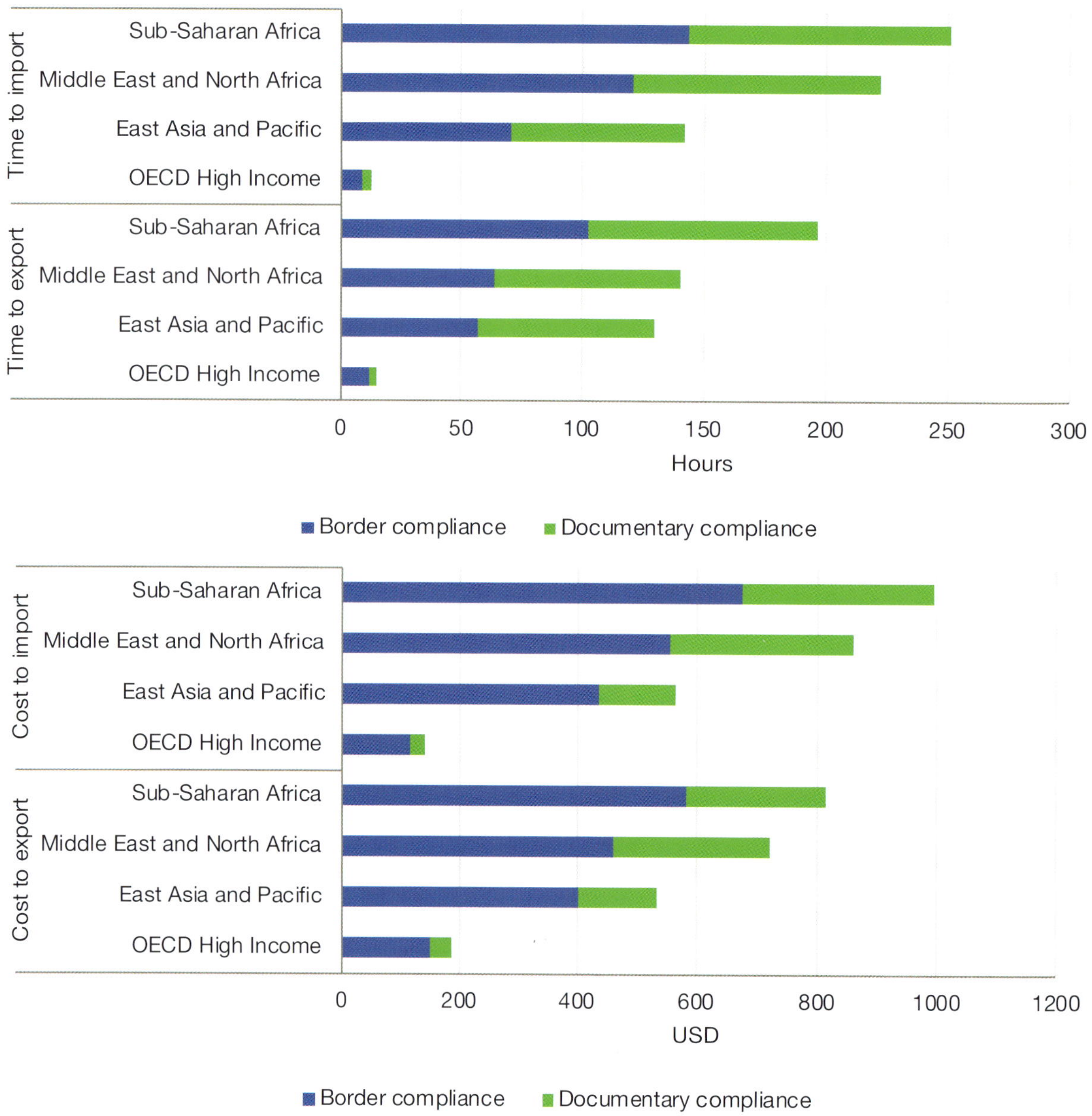

Source: World Bank (2017)

Despite frequent, strong high-level declarations of political commitment, facing diverse impediments, progress toward the goal of deeper economic integration has heretofore proven insufficient and elusive.

Figure 7: REC trade values by partner

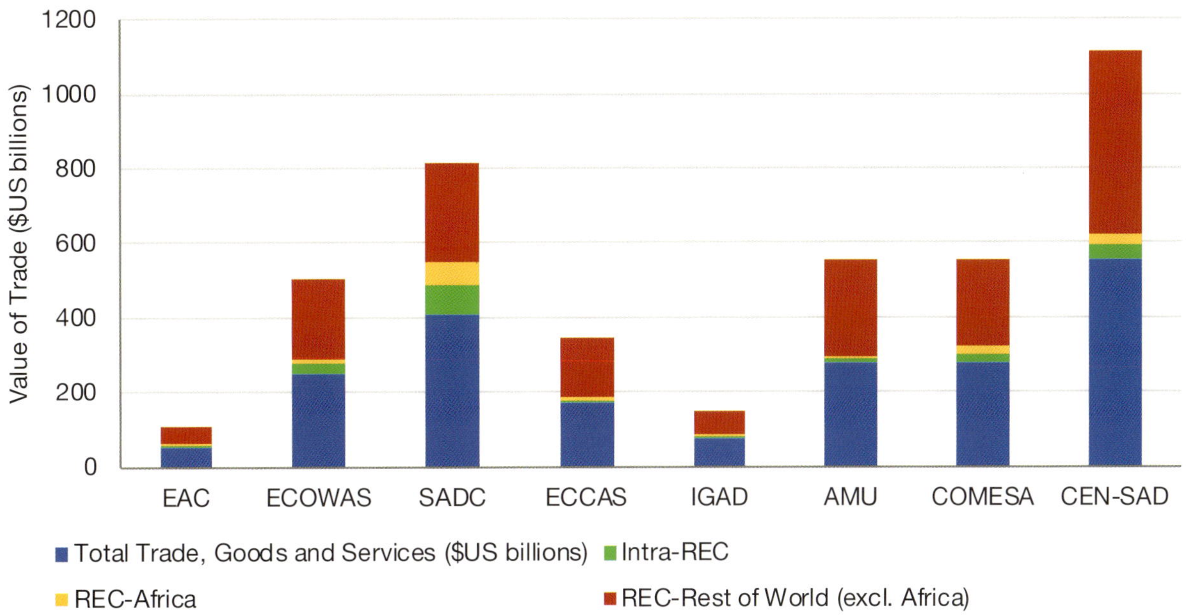

Source: UNCTAD (2017)

administrative capacity to make a compelling analytical case for integration, or to design, implement and monitor multi-faceted programs to encourage trade and integrate markets.

These constraints have prevented Africa from realizing its ambitious regional integration plans. African economies have remained relatively fragmented and high cost, cutting into competitiveness, penalizing producers, exporters and consumers. They further hindered firms' ability to operate in lean, just-in-time production mode needed to effectively participate in global value chains.[54]

While these challenges make intra-regional trade and integration a particular challenge, with growing population, rising incomes, increasing demand for foodstuffs, manufactures, and quality services there is significant potential for deeper regional economic integration in trade and investment in regional value chains.[55]

The way forward: Action agenda

There is little disagreement on the goal for Africa to achieve greater scale and depth, and to promote productivity and competitiveness through greater integration. Yet despite frequent, strong high-level declarations of political commitment, facing diverse impediments, progress toward the goal of deeper economic integration has heretofore proven insufficient and elusive.

African countries can make significant progress toward this goal by adopting a flexible, pragmatic approach, driven by economic imperatives, by focusing on those hard and soft infrastructure reforms that connect African economies and facilitate their participation in global markets and value chains.

54. In addition, cross-border spillovers of insecurity, fragility and unpredictability have significant adverse effects on the scale intra-regional flows of goods, services and persons.

55. Furthermore, deeper integration would benefit the poorer consumers, foodstuff producers and traders and small-scale traders (often women).

Move forward around a few key corridors and possibly around a small number of sectors/sub-sectors.

Figure 8: Africa REC membership

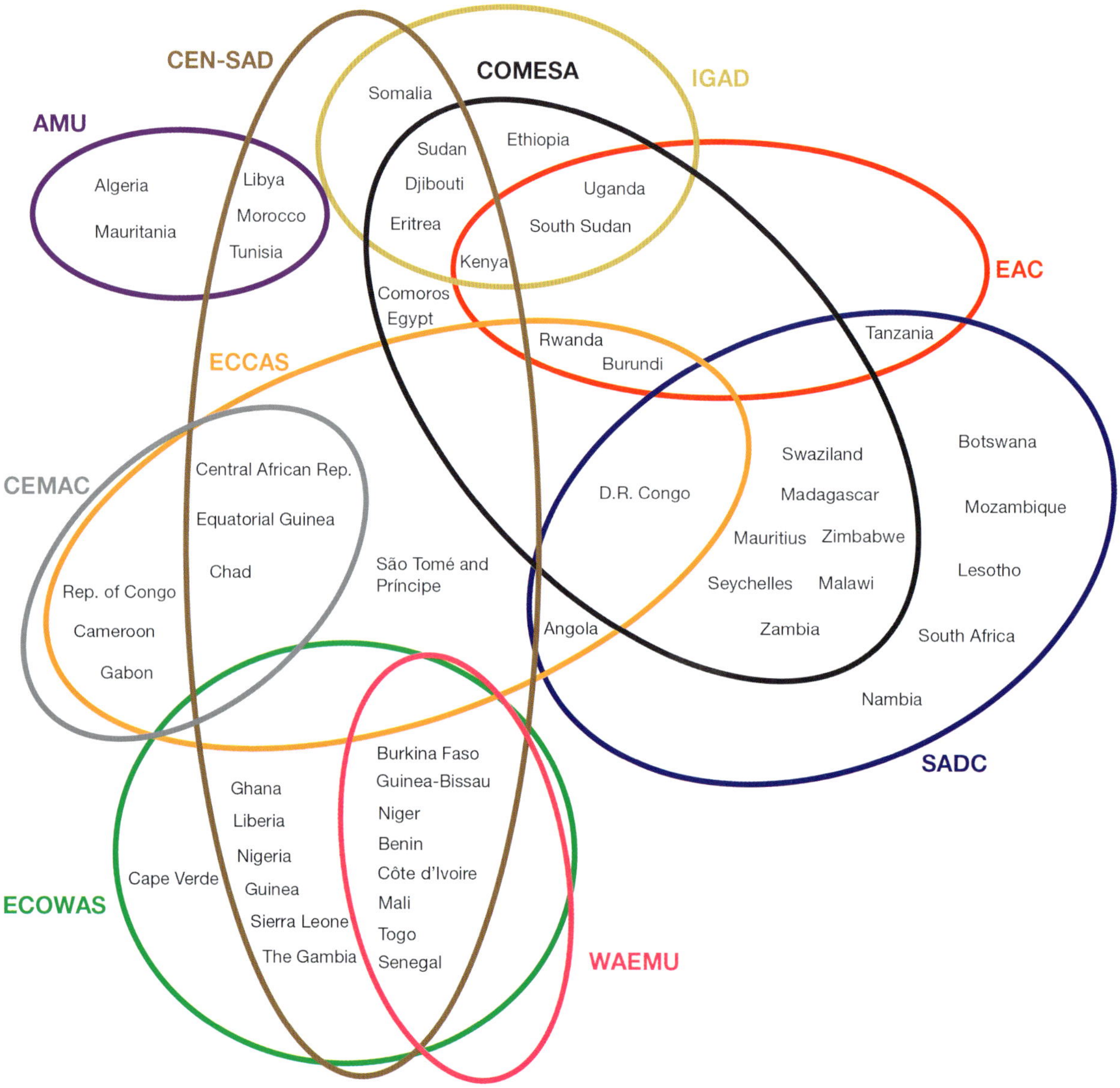

Build broader coalitions in favor of integration by engaging private sector representatives (business councils and consumer interest groups) in the design, development and implementation of such corridors.

1. First, adopt a variable geometry approach whereby a subset of like-minded countries take action on a focused agenda—while remaining flexible and open to inviting other countries that operate at different speeds to join in over time—instead of (or in parallel to) the more politically driven linear and comprehensive approach.
2. Second, move forward around a few key corridors and possibly around a small number of sectors/sub-sectors; an approach that has the advantage of engaging fewer players that need to reach agreement on few critical infrastructure investments, and a more limited range of policy issues.
3. Third, build broader coalitions in favor of integration by engaging private sector representatives (business councils and consumer interest groups) in the design, development and implementation of such corridors. Private participation in the build-out phase, and certainly private expertise in management of the key corridor assets can be envisaged for many of the infrastructure investments.
4. Fourth, continue policy reforms in tariffs and regulations to substantially reduce time and cost.
    - i. Continue lowering and simplification of tariff regimes. As we have seen, despite a reduction of the average tariff levels in the past two decades, and a trend to simplify the structure, Africa's tariffs remain higher and more complex than other emerging economies. In addition, extensive recourse to "exemptions" by a number of large economies of the continent that could have been engines of trade and growth have in contrast effectively slowed growth of regional trade. Further progress is certainly necessary and possible.
    - ii. Open markets to tradable services. Services, whether professional services (accounting, brokers, legal, banking, insurance), communications services (fixed, mobile, broadband), or transport services (road, air, rail, maritime) are critical contributors to raise Africa's manufacturing productivity and competitiveness.
    - iii. Address other impediments that act like non-tariff barriers and influence production and investment choices to enable countries to reap real benefits from improved physical infrastructure[56] and lowered formal trade barriers. These include items such as the number, complexity and differences in or duplication of documentation and processing steps; differences in norms, standards, certification requirements, sanitary and phytosanitary measures, marking, labeling and packaging requirements. Simplifying, harmonizing and automating would yield substantial benefits at relatively little investment cost.
    - iv. Deal with illegal rent-seeking behaviors especially along the priority trade corridors. Complexity, lack of automation, and differences in rules and regulations increase the chance for interpretation and discretion, and in turn the opportunity for rent seeking. Progress is possible: When Senegal and Mali signed a border cooperation agreement that reduced the number of checkpoints from 25 to 4, transport times quickly declined from 7-10 days to just 1-2 days.[57]

56. A systematic review of such measures by member country is presented in WTO/Trade Policy Review(s) under the headings of measures affecting Import, Exports, and Production and Trade.
57. World Bank. (2009a). *Doing Business in Landlocked Economies*.

Regional institutions and development partners must support this process in a coordinated manner by bringing together governments and private sector interests (producers and consumers) to identify impediments to greater scale, competitiveness and economic integration.

5. Fifth, continue complementary reforms aimed at improving investor protection, predictability, reliability and timeliness—features that are essential for production of tradables (and for participating in global value chains)—to reduce supply side constraints and to encourage production of tradable goods and services. Many of these are reforms along the lines of Doing Business (such as registration, credit, contract enforcement and IPR) and fall within the domain of national decision, and can be undertaken without awaiting agreement at the regional level. Harmonizing as much as possible such business regulations and investment codes, etc., at the sub-regional level would further encourage scale economies;
6. Sixth, regional institutions and development partners must support this process in a coordinated manner by bringing together governments and private sector interests (producers and consumers) to identify impediments to greater scale, competitiveness and economic integration. Regional and national institutions' analytical capacity needs support and strengthening inter alia to (a) set out those minimum threshold conditions that countries would need to meet before coming on board to variable geometry platforms without endangering overall viability/progress; (b) to rigorously assess the dynamic effects of integration on winners and losers; (c) to advise on the establishment of a credible transitional compensation mechanism; (d) to set out a framework for determining the appropriate scale (dimension) as well as the respective cost, benefit and debt service obligations of intra-regional projects to individual member countries; (e) to explore risk management tools for long-term multi-country project undertakings; and (f) to support a supra-national monitoring and dispute resolution mechanism.

Conclusion

As some of the encouraging recent African initiatives and the successful Asian experiences have shown, Africa can significantly deepen regional economic integration by adopting a flexible, bottom-up approach driven by economic objectives, focusing on a few corridors and clusters. This approach, as recommended by the agenda for action of this report, will increase the scale and depth of regional markets and link Africa more firmly and competitively into global value chains and markets.

Washington: World Bank.

In East Asia, regional economic cooperation was advanced through bilateral and multi-country negotiations, which took a pragmatic, business-oriented approach of developing key industry and manufacturing segments, and key corridors within and across borders.

Box 1: Asian and European approaches to regional cooperation and integration

East Asia and Europe offer two different models of regional economic cooperation and integration. In East Asia, regional economic cooperation was advanced through bilateral and multi-country negotiations, which took a pragmatic, business-oriented approach of developing key industry and manufacturing segments, and key corridors within and across borders. The state played a supportive and active role through policies that provided macro-financial stability, a competitive exchange rate, and maintained a reliable, predictable policy environment that allowed for significant domestic and foreign investment in manufacturing and industry. The corporate sector benefited substantially from a partnership with the active state, and in turn, acted as an important lobby for continued openness, competitiveness and deepening of trade.

In the earliest stages, a few technically advanced, capital rich countries—initially Japan—and large industrial conglomerates with access to term financing from public institutions were the main drivers of regional economic cooperation with the newly industrialized economies of the region, starting with Korea, Singapore, Taiwan (PoC) and Hong Kong (SAR), followed in the next decade by China, Thailand and Malaysia. Within this context, large industrial enterprises from the technologically more advanced economy shifted production processes to the next tier of regional countries, accompanied by substantial direct investment flows, and even more importantly, by the purposeful transfer of technology. Over time this resulted in the establishment of integrated network-type connections and complementary industrial clusters, giving Asian countries the ability to actively participate in and shape all aspects of global value chains.

In contrast, European integration born in the years after the world war, was heavily motivated by a top-down political desire to balance adverse effects of nationalism by closely binding together European economies and by creating strong supra-national institutions. Today Europe represents an integrated space of 28 members, a population of nearly 500 million, accounting for nearly one-fifth of global GDP.

Critical to the advancement of the European experience has been the willingness of founding countries to cede some of their sovereignty in favor of shared supra-national institutions with authority to set policy, regulate and enforce decisions in a broad range of public policy areas. Equally important to progress toward regional integration has been that France and Germany, the two major economies of Europe (and past combatants) joined forces to drive the European project forward over decades of domestic political cycles. A body of common policies and regulations served to guide new members' convergence (accession) while a generous compensation mechanism allowed new members to integrate with minimal short-term disruption to their economies. Finally, Europe set out a model of "multi-speed" integration whereby enlargement and deepening of the regional model proceeds flexibly with new members able to sign on to different aspects of the integrated European model (for instance common currency, or visa-free zone) at different speeds.

What Asian and European experiences have in common is that they were led by large forerunner states, which maintained supportive public policies, built sound infrastructure and invested in good human capital. The regions offered complementarity in cost structure that allowed for significant direct investment and transfer of technology from the costlier economies to the less advanced, lower cost economies to integrate in GVCs. The paths differed in regard to the top-down, politically inspired approach of Europe that favored convergence – albeit at flexible speeds - with supra-national policies, regulations and institutions, as compared to the more bottom-up, economically motivated and focused Asian integration which did not call for the dilution of sovereign prerogatives. Some of these features provide hints of paths that Africa may also wish to pursue.

Note: There is an extensive literature that analyzes the record and features of East Asian and European cooperation and integration models. See for instance: ADB (2013, 2010), Kasahara (2013), Rana (2006), Cameron (2010), Moghadam (2014), and Spolaore (2013). This high-level summary merely seeks to highlight some of the distinguishing features without attempting to be comprehensive.

European integration born in the years after the world war, was heavily motivated by a top-down political desire to balance adverse effects of nationalism by closely binding together European economies and by creating strong supra-national institutions.

Table 1: Basic statistics of RECs

REC; Year founded	# of members	Total GDP (current $US billion)	% of Africa GDP	Largest economy, GDP (current $US billion), and % of REC GDP	Total population (million)	% of Africa pop.	Total trade, goods and services ($US billions)	Volume of intra-REC trade (merchandise, $US billions)	Volume of REC-Africa trade (merchandise, $US millions)	Volume of REC-Rest of World trade (merchandise, $US billions)
EAC; 1967, 2000	6	144.8	6.4	Kenya, $61.4 billion, 42.4%	173.7	14.7	53.8	5.4	5.2	48.4
ECOWAS; 1975	15	658.3	29	Nigeria, $490.2 billion, 74.5%	372	31.4	251.9	24.8	15.1	227.1
SADC; 1980, 1992	15	611.7	27	South Africa, $313 billion, 51.2%	248.4	21	406.4	77.8	62.1	328.6
ECCAS; 1983	10	191.8	8.5	Angola, $103 billion, 53.7%	140.3	11.8	171.7	2.7	15.7	169.1
IGAD; 1986	8	246.1	10.9	Sudan, $83.6 billion, 34%	254	21.4	74.1	4.7	5.4	69.5
AMU; 1989	5	362.1	16	Algeria, $172.3 billion, 47.6%	956.4	8.1	277.8	11	6.4	266.7
COMESA; 1994	19	729.4	32.2	Egypt, $330.8 billion, 45.3%	445.1	37.6	278.1	21.7	23.7	256.5
CEN-SAD; 1998	28	1312.5	57.9	Egypt, $330.8 billion, 25.2%	613.4	51.8	556.4	39.6	26.8	516.8

Note: EAC was originally founded in 1967, dissolved in 1977, then reformed in 2000. SADC was originally founded in 1980 as the Southern African Development Coordination Conference (SADCC), then reformed as SADC in 1992.
Source: IMF (2017); UNCTAD (2017); UNECA (2016)

Chapter 11

New Threats to Africa's Stability and Growth

Serge Michailof

Africa is doing better than 15 years ago

Any productive discussion of Sub-Saharan Africa must take into account its great diversity. Africa's ecosystems are as diverse as its peoples and the legacies of its colonial past. The continent is equally diverse in terms of its countries' economic situations and income levels. The US$20,000 average annual income of an inhabitant of Equatorial Guinea, for example, contrasts starkly with the US$400 of a resident of Niger.

Despite this diversity and the obvious differences across countries, trends in Sub-Saharan Africa were fairly similar between 1970 and 1990. These years were marked by weak long-term economic growth, chronic productivity deficits, largely rentier-based economies, wide-ranging demographic changes, strong urbanization, stalled industrialization, and the persistence of poverty traps. It is often forgotten that these same countries, after winning independence, enjoyed rapid growth from the 1960s until the oil crisis of 1973.

Since the new millennium however, many countries in Sub-Saharan Africa have experienced growth rates that stand in sharp contrast to the previous two decades of stagnation. Of the ten countries with the highest levels of growth in the world in the first decade of the new millennium, five—Angola, Ethiopia, Chad, Mozambique, and Rwanda—were in Africa, all averaging growth above 7 percent; at that rate, an economy doubles in size in ten years. In fact, almost everywhere on the continent, trade, mass distribution, construction, and services have seen spectacular growth. In 15 years, African market capitalization has almost quadrupled, private equity has boomed, and migrant remittances and foreign direct investment have far exceeded official development aid. The so-called "awakening" of Côte d'Ivoire since President Ouattara took office in 2011 is a stunning case in point.

The reasons for this widespread success are well established. They begin with the high prices of raw materials stimulated by the extraordinary growth of China until 2013, which increased revenues from exports. This economic success was reinforced by major infrastructure projects, including the construction of highways and freeways, expansion of ports, rehabilitation of major railroads, and commissioning of numerous power stations. The growth of new information and communications technologies and of the financial sector over the past two decades has been similarly spectacular. Today, even the smallest market trader has two, three, or even four mobile phones in his or her pocket. A scene in the remarkable film Timbuktu that shows a Tuareg child trying to get a signal at the top of a sand dune underscores the importance of the mobile phone in even the poorest communities.

Africa's economic success is also grounded in the macroeconomic stability that was rediscovered following the instability of the 1980s and 1990s. Throughout the 1980s, severe structural adjustments sometimes provoked social disasters that led to collapses in the public services responsible for education and health. In some countries, they also caused breakdowns in state structures and major increases in corruption. Yet the adjustments ultimately resulted in the restoration of balanced budgets and external accounts that for more than a decade had accumulated enormous deficits. The adjustments made it possible to lower inflation and more broadly implement rigorous budgeting thanks to the rise of a new generation of technocrats accustomed to working with the Bretton Woods institutions. For the countries on this path, the cancellation of most of their external debt, which had risen to unsustainable levels, greatly facilitated these budgetary adjustments.

What are the threats?

Today, many observers agree that the growth of the past 15 years will continue, albeit less rapidly because of the decline in commodity prices and the slowing of the Chinese economy. However, two new clouds loom on the African horizon.

The first is the contrast between successful countries and those seemingly doomed to failure. While

Areas that have not benefited from economic growth now face long-run stagnation and the risk of entering alarming cycles of violence.

certain countries have seen remarkable growth, others remain plagued by poverty, disastrous management of public affairs, and unresolved internal conflicts. The Central African Republic, Somalia, and South Sudan are well-known cases.

The second is that even the successful countries have not been able to prevent the emergence of deep social and geographical inequalities, which are often accompanied by rising tensions and increased insecurity. In many cases, these phenomena combine with an erosion of authority as the state loses control over peripheral regions, which become lawless zones.

The continent's extraordinary economic successes led to the development of urban infrastructure, the proliferation of skyscrapers, traffic jams of Mercedes and SUVs, and the emergence of not only an opulent class of millionaires but also an authentic middle class. But these impressive developments tend to be limited to particularly dynamic regions and to the capitals. The businesspeople who invest there often forget that the peripheries of these capitals mostly comprise miserable shantytowns and poorly integrated neighborhoods that lack public services such as roads, drainage, drinking water, and electricity. Areas that have not benefited from economic growth now face long-run stagnation and the risk of entering alarming cycles of violence.

Without doubt, the destabilization of the North East of Nigeria is the most emblematic.

The Nigerian economic boom has not prevented the emergence of a caliphate in the north of the country. Nigeria, whose economy largely stagnated from the late 1960s to 2000, experienced remarkable growth afterwards until the 2014 collapse in oil prices. This growth coincided with the end of military regimes and, combined with a change in statistical procedures, made it the largest economy in Africa. Nigeria is currently the seventh most populous country in the world, with 190-million inhabitants. It is on track to become a global giant by 2050, the third most populous country (after China and India), with 400-million inhabitants, and one of the world's twenty largest economies. It recently had a non-permanent seat on the UN Security Council.

Nigeria is a working democracy. The most recent elections, in March 2015, saw the replacement of President Goodluck Jonathan, who hailed from the south of the country, by General Muhammadu Buhari, a man from the north. The education system is fairly good, the administrative elites are for the most part highly qualified, and some institutions (though not all) function remarkably well. Nigeria was also one of only two African countries affected by Ebola that was able to rapidly and effectively contain the epidemic (the other being Senegal). Still, it suffers extraordinary inequality between the largely deprived north, where per-capita income is among the lowest in the world, and the capital city and the south, both of which have experienced an economic boom.

The troubling issue today is that despite its considerable financial resources, administrative structures, and sizable military budget, the Nigerian government is unable to guarantee security in the Niger River Delta, where mafia gangs rule, and has allowed maritime piracy to develop to the extent that the Gulf of Guinea is now more dangerous than the Somali coast. In recent years it has also largely lost control of the North east of the country, a territory ravaged by the armed group Boko Haram.

The destabilization threat is becoming regional.

Naturally, the advances made by Boko Haram are of great concern to the neighboring countries of Chad, Niger, and Cameroon. Chad feared economic suffocation because Boko Haram was threatening its main access route to the sea via Douala and north Cameroon. At the end of 2014, Chad, Niger, and Cameroon decided to commit their forces to loosening this stranglehold, but with mixed success. The offensive resulted in the destruction

While seriously weakened, Boko Haram now still poses a threat to the region.

of Boko Haram's most visible military structure, especially its armored equipment and its ability to mount coordinated offensives. In spite of its claim of having established a caliphate, Boko Haram, unlike ISIS, is incapable of administering the regions under its control. None of its stated objectives—to 1) establish a caliphate covering all of northern Nigeria, southern Chad, southeastern Niger, and northern Cameroon, 2) impose an extreme version of Sharia law, and 3) eradicate all Western traces, in particular public education—was achieved. In fact, the nihilistic savagery apparent in the movement is reminiscent of the infamous LRA, the Lord's Resistance Army, which has long terrorized northern Uganda. It is difficult to imagine its sustainability as an organized movement, as its activities are now largely confined to looting and massacres. But it is still active around Lake Chad, and it is too early to think that the threat has been conclusively removed. Such mixed results after a coordinated offensive by the armies of four countries—supported by the UK, the US, and France—justify probing the reasons for the emergence and expansion of a movement of such magnitude in the richest and most powerful country in Africa.

Northern Nigeria was a land of jihad throughout the 19th century, and its impact was felt as far away as Mali and Senegal. The Sokoto Caliphate led by Usman dan Fodio, which emerged at the beginning of the 19th century, covered the whole of what is now northern Nigeria, southern Chad, and northern Cameroon. It even exercised nominal sovereignty over a group of emirates covering part of present-day Mali and Burkina Faso. In addition, the establishment of Pax Britannica gave rise to a series of revolts led by preachers throughout northern Nigeria, particularly in the northeastern states, where Boko Haram is currently established. This rebellion thus has historical and religious roots.

It is surprising that the Boko Haram movement started out in 2000 as a tiny Islamic sect comprising only a few dozen followers, all strongly influenced by the Wahhabi teachings disseminated by Saudi Arabia. This marginal sect, ridiculed by some for its isolationism and sectarianism, became progressively more radical after 2003 and adopted an ideology rejecting what it considered the remnants of colonial influence, in particular Western-style education and both national and local forms of government.

Although its aim is to establish an Islamic state "purified" of all Western influence, Boko Haram's success is largely explained by the deprivation in northern Nigeria. Poverty in the north of the country, which stems from extreme population density, the consequent environmental crisis in the countryside, and the lack of prospects and employment for young people, allowed Boko Haram to prosper. Even viewed from an airplane, the overexploitation of land in the region, with the disappearance of fallow land due to demographic pressure, is striking. As in many other countries, the struggle for access to land is often the source of violent conflict. Boko Haram has skillfully played on such tensions, as well as on inter-ethnic and inter-religious rivalries. Since 2009, it has established links with jihadist networks in Niger, Mali, Libya, Algeria, and even Somalia.

While seriously weakened, Boko Haram now still poses a threat to the region. The linguistic and ethnic proximity between Niger and Nigeria along their 1,500-kilometer shared border means that insecurity in northeastern Nigeria is gradually corrupting southeastern Niger in the Diffa region, which is of considerable concern to Niger officials, who fear it could jeopardize the unity of the country[1]. They are well aware that the threat cannot be addressed by military means alone but demands a rapid acceleration of economic and social development programs at the local level.

The example of Boko Haram shows that a new type of menace is emerging in Africa.

A new kind of threat is now emerging that is likely to spread to the many regions in Africa that, like northeastern

1. In June 2016, the military base of Bosso close to Diffa was taken over by Boko Haram fighters and 32 soldiers from Niger were killed.

These new threats are emerging in countries subject to tensions that neither national institutions nor failing political processes are able to manage.

Nigeria, have lagged as development has left them behind [2]. For a long time, the power elites in Africa assumed that the main danger came from rebellious armies or from the streets of deprived neighborhoods. To deal with these dangers, they reinforced the presidential guards built on tribal loyalties and instituted populist policies ranging from low-cost cereal imports to subsidies for diesel fuel. Yet rural people in peripheral regions were largely forgotten; their political weight did not count, or their votes were bought by unscrupulous politicians. Their isolation was reinforced by populist policies and the lack of all-season highway infrastructure.

This new type of threat is arising in places where radical Islam has replaced the secular ideologies of the 20th century (Marxism, fascism), which had barely penetrated Africa. It gives the populations of these regions simplistic explanations for the misery into which they are plunged and pushes them to believe that the West is responsible for their ills.

Conflicts in Africa are not a new phenomenon—quite the contrary. There were many conflicts, some of them devastating, in the decades following independence. These included attempts at secession (Biafra) and long secessionist struggles (South Sudan, Eritrea), and some arose in the context of difficult decolonization (Angola, Mozambique, Guinea Bissau). Many (Ethiopia, Somalia) took place in the context of the Cold War and were supported by external players. Some of these conflicts were consequences of implosions of the economy and the state apparatus (DRC) or the outcome of ethno-political crises (Rwanda). The rarest type consisted of classic conflicts between states, such as the one that once gripped Burkina Faso and Mali.

These wars and conflicts can be categorized according to various typologies, but they were essentially the result of internal political clashes and were only marginally driven by global ideologies. Even when regional coalitions were involved, as for example in the DRC, each conflict was essentially unique in that it was linked to the specific characteristics and internal political tensions of a particular state.[3]

With the end of the Cold War a quarter-century ago, these countries generally felt secure against external threats, and their military budgets remained at low levels.[4] But for at least a decade now, new threats have developed from the depths of the forgotten countryside.

The nature of the threats hanging over many African countries has changed.

These new threats are emerging in countries subject to tensions that neither national institutions nor failing political processes are able to manage. Large-scale challenges weaken state structures created too recently to have developed deep roots. One striking characteristic is the similarity of the tensions and challenges that have appeared simultaneously in many countries, sometimes regardless of highly satisfactory rates of economic growth.

The causes are very often the coincidence of strong demographic growth, a narrow economic base principally focused on fairly unproductive agricultural activities, vast territories that are difficult for a weak state apparatus to control, populations fragmented into ethnic or religious groups, and the presence of a large Muslim population subjected for several decades to strong Salafist propaganda supported by active social actions. The considerable underemployment among young men entering the labor

2. A full analysis of this issue has been recently developed in Ferdi. (2016). *Linking security and development—A Plea for the Sahel.* Clermont-Ferrand: Ferdi.

3. Francophone Africa was for the most part spared large-scale conflicts, if we omit the particular case of Chad as well as that of the former Belgian colonies of the DRC, Rwanda, and Burundi. The reasons probably lie in a relatively well-managed decolonization process, a concern on the part of the elites in power for appeasement of ethno-political tensions through diverse redistributions, and by the role played at the regional level by structured organizations such as WAEMU or the CFA franc zone. One final factor was the existence of defense agreements with France, which constituted de facto protection against external aggression but which until recently were perceived by local elites as insurance against internal uprisings.

4. To some extent, the situation is comparable to Western Europe, where the US shield and membership of NATO have led to a steady decline in military contributions.

These countries or regions...are currently subjected to destabilization attempts conducted on their poorly governed peripheries by jihadist groups.

market[5] has also sometimes been heightened by marginalization or by economic or political discrimination.

These countries or regions, often described as "fragile," are currently subjected to destabilization attempts conducted on their poorly governed peripheries by jihadist groups. These groups control specific economic circuits dealing with illicit trafficking, including weapons, cigarettes, drugs, and migrants. Apart from the northeast of Nigeria, as described above, these threats at present mostly concern the countries of the Francophone Sahel—Mali, Niger, Chad, Burkina Faso, and Mauritania—which have grouped together to confront them as the G5, but also countries located near these at-risk areas, including Senegal, Côte d'Ivoire, and Cameroon, as well as those close to the "failed" states of Somalia and South Sudan, including the border regions of Kenya and Ethiopia. Thus, the entire Sahel-Saharan belt and its neighboring areas to the south, from Senegal to Kenya, are affected.

A series of events in 2012 and 2013 brought to light the severity of these threats. First, with the collapse of the Malian army, the whole north of Mali was taken over by jihadist groups. Emboldened by their victory, they soon attempted to take control of the south of the country but were stopped by the intervention of the French army. At the same time, the well-funded Nigerian Army was unable to regain control of the area where Boko Haram was active. In short order, the ideological, financial, technical, and sometimes military links among these groups became apparent, particularly Al-Qaeda in the Islamic Maghreb (AQIM), Ansar Dine and Mujao in Mali, and Boko Haram in Nigeria. The symbolic attachment of jihadist groups in the Sahel and Nigeria to Al-Qaeda or ISIS signaled a connection to similar centers of jihad in the Middle East and sometimes even Afghanistan.

These new threats are evidenced by the presence of armed groups, often of foreign origin, linked to fundamentalist Islam that take advantage of local tensions to slip into lawless, peripheral areas of fragile states. They result in a rising incidence of illicit roadblocks and taxation of road users, cattle rustling, assaults and kidnappings of traders, followed by targeted assassinations of hostile local authorities and punitive attacks on recalcitrant villages. These actions clearly demonstrate the breakdown of the local state apparatus.

This first phase is frequently followed by terrorist acts carried out by young suicide bombers in local markets or capital cities. Less spectacular but even more serious is the everyday insecurity that is becoming widespread[6], which paralyzes travel and can lead to the collapse of the local economy. At the same time, in some cases such as in Mali, attempts are made to set up parallel "proto-state" structures that provide justice and security but impose religious and social norms on the population.

These new threats are troubling for many reasons.

These threats emerge in regions facing the serious problems previously described. The threats primarily affect low-income countries with limited tax revenues. These countries have so far not faced major threats and have largely neglected their military structures as well as their overall security and state structures. Most disturbing are the links between demography and natural resources, weaknesses and sometimes serious dysfunctions in the state apparatus, the lack of agricultural modernization and associated environmental degradation, and the lack of jobs and opportunities for young people who, lacking alternatives, easily become involved in illegal trafficking or armed actions.

The main victims of these threats are civilians, who are often unaccounted for because of an absence of local administration and records. In practice, clashes between armed groups and local armed forces are limited because

5. Beyond the obvious cultural, historical, and geographical differences, the astonishing similarity of these characteristics has led me to compare the conflicts that now affect much of the Sahel with the case of the Afghan conflicts.

6. We may recall here the transfer of the Paris-Dakar Rally to Latin America in 2009 for security reasons.

These zones of insecurity behave like metastasizing cancers...taking advantage of local ethno-political tensions and problems to insert themselves and grow in fragile neighboring countries.

they are asymmetric; control of entire territories and the populations residing in them is often achieved through a process that does not become visible for many years.[7] For jihadist groups, controlling territories and evicting state structures so as to conduct their trafficking, and undermining the morale of local armed forces through harassment, are more important than defeating them, which often is not within their capabilities.

Many armed groups that threaten these fragile countries have support networks and logistical bases in neighboring countries that are subject to even greater insecurity and are virtually inaccessible, as is the case of Fezzan in Libya and in parts of Somalia. Finally these threats have a very strong ideological dimension based on a radical Islamism supported by foundations and networks in the Persian Gulf and promoted by skilled jihadist propaganda backed by considerable financial resources and expertise. They are part of an arc of crisis that runs from Afghanistan to Mauritania through Iraq, Syria, the Sinai, and Libya, where failed democratic efforts, external interventions such as in Iraq and Libya, religious conflicts, misgovernment, economic failure, and mass unemployment or underemployment have accumulated in multi-ethnic or multi-confessional contexts.

These zones of insecurity behave like metastasizing cancers—exporting terrorism, arms trafficking, and jihadist propaganda, and taking advantage of local ethno-political tensions and problems to insert themselves and grow in fragile neighboring countries. If they are not swiftly controlled, these threats risk spilling over from their areas of origin and causing regional destabilization, which can spread terrorism and give rise to widespread insecurity in neighboring countries, even those with relatively well-structured state systems.

The ongoing decline in security in the north and now in the center of Mali clearly threatens the Malian state. But it also threatens western Niger, as evidenced by the October 2016 attack on the Tassalit camp in which the Niger army lost 22 soldiers. The spreading insecurity in Mali also threatens Mauritania and potentially Senegal as well as Burkina Faso and northern Côte d'Ivoire. Boko Haram is likely to survive as a serious regional threat if the economic and social roots of the insurgency are not eradicated. The situation around Lake Chad is similar to the threat created in East Africa by the Shebabs, which are based in Somalia and promote insecurity in northeastern Kenya and along the entire coast of the Indian Ocean as far as Tanzania.[8]

The ideological, religious, social, and ethnic dimensions of these conflicts make them difficult to defeat.

In the Sahel, as General Clément Bollée recently pointed out,[9] "the deterioration of the situation has accelerated exponentially when the various threats have combined their interests. Thus, when traffickers, highway bandits, autonomists, jihadists, et cetera, could reconcile their interests, the scale of the threat dramatically increased, whereas the previous compartmentalization that existed between the threats helped to keep them at low intensity." Just as a series of small waves, through the resonance phenomenon, can create a monster wave, this overlapping of formerly isolated threats now causes a greater threat of unexpected magnitude and reach.

A significant part of the African continent now faces a variety of threats whose determinants are not only linked to local politics or specific to the continent but are also found in other multi-ethnic or multi-religious countries in the Middle East, the Caucasus, and Central Asia. These threats reflect the messianic ideology of jihadism, with its hatred of the West and its values, and are fostered by

7. To take the Afghan example, the calmest areas are those that are well controlled by the Taliban. As the Afghan state no longer has the means to challenge the Taliban in these areas, the Taliban has no interest in fomenting disorder.

8. The Ethiopian army, which is essential to the maintenance of minimum order in Somalia, is currently withdrawing many of its troops from the country to deal with rural uprisings in Ethiopia itself.

9. Former commander of the French Unicorn force in Côte d'Ivoire in an exchange with the author.

Facing up to these new threats entails both extinguishing the flashpoints and also—and above all—neutralizing the powder kegs.

poverty, mass underemployment, a loss of bearings and hope for young people, the absence of the state, and missing or inept local government.

The collapse of the great secular ideologies of the 20th century was thus succeeded—and in spectacular fashion since September 11, 2001—by a new religious ideology that clearly identified its enemies: apostates, the West and its education system and culture, and local elites corrupted by Western culture. This ideological phenomenon has an ethnic dimension and is heightened by tensions linked to conflicts over land and access to water. Conflicts among individuals (such as the one illustrated in the film Timbuktu, mentioned above, in which a farmer bumps heads with a breeder whose cow had eaten the farmer's lettuce) now easily take on an ethnic dimension—for example, setting Fulani and Bambaras against each other in central Mali.

Throughout the Sahel, this new situation gives rise to multiple flashpoints in regions that are basically powder kegs—places ripe for conflict as a result of poverty, despair on the part of young people, and proliferating economic and social problems in a context of increased circulation of information. The question facing the countries directly affected by this phenomenon and their neighbors is how to deal with these new threats.

How should the new threats be confronted?

Facing up to these new threats entails both extinguishing the flashpoints and also—and above all—neutralizing the powder kegs. Essentially, extinguishing the flashpoints requires military means. Dismantling the powder kegs requires the implementation of complex strategies combining security measures, political action, social actions, ambitious development programs, and a vigorous ideological struggle. Let us first consider the problem of how to deal with flashpoints.

Existing flashpoints must be extinguished as quickly as possible.

Flashpoints threatening to spread very swiftly may require external military intervention, as was the case when French forces conducted high-impact operations to stop a military offensive led by jihadist groups in Mali in 2013. This case is probably exceptional, as the fighting took place in a semi-desert environment where air support and heavy weaponry could be used without the risk of collateral damage. The involvement of foreign military forces in densely populated areas as presently in the center of Mali raises more complex issues. Clearly this type of conflict can neither be settled by foreign armies nor solved by military means alone. "Winning the war is not enough to win the peace," the chief of staff of the French armed forces, General de Villiers, wrote recently.[10] Clearly, the destruction of the main rebel armed forces alone does not resolve the conflict. On the contrary, the cancer is likely to spread and expand if the underlying problems—the powder keg—are not addressed. Moreover, experience shows that these conflicts are rarely resolved in a few months but rather require decades. And it is illusory to expect that foreign forces should remain involved in a conflict of this kind for decades.

What can be expected for these countries is similar to what is taking place in central Mali and around Lake Chad. In these regions, various small armed groups take advantage of the local weakness of the state to exploit economic, social, and political difficulties to establish a foothold in densely populated areas; if foreign armies were to intervene, they would be perceived as occupying forces. Clearly, action limited to extinguishing flashpoints by "neutralizing" jihadists (to use the official wording), though necessary, is

10. Le Monde. (20 January 2016). Gagner la guerre ne suffit pas à gagner la paix. *Le Monde*.

Defusing the powder kegs cannot wait for political consensus.

insufficient; a powder keg that is not defused will produce more jihadists than the armed forces will be able to eliminate. This is what occurred in Afghanistan.

Defusing the powder kegs cannot wait for political consensus.

Defusing these powder kegs involves the implementation of complex strategies that combine political action, security measures, social actions, ambitious development programs, and ultimately an ideological struggle.

Politically, it will be necessary sooner or later to reach balanced political agreements designed to reduce the tensions that have accompanied or contributed to the conflict. These tensions are very often linked to perceptions of marginalization and, in some cases, to severe discrimination. This was the case of some Tuareg revolts in both Mali and Niger, and it seems clear that this sense of political and economic marginalization is behind the recent formation of the Macina Liberation Front by Fula groups in central Mali.

The sooner political agreements can be reached, the easier it will be to resolve the conflict. But if these political negotiations drag on, as is currently the case in Mali, the conflicts have every chance of becoming entrenched, especially if, as is often the case, certain actors benefit from them. It is generally very difficult to reach a political consensus at the outset of or during a conflict, as hoped by many observers and by impatient public opinion in the international community, which underestimates the depth of the political tensions affecting these countries.

Unfortunately, it is often necessary to wait until the conflict unfolds like a Greek tragedy before a political agreement can be reached. This also means that political agreements cannot be a prerequisite for launching security, social, and development actions. This is very important because reaching political agreement or relative consensus is always difficult, if not impossible, in acute conflicts, but a stabilization strategy cannot wait.[11]

Beyond political agreements, defusing these powder kegs also requires addressing the multiple challenges faced by the regions concerned. This can sometimes be difficult or even impossible in the absence of security. Combined civilian and military actions, the execution of which is entrusted to specialized military teams or mixed civilian and military teams, can then be envisaged, as was the case in Afghanistan with the Provincial Reconstruction Teams (PRT). However, the lesson to be drawn from this inconclusive experience is that this type of action can only be carried out on a temporary basis until normal development programs can be implemented. The two main lessons are: 1) that these civilian-military programs must secure the strengthening of local governance structures and not replace them; and 2) that the financial resources made available to them must be significant without being excessive.[12] The objective must always be to hand over social and development programs to development agencies and local civilian authorities as soon as possible.

In addition, while insecurity constitutes a major obstacle to development agencies in the field, it is important to address the key problems in regions close to the areas of greatest insecurity to halt the spread of the conflagration. We will return to these issues, which involve major changes to the objectives and working methods of the principal aid

11. In Côte d'Ivoire, in 2011, when the tensions and disagreements among the parties to the conflict were still extreme, priority was given to disarmament, demobilization, and reintegration programs as well as an ambitious reform of the security sector even as politicians were still involved in discussions. Where the external partners strive to obtain the agreement of all parties before acting (as in the case of Mali and the CAR), the situation solidifies, then degrades.

12. The resources were insufficient in the early years in Afghanistan and subsequently excessive, resulting in a great deal of waste and in marginalization of local authorities. Today they are ridiculously low for the Barkhane operation, at €300,000 for 2016.

On the security front, it is important to first regain control of regions and populations that are outside the authority of the central state.

donors, but first we should specify the actions that must be taken in terms of security.

Are United Nations peacekeeping forces the solution to restoring security?

Assessment of the performance of UN peacekeeping forces in the face of these new threats is critical. These forces can help maintain a minimum level of security in a region if the situation has not become too degraded, but their operational capacities are low. For example, the main concern of the MINUSMA force in Mali today is the protection of its own bases and of key roads to ensure their supply chain[13]. One reason for the weak capabilities of these forces stems in part from their heterogeneity (29 countries were represented in MINUSMA in Mali in 2016—many of them with a merely symbolic force). But the main reason for their weak capability is the poor quality of troops sent by the countries providing the forces. These countries receive good income from the United Nations while sending untrained and unmotivated personnel who are sometimes not fully equipped. As a result, providing troops to the UN has become a profitable business for some countries.

It is thus reasonable to question the cost-effectiveness of these forces, whose cost in Mali exceeds US$1 billion per year, especially if their maintenance over 15 years proves necessary, as is the case, for instance, in the DRC. In addition, the mandate of these forces is often inadequate to the situation and may give rise to varying interpretations on the ground resulting in culpable inaction.[14] These constraints do not allow the forces to carry out pre-emptive actions or even engage in aggressive responses if they are attacked.[15]

On the other hand, as General Lamine Cissé[16] pointed out to the author, if this type of force is made up exclusively of regional African contingents, they are able to equip and train themselves while incorporating rules concerning respect for fundamental rights as well as in operations involving forces of diverse origins. These assets would give them greater efficiency both on the spot, where they are easier to motivate than when they return to the armies of their countries of origin, and in future African regional permanent forces.

The rapid strengthening of all local sovereign institutions of the threatened countries is essential.

On the security front, it is important to first regain control of regions and populations that are partially or completely outside the authority of the central state. Beyond any external military intervention, this requires responding to the state's shortcomings and not only strengthening the national armed forces, but also consolidating—or in some difficult cases entirely rebuilding—the other state sovereign institutions. This type of consolidation can be part of an ambitious program of security-sector reform, the scope of which must be expanded beyond current practice.[17]

It is very often the weakness, the absence, sometimes even the decay and irresponsible behavior of these state institutions that led to the insecurity in the first place and, in some cases, to the establishment of parallel authorities. The objective of strengthening the state apparatus is easy

13. A country that sends a battalion as part of a United Nations peacekeeping operation receives about US$50 million per year. The salaries it pays its soldiers must be between US$2 million and US$4 million, or sometimes less if expatriation and risk premiums are not paid, as has been known to happen. This demonstrates the profitability of what for some countries becomes a business. Note that the discrepancies between billed and actual costs mean that private security companies (which are also interested) could offer a much better service for less.

14. It is for this reason that the head of UNMISS in South Sudan has recently been relieved of his duties after allowing a massacre of civilians to take place before his eyes.

15. In these conditions, what can the level of motivation be, for example, for the Bangladeshi soldiers locked up in their bastion in Kidal in northern Mali or traveling in the desert on impossible roads without ever coming across the enemy but who witness the death of their brothers-in-arms who step on improvised mines or are subjected to incoming mortar shells at night? In any case, the MINUSMA force has suffered significant losses in Mali, with more than 100 deaths since it was set up in 2013, revealing the inadequacy of its mandate and of the structure of forces relative to the enemy they are expected to fight and its modes of action.

16. Former chief of staff of the Senegalese army and former commander of the United Nations office in West Africa.

17. Often, this type of reform covers only the army and sometimes the police.

A true reform of the security sector requires a profound reform of the human resources management practices in the pillars of security.

to identify, but the implementation of such programs poses difficult technical, political, and financial problems.

At the technical level, rehabilitating the relevant institutions generally requires much more than training and equipment programs.[18] The process require reintroduction of the principles on which the effectiveness of institutions has always been based: rigorous selection of management at all levels on the basis of merit; promotion based on performance; and the introduction of modern human-resource management methods. These are based on results-oriented management requiring clear job definitions, skills reviews to eliminate unfit personnel and organizational structures with clear lines of responsibility. These steps often require targeted salary increases to attract and retain specialized or managerial staff.

The greatest obstacle is political in nature because this type of reform requires abandoning practices that are common in these sensitive institutions, where loyalty and clientelism often take precedence over capability. A true reform of the security sector for instance requires a profound reform of the human-resources management practices in the pillars of security (armed forces, police forces, local government). No lasting results can be expected where clientelism, ethnicism, and corruption reign supreme.[19] The quality of every institution—and the institutions responsible for security are no exception—depends above all on their personnel and especially on the quality of those who lead them.

A final difficulty is the financing of such programs, which are anathema to international aid. The statutes of some multilateral aid organizations prohibit them from funding anything connected to military and security matters, and their internal rules sometimes even prohibit them from funding the local civil administration. These multilateral organizations have long funded such institutional restructuring programs in their usual areas of intervention, and ministries of finance, ministries of education, and energy companies have been made operational again thanks to these major aid institutions. The paradox is that these aid institutions recognize that there can be no development without security and no security without development. Yet they apply rules and practices that clearly contradict their own observations.

Among multilateral bodies, only the EU is beginning to get involved in these issues and, in particular, to fund training programs for security forces such as the EUTM program in Mali. However, if funding is confined to this type of expenditure or, as is currently envisaged, to non-lethal equipment without providing for proper military equipment, soldiers' pay, construction of satisfactory barracks, and, above all, the means of maintaining civilian control over military forces, such funding remains inadequate. For now, the EU remains hesitant, and its expertise in this field is very limited.[20]

The poorest countries lack the resources to carry out this strengthening of their state apparatus.

A major difficulty is that Least Developed Countries (LDCs), which include the Sahelian countries, cannot finance both their development[21] and state apparatus able to meet the threats they now confront, aware that state apparatus must be deployed throughout their territories. In the characteristic case of Niger,[22] the country was forced

18. The limits of such programs have been seen in the case of the Afghan police, which after 15 years of programs of training and provision of equipment remains the mafia it was in early 2002.

19. For example, the vehicles bought at great expense are plundered (as was the case in Iraq) or their tires found for sale in the market (as is still the case in Mali), arms and ammunition are resold, and the units that on paper are ready to fight are in fact ghost troops, like those that fled before the jihadists in Mosul in 2014.

20. Through the mobilization of the human resources of their own state institutions, bilateral donors (US, UK, France, and Germany) have the best expertise in this field. But with the exception of the US, which is far less concerned than Europe with security in Africa, and of Great, which has little interest in Francophone countries, these countries have limited resources with which to finance support for capacity-building and institutional restructuring.

21. Social expenditures are currently exploding because of demographics: 40 percent to 50 percent of the population is under 15 years of age.

22. This is the first country in the world to have benefited from a detailed analysis by the World Bank of the sustainability of its security spending based on various assumptions about its pace of growth. The analysis, carried out in 2015 based on data from 2013, showed that if security expen-

International responsibility for the security expenditures of the poorest countries is essential but currently impossible.

to multiply its military spending by a factor of 3.7 between 2009 and 2015. Neither Niger nor Mali nor the other countries of the Sahelian sub-region possess economies or tax bases that would enable them to meet their immense social and economic needs as well as the emergencies they are forced to face in terms of security.

These countries have a fiscal capacity that rarely exceeds 17 to 18 percent of their GDPs. Faced with these threats, they are forced to reduce development spending to finance overall security spending, which is now approaching 6 to 7 percent of GDP in many places and as much as 9 percent in Chad. Even this level of security expenditure is insufficient to cope with the new threats they face. These exceptional costs tend to reduce the resources allocated to economic and social development, thus increasing future risks without guaranteeing security. These countries are therefore caught in a double impasse that is both budgetary and security-related.[23] As a result, they risk falling into conflict traps. Only countries with significant oil or mining revenues—as was the case of Chad prior to the collapse of oil prices, which largely explains its army's capabilities—or dynamic economies can finance the security costs to meet these threats.

International responsibility for the security expenditures of the poorest countries is essential but currently impossible.

Responsibility by the European Union or a group of donor countries for at least part of the security costs of these countries is the most urgent measure needed to prevent further deterioration of security from paralyzing the massive development effort that lies ahead, especially in the rural sector. This support should not be limited, as it is now, to training personnel and supplying miscellaneous equipment. Instead, it should include paying wages, reforming human-resources management, fully equipping units with appropriate equipment, and reforming governance of the security forces.

The problem for the international community is not financial. With sound management, equipping, training, and funding a Sahel battalion for one year costs about US$15 million.[24] Instead of setting up high-cost peacekeeping forces, the United Nations would be better off funding local security forces—on the condition that it oversee their complete reorganization. The rehabilitation and reconstruction of the Malian army, for example, certainly would not cost the billion dollars a year mobilized for the UN peacekeeping force. Moreover, the conditions likely to accompany funding from aid institutions—on the order of one quarter of this amount—intended for such reconstruction could be very helpful in reordering the governance of these forces, an outcome the provision of training courses and the donation of a few armored personnel carriers can never hope to achieve.

The international community's responsibility for a large part of the security costs of these countries can be justified for three reasons: 1) financially, it would be far less expensive than a foreign military intervention,[25] (moreover, the political cost would be much lower because the international community does not take kindly to the return of its children in coffins); 2) the security of these vast regions constitutes a regional or even global public good and therefore justifies a cost sharing approach; and 3) this is the only

ditures were to increase over the period 2013–2016 at the same rate as 2009–2012 (154 percent), the budget deficit would become intolerable. However, the country's security spending in 2016 has already exceeded the World Bank's most pessimistic expectations.

23. Recall that it was the American refusal until the arrival of General Petraeus in 2008/2009 to accept financial responsibility for the Afghan army or to seriously attempt to reform the police that now make the latter a mafia enterprise. It is, therefore, the entire state apparatus of these Sahelian countries—including the army, police, local administration, justice, and customs—that urgently needs consolidating and funding.

24. Recall that the cost of MINUSMA for Mali alone is on the order of US$1 billion per year, that the cost of the Barkhane operation is more than US$650 million, and that the budget of the 11th European Development Fund (EDF) covering the 2014–2020 period is €30 billion.

25. A Western military intervention would in any case lead to an impasse in view of the available forces, the size of the territories in question, their populations, and the inevitable friction between the population and armed forces from very different cultures, sometimes representing the former colonial power. The Sahel represents about 7 million square kilometers and will have a population of 150 million in 10 years. The Barkhane force consists of 4,000 men.

Funding the security needs of low-income countries can be carried out without the direct funding of military expenditures by aid partners.

credible way to ensure the security of these areas and to avoid a process of what might be termed "Afghanization."

Opposition to this reasoning is considerable: Within multilateral aid organizations, legal experts rely on 70-year-old statutes that challenge any involvement of donors in the security sector; Officials at these agencies also fear that resources devoted to security will reduce those devoted to traditional development activities and take a dim view of new demands on limited budgetary resources; Finally public opinion and representatives of civil society argue that aid is not meant to fund security, security budgets have a reputation for being particularly opaque, and funding them under these circumstances represents a gift to corruption. Given these conditions, it will clearly take time and considerable lobbying if there is to be any hope of altering the practices of the principal donors.

In spite of this pessimistic observation with regard to the short term, it is important that the governments of the countries concerned, especially the Sahelian countries, exert pressure on the multilateral aid institutions via the international community to demonstrate the obvious contradiction between their analyses, which show that there can be no development without security, and their practice of ignoring this question. The OECD Development Assistance Committee (DAC) is already well aware of this contradiction and is conducting work on the subject,[26] which makes it possible to anticipate some progress, even if it remains very timid for the time being.

In the World Bank study of the sustainability of security spending in Niger, the first of its kind in a country facing particularly serious threats, the goal was to achieve agreement among the major multilateral partners within three to five years to fund at least non-military security spending, focusing primarily on local administration and justice, followed by equipping police and similar forces such as the "garde nomade."

Provision of international funding for local security costs implies their rationalization and transparency.

Funding the military and security needs of low-income countries subject to these new threats can be carried out without the direct funding of military expenditures by aid partners. The solution would be to show the actual amounts of these costs and to fund the increased deficits as budget support, whether unallocated (ideally) or even allocated to social or development expenditure, which would create room for maneuver in the budget. In this case, the fungibility of budgetary resources allows for the indirect funding of security spending.[27] However, this mechanism involves finding solutions to various problems.

First, to reassure donors, these countries should abandon the purely reactive approach to emergencies that currently holds sway and introduce mechanisms for the rational programming of security expenditure based on accurate threat analyses. Second, a satisfactory level of transparency must be introduced into the security sector by preparing security analyses or white papers that accurately identify threats and ways to deal with them.

This effort should result in multi-year military programming that sets out requirements for both the military and the other state security institutions.[28] Subsequently, it is important to move away from an accounting approach that leads most of the countries concerned, all of which are under IMF supervision, to scale their security budgets in line with their available resources and not in accord

26. See Annex 2 of OECD. (19 February 2016). DAC High Level Meeting Communiqué.

27. For example, the Algerian government met the budgetary cost of a large part of its security expenditure linked to the outbreak of the civil war in 1993–1994 with indirect financing through the IMF.

28. It is desirable that the countries concerned validate the importance of this work by the partners who support their military efforts, in particular France, the US, Germany, and the UK, depending on the case. However, this approach requires still greater transparency in security budgets—including the military budget—which must be capable of being audited by the financial partners, as is commonly the case with the education and health budgets that receive funding.

Properly addressing these challenges will require a kind of "Marshall Plan" aimed at the social and economic upgrading of these countries.

with the nature and extent of actual threats.[29] They tend to respond to security emergencies with supplementary budgets that widen deficits and lower development spending. This highly constrained and unplanned budgetary approach does not provide an effective response to real security needs.

Implementation of these principles requires a high level of awareness among bilateral partners—in particular France, Germany, the UK, the Nordic countries, and the US—as well as EU bodies. They must recognize the crucial problem of security in these regions, the inevitability of increased budget deficits linked to the military and security efforts required, and the need for external funding of these deficits on a multi-annual basis in order to avoid financial gaps and security impasses each year.

Once such an agreement has been reached in principle in the Sahelian countries' negotiations with the leading European governments, it is also desirable that these countries raise awareness among the governments with influence in both the IMF and the World Bank, in particular the US, Canadian, Japanese, and Chinese governments. It would then be easier, in negotiations with the Bretton Woods institutions, to integrate the real costs of security expenditure into budgets and anticipated financial operations with greater transparency. If the corresponding financial gaps can be covered by bilateral aid or by the European Union, the agreement of the IMF and the World Bank should be easy to obtain.

The restoration of security is impossible without seriously addressing the full range of social and development challenges.

The cases of Boko Haram and Mali show security cannot be ensured solely by reinforcing security measures and that it is essential to respond at the same time to the immense social and development challenges. In the case of Nigeria, the rapid expansion of Boko Haram was linked first of all to poverty, the lack of employment prospects and social integration for the vast numbers of young men who, lacking any alternative, may become involved in illegal trafficking or enlist in armed groups. Even a superficial examination of the social and economic situations in most of the rural areas of the Sahel reveals the magnitude of the challenge confronting the region.

Properly addressing these challenges will require a kind of "Marshall Plan" aimed at the social and economic upgrading of these countries and especially of their deprived rural areas. Such an effort implies the simultaneous launching of vigorous sets of development programs, in particular for rural and municipal development, education and basic technical training, infrastructure development, and access to drinking water and electricity. Most of these initiatives will have to be financed by international aid, at least in the poorest countries. Yet their implementation will require that local politicians pay them much greater attention than in the past and focus on effectiveness and results on the ground rather than on the fanfare associated with project launches.

Donors are beginning to respond to this need: Development aid to the Sahel now reaches about US$4 billion per year. Does this increased development aid represent a magic weapon for lowering insecurity? There is a tendency to mock aid and to minimize its importance, and most African leaders would like to do without it. At the global level—about US$130 billion a year—development aid has become almost marginal compared to private-investment flows to developing countries or remittances from migrants. Yet these figures mask the important role it still plays in LDCs and all very poor countries; as in the case of the Sahel, apart from the mining and oil sectors, private investment has been notably absent.

For the very poor countries of the Sahel, international aid easily represents 8 to 10 percent of their GDP, about 60

29. Following this accounting reasoning, the Afghan army was sized to very insufficient levels (about 30,000 men until 2006 and 50,000 until 2007/2008), leaving foreign forces with the responsibility of fighting the rebellion. Given the extent of the rebellion, in 2008 General Petraeus estimated the need to urgently build a local force of 350,000 men.

Donors follow their own logic, and their actions rarely respond to the priorities arising from the security situation.

to 90 percent of their investment budgets, 60 to 70 percent of their net foreign revenues, and close to 40 percent of their tax revenues. Well-targeted and well-managed, these transfers should significantly contribute to the economic development of beneficiary countries, where it is important to engage young people as quickly as possible and thus reduce the temptation to join the ranks of traffickers linked to jihadist groups.

The example of aid in Afghanistan is inconclusive, however. The evolution of insecurity in that country is instructive, as it has been linked to factors similar to those found in the Sahel. The total volume of aid to Afghanistan has been colossal, in some years exceeding the GDP of the whole country; aid strictly reserved for development between 2009 and 2012 exceeded 50 percent of GDP. Despite levels of development aid that in some years exceeded the amounts disbursed by the World Bank for all of Sub-Saharan Africa, the results are disturbing: After 15 years of sometimes massive aid efforts, Afghanistan still ranks 171st out of 190 on the Human Development Index. Insecurity reigns even in the embassy district at the heart of Kabul. Kunduz, an important provincial capital, has been occupied twice by the Taliban. No road can be traveled safely, and the government truly controls little more than the key cities. Given its instability, what lessons can Africa learn from this clear failure of aid in Afghanistan?

Donors follow their own logic, and their actions rarely respond to the priorities arising from the security situation.

In Afghanistan, the need to combine the four most urgent tasks—establishing security, maintaining it, simultaneously building a state apparatus, and promoting rural development to create jobs—had, at the time of the US intervention in 2001, not been conceptualized at all. The aid needs were immense, and donors largely did as they pleased. Until the arrival of General Petraeus, there were no clear common objectives between military and development institutions. It now seems clear that aid to the country has suffered from a serious lack of coherence linked to a total lack of strategic direction in the allocation of resources at both the sectoral and the geographic levels. As in many Sahelian countries, the Afghan population was 75 percent rural, yet of the US$15 billion disbursed by donors between 2002 and the end of 2007, only about US$500 million—roughly 3.3 percent of the total—was spent on agriculture. At a press conference in Paris at the end of 2010, General Petraeus openly acknowledged this problem and assured the meeting that civilian aid spending in rural Afghan areas now exceeded US$800 million a year.

Yet how much time was wasted! In Afghanistan, as in the Sahel, the inadequacy of efforts in agriculture, the only sector in which massive job creation is possible in the short term, has been notable, despite the efforts of some donors.[30] Just as in the Sahel, young people cannot find employment where they live. They stream into the cities, where they join the masses of the urban unemployed. Following the departure of the international forces and the jobs that were linked to their presence, their main options are to participate in the networks of the opium economy[31] or to enlist with the Taliban, which offers attractive wages. As noted as early as 2009 by an Afghan tribal chief quoted in the New York Times: "The vast majority of the Taliban in my area are young men who need jobs. We just have

30. These include the World Bank, which financed a remarkable small-scale irrigation-development program over a period of 12 years as well as a successful community-development program. However despite the sometimes astonishing efforts of villagers, many Afghan valleys are still faced with a Malthusian tragedy heightened by the return of many of the 5 million refugees in Pakistan and Iran.

31. The drug economy is now deeply rooted in the Afghan countryside and is a source of funding for the rebellion and the local power structure. Drug networks have also penetrated the upper levels of the political hierarchy. This represents a turnover of between US$3 billion and US$5 billion depending on the year, employing more than 400,000 farmers. The phenomenon is similar to that in the Sahel, where unemployed young men in the rural sector are increasingly attracted to illicit trafficking in cigarettes, cars stolen in Europe, cocaine imported from Latin America and destined for Europe, and the transportation of migrants attracted by the European mirage.

African leaders need to learn to discipline donors and to guide funding toward their own priorities.

to give them work; if we can put them to work, we will weaken the Taliban."[32]

The lesson to be learned is that in a country where agriculture is the main source of employment, any security-stabilization process must be accompanied by massive investments of international aid in rural development, including small-scale irrigation projects, roads, soil protection and restoration, rural electrification, and the like. Community-driven development approaches have produced effective results in many places, but steering international aid in these countries toward this sector and multiplying such investments in the rural sphere requires the capacity to strategically guide and direct international aid resources.

African leaders need to learn to discipline donors and to guide funding toward their own priorities.

Those responsible for delivering aid in the Sahel clearly have not drawn conclusions from the consequences of donors' forgetting agriculture and rural development in Afghanistan. Nor have they perfected methods for strategically steering flows of aid so they respond to the urgent needs in the countryside. According to Professor Brunet-Jailly's analysis of the aid that was promised at the donor meeting for Mali (Paris, October 2015), of the euros 3.4 billion pledged, only 3.7 percent was allocated to the development of agriculture and livestock,[33] this in a country that is 80 percent rural—a repeat of what happened in Afghanistan.

This example (among others) shows that donor coordination does not work in fragile countries that may prefer to receive aid they know is useless over conducting frank negotiations with donors to impose their own priorities. These countries are often in situations of such dependency regarding aid that they do not dare to challenge donor choices. Whole forests have been pulped to print reports on the problem of aid coordination, and myriad experts have been mobilized on this subject at major international conferences (Paris in 2005, Accra in 2008, Busan in 2011). These conferences defined a set of best practices, but the practices rarely have been followed in fragile countries with weak and largely disorganized governments.

Some countries are very well structured administratively and politically—for example Côte d'Ivoire, Morocco, and Vietnam—and local authorities take a dim view of any attempt at coordination on the part of the donors that support them. They see this as a donor syndicate trying to dictate their policies. These countries are coordinating the donors themselves, and this is a very good thing.

In fragile countries with little administrative structure, and especially in "failed" states, the situation is clearly very different. There, coordination is supposed to take place first among donors to avoid duplication, errors, and the omission of specific sectors, and above all to place their actions within the framework of an overall strategy. But experience shows[34] that this coordination is limited mostly to exchanges of superficial information and is only rarely reflected in real strategic direction designed to guide resources to where they will be most useful. In countries where budget-planning mechanisms are failing, the laudable principles developed at the above-mentioned international conferences are ineffective, especially as the problem of aid coordination is difficult to solve without serious involvement by local political authorities at the highest level.

The dispersal of local centers of responsibility seriously undermines the effectiveness of aid.

In fragile countries, the first difficulty arises as a result of the dispersal of decision-making centers concerned with international aid. These consist of central actors, where the

32. Hajji Fazul Rahim, quoted in Filkins, D. (27 November 2009) Afghans offer jobs to Taliban rank and file if they defect. *New York Times*.
33. Brunet-Jailly, J. (18 January 2016). 3,4 milliards d'euros pour quoi faire?. *Mediapart*.

34. And the recent case of Mali, where only 3.7 percent of resources is devoted to agricultural development, provides further proof.

African governments must organize the strategic planning of aid resources.

responsibilities are already divided among the ministries of finance, budget, planning, and foreign affairs. There are also at least a dozen peripheral actors, namely the sectoral ministries. Each of these actors interacts with certain donors from among the dozens of major donors and the thousands of small NGOs, ignoring others, while each of the sectoral ministries tries to attract donors to finance what it sees as its own priority operations. The result is extraordinary disorder.

As might be expected, the international conferences recommended that a senior national official be put in charge of directing aid, but this very rarely occurs. Solving the problem requires the involvement of African leaders. One option is for the Prime Minister to take responsibility for coordinating aid. In many countries, however, this is a key position and the Prime Minister is already overwhelmed; in others, the position does not exist or is purely political, filled by a major figure not inclined to get involved in mere stewardship. Sometimes this position is even entrusted to an opponent and endowed with a merely symbolic power.

In these common situations, finance ministers often try to impose some order. But unless their role in the aid area is clearly defined in the framework that sets out the functions and responsibilities of members of the government, they can expect trouble. This was precisely the case of Afghanistan's Ashraf Ghani, Minister of Finance in 2002–2004,[35] who, thanks to his background at the World Bank, had the experience required for the task. A book written by Ashraf Ghani (with Clare Lockhart) after his departure from the Ministry of Finance and published in 2008 devotes an extraordinary chapter to the role of aid. In it he wrote:

"From the user's perspective, the fragmented system is costly. Ministers who are responsible for coordinating policy must create consensus not only with other cabinet ministers but also with dozens of donors and hundreds of NGOs, each with their own budgets, priorities, rules, and preferences. In Afghanistan, the Minister of Finance in the post-Taliban period spent more than 60 percent of his time on coordination. Had the aid system united around a single flow of financing and rules, the number of reforms carried out within the government's core systems would have risen exponentially. Moreover, each donor agency tends to build alliances with different ministries, further fragmenting cabinet unity. Instead of becoming catalysts for orderly policy management, donors become instruments of division and chaos."[36]

What he did not say is that any Minister of Finance who attempts this coordination risks attracting the wrath of his colleagues, who find it difficult to accept that one among them would grant himself the considerable power arising from control of flows of international aid. This happened to Ashraf Ghani, who had to leave the government in December 2004 after a serious falling-out with his colleagues. In the absence of a prime minister truly concerned about the coordination of aid policy—such as Kablan Duncan in Côte d'Ivoire, whose teams followed these issues week after week and provided him with updates—institutional and political problems impede the management of aid according to the precepts from the international conferences. Instead, aid is dispersed according to the donors' preferences rather than addressing the critical problems.

African governments must organize the strategic planning of aid resources.

The current, widespread solution—which does not work satisfactorily, either—consists of the preparation of a Poverty Reduction Strategy Paper to which the actions of the various donors must conform. In countries lacking the capacity to carry out the process, this work is often entrusted to teams of foreign consultants. These efforts most often result in formal actions aimed at donor conferences, which throw up so many priorities that there is

35. Currently President of the Islamic Republic of Afghanistan.

36. Ghani, A. & Lockhart, C. (2008). *Fixing Failed States*. Oxford: Oxford University Press.

The availability of significant resources is necessary but not sufficient; the resources must be put to good use.

no priority. Moreover, establishing the fight against poverty as the sole objective does little to solve security problems.

This approach leaves donors free to hunt around for projects, choosing from the long list presented to them one that best corresponds to the preferences of their backers and pressure groups. As a result, their institutional and political constraints—instead of the most obviously urgent needs of the country—decide their programs of action. Typically, they focus on social sectors that are rarely controversial, usually forgetting the urgency of rural employment and the importance of rural infrastructure and services. Ultimately, each donor acts as it pleases. In the words of an ambassador I met in Kabul in 2007, "Managing international aid is like herding cats." Sometimes a donor representative assumes the role of aid coordinator—in practice, it is often the UNDP representative—and holds coordination meetings to which the aid agencies often send their most junior staff.

Given donors' distrust of national financial circuits, a good short term alternative would be for donors to pool their resources into a fund under a specific governance structure. This pooling could take the form of what is commonly referred to as a "trust fund" that corresponds to one or more parallel budgets jointly managed by a group of donors and the ministries directly concerned. Donors contribute to the financing of this parallel budget pending the strengthening of local capacities. The government's objectives could then be clearly defined and the use of aid brought under control. This formula, which responds to Ashraf Ghani and Clare Lockhart's[37] desire to see a unified flow of resources and common rules, was used very effectively in Afghanistan with the creation of the Afghanistan Reconstruction Trust Fund. Unfortunately, it involved only a very small fraction of international aid.

African governments must rebuild their failing administrations so they can drive ambitious social and development programs.

The availability of significant resources is necessary but not sufficient—the resources must be put to good use. We must not be deluded: Governments in insecure countries will also have to rebuild their failing public administrations if they are to make effective use of both international aid and their own budgetary resources. The transformation of weak Sahelian governments into genuine administrations for development on the Singapore model is a difficult undertaking, which often fails as a result of being riven by clientelist practices.

It is indeed necessary to resolve such cross-cutting issues as the status of civil servants, salary scales, or the possibility of using contractors or local consultants for highly specialized tasks. Above all, it is necessary to make profound changes in the rules and practices of personnel management relating to recruitment, promotion, and remuneration and to align them with principles of merit and performance. Such reforms inevitably upset existing hierarchies but also ultimately determine the effectiveness of any public or private institution.

One easy alternative is to rapidly reinforce within an administration such key functions as administrative and financial departments, information technology, and certain technical departments. Experience shows, however, that this approach produces mixed results, and it is infinitely more efficient to transform some essential administrations into institutions of excellence, addressing them one after another. This type of transformation is possible within a reasonable time frame if the political will is clear and significant technical and financial resources are mobilized. Such steps should be limited to a few key institutions whose functioning will be critical to the implementation of reforms

37. Ghani & Lockhart (2008)

African governments will have to consolidate or rebuild their state apparatus and negotiate support from the international community for this purpose.

and development programs. These are usually the financial ministries (finance, planning, and budget), the ministries of agriculture and rural development, energy, infrastructure, and education and technical training. The sovereign institutions should of course also be part of the process.

The agenda for facing these new threats is ambitious and hard to implement

African governments will have to consolidate or rebuild their state apparatus and negotiate exceptional financial, technical, and political support from the international community for this purpose.

To ensure the security of their territories, they will have to extinguish the flashpoints to the extent possible through their own strengthened military means without expecting to rely on foreign or United Nations forces. They will also have to complement this military approach by considerably reinforcing their entire state apparatus. They must overcome the double fiscal and security impasse that forces them to choose between security and development spending. They must not only rebuild their failing state institutions but they must also reconstitute a strong nucleus of institutions with economic and social mandates if these are revealed, as is likely, to be largely failing. Absent the reorganization of key administrations, countries may find themselves unable to launch the necessary investment programs and impose the necessary reforms.

They will have to regain control of international-aid spending in order to reorient it, to the extent possible, toward the factors that fuel insecurity, particularly rural poverty.

Given that the vast majority of those with the lowest incomes live in rural areas and make a living from agriculture or raising livestock, any effort to generate massive employment and reduce poverty in these countries will require the stimulation and modernization of agro-pastoral systems and the rural world. This goal must be both long-term and ambitious, as these countries also suffer the effects of global warming. They urgently need to revitalize and intensify their traditional rain-dependent cereal crops. This requires significant public investment in soil defense, protection, and restoration, rural roads, market organization, agronomic research, adapted farming practices, more widespread use of animal-drawn cultivation, and more ecological agricultural practices. They will also need to pursue and accelerate investments in irrigation, especially small-scale systems, and restructure their transhumant and sedentary livestock systems.

The aim should be twofold: to ensure food security in the medium term and to increase the number of jobs in more intensive agriculture and livestock farming and associated support functions both upstream and down. Achieving these goals will require enormous efforts in many areas, including literacy, targeted training, legal and regulatory measures, and investment in rural areas in parallel with sustained efforts to expand drinking-water infrastructures and rural electrification. These actions will require innovative, decentralized approaches that have been successfully implemented in other countries.

These countries will have to undertake wide-ranging reforms of their education systems and vocational and technical training programs.

The aim must be to facilitate the job integration of young people in their own countries, in the sub-region and, where appropriate, in migration outside the continent. It is also to provide these countries with the necessary human capital to secure an economic upswing. They will most likely need to focus on primary education, reorient secondary and tertiary education toward vocational, technical, and scientific subjects, launch ambitious adult-literacy programs associated with basic-skills training programs for artisans in the informal sector, and revitalize post-primary

The creation of jobs demanded by their level of demographic dynamism also means facilitating the development of a dynamic private sector.

education. Such programs constitute huge challenges for the countries concerned; they will not be able to fund them alone. It will therefore be necessary to remobilize development partners in this area.

The massive creation of jobs demanded by their exceptional demographic dynamism also means facilitating the development of a dynamic private sector.

This objective will require a radical rethinking of the generally restrictive business environments and rapidly enhancing the availability, quality, and cost of using basic infrastructure. These cross-cutting measures will have to be supplemented by various programs that may give rise to ripple effects such as the implementation of support programs for training and equipment in the informal services sector and urban and rural handicrafts.

These multiple efforts will remain insufficient if the rate of population growth is not brought down to a level compatible with countries' economic capacities.

Population growth is so high in all these regions, and natural resources so limited, that these countries cannot expect economic growth, urbanization, income growth, and girls' education to spontaneously reduce the birth rate. They have no choice but to implement population policies.

The implementation of such policies will require major changes in current norms and values in the sub-region, which in turn will require exceptional communication and pedagogical efforts. Programs aiming to control demography in the Sahel have been prepared and adopted in the past, but have never really been implemented. Yet other poor countries with rural majorities and of Muslim faith, such as Bangladesh, have found ways to achieve this. The countries of the Maghreb, and also Egypt, Saudi Arabia, and Iran, have all succeeded. As in these countries, several levers that are immediate determinants of fertility are available to authorities. These principally include access to modern contraceptive techniques, dissuading the practice of early marriage, and lengthening the period of breastfeeding. They should be used simultaneously.

Finally, it is imperative that governments engage in a courageous struggle against Islamic fundamentalism and jihadist ideology.

The restoration of security throughout the region implies an important ideological dimension that cannot be underestimated. For more than 30 years, Salafist preachers returning from the Haj have traveled across the rural Sahel. Throughout that period, funding from Saudi Arabia has enabled the proliferation of mosques and Koranic schools, which thanks to the building of major works and prestige investments, has bought the support—or at least the neutrality—of the political elites, for the expansion of a conception of Islam that does not reflect the tolerant tradition of local Sufism.[38] African leaders must regain control of this phenomenon and halt the process of radicalization and intolerance that prepares young people for jihadism. This task may well be the most difficult of all because political leaders with the courage to engage in this ideological battle will have to confront the hatred of the preachers of intolerance in the mosques, the markets and the poll booths. They may even have to fear for their lives. However, this struggle, which must necessarily accompany

38. Classic reference works such as L'Islam Noir by Vincent Monteil or L'Islam au Sénégal by Moriba Magassouba are no longer representative of the reality of today's Islam in the Sahel.

The success of such a comprehensive response to the security challenge presupposes that these programs constitute an interdependent and indivisible whole.

any demographic reduction-and-control program, cannot be avoided.

The success of such a comprehensive response to the security challenge presupposes that these programs constitute an interdependent and indivisible whole.

These ambitious programs must be implemented almost simultaneously and cannot be approached in a selective manner. In fact, the interconnections among the programs constitute the key to initiating a chain of virtuous circles. This type of comprehensive response to the security challenge is inevitably a lengthy undertaking that will require significant additional resources from financial partners over the long term. But such a mobilization does not require excessive amounts and is perfectly possible and realistic. Yet it is necessary that government officials demonstrate the political will to act simultaneously on the various axes by building political coalitions adapted to the scale of the challenges they face. These challenges are considerable, and the agenda for action is extraordinarily difficult. But this program of action is essential.

Epilogue

Harinder S. Kohli and Hiroshi Kato

The overarching message of this book is that creating meaningful jobs for Africa's coming youth bulge is the single most important challenge facing Africa. It is also the vehicle to meet the fast-rising aspirations of Africans and put the continent on a faster track to achieve convergence with the rest of the world.

During the next decade, Africa's working-age population will increase by some 200 million. In addition to employment for these new job seekers, millions of Africans currently unemployed or underemployed need meaningful jobs and better income. The number of jobs that need to be created will rise further in each subsequent decade. To meet this unprecedented challenge, the region must significantly raise its economic growth rate and achieve per capita growth averaging 3.5 percent or more, as a few countries have successfully done since 2010 and as high-performance Asian economies did in the 1970s and 1980s. In addition, this higher growth needs to be much more inclusive to tackle current inequities and widespread poverty. In our view, Africa's future political and social stability and well-being depend on this higher, inclusive growth.

Accelerating the demographic transition and moderating population growth is a fundamental challenge in most countries in Sub-Saharan Africa. It is imperative to confront this challenge for two reasons. First, irrespective of what is done to promote job creation, it seems highly unlikely that "good" jobs can be created at the pace required to match projected growth in the working-age population. Second, whether a country has a population growth rate of 3. percent or 1. percent makes a huge difference in the improvement in per capita income for the same economic growth over the long term. In much of East Asia, population growth rates have fallen to between 1 and 1. percent, while economic growth rates have averaged 6 to 7 percent. As result, absolute poverty has been effectively eradicated and living standards have improved rapidly. Africa can and should aim at similar results.

To achieve the much higher per capita income growth of 3.5 percent (for high population growth countries, this would mean an absolute economic growth rate of 6 percent or higher over many decades) countries will need to achieve much higher investment rates, dramatically raise productivity, and significantly improve the quality of human capital. Given the tougher global economic environment, the region would also need to become more self-sufficient in terms of resource mobilization. Domestic saving rates would need to rise from an average of about 17 percent today to about 30 percent (developing Asia is at around 40 percent). Economies would need to become more open to each other (through deeper regional cooperation) and to the rest of the world. Improving the quality of education would be of utmost importance.

Rural transformation remains central in Sub-Saharan Africa. The majority of Africans still live in rural areas and almost four-fifths of the absolute poor are concentrated there. There is tremendous scope to improve agricultural productivity and crop yields. As part of this transformation, new value chains between farmers and urban consumers would create well-paying jobs and service industries. Indeed, in the near term, agriculture and related activities could be a major source of much-needed jobs, particularly in the low-income countries and small economies.

It is obvious that only the private sector can create most of the needed jobs and provide the spark for accelerating Africa's growth. Governments should nurture private enterprise, rather than hinder it. African entrepreneurs need a competitive environment and the rule of law, not crony capitalism. Governments can create such conditions by improving the business environment, overcoming the current infrastructure bottlenecks, planning and managing cities that work, and deepening regional integration, as discussed in detail in this book.

Climate change is already having an adverse affect on Africa. Even though carbon emissions by African countries are small and did not contribute much to global warming, Africa must cope with the reality of climate change and adapt accordingly. The current droughts in eastern and southern Africa are wake-up calls for the entire continent.

The political will to adopt and implement bold policy reforms is decisive in determining a country's success.

The most urgent task is to make agriculture more resilient. Only 5 percent of the current crop area is irrigated and most small farmers are at the mercy of increasingly variable weather patterns. Rising sea levels are also threatening low-lying coastal cities and islands. Climate change is real and here to stay. Adaptation to climate change must become an integral part of the national policy agenda.

Fragility, and the associated vulnerability to extremists, is the other unfortunate reality that threatens the social and political fabric of a large number of African countries, particularly in the Sahel. Unless successfully confronted now, it could spread further given the lack of jobs and the inequities in other African countries. Fragility is both a security and a development problem and must be treated as such. Reducing fragility and the associated vulnerabilities requires a program of action that will rebuild confidence in the governance system, restore the legitimacy of the state apparatus, help reduce rural poverty, reform the education systems, create new jobs, and bring down the rate of population growth.

The political will to adopt and implement bold policy reforms is decisive in determining a country's success. It is also the scarcest commodity in the region. Many of today's high-performing countries, both in Africa and elsewhere, have leaders with a single-minded focus on economic and social development and a willingness to take politically difficult decisions. The same was true in East Asia when its growth accelerated. For the rest of Africa to emulate these success stories, their leaders—in politics, business, and civil society—will need to show similar political will.

Creation of this political will, crucial for reducing poverty and inequality, also includes a human development paradigm. This will require much greater emphasis on civil rights, public deliberations and participatory approaches to development, and on the role of bottom-up planning processes in organizations at the grassroots level.

Should the vast majority of African countries—including its largest economies—achieve the aspirational scenario, with an average per capita growth of around 4 percent between now and 2060, the region would be transformed. Its per capita would have risen five-fold to $25,515 (2015 PPP), its share of global GDP increased from 3 percent to almost 12 percent, and its poverty rate fallen to 2.4 percent. The world would have conquered the final development frontier. On the other hand, under a business-as-usual scenario, Africa's GDP and per capita income would be 54 percent of that of the convergence scenario, its share of global GDP stuck at only 5.7 percent, and its poverty rate still in double digits at 13.9 percent.

The difference between the two scenarios is staggering. It is, therefore, incumbent upon African leaders and the region's development partners to do everything possible to realize the aspirational scenarios outlined in this book.

References

ADB. (2010), *Toward Sustainable and Balanced Development: Strategy and action plan for the Greater Mekong Sub-region North-South Economic corridor*. Manila: ADB.

ADB. (2013). Regional Cooperation and Integration: Experiences in Asia and the Pacific. Conference Proceedings.

Africa-America Institute. (2015). *The State of Education in Africa 2015*.

African Development Bank. (2011). *Programme for Infrastructure Development in Africa (PIDA)*. Abidjan: AfDB.

African Development Bank. (2015). *African Competitiveness Report*. Abidjan: AfDB.

African Development Bank. (2016). *Strategy for Agricultural Transformation in Africa, 2016-2025*. Abidjan: AfDB.

Agénor, P. & Canuto, O. (2012). Access to Infrastructure and Women's Time Allocation: Evidence and a Framework for Policy Analysis. *Policy Paper* (45). Retrieved at http://www.academia.edu/download/30369707/Agenor_OC_Infra_Gender_Growth-P45.pdf.

Ahlers, T. Kato, H., Kohli, H., Madavo, C., & Sood. A. (eds.). (2014). *Africa 2050: Realizing the Continent's Full Potential*. New Delhi: Oxford University Press.

Airport Council International. (31 March 2014). *Preliminary World Airport Traffic and Rankings 2013*. Retrieved at http://www.aci.aero/News/Releases/Most-Recent/2014/03/31/Preliminary-World-Airport-Traffic-and-Rankings-2013--High-Growth-Dubai-Moves-Up-to-7th-Busiest-Airport-.

Alkire, S., and Housseini, B. (2014). *Multidimensional Poverty in Sub-Saharan Africa Levels and Trends*. Oxford: Oxford Poverty & Human Development Initiative. Retrieved at http://www.ophi.org.uk/wp-multidimensional-poverty-in-sub-saharan-africa-levels-and-trends/.

Angel, S. (2012). *Planet of Cities*. Cambridge, MA: Lincoln Institute of Land Policy.

Angel, S., Blei, A., Parent, J., Lamson-Hall, P. & Galarza Sánchez, N. with Civco, D., Qian Lei, R. & Thom, K. (2016). *Atlas of Urban Expansion, 2016 Edition, Vol. 1: Areas and Densities*. NYU Urban Expansion Program at New York University, UN-Habitat, and the Lincoln Institute of Land Policy.

Angel, S., Lamson-Hall, P., Madrid, M., Blei, A., & Parent, J. with Galarza Sánchez, N. & Thom, K. (2016). *Atlas of Urban Expansion, 2016 Edition, Vol. 2, Blocks and Roads*. NYU Urban Expansion Program at New York University, UN-Habitat, and the Lincoln Institute of Land Policy.

Aryeetey, E. and Oduro, A. D. (1996). Regional Integration Efforts in Africa: An Overview. In *Regionalism and the Global Economy: The case of Africa*. The Hague: FONDAD.

Aspen Institute. (24–25 March 2005). Trade Facilitation to Promote Intra-African Trade, Committee on Regional Cooperation and Integration. Addis Ababa: UNECA.

Banerjee, A., Duflo, E., & Hornbeck, R. (2014). (Measured) Profit Is Not Welfare: Evidence from an Experiment on Bundling Microcredit and Insurance. *NBER Working Paper* (20477).

Banerjee, S. & Morella, E. (2011). *Africa's Water and Sanitation Infrastructure—Access, Affordability, and Alternatives*. Washington: World Bank.

Banerjee, S., Diallo, A., Foster, V. & Wodon, Q. (2009). Trends in Household Coverage of Modern Infrastructure Services in Africa, *Policy Research Working Paper* (4880). Washington: World Bank.

Banerjee, S., Foster, V., Ying, Y., Skilling, H., Wodon, Q. (2010). Cost Recovery, Equity, and Efficiency in Water Tariffs: Evidence from African Utilities, *Policy Research Working Paper* (5384). Washington: World Bank.

Basu, A. and Fajgenbaum, J. (2014). Chapter 9, Maintaining Macroeconomic Stability and Increasing Resiliency in Ahlers, T., Kato, H., Kohli, H., Madavo, C., & Sood, A. (eds.). *Africa 2050: Realizing the Continent's Full Potential*, New Delhi: Oxford University Press.

Baum, D., Lewis, L., Lusk-Stover, O. & Patrinos, H. (2014). What Matters Most of Engaging the Private Sector in Education: A Framework Paper. *Systems Approach for Better Education Results (SABER) Working Paper Series* (8). Washington: World Bank.

Beegle, K., Christiansen, L., Dabalen, A., & Gaddis, I. (2016). *Poverty in a Rising Africa*. Washington: World Bank.

Berner, E., Gomez, G., & Knorringa, P. (2012). Helping a Large Number of People Become a Little Less Poor': The Logic of Survival Entrepreneurs. *European Journal of Development Research 24*(3): 382.

Binswanger, H., Khandker, S., & Rosenzweig, M. (1993). How Infrastructure and financial institutions affect agricultural output and investment in India. *Journal of Development Economics 41*(2): 337–366.

Binswanger-Mkhize, H. & McCalla, A. (2009). *The changing context and prospects for agricultural and rural development in Africa*. Rome: IFAD.

Black, RE, Victora, C., Walker, S., Bhutta, Z., Christian, P., de Onis, M., Ezzati, M., Grantham-McGregor, S., Katz, J., Martorell, R., & Uauy, R. (2013). Maternal and child undernutrition and overweight in low income and middle income countries. *Lancet 382*: 427–51.

Bloom, N., Eifert, B., Mahajan, A., McKenzie, D., & Roberts, J. (2013). Does Management Matter? Evidence from India. *The Quarterly Journal of Economics 128*(1): 1–51.

Bloomberg. (2013). What Africa Can Teach Us About the Future of Banking. Bloomberg.

Bloomberg. (2016). Emerging Markets Bond Index. Retrieved at http://www.bloomberg.com/quote/BEMS:IND.

Boeing. (2015). *World Air Cargo Forecast 2014-2015*. Retrieved at http://www.boeing.com/resources/boeingdotcom/commercial/about-our-market/cargo-market-detail-wacf/download-report/assets/pdfs/wacf.pdf.

Bold, T., Filmer, D., Martin, G., Molina, E., Stacy, B., Rockmore, C., Svensson, J. & Wane, W.. (2017 January). What Do Teachers Know and Do? Does It Matter? Evidence from Primary Schools in Africa. *Policy Research Working Paper (7956)*. Washington: World Bank.

Bond, J. & Fajgenbaum, J., (2014). Chapter 12: Harnessing Natural Resources for Diversification in Ahlers, T., Kato, H., Kohli, H., Madavo, C., & Sood, A. (eds.). *Africa 2050: Realizing the Continent's Full Potential*, New Delhi: Oxford University Press.

Brenton P., and Gözde, I. (2012). *De-fragmenting Africa: Deepening Regional Trade Integration in Goods and Services*. Washington: World Bank.

Brenton, P. & Hoffman, B. (eds.). (2016). *Political Economy of Regional Integration in Sub-Saharan Africa*. Washington: World Bank.

Brookings Institution. (2015). *Ending Rural Hunger*. Washington: Brookings Institution.

Bruegel. (2016). Real effective exchange rates for 178 countries: a new database.

Brune, L., Giné, X., Goldberg, J., & Yang, D. (2015). Facilitating Savings for Agriculture: Field Experimental Evidence from Malawi. *NBER Working Paper* (20946).

Brunet-Jailly, J. (18 January 2016). 3,4 milliards d'euros pour quoi faire?. *Mediapart*. Retrieved at https://blogs.mediapart.fr/joseph-brunet-jailly/blog/180116/34-milliards-deuros-pour-quoi-faire.

Bruns, B., Filmer, D. & Patrinos, H. (2011). Making Schools Work. New Evidence on Accountability Reforms. *Human Development Perspectives*. Washington: World Bank.

Buckley, R., Clarke Annez, P., & Spence, M. (eds.). (2008). *Urbanization and Growth*. Washington: World Bank.

Cameron, F. (2010). *The European Union as a Model for Regional Integration*. New York: Council on Foreign Relations.

Castellano, A., Kendall, A., Nikomarov, M., & Swemmer, T. (2015). *Powering Africa*. McKinsey.

Centennial Group International. (2017). Unpublished data.

Christ, N. & Ferrantino, M. (2009). Land Transport for Exports: The Effect of Cost, Time and Uncertainty in Sub-Saharan Africa. *Office of Economics Working Paper, U.S. International Trade Commission* (2009-10-A).

De Melo, J. (26 August 2015). Regional integration arrangements in Africa: Is large membership the way forward?. *Brookings Africa in Focus Blog*. Retrieved at https://www.brookings.edu/blog/africa-in-focus/2015/08/26/regional-integration-arrangements-in-africa-is-large-membership-the-way-forward/.

De Melo, J. and Tsikata, Y., (2014) Regional Integration in Africa: Challenges and prospects. *UN University-WIDER, Working Paper* (37).

Dinh, H., Palmade, V., Chandra, V., Cossar. F. (2012). *Light Manufacturing in Africa: Targeted Policies to Enhance Private Investment and Create Jobs*. Washington: World Bank.

Duranton, G. (2015). Growing through Cities in Developing Countries. *World Bank Research Observer 30*(1): 39–73.

Dutt, P. & Traça, D. (2009). Corruption and its impact on trade: Extortion or evasion?. *VoxEU*. Retrieved at http://voxeu.org/article/when-corruption-boosts-trade.

Eifert, B., Gelb, A., & Ramachandran, V. (2005). Business Environment and Comparative Advantage in Africa: Evidence from the Investment Climate Data. *Center for Global Development Working Paper 56*.

EM-DAT. (2016). Centre for Research on the Epidemiology of Disasters. Brussels: Université de Louvain. Retrieved at http://www.emdat.be/.

European Commission, IMF, OECD, UN, and World Bank. (2009). *System of National Accounts 2008*. UN: New York.

Evans, D. & Popova, A. (2014). Cash Transfers and Temptation Goods: A Review of Global Evidence. *World Bank Policy Research Working Paper* (6886).

Fajgenbaum, J. (2012). Macroeconomic Management—Implementing Responsible Fiscal and Monetary Policies. In Loser, C., Kohli, H. & Fajgenbaum, J. (Eds), A *New Vision for Mexico 2042: Achieving Prosperity for All*. New Delhi: Sage.

FAO. (2012). Agricultural Area and Permanent Crop Tables 2000. Rome: Statistics Division, FAO.

FAO. (2016a). FAOSTAT. Retrieved at http://www.fao.org/faostat/en/#home.

FAO. (2016b). *The State of Food and Agriculture: Climate Change, Agriculture and Food Security*. Rome: FAO.

FAO, IFAD, WFP. (2015). *Achieving Zero Hunger*. Rome: FAO, IFAD, WFP.

Ferdi. (2016). *Linking security and development—A Plea for the Sahel*. Clermont-Ferrand: Ferdi.

Filkins, D. (27 November 2009) Afghans offer jobs to Taliban rank and file if they defect. *New York Times*.

Filmer, D. & Fox, L. (2014). *Youth Employment in Sub-Saharan Africa*. Washington: World Bank.

Fischer, R.A., Byerlee, D., & Edmeades, E.O. (June 2009). Can Technology Deliver on the Yield Challenge to 2050. *Expert Meeting on How to Feed the World in 2050*. Rome: FAO.

Foster, V. & Briceño-Garmendia, C. (eds.). (2010). *Africa's Infrastructure: A Time for Transformation*, Washington: World Bank.

Fouroutan, F. (1992). Regional Integration in Sub-Saharan Africa: Past Eperience and Future Prospects. In de Melo, J. & Panagariya, A. (eds.), *New Dimensions in Regional Integration*. Cambridge: Cambridge University Press.

Fox, L. (2016). What Will It Take to Meet the Youth Employment Challenge in Sub-Saharan Africa?. *GLM | LIC Working Paper* (10).

Fox, L. & Pimhidzai, O. (2013). *Different Dreams, Same Bed: Collecting, Using, and Interpreting Employment Statistics in Sub-Saharan Africa—The Case of Uganda*. Washington: World Bank.

Fox, L., Senbet, L., & Simbanegavi, W. (2016). Youth Employment in Sub-Saharan Africa: Challenges, Constraints and Opportunities. *Journal of African Economies 25*(suppl_1): i3–15.

Fox, L. & Thomas, A. (2016). Africa's Got Work to Do: A Diagnostic of Youth Employment Challenges in Sub-Saharan Africa. *Journal of African Economies 25*(suppl_1): i16–36.

Fredriksen, B. & Kagia, R. (2014). Breaking the Human Capital Barrier. In Ahlers, T., Kato, H., Kohli, H., Madavo, C. & Sood, A. (eds.). *Africa 2050 Realizing the Continent's Full Potential.* New Delhi: Oxford University Press.

Gelb, A., Meyer, C., & Ramachandran, V. (2013). Does Poor Mean Cheap? A Comparative Look at Africa's Industrial Labor Costs. *Center for Global Development Working Paper* (325).

Ghani, A. & Lockart, C. (2008). *Fixing Failed States*. Oxford: Oxford University Press.

Glatzel, K & the Montpellier Panel. (2014). No ordinary matter: Conserving, restoring, and enhancing Africa's soils. *Agriculture for Impact*.

Glick, P., Huang, C., & Mejia, N. (2015). *The Private Sector and Youth Skills and Employment Programs in Low-and Middle-Income Countries*. Washington: World Bank.

Gore, C. (2015). Climate Change Adaptation and African Cities: Understanding the Impact of Government and Governance on Future Action. Ch. 11 in Johnson, C., Toly, N., & Schroeder, H. (eds.), *The Urban Climate Challenge—Rethinking the Role of Cities in the Global Climate Regime*. London and New York: Routledge.

Grimm, M. & Paffhausen, A. (2015). Do Interventions Targeted at Micro-Entrepreneurs and Small and Medium-Sized Firms Create Jobs? A Systematic Review of the Evidence for Low and Middle Income Countries. *Labour Economics 32*: 67–85.

Gutman, J., Sy, A., & Chattopahyay, S. (2009). *Financing African Infrastructure – Can the World Deliver?* Washington: World Bank.

Gwilliam, K., Foster, V., Archondo-Callao, R., Briceno-Garmendia, C., Nogales, A., & Sethi, K. (2008). Africa Infrastructure Country Diagnostic: Roads in Sub-Saharan Africa. *AICD Background Paper*. Washington: World Bank.

Hanushek, E. & Woessmann, L. (2015). *The Knowledge Capital of Nations. Education and the Economics of Growth*. CESifo Book Series. Cambridge, MA: The MIT Press.

Harmon, L. M., Simataa B., & van der Merwe, A., (July 2009). Implementing Facilitation on Trade and Transport Corridors. Proceedings of the 28th South African Transport Conference (SATC), Pretoria.

Hartzenberg, T. (2011). Regional Integration in Africa. Trade and Law Center for South Africa (Tralac), *WTO Economic Research and Statistics Division Staff Working paper (*ERSD-2011-14).

Henderson, J., Storeygard, A. & Deichmann, U. (2016). Has climate change driven urbanization in Africa?. Retrieved at http://www.lse.ac.uk/geographyAndEnvironment/pdf/HasClimateChangeDrivenUrbanisationHenderson.pdf.

Hicks, J., Kremer, M., Mbiti, I., & Miguel, E. (2015). Vocational Education in Kenya—A Randomized Evaluation. Retrieved at http://www.3ieimpact.org/media/filer_public/2015/07/21/gfr_ow164_vocational_education_in_kenya.pdf.

Hirshleifer, S., McKenzie, D., Almeida, R., & Ridao-Cano, C. (2015). The Impact of Vocational Training for the Unemployed: Experimental Evidence from Turkey. *The Economic Journal 126*(597).

ICA. (2015). *Infrastructure Financing Trends in Africa – 2015*. Abidjan: Infrastructure Consortium for Africa.

IEA. (2015). *World Energy Outlook 2015*. Paris: IEA.

IFAD. (September 2016). *Rural Development Report 2016: Fostering Inclusive Rural Transformation*. Rome: IFAD

IFPRI. (2014). *Total and Partial Factor Productivity in Developing Countries*. Washington: IFPRI.

ILO. (2016). *World Employment and Social Outlook 2016: Trends for youth*. Geneva: ILO.

IMF. (2016). *Primary Commodity Prices Database*. Washington: IMF.

IMF. (2017). *World Economic Outlook*. Washington: IMF.

Ingram, G. (2016). Demographics and Urbanization, Ch. 3 in *The World in 2050: Striving for a More Just, Prosperous, and Harmonious Global Community*, Kohli, H. (ed.). New Delhi: Oxford University Press.

Ingram, G., Liu, Z., Brandt, K. (2013). Metropolitan Infrastructure and Capital Finance. In Bahl, R., Linn, J., & Wetzel, D. (eds.) *Financing Metropolitan Governments in Developing Countries.* Cambridge, MA: Lincoln Institute of Land Policy, 339–366.

Intergovernmental Panel on Climate Change. (2014a). *Climate Change 2014 Synthesis Report Summary for Policymakers, Contribution of Working Groups I, II and III to the Fifth Assessment Report of the Intergovernmental Panel on Climate Change*. Cambridge, UK and New York: Cambridge University Press.

Intergovernmental Panel on Climate Change. (2014b). *Climate Change 2014: Impacts, Adaptation, and Vulnerability. (Report of Working Group II)*, Cambridge, UK and New York: Cambridge University Press, pp. 1199-1265.

International Telecommunication Union. (2014). ICT Statistics. Geneva: International Telecommunication Union.

Ismail, O. (2016). What Is in a Job? The Social Context of Youth Employment Issues in Africa. *Journal of African Economies 25*(suppl_1): i37–60.

Kasahara, S. (2013). *The Asian Developmental State and the Flying Geese Paradigm*. UNCTAD Discussion Paper (213).

Kathuria, S. & Shahid, S. (2015). *Opening up markets to neighbors: Gains from smaller countries in South Asia*. Washington: World Bank.

Keefer, P. & Knack, S. (2002). Polarization, Politics and Property Rights: Links between Inequality and Growth. *Public Choice 111*(1–2): 127–154.

Keefer, P., Sahnoun, H., Sy, A., Hussain, S., & Schiffbauer, M. (2015). *Jobs or Privileges: Unleashing the Employment Potential of the Middle East and North Africa*. Washington: World Bank.

Kharas, H. (2010). The Emerging Middle Class in Developing Countries. *OECD Development Centre Working Paper* (285).

Kharas, H. & Linn, J. (2013). External Assistance for Urban Finance Development: Needs, Strategies, and Implementation. In Bahl, R., Linn, J., & Wetzel, D. (eds.) *Financing Metropolitan Governments in Developing Countries.* Cambridge, MA: Lincoln Institute of Land Policy, 393–420.

Kochhar, R. (2015). *A Global Middle Class Is More Promise than Reality*. Washington: Pew Research Centre. Retrieved at http://www.lisdatacenter.org/wps/liswps/641.pdf.

Kohli, H. (ed.). (2016). *The World in 2050: Striving for a more just, prosperous, and harmonious global community*. New Delhi: Oxford University Press.

Lamson-Hall, P., Degroot, D., Martin, R., Fafesse, T., Angel, S. (2015). *A New Plan for African Cities: The Ethiopia Urban Expansion Initiative*. Retrieved at http://marroninstitute.nyu.edu/uploads/content/A_New_Plan_for_African_Cities_Oct_19_2015.pdf.

Le Monde. (20 January 2016). Gagner la guerre ne suffit pas à gagner la paix. *Le Monde*. Retrieved at http://www.lemonde.fr/idees/article/2016/01/20/gagner-la-guerre-ne-suffit-pas-a-gagner-la-paix_4850136_3232.html.

Levy, B. (2014). *Working with the Grain: Integrating Governance and Growth in Development Strategies*. Oxford: Oxford University Press.

Maddison. (2013). The Maddison Project. Retrieved at http://www.ggdc.net/maddison/maddison-project/home.htm.

Maloney, W. (2004). Informality Revisited. *World Development 32*(7): 1159–78.

Malpel, J. (2016). PASEC 2014: Education System Performance in Francophone Sub-Saharan Africa. *Programme d'Analyse des Systèmes Educatifs de la CONFEMEN*. Dakar: PASEC.

Martell, C. & Guess, G.M. (2006). Development of Local Government Debt Financing Markets: Application of a Market-based Framework. *Public Budgeting and Finance 26*(1), Blackwell Synergy.

Marx, B., Stoker, T., & Suri, T. (2013). The Economics of Slums in the Developing World. *Journal of Economic Perspectives 27*(4): 187–210.

McCluskey, W. & Franzsen, R. (2013). Property Taxes in Metropolitan Cities. Bahl, R., Linn, J., & Wetzel, D. (eds.) *Financing Metropolitan Governments in Developing Countries.* Cambridge, MA: Lincoln Institute of Land Policy, 159–181.

McGranahan, G., Balk, D., Anderson, B. (2007). The rising tide: assessing the risks of climate change and human settlements in low elevation coastal zones. *Environment & Urbanization*, International Institute for Environment and Development (IIED) *19*(1), pp. 17–37.

McKinsey Global Institute. (2016 March). Digital Globalization: The new era of global flows.

McKinsey Global Institute. (2016 June). Bridging global infrastructure gaps.

Moghadam, R. (2014). Europe's Road to Integration. *Finance & Development (IMF)* 51(1).

Musgrave, R. (1959). *The Theory of Public Finance*. New York: McGraw-Hill.

NEPAD. (2016 May). *Move Africa: Launch of Initiative*. Midrand, South Africa: NEPAD.

Newman, C., Page, J., Rand, J., Shimeles, A., Söderbom, & Tarp, F. (2016). *Made in Africa – Learning to Compete in Industry*. Washington: Brookings Institute.

Nosal, L., & Saltane, V. (2016 January). Harmonization strike a chord of success: Doing Business in OHADA economies. *IFC SmartLessons*.

OECD. (19 February 2016). DAC High Level Meeting Communiqué. Retrieved at https://www.oecd.org/dac/DAC-HLM-Communique-2016.pdf.

OECD. (2016a). *African Economic Outlook 2016*. Paris: OECD. Retrieved at http://www.oecd.org/dev/african-economic-outlook-19991029.htm.

OECD. (2016b). Education at a Glance. *OECD Indicators*. Paris: OECD.

OECD. (2016c). Program for International Student Assessment (PISA). Retrieved at http://www.oecd.org/pisa/.

OECD & World Bank. (2015). *Inclusive Global Value Chains*. Report prepared for submission to the G20 Trade Ministers Meeting, Istanbul.

Perkins, D. & Robbins, G. (2011 March). The Contribution to Local Enterprise Development of Infrastructure for Commodity Extraction Projects: Tanzania's Central Corridor and Mozambique's Zambezi Valley. *Making Most of Commodities Programme (MMCP) Discussion Paper* (9).

Port Regulators of South Africa. (2016). Port Benchmarking Report: SA Terminal 2015/2016. Retrieved at http://www.portsregulator.org/images/documents/SA-port-benchmarking-report-2015-16.pdf.

Puentes, R. & Tomer, A. (2014). *Getting Smarter about Smart Cities*. Washington: Brookings Institution.

Rana, P. (2006). Economic Integration in East Asia: Trends, Prospects, and a Possible Roadmap. *ADB Working Paper Series on Regional Economic Integration*, 2.

Rand Corporation. (2012). Teachers matter: Understanding teachers' impact in student achievement. (CP-693/1).

Ratti, C. (2016). Five Smart City Innovations for Africa. *Africa.com*. Retrieved at http://www.africa.com/five-smart-city-innovations-africa/.

Reinsdorf, M. (2009). *Terms of Trade Effects: Theory and Measurement*. Washington: Bureau of Economic Analysis, Dept. of Commerce.

Rodrik, D. (2015). Premature deindustrialization. *Kennedy School of Government, Harvard University Working Paper*.

Sandefur, J., Birdsall, N., & Moyo, M. (2016). *The Political Paradox of Cash Transfers*. Washington: Center for Global Development. Retrieved at http://www.cgdev.org/blog/political-paradox-cash-transfers.

Satterthwaite, D., Huq, S., Reid, H., Pelling, P. & Romero Lankao, P. (2009). Adapting to climate change in urban areas: the possibilities and constraints in low- and middle-income nations in *Adapting Cities to Climate Change. Understanding and Addressing the Development Challenges*, Bicknell, J., Dodman, D., & Satterthwaite, D. (eds.). Abingdon, UK and New York: Earthscan.

Schlendker, W & Lobell, D.B. (2010). Robust negative impacts of climate change on African agriculture. *Environmental Resources* 5(1).

Southern and Eastern Africa Consortium for Monitoring Educational Quality (SACMEQ). (2016). Retrieved at http://www.sacmeq.org/.

Spolaore, E. (2013). What Is European Integration Really About? A Political Guide for Economists. *NBER Working Paper* (19122).

Stifel, D. & Minten, B. (2003). Transactions costs and agricultural productivity: Implications of Isolation for rural poverty in Madagascar. Background paper for the Northeast Universities Development Consortium Conference, Yale University, New Haven, Connecticut, October 17–19.

The Economist. (16 April 2016). Obstacle Course: Africa's trade suffers from dismal infrastructure, lack of investment and corruption. *The Economist*.

The Economist. (4 June 2016). Railways in Africa: Puffed out. *The Economist*.

Theunynck, S. (2009). School Construction Strategies for Universal Primary Education in Africa. *Africa Human Development Series*. Washington: World Bank.

Thorpe, J. & Maestre, M. (2015). *Brokering Development: Enabling Factors for Public-Private Partnerships in Agricultural Value Chains*. Rome: IFAD and the Institute of Development Studies.

Thurlow, J. & Wobst, P. (2004). The Road to Pro-poor growth in Zambia: Past Lessons and Future Challenges. *IFRPI Development Strategy and Governance Division Discussion Paper* (16).

Trends in International Mathematics and Science Study (TIMSS). (2015). Trends in International Mathematics and Science Study (TIMSS). Retrieved at https://nces.ed.gov/timss/countries.asp.

Tripney, J., Hombrados, J., Newman, M., Hovish, K., Brown, C., Steinka-Fry, K., Wilkey, E. (2013). Technical and Vocational Education and Training (TVET) Interventions to Improve Employability and Employment of Young People in Low-and Middle-Income Countries: A Systematic Review. Retrieved at http://eprints.ioe.ac.uk/17713/1/Tripney_et_al_2013_TVET_Interventions_for_Young_People_in_LMICs.pdf.

UNCTAD. (2017). UNCTADSTAT. Retrieved at http://unctadstat.unctad.org.

UNECA. (Various). Assessing Regional Integration in Africa. Addis Ababa: UNECA.

UNECA. (2010). *Assessing Regional integration in Africa IV: Enhancing Intra-African Trade*. Addis Ababa: UNECA.

UNESCO. (2013). *The Global Learning Crisis: Why Every Child Deserves a Quality Educatio*n. Paris: UNESCO.

UNESCO. (2016). UNESCO Institute for Statistics. Retrieved at http://uis.unesco.org/.

UNIDO. (2016). Statistical databases. Retrieved at http://www.unido.org/resources/statistics/statistical-databases.html.

United Nations. (2014). *World Urbanization Prospects: The 2014 Revision*. New York: Department of Economic and Social Affairs, Population Division, CD-ROM edition.

United Nations. (2015). *World Population Prospects: The 2015 Revision*. New York: Department of Economic and Social Affairs, Population Division, CD-ROM edition.

Uwezo. (2013). *Are Our Children Learning? Literacy and Numeracy across Eastern Africa*. Nairobi: Uwezo.

Walker, M. (2016). Smart Cities in Africa: Hype or Hope? Retrieved at http://idc-cema.com/eng/trendspotter/63734-smart-cities-in-africa-hype-or-hope.

World Bank. (1994). *World Development Report 1994: Infrastructure and Development*. Washington: World Bank.

World Bank. (2003). *World Development Report 2004. Making Services Work for Poor People*. Washington: World Bank.

World Bank. (2008). *World Development Report 2008: Agriculture for Development*. Washington: World Bank.

World Bank. (2009a). *Doing Business in Landlocked Economies*. Washington: World Bank.

World Bank. (2009b). *World Development Report 2009*. Washington: World Bank.

World Bank. (2013a). Service Delivery Indicators. Retrieved at http://datatopics.worldbank.org/sdi/. Washington: World Bank.

World Bank. (2013b). *World Development Report 2013: Jobs*. Washington: World Bank.

World Bank. (2014). *Logistic Performance Index 2014*. Washington: World Bank.

World Bank. (2015). *Women, Business and the Law 2016: Getting to Equal*. Washington: World Bank.

World Bank. (2016a). *Africa Enterprise Surveys*. Washington: World Bank.

World Bank. (2016b). *Enabling the Business of Agriculture*. Washington: World Bank.

World Bank. (2016c). *World Commodity Outlook, April 2016*. Washington: World Bank.

World Bank. (2016d). World Development Indicators. Washington: World Bank. Retrieved at http://databank.worldbank.org/data/.

World Bank. (2017). Doing Business rankings. Washington: World Bank. Retrieved at http://www.doingbusiness.org/.

World Economic Forum (WEF). (2017). *Global Competitiveness Report*. Retrieved at http://reports.weforum.org/global-competitiveness-report-2015-2016/competitiveness-rankings/.

WTO. (2016). WTO statistics. Retrieved at http://stat.wto.org/Home/WSDBHome.aspx?Language=E.

Yazbeck, A., Raja, S., & Canning, D. (2015). *Africa's Demographic Transition*. Washington: World Bank; Paris: Agence Française de Développement.

Yepes, T., Pierce, J., & Foster, V. (2008). Making Sense of Africa's Infrastructure Endowment: A Benchmarking Approach. *World Bank Policy Research Working Paper* (4912).

About the Editors and Contributors

Editors

Theodore Ahlers

Theodore Ahlers is an economist with extensive experience in Europe & Central Asia, the Middle East & North Africa, and sub-Saharan Africa. Over the last 25 years, he held numerous economist and senior management positions at the World Bank, including Strategy and Operations Director for Europe & Central Asia (2007–12), Maghreb Department Director (2002–07), and Strategy and Operations Director for Africa (2000–02). He holds a PhD in Development Economics from Tufts University, Fletcher School.

Harinder S. Kohli

Harinder S. Kohli is the Founding Director and Chief Executive of Emerging Markets Forum as well as Founding Director, President, and CEO of Centennial Group International, both based in Washington, DC. He is the Editor of *Global Journal of Emerging Markets Economies*. Prior to starting his current ventures, he served over 25 years in various senior managerial positions at the World Bank. He has written extensively on the emergence of Asia, Latin America, Africa and other emerging market economies; financial development; private capital flows; and infrastructure. He is an author and co–editor of *Africa 2050: Realizing the Continent's Full Potential* (2014), *India 2039: An Affluent Society in One Generation* (2010), *Latin America 2040—Breaking Away from Complacency: An Agenda for Resurgence* (2010), *A Resilient Asia amidst Global Financial Crisis* (2010), *Islamic Finance* (2011), *Asia 2050: Realizing the Asian Century* (2011), and *A New Vision for Mexico 2042: Achieving Prosperity for All* (2012). He led Centennial Group teams that helped ADB and CAF develop their long–term corporate strategies. He finished a year–long EMF study on the long–term prospects and challenges faced by emerging market economies worldwide and the first edition of the book *The World in 2050: Striving for a More Just, Prosperous, and Harmonious Global Community* was released in Paris in April 2016, with a second edition released in London in January 2017.

Contributors

Kaisa Alavuotunki

Kaisa Alavuotunki is a Senior Development Effect Adviser at Finnfund (a Finnish development finance company). She has a PhD in Economics from Aalto University in Helsinki. She has conducted research on impacts of development aid and implications on adaption of value added tax, and, as a consultant, worked extensively on economic impact assessments and evaluations.

James Bond

James Bond is based in Washington, DC and specializes in infrastructure, energy, and climate change. His positions include Senior Advisor to Centennial Group International; Senior Advisor to African Development Bank; and Non–Executive Director with Helios SE. He is member of the Board of Trustees of the Global Heritage Fund.

Until 2016, Bond was Senior Advisor to the Green Climate Fund, where he participated in launching the Fund; designing financial instruments; and fund raising. In 2014 the Fund raised $10.2 billion.

At the African Development Bank, Bond contributed to the launch of the Bank's partial risk guarantee, including for the Kenya Lake Turkana Wind Project.

Bond's positions in the World Bank Group include Chief Operating Officer of MIGA, where he oversaw the introduction of a range of new products, leading to a more than doubling of business volume. Bond has been World Bank Country Director in West Africa, and for Indian Ocean countries, based in Madagascar. His sector responsibilities at the World Bank have included Director of Energy; Director of Agriculture for Africa, and Sector Manager for telecoms. At IFC, James was Director of the Mining Department.

Before joining the World Bank Group, James spent nine years with the oil major Total in Paris, and two with

Gold Fields. James has a Doctorate in economics from Pantheon–Sorbonne; a Masters in energy economics from ENSPM; and a Bachelors in chemical engineering from University of Witwatersrand. He holds a Légion d'Honneur from France and an Ordre du Mérite from Madagascar.

Kevin Cleaver

Kevin Cleaver was the International Fund for Agricultural Development (IFAD)'s Associate Vice–President, in charge of its programmes. He joined IFAD in September 2006.

Before IFAD, he held several key positions in the World Bank, including: Director, Africa Technical Department, Africa Region; Director, Environmentally and Socially Sustainable Development, Europe and Central Asia Region; and, the most recent position, Director, Agriculture and Rural Development for the World Bank Group. He represented the World Bank on the Executive Committee of the Consultative Group on International Agricultural Research (CGIAR) and participated in mobilizing funds for all of the environmentally and socially sustainable development network's global programmes.

While at the World Bank, Cleaver was recognized as an outstanding manager and was the recipient of the "Good Manager" award from the World Bank Staff Association in 2001. He helped create an effective system of knowledge sharing, knowledge management, and staff learning in the World Bank's Environmentally and Socially Sustainable Development Network.

Cleaver has a long and distinguished career in agriculture and rural development, with many books and articles published on agricultural development. He spent several years working and living in Sub–Sahara and North Africa. He holds a BA in International Relations from the University of Pennsylvania, Philadelphia, a Master's degree in International Law and Diplomacy, and a PhD in Economics from the Fletcher School, Tufts University. He has also completed an Executive Development Management Programme at the Harvard Business School.

Louise Fox

Louise Fox is currently USAID's Chief Economist. In this role, she guides the Agency on economics–based decision making and is responsible for keeping USAID's economists on the cutting edge of ideas in development economics.

Before joining USAID, Fox served as a Visiting Professor of Development Economic Policy at the University of California, Berkeley, and as a consultant in development economics, specializing in employment, labor markets, gender, social service delivery and poverty reduction. Prior to joining UC Berkeley, Fox had a distinguished career at the World Bank where she advised governments in Africa, Latin America, Asia and Eastern Europe on how to develop, implement, and evaluate effective policies for employment, social security and poverty reduction.

Her most recent published work has been on the topics of poverty reduction and inclusive growth, the political economy of poverty reduction, and on employment, labor markets, and labor regulation, all with respect to Sub–Saharan Africa. She has also published in the areas of pension reform, reform of child welfare systems, social protection, public expenditures in the social sectors and poverty reduction, female–headed households and child welfare, stabilization policies and poverty reduction, the social costs of adjustment, and the economic history of poverty and inequality in Brazil. Her most recent book is *Youth Employment in Sub–Saharan Africa*, published by the World Bank in 2014.

Fox received a Bachelor's degree in international relations and affairs from UC Berkeley and a PhD. in economics from Vanderbilt University.

Gregory K. Ingram

From mid–2005 through mid–2014, Gregory K. Ingram was President and CEO of the Lincoln Institute of Land Policy, a private operating foundation in Cambridge, MA, carrying out training, research, and policy evaluation on the taxation, development, regulation, and planning of land and its uses. Prior to that he was Director–General, Operations Evaluation for the World Bank Group where he was responsible for evaluating operations, policies, and programs at the World Bank, the International Finance Corporation, and the Multilateral Investment Guarantee Agency. At the World Bank, his other positions included Director of the Development Research Department; Staff Director for the World Development Report 1994, Infrastructure for Development; and Economic Adviser in the Urban Projects Department. Before joining the World Bank, he was Associate Professor of Economics at Harvard University. He has published in the areas of housing and land markets, transportation, urban economics, infrastructure, evaluation, environment, land policy, and development. He holds a PhD. in economics from Harvard University; a BA and MA in philosophy, politics, and economics from University of Oxford; and a BS in civil engineering from Swarthmore College.

Hiroshi Kato

Hiroshi Kato is Senior Vice–President of the Japan International Cooperation Agency. Since joining JICA in 1978, he has served at various positions, including the General Affairs Department, the Planning Department, and the Southeast Asia Department. Prior to his current position, he was Director of the JICA Research Institute. He graduated from the University of Tokyo in 1978 majoring in Asian History. He later earned his master's degree in Public Administration from the John F. Kennedy School of Government, Harvard University in 1988. He has been on the board of directors of the Japan Society for International Development since 2002.

Alden LeClair

Alden LeClair is a Project & Research Associate at Centennial Group International and the Emerging Markets Forum. While at Centennial and EMF, he has worked on projects for a number of different clients, including the African Development Bank, the Japanese International Cooperation Agency, the Islamic Development Bank, and the Government of Niger. He previously co–authored a chapter, "Alternative long–term scenarios," in *The World in 2050: Striving for a more just, prosperous, and harmonious global community* (Oxford University Press, 2016). He is currently pursuing a Master's in Global Human Development and holds a BSFS in International Politics with a Certificate in African Studies, both from the Walsh School of Foreign Service at Georgetown University.

Claudio Loser

Claudio Loser is Founding Director and Chief Executive Officer of Centennial Latin America. He is a well–known authority on Latin American economies and institutions. During his career at the International Monetary Fund he held many senior positions, including Director of the Western Hemisphere Department. Under his leadership, the Department was actively involved in a wide range of surveillance, technical assistance, and research activities. Recently he has worked closely with Latin American Development Bank (CAF), Asian Development Bank, JICA, JBIC, and with a number of other financial corporations, dealing with developments in Latin America and the evolving relations between these countries and the IMF. He is a Senior Fellow at the Inter–American Dialogue, a Washington–based forum for opinion leaders and policymakers on Western Hemisphere affairs. He teaches Latin American Development issues and finance at the George Washington University. He has published in many journals, mostly on Latin American economic issues. He graduated from the University of Cuyo, Argentina and received his Masters of Arts and PhD from the University of Chicago in 1967 and 1971, respectively.

Serge Michailof

Serge Michailof has recently published a best–selling book: *Africanistan, l'Afrique en crise va–t–elle se retrouver dans nos banlieues?* (Fayard, 2015), which will be soon updated and released in English, entitled *Africanistan, the new land of Jihad* (Oxford University Press, forthcoming). He is presently Associate Researcher at IRIS, one of the leading think tanks in geopolitics in Paris. He has previously been teaching economic development at the elite Science Po School in Paris for ten years, also working as an international consultant on fragile states and post conflict reconstruction with a specific focus on institution and state building. Previous positions included Executive Director for Operations of the French Development Agency (AFD) from 2001 to 2005, eight years as Regional Director and Senior Advisor at the World Bank in Washington from 1993 to 2001. During a 50 year career dedicated to development he has worked in more than 65 different countries. His publications can be consulted on his website: www.sergemichailof.fr.

Ritva Reinikka

Ritva Reinikka currently chairs the Delivery Board of the Research on Improving Systems of Education (RISE) for the UK's Department for International Development as well as of the Steering Committee for the Africa–wide Service Delivery Indicators Initiative. She was formerly a director at the World Bank where she held various positions for two decades in the Africa region, the Middle East and North Africa region, and the Development Research Group. Her most recent assignment was director for human development in the Africa region. She was also co–director of the 2004 World Development Report Making Services Work for Poor People.

Prior to joining the World Bank, she held research and operational positions at the Centre for the Study of African Economies in the University of Oxford, the Helsinki School of Economics, UNICEF, and Finland's Ministry for Foreign Affairs.

She has published widely in peer–reviewed journals and policy–oriented outlets on public economics, service delivery in education, health care, and infrastructure, governance, micro foundations of growth, and international trade. She holds a D.Phil in Economics from the University of Oxford.

Hasan Tuluy

Hasan Tuluy brings a wide experience in Africa, the Middle East, and Latin America and the Caribbean, particularly on issues of development strategy and policy, trade and regional integration. He led the team for Centennial's Niger 2035 project, as well as serving as an Adviser to the World Bank on the project, "Libya: Transitional Assistance, Consensus Building." He previously served as Vice President, Latin America and the Caribbean Region at the World Bank, where he managed the Bank's relations with 32 countries and several regional institutions. He also served as Vice President for Human Resources for the World Bank, and as COO for the Multilateral Insurance Guarantee Agency (MIGA). Prior to that he was Director of Operations & Strategy, Middle East North Africa Region, where he oversaw regional strategy, advisory and lending support and managed the cross cutting operational services department.

Ieva Vilkelyte

Ieva Vilkelyte is a Senior Research Assistant at Centennial Group International. She is a graduate of Georgetown University, where she earned a BA in Economics.

Index